D0421580

an dáta is déanaí atá

Making Sense of
Factor Analysis

Making Sense of
Factor Analysis

The Use of Factor Analysis for Instrument Development in Health Care Research

Marjorie A. Pett • Nancy R. Lackey • John J. Sullivan

SAGE Publications
International Educational and Professional Publisher
Thousand Oaks ▪ London ▪ New Delhi

i16635437

For information:

Sage Publications, Inc.
2455 Teller Road
Thousand Oaks, California 91320
E-mail: order@sagepub.com

Sage Publications Ltd.
6 Bonhill Street
London EC2A 4PU
United Kingdom

Sage Publications India Pvt. Ltd.
B-42, Panchsheel Enclave
Post Box 4109
New Delhi 110 017 India

Printed in the United States of America

Library of Congress Cataloging-in-Publication Data

Pett, Marjorie A.
Making sense of factor analysis : the use of factor analysis for instrument development in health care research/Marjorie A. Pett, Nancy R. Lackey, John J. Sullivan.
    p. cm.
Includes bibliographical references and index.
ISBN 0-7619-1949-X (cloth) -- ISBN 0-7619-1950-3 (pbk.)
    1. Medicine—Research—Statistical methods. 2. Medical care—Research—Statistical methods. 3. Factor analysis. I. Lackey, Nancy R. II. Sullivan, John J. III. Title.
R853.S7 P479 2003
610′ .7′ 27--dc21

                                2002156318

03   04   05   06   10   9   8   7   6   5   4   3   2   1

Production Editor:	Sanford Robinson
Editorial Assistant:	Karen Wiley
Typesetter:	C&M Digitals (P) Ltd.
Copy Editor:	Connie Adams
Indexer:	Pilar Wyman
Cover Designer:	Michelle Lee
Cover Illustrator:	Mark Pett

Contents

Acknowledgments

There are many people to whom we are indebted for helping to make this text a reality. First, we would like to thank the administration, faculties, and staff of the Colleges of Nursing at the University of Utah and University of Memphis for their continued support and patience for our, at times, mystical academic endeavors.

We are appreciative as well of the many graduate students in the Colleges of Nursing, Health, Business, and Social Work who "volunteered" numerous hours critiquing various drafts of the manuscript. Thanks in particular to Sungu Armagan, Gerrie Barnett, Judy Berry, Monte Butler, Kara Diersing, Alexa Doig, Manuel Ferreira, Mary Jayne Johnson, Yu-Chen Kao, Charles Krog, Mike Lyman, Laurence Marsh, Jason McCreary, Catherine McDonald, Brian Pilling, Ron Ramsing, Pat Ravert, Tessie Rose, Kristine Tanner, and Wei-Chen Tung. Your many suggestions for improving the clarity of this text were extremely helpful.

We are also indebted to the staff and reviewers at Sage Publications and to Heidi Van Middlesworth and Sanford Robinson in particular, who guided this manuscript toward fruition. Many thanks to our families as well for their patience and support throughout the process. Thank you, Mark Pett, for your willingness to illustrate the cover of this book.

Finally, to John Sullivan, our coauthor, colleague, mentor, and friend: You died before the final draft was sent to press. Yet, without you and our weekly meetings, we would still be in the talking stages. Thanks, John, wherever you are. It is to your memory that we dedicate this book.

In Memory of John J. Sullivan, Ph.D., 1919-2001

Remember
When you remember me
It means that you have carried something of who I am with you,
That I have left some mark of who I am on who you are.
It means that you can summon me back to your mind
even though countless years and miles may stand between us.
It means that if we meet again, you will know me.
It means that even after I die
You can still see my face and hear my voice,
and speak to me in your heart.

— *Frederick Buechner*

Introduction

Let us suppose that you are a health care practitioner working in the field of medical genetics and cancer-risk counseling. Your interest is in developing programs of interventions to aid individuals who are considering undergoing genetic testing for inheritable cancer. In particular, you are interested in identifying decision-making concerns among women who are at familial risk for breast cancer. By identifying these concerns, you will be better able to devise counseling programs that are specific to this vulnerable group.

You and your colleagues scour the health care literature. You identify a number of recent publications that have undertaken excellent qualitative studies of decision-making issues related to genetic testing among individuals at risk for various forms of cancer (e.g., Croyle, 1995; Jacobsen, Valdimarsdottir, Brown, & Offit, 1997; Kelly, 1992; Kinney et al., 2000; Lerman, Marshall, Audrain, & Gomez-Caminero, 1996; Smith & Croyle, 1995). Unfortunately, there do not appear to be any standardized scales available that would provide you and your colleagues with a reliable, valid, and easy-to-use assessment of the genetic testing and cancer outcome concerns of this population. A review of the instrument development literature also indicates that the scales that are available to address patient concerns are not entirely relevant for use with women at familial risk for breast cancer. It is apparent to you and your colleagues that the structure of this construct called *concern* that has been identified so aptly for other populations (e.g., adult caregivers of cancer patients) needs to be reexamined and redefined for your population of interest.

Sound familiar? It should. Health care practitioners and researchers have become increasingly aware of the need for greater specificity and clarity of a number of behavioral constructs that are prevalent in their disciplines, such as the structure of temperament, the dimensions of sleep, and the needs of specific patients and their families. To address this problem, these individuals are seeking to develop more sensitive instruments for data collection that clearly define and clarify the structure of their constructs of interest. Toward this end, the methods of factor analysis are being used more frequently to assist in the development of these instruments.

Unfortunately, factor analysis is not a unidimensional approach that is easily understood even by the most experienced of researchers. Despite the apparent singularity of its name, factor analysis involves a series of complex statistical techniques that involve higher-order mathematics. There is also much subjectivity, artistry, and "laying on of hands" involved in this complex method. Clearly communicating one's approach to decision making and the results of these analyses is not an easy task. It has even been our observation that, on occasion, researchers have misreported the results of their analyses. Most statistical computer packages provide adequate instructions for using factor analysis. What is not available is a detailed discussion of the numerous practical and theoretical decisions that need to be made in order to knowledgeably run and accurately interpret the outcomes of these overwhelmingly fast, sophisticated computer programs.

The temptation among statistically challenged health care professionals who desire to develop scales to measure their domains of interest may be to hand their data to professional statisticians who would then run the factor analyses for them and interpret the results of these machinations. Unfortunately, not all statisticians are trained in measurement theory and may in fact have limited knowledge of the intricacies of test construction. They may also be unaware of the dynamics of your population of interest. As a result, the artistry that is so important in factor analysis may be diminished and the important interrelationships among clinical concerns, test construction, and the application of factor analysis to test construction may be lost.

ORGANIZATION OF THE TEXT

The purpose of this text is to provide clinicians and researchers with a practical understanding of the complex statistical procedures involved in factor analysis. The emphasis of this text will be on the use of factor analysis as a procedure to construct tests, to develop instruments, and to check the reliability and structure of existing instruments in health care research. The important interrelationship between factor analysis and test construction will be emphasized and discussed in detail.

Step-by-step descriptions of the approach to analyzing data using statistical computer packages (e.g., SPSS for Windows and SAS) will be presented. Because of space limitations and to avoid confusion, we have limited our presentation in the main body of the text to printouts obtained from SPSS for Windows. The corresponding SAS examples can be found in Appendix B. References to SAS examples in each of the chapters will be cited in parentheses following the SPSS for Windows examples. The same circled numbering system (e.g., ①) will be used for both programs when discussing similar points related to the generated output. To obtain copies of the actual data set in SPSS® and Excel™, go to www.sagepub.com/books/0761919503.htm and click on Additional Materials.

If you are interested in learning more about SAS and its factor analysis programs, there are several excellent resources available. These include Cody and Smith (1997), Delwiche and Slaughter (1998), Der and Everitt (2002), and Hatcher (1994). Additional resources for SPSS for Windows include Gardner (2001), Green, Salkind, and Akey (2000), and SPSS, Inc. (2002).

To facilitate your understanding of factor analysis, we will walk you through this process using our genetic testing example whenever possible. Interpretations of the factor analysis output generated from the statistical packages and assistance with approaches to reporting and interpreting the findings will be offered. Additional published examples of the application of this procedure in health care research will be provided. References to the "experts" in the factor analysis and instrument development literature will also be given throughout the text.

This text is intended for use by beginning or advanced health care researchers from a variety of disciplines (e.g., exercise and sports science; health sciences; medicine; nursing; parks, recreation, and tourism; psychology; and social work) whose goals are to

- become more knowledgeable about the use of factor analysis in health care research without necessarily becoming a specialist,
- gain a greater understanding of what the specialists (e.g., expert writers on factor analysis or consultants who have undertaken such analyses) are saying regarding factor analysis,

- understand journal articles that report the use of factor analysis in test construction and instrument development,
- create or examine the reliability and structure of a particular health care instrument, and
- accurately interpret and report computer output generated from a factor analysis run.

To help you achieve these goals, we have organized this text into eight chapters and five appendices. Chapter 1 presents an overview of factor analysis and its history and development. Chapter 2 examines issues related to the initial development of the instrument. In Chapter 3, we introduce you to the various matrices that are critical to factor analysis. Chapters 4 and 5 outline the various approaches to extracting the initial factors and then the logic and merit of factor rotation. Interpreting and naming the factors are the focus of Chapters 6 and 7. The text concludes with Chapter 8, in which we suggest ways to present and report the results of the factor analysis and discuss issues related to replication of study findings to corroborate the dimensions of the construct that has been identified.

In the appendices, we present you with additional source materials that may be useful as you proceed through this text. Sound a bit daunting? The material may overwhelm you at first, but we are optimistic that the processes of factor analysis will become more understandable to you as you read on. So, without further delay, let us proceed to Chapter 1.

1

An Overview
of Factor Analysis

Not all science is hypothesis testing. Sometimes we are interested in the structure of a particular phenomenon. Factor analysis provides us with the means to undertake a structural analysis of that problem. In the Introduction, for example, we identified a construct we wished to explore in greater depth: the concerns of individuals who are considering undergoing genetic testing for cancer. Our interim goal is to develop an instrument of data collection that would adequately measure and reflect the structure of this construct. Ultimately, we would like to formulate programs of intervention that would address the specific concerns of individuals who make up this population.

A review of the literature indicates that there may be several different but possibly interrelated subdimensions of concerns about genetic testing contained within this single construct. Through our knowledge of the theoretical literature as well as discussions with health care providers and persons considering undergoing genetic testing, we have identified a large set of items or statements, which may—or may not—reflect the dimensions of concerns related to genetic testing. We intend to present these statements to a large group of potential recipients of genetic testing, to receive their feedback about the importance of these concerns to them, and to simplify the instrument into a user-friendly, easy-to-complete form that could be used in future research.

Although these tasks appear, on the surface, to be easily accomplished, there are a number of questions related to instrument development that need to be answered prior to undertaking the study. For example, how will we select these items? Do those selected items cover the subject completely? How many items should there be? To how many subjects should we administer this instrument?

Once we have determined the sample size and number and content of the items, we will need to identify the most appropriate statistical analyses that should be used with the collected data. A review of the measurement literature suggests that *factor analysis* might be a useful tool to analyze the structure of this construct, called Concerns About Genetic Testing. How can we use factor analysis, and what are the processes underlying this procedure? How is factor analysis different from other statistical procedures (e.g., the *t* test, analysis of variance [ANOVA], and multiple regression)? A number of statistical computer packages offer fast, economical factor analysis programs. What are the differences and similarities between these programs? How do we decide on the best program to use and, once we have done that, how would we interpret the results reported in the computer printouts?

We realize that these may be daunting questions to which you would like immediate answers. Why are sample size and number of items important to us? What is meant by the "structure" of a construct, and what is its relevance to factor analysis? In these next chapters, we hope to provide you with answers to these puzzling questions.

CHARACTERISTICS OF FACTOR ANALYSIS

Factor analysis is not a single statistical method. Unlike the *t* test or ANOVA, it is not a test of differences between groups of subjects. Rather, factor analysis represents a complex array of structure-analyzing procedures used to identify the interrelationships among a large set of observed variables and then, through data reduction, to group a smaller set of these variables into dimensions or *factors* that have common characteristics (Nunnally & Bernstein, 1994).

What is a factor? Most simply summarized, a factor is a linear combination or cluster of related observed variables that represents a specific underlying dimension of a construct, which is as distinct as possible from the other factors included in the solution (Tabachnick & Fidell, 2001). As you will read in Chapter 8, Leske (1991) used the techniques of factor analysis to identify five underlying dimensions or factors related to the Critical Care Family Needs Inventory (CCFNI), an instrument designed to assess the needs of family members of the critically ill. She labeled these distinct CCFNI factors as *needs for support, comfort, information, proximity,* and *assurance.*

In the genetic testing example, the methods of factor analysis will help us examine the interrelationships among the items or statements that we believe are measuring this construct called Concerns About Genetic Testing, and then to identify its subdimensions. Our ultimate goal in using the methods of factor analysis is to arrive at a parsimonious or reduced set of factors that summarizes and describes the structural interrelationships among the items in a concise and understandable manner (Gorsuch, 1983).

Factor analysis can be used for theory and instrument development and assessing construct validity of an established instrument when administered to a specific population. Once the internal structure of a construct has been established, factor analysis may also be used to identify external variables (e.g., gender and social status position) that appear to relate to the various dimensions of the construct of interest (Nunnally & Bernstein, 1994).

EXPLORATORY VERSUS CONFIRMATORY FACTOR ANALYSIS

There are two basic types of factor analysis: exploratory and confirmatory. *Exploratory factor analysis* (EFA) is used when the researcher does not know how many factors are necessary to explain the interrelationships among a set of characteristics, indicators, or items (Gorsuch, 1983; Pedhazur & Schmelkin, 1991; Tabachnick & Fidell, 2001). Therefore, the researcher uses the techniques of factor analysis to explore the underlying dimensions of the construct of interest. This was the approach that Leske (1991) used in her conceptualization of the dimensions of needs of families of the critically ill. EFA is the most commonly used form of factor analysis in health care research. It is what we will use to examine the dimensions of Concerns About Genetic Testing.

In contrast, *confirmatory factor analysis* (CFA) is used to assess the extent to which the hypothesized organization of a set of identified factors fits the data (Nunnally & Bernstein, 1994; Pedhazur & Schmelkin, 1991). It is used when the researcher has some knowledge about the underlying structure of the construct under investigation. CFA could also be used to test the utility of the underlying dimensions of a construct identified through EFA, to compare factor structures across studies, and to test hypotheses concerning the linear structural relationships among a set of factors associated with a specific theory or model. Pett, Wampold, Turner, and Vaughan-Cole (1999), for example, used CFA to test a hypothesized model predicting the paths of influence of divorce on young children's psychosocial adjustment.

When undertaking a factor analysis using EFA, it is common practice to use more traditional statistical computer packages (e.g., SPSS, SAS, and BMDP) for the statistical analyses. CFA, on the other hand, requires a comprehensive analysis of covariance structures (Byrne, 1989). This form of measurement model is available in *structural equation modeling* (SEM). LISREL (Jöreskog & Sörbom, 1989) and EQS (Bentler, 1985) are two statistical computer packages that are used to undertake SEM analyses.

ASSUMPTIONS OF EXPLORATORY FACTOR ANALYSIS

Because the focus of this book is on beginning instrument development in health care research, we will concentrate on exploratory factor analysis. Before we begin that exploration, there are some assumptions about EFA that need to be considered.

A basic assumption of EFA is that within a collection of observed variables, there exists a set of underlying factors, smaller in number than the observed variables, that can explain the interrelationships among those variables (Kim & Mueller, 1978). Because the initial steps of factor analysis are performed using Pearson product moment correlations, many of the assumptions relevant to this parametric statistic are applicable to factor analysis (e.g., large sample sizes, continuous distributions, and linear relationships among items).

Some of the assumptions related to the Pearson product moment correlation, however, are violated in factor analysis. As you will see in Chapter 2, the response categories for each individual scale item are most often constructed using dichotomous *yes, no* responses or are based on ordinal-level Likert scales. Tabachnick and Fidell (2001) also argue that normality of distributions is not critical if the researcher's intent is to explore, summarize, and describe relationships among variables. If, on the other hand, the goal is to identify the number of factors that underlie the items being examined, then multivariate normality is an issue about which to be concerned. *Multivariate normality* implies that all of the variables being considered and the linear combinations of those variables are normally distributed. Hair, Anderson, Tatham, and Black (1995), Pett (1997), and Tabachnick and Fidell (2001) offer extensive discussion and advice concerning approaches to screening data for both univariate and multivariate normality. As these issues arise throughout the chapters, we will discuss various approaches to evaluating these assumptions.

HISTORICAL DEVELOPMENTS OF FACTOR ANALYSIS

Factor analysis owes its earliest development to several groups of British and American psychologists whose work from 1900 to the late 1930s focused on addressing problems related to the structural modeling of such constructs as the dimensions of human intelligence (e.g., Garnett, 1919; Pearson, 1901; Spearman, 1904, 1923, 1927, 1929; Thurstone, 1935, 1937a, 1937b; Wilson, 1928). Unfortunately, the wide expanse of the Atlantic Ocean not only separated two continents, it also divided these psychologists into two separate camps that, at times, either ignored or vociferously challenged the other's contributions (Harman, 1976; Mulaik, 1986).

In Britain, Spearman and his colleagues (e.g., Burt, 1939, 1941; Garnett, 1919; Ledermann, 1937, 1938; Spearman, 1904, 1922, 1923, 1927, 1928, 1929, 1930a, 1930b; Thomson, 1934, 1936, 1938) pursued the concept of the two-factor *g* theory of human intelligence. Briefly, supporters of this two-factor theory of intelligence initially argued that all intercorrelations among tests of mental ability could be explained by two factors: (1) a single general factor, or *g* factor, that represented *general intelligence* and (2) a unique factor that was associated with a particular test. Because these unique factors are uncorrelated with one another, the *g* factor accounted for all the correlation among tests of mental abilities (Nunnally & Bernstein, 1994). Although this two-factor theory was later modified to include group factors as well (Garnett, 1919;

Spearman, 1927), much of the development of early factor analysis could be attributed to the search for the existence of a single general factor of intelligence (Burt, 1966; Harman, 1976).

In the United States, the group of Thurstone and his students (a.k.a., the Thurstonians) challenged the adequacy of Spearman's two-factor theory to describe tests of mental abilities. Like Garnett (1919), they developed the concept of multiple-factor analysis and applied these methods to a variety of psychometric problems (Thurstone, 1931, 1940, 1947, 1948, 1954). Mulaik (1986) notes that although the British psychologists made significant contributions to the early development of factor analysis, once the Thurstonians arrived on the scene in the early 1930s, the United States became a major center for the development of factor analysis procedures. This dominance continued until the late 1960s and 1970s, when a number of prominent European psychometricians (e.g., Jöreskog and Sörbom from Scandinavia) made major contributions to the field (Jöreskog, 1967, 1969, 1970; Jöreskog & Goldberger, 1972; Sörbom, 1974).

A search of the psychology literature via PsycINFO for the use of factor analysis as a statistical technique during the 100-year period 1901-2000 indicated that many of the earliest references to the procedure were organized around discussions and critiques of the theory and mathematics of Spearman's two-factor g theory of intelligence (e.g., Dodd, 1929; Meili, 1930; Miner, 1912, 1920; Spearman, 1922, 1923, 1927, 1928, 1929, 1930a, 1930b; Spearman & Holzinger, 1924; Wilson, 1928). Other highlights of early factor analysis history include Thurstone's (1931) first textbook on test theory and, in 1936, the first issue of the journal *Psychometrika*, which was published by the Thurstone group to provide a forum for their research and theoretical interests (Mulaik, 1986).

Since the 1930s, the use of factor analysis in psychology research has rapidly expanded. It should be noted that although factor analysis has had its fair share of fervent supporters, it has also been met with concerned challengers (Steiger, 1996). Figure 1.1 outlines the geometric growth in the use and examination of factor analysis as a research tool as reported in PsycINFO between 1930 and 2000.

Prior to the 1950s, the use of factor analysis was relatively stable, with fewer than 100 publications on the subject being reported in PsycINFO annually. Since the 1950s, there has been a rapid acceleration in the use of factor analysis. Several possible reasons for this phenomenon that are related to psychometrics have been suggested (Gulliksen, 1974; Mulaik, 1986) and include

Figure 1.1 References to Factor Analysis in PsycINFO, 1930 to 2000

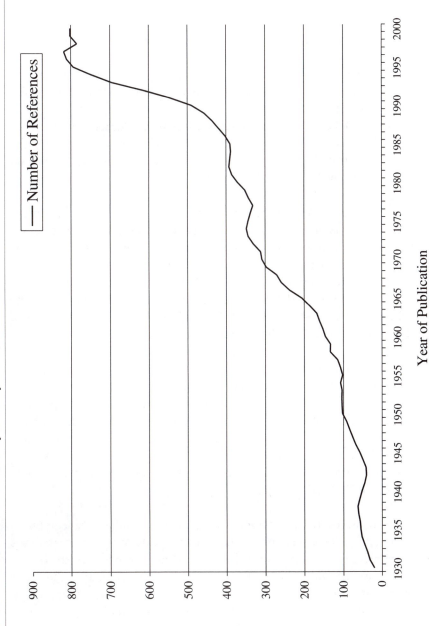

- the use of factor analysis by Thurstone and his colleagues during World War II to develop selection and criterion variables for use by the military;
- the development in the 1950s of electronic digital computers, which rapidly became readily accessible tools on university campuses;
- the generating of algorithms to compute eigenvalues and eigenvectors, two related elements that are critical to statistical analyses of matrices; and
- the development in the early 1960s of the Varimax rotation, an important time-saving solution to rotations for uncorrelated factors, followed by the development of the Oblimax and Oblimin rotations for correlated factors.

The important contribution of computers to the rapid rise in the use of factor analysis cannot be overstated. Without computers, factor analysis involved extremely labor-intensive computations. During the 1940s and 1950s, for example, the mere undertaking of a factor analysis was often enough to serve as a Ph.D. dissertation (Steiger, 1996). Gulliksen (1974), an outstanding theoretician who worked at the Educational Testing Service at Princeton, illustrates the dimensions of this problem with the following comments:

> I was a research assistant for a year working on Thurstone's first study of primary mental abilities. The computational work in resolving a battery of about 50 tests into seven primary mental abilities meant that I was supervising a group of about 20 computer clerical workers for about a year. I recall Thurstone lamenting that his Ph.D. candidates would not be able to do factor analysis dissertations because it would not be practical to employ such a crew for each Ph.D. thesis. (p. 251)

The arrival of mainframe computers on university campuses during the 1970s enabled researchers to undertake factor analyses more rapidly and efficiently. Still, given the slowness and restricted use of mainframe computers, such analyses continued to be labor intensive, time-consuming, and expensive by today's standards. It was not until the 1980s, with the advent of personal computers, that factor analysis became a readily available and popular research tool.

For example, Gulliksen (1974) observed that in early 1970, a research worker from the Civil Service came to him for help in analyzing a set of attitude scales:

> He came up one afternoon, with his data on punched cards, and we started about 4:00 p.m. to run the preliminary error-detecting program, and we corrected the cards whenever errors were found. In all, including the scaling, correlations, factor analyses, and rotations, although the job was somewhat larger than the primary mental abilities one, we were finished about 3:00 a.m. the next morning. (p. 251)

Today, assuming no errors in the data, the same job would probably take only a few seconds!

USES OF FACTOR ANALYSIS
IN HEALTH CARE RESEARCH

A review of other health care disciplines during the past 15 years indicates similar dramatic increases in the use of both exploratory and confirmatory factor analyses. A review of the published articles in PsycINFO indicated more than twice as many published studies reported having used factor analysis in 2000 ($n = 800$) compared with 1985 ($n = 319$).

The rise has been even more dramatic in those health care disciplines that do not have the rich psychometric history that psychology and education enjoy. For example, for this same 15-year period, the number of research articles reporting the use of factor analysis in the nursing and allied health literature (CINAHL) increased by more than 16,000%, from 2 in 1985 to 326 in 2000. Notable increases in the reported use of factor analysis were also noted in the medical literature (MEDLINE: $n = 97$ in 1985 to $n = 365$ in 2000, 276%; HEALTHSTAR: $n = 74$ in 1985 to $n = 377$ in 2000, 409%). Although the reported uses of factor analysis in the research literature search bases SPORT Discus and AGELINE have remained relatively low ($n = 111$ and $n = 28$, respectively, during 2000), these numbers still represent increases of 311% and 180% for each search base from 1988 figures ($n = 27$ for SPORT Discus and $n = 10$ for AGELINE).[1]

What has contributed to this continued increase in the use of factor analysis in the health sciences in particular? Several possibilities come to mind:

- Increased researcher interest in the complex organizational structure of various health-related constructs
- Recent developments in the use of confirmatory factor analysis and structural equation modeling
- Greater sophistication concerning statistics on the part of some health care researchers from all disciplines and levels of expertise
- Increased availability of inexpensive but powerful personal computers, which can undertake analyses quickly and inexpensively
- Availability of increasingly user-friendly statistical computer packages

Unfortunately, enhanced user understanding and expertise with regard to measurement theory and factor analysis have not always accompanied the increased use of this statistical method in health care research. Our experience indicates that with the exception of psychology and education, few graduate programs in the health sciences provide their students with strong backgrounds in either of these areas. As Kline (1994) has lamented, "With the advent of powerful computers and the dreaded statistical packages which go with them, factor analysis and other multivariate methods are available to those who have never been trained to understand them" (p. 1).

As a result, we are seeing improper use and reporting of analyses that have been generated from this technique. It is our hope that this text will help to resolve this unfortunate situation by providing you with a clearer understanding of the logic and techniques involved in using factor analysis as a statistical tool for research in the health sciences.

DECISION-MAKING PROCESS IN EXPLORATORY FACTOR ANALYSIS

Regardless of statistical package or level of expertise of the researcher, there are eight basic steps to exploratory factor analysis (Figure 1.2). These steps include specifying the problem, generating the items, assessing the adequacy of the correlation matrix, extracting the initial

Figure 1.2   A Block Diagram of the Decision-Making Process
in Exploratory Factor Analysis

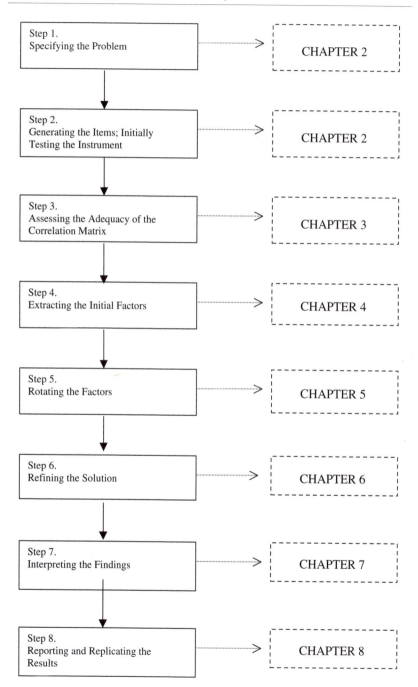

factors, rotating those factors, refining the solution, interpreting the findings, and, finally, reporting and replicating the results. These are the steps that we will examine in considerable detail in Chapters 2 through 8.

NOTE

1. The year 1988 is reported here because it is the initial year of reporting for SPORT Discus.

2

Designing and
Testing the Instrument

The development of valid and reliable instruments takes time, patience, and knowledge and is not the research focus of most investigators. It is only when reliable and valid instruments are not available to measure a particular construct of interest that we might turn our attention, albeit reluctantly, to instrument development. It is unfortunate that a limited interest in and knowledge about the process of instrument development has led to a proliferation of unreliable and invalid instruments in the health care arena (Rempusheski, 1990).

This does not have to be your experience. With careful preparation and testing, it is possible to produce, under most circumstances, reliable and valid measures of a construct. One of the first steps in this process is to prepare an instrument that can be evaluated using factor analysis. In this chapter, we will examine various measurement frameworks that can be used to guide the design of an instrument. Then we will examine the role of latent variables in instrument development. Finally, we will address issues related to specifying the problem, generating the items, developing the form of an instrument, and initially administering an instrument to a selected group of subjects. Throughout the chapter, we will be using as our example the Concerns About Genetic Testing construct that we identified in Chapter 1.

Although the terms *measurement* and *instrumentation* are often used interchangeably in research, they are different. *Measurement* is the process of assigning "numbers to objects, events or situations in accord with some rule" (Kaplan, 1963, p. 177). The main purpose of measurement is to produce reliable evidence that can be used in evaluating the outcomes of research. *Instrumentation*, a component of measurement, is the development of a measurement device—scale, instrument, test, or tool—following specific rules of psychometrics. These rules ensure that the assignment of numbers to values or categories is consistent across subjects, events, and studies for the purpose of producing reliable and valid evidence that can be used in evaluating the outcomes of research (Burns & Grove, 2001).

TYPES OF MEASUREMENT FRAMEWORKS

Before an instrument can be developed, the researcher must identify and select the type of framework that will guide the design and interpretation of the results obtained through use of the instrument. There are two major frameworks for instrument development: criterion-referenced and norm-referenced frameworks (Waltz, Strickland, & Lenz, 1991).

Criterion-Referenced Frameworks

Criterion-referenced instruments are also referred to as *predictive indexes* (Mishel, 1998; Waltz et al., 1991). The purpose of a criterion-referenced measure is to determine what an individual knows or does not know, can or cannot do. More specifically, criterion-referenced instruments are developed to assess the effectiveness of a given intervention in achieving specific learning objectives. They are designed to meet the needs of programmed instruction and mastery learning (Ebel, 1979; Kline, 2000a; Waltz et al., 1991). Achievement tests are examples of criterion-referenced instruments.

Before a criterion-referenced instrument can be developed, the researcher must determine a set of target behaviors or specific knowledge that an individual needs to know in order to perform a specific task or achieve a desired outcome (Waltz et al., 1991). Items are then developed from this set of target behaviors or knowledge and put in a specified instrument format. This criterion-referenced framework provides an indication of whether or not a set of specific objectives has been attained or a set of target behaviors has been mastered.

Criterion-referenced instruments are used for formative evaluation and to guide the process of learning. The content for such instruments is based on a specified content domain. The instruments generally have several items per objective, and the items tend to be very specific and narrow. These instruments are developed to match a particular instructional situation (Isaac & Michael, 1981). Kline (2000a, 2000b) argues that the value of such tests depends not so much on the tests' psychometric virtues (e.g., validity and reliability) as on the quality of the items representing the content to be mastered.

Norm-Referenced Instruments

Norm-referenced instruments are used to discriminate between participants, predict the results of some tests, or evaluate change over time (Mishel, 1998; Waltz et al., 1991). These instruments are designed such that differences among people who possess differing quantities of a characteristic can be portrayed along a continuum of values. Variance is a key feature of a norm-referenced instrument.

The Concerns About Genetic Testing Scale (CGTS) (Appendix A) is a norm-referenced instrument that was designed to measure a specific characteristic, *concerns regarding genetic testing,* among subjects who may differ in the amount and type of concern they have about genetic testing. The goal of administering the CGTS is to obtain a range of scores along a continuum regarding respondent concerns about genetic testing. If this goal is obtained, the distribution of scores should resemble a normal curve. This will help us to differentiate one subject's concerns about genetic testing from the concerns of other subjects or a norm group.

The majority of personality, attitudinal, affective, and cognitive constructs are measured using norm-referenced frameworks. For that reason, the norm-referenced framework will be the focus of our discussion concerning instrument development. The levels of measurement of the item scores generated by norm-referenced instruments can be interval or ratio and can be evaluated using factor analysis.[1] The Adolescent-Coping Orientation for Problem Experiences (A-COPE) (McCubbin, Thompson, & McCubbin, 1996), the SF-36 Health Survey (SF-36) (Ware, Snow, & Kosinski, 2000), the Beck Depression Inventory

Beck, Steer, & Garbin, 1988), and the Symptom Checklist-90-Revised (SCL-90-R) (Derogatis, Lipman, & Covi, 1973) are four examples of well-known norm-referenced instruments used in health care research.

The terms *norm-referenced* and *standardized* are not to be used synonymously. There are several types of norm-referenced tests, and a standardized test is just one of them. A standardized test has established norms that have been set up using clearly defined populations (Kline, 2000a). Standardized tests are often used for diagnostic and screening purposes. The Minnesota Multiphasic Personality Inventory (MMPI) (Hathaway, 1942) is an example of a standardized norm-referenced test.

THE USE OF LATENT VARIABLES IN INSTRUMENT DEVELOPMENT

When we develop a scale, we are less interested in the scale items than we are in the construct they purport to measure. As DeVellis (1991) has aptly stated, "Scale items are usually a means to the end of construct assessment … they are necessary because many constructs cannot be assessed directly" (p. 2).

Because constructs are not directly observable, they are often referred to as *latent variables*. The latent variable, or construct, is presumed to cause an item (or a cluster of items) to take on a certain value for a specific subject at a specific time. "When we examine a set of items that are presumably caused by the same latent variable, we can examine their relationships to one another" (DeVellis, 1991, p. 13).

Measurement can be direct or indirect. *Direct measurement* occurs when one can measure concrete factors such as height, weight, head circumference, temperature, time, heart rate, and respiration. Advances in technology allow us to measure many physiological, biological, and chemical functions using standardized equipment such as the sphygmomanometer for blood pressure or the thermometer for body temperature. The National Bureau of Standards defines the standards for many of these measures. When using physiological measures, the researcher is more concerned with accuracy, selectivity, precision, sensitivity, and error than with reliability and validity (Burns & Grove, 2001).

Indirect measurement applies to measurement of abstract ideas or constructs. Pedhazur and Schmelkin (1991) define constructs as "theoretical constructions, abstractions, aimed at organizing and making sense of our environment" (p. 52). Examples of such constructs are uncertainty, anxiety, pain, sorrow, grief, coping, health, illness, quality of life, and concerns about genetic testing. Abstract constructs cannot be directly observed but are measured through the use of attributes or indicators derived from construct clarification and definition.

Attributes are those characteristics or features of a construct that one observes over and over again. They are much like the criteria that health care practitioners would use to make differential diagnoses in their clinical practices. Attributes help us to name a specific pheno-menon (construct) and to differentiate it from a related one. Because of the complexity and abstractness of these constructs, it is helpful to identify clusters or categories of attributes. Such clusters or categories will often give the researcher greater insight into the nature of the con-struct. Unfortunately, because of the complexity and abstractness of a given construct, rarely can an instrument be developed that measures all of its aspects (Walker & Avant, 1995).

The items that are measured on an instrument are the observed or empirical indicators for the attributes of the construct. Observed or empirical indicators are defined as specific and concrete items that are used to measure constructs in the real world (Fawcett, 1997). Empirical indicators are useful in instrument development because they can be linked to the theoretical base of the construct and will contribute to the content and construct validity of the new instrument (Walker & Avant, 1995).

Pain, for example, is an abstract construct that cannot be observed directly. We can assume, however, that a patient who has undergone abdominal surgery less than 24 hours ago, is lying in bed with a drawn look, and is taking frequent shallow breaths is in pain. The abstract con-struct pain may cause each of the observed indicators, a drawn look on the patient's face and frequent shallow breaths. Each of these observed indicators could be measured. To understand this construct, we will look for the patterns of interrelationships between those observed indi-cators and the domains of the latent variable (McCutcheon, 1987).

IDENTIFYING EMPIRICAL
INDICATORS OF LATENT VARIABLES

In order to measure latent variables of the construct of interest, the researcher needs to identify those empirical indicators of the con-struct that can be observed and stated as declarative statements in a designated measurement format. There are several steps to this process and several methods through which these empirical indicators can be identified. These steps include (1) determining the construct or phenomenon of interest, (2) conceptualizing and operationalizing the construct, (3) conducting an integrated review of the literature, and (4) undertaking a concept analysis of the construct.

Determining the Construct or Phenomenon of Interest

Many times, researchers think they know exactly what phenomenon or construct they want to measure until they start generating indicators, or items, related to the construct. It is important, therefore, to carefully conceptualize and operationally define the observed indicators of the construct of interest in the initial phase of scale development. Without careful conceptualization, the resulting instrument will likely have poor construct validity.

There are a number of questions that the researcher needs to address when conceptualizing and operationalizing the content of the instrument:

What is the purpose of the instrument? The researcher needs to describe exactly what the instrument will measure.

What other constructs are related to the concept of interest? Can the concept of interest or phenomenon be clearly distinguished from those that are related to it? This is not an easy task if the construct of interest is complex and abstract.

Will the instrument measure the construct broadly or will it focus on a specific aspect of the concept? The researcher must carefully answer these questions before the actual development of the instrument can occur. These answers can help the researcher to determine both the specific construct of interest and its empirical indicators.

Conceptualizing and Operationalizing the Construct

Conceptualization is a mental process of thoughts, feelings, and ideas that enables the researcher to identify empirical meaning (Chinn & Kramer, 1999). Conceptual definitions give the general or theoretical meaning to the construct. To *operationalize* a construct is to define a construct in such a way that it can be measured or identified (Vogt, 1993). Observable or empirical indicators are the end products of the operational process (Keck, 1998). Empirical indicators become the items or categories of items on the instrument.

Some of the constructs that we want to measure are derived from conceptual or theoretical frameworks. These frameworks can help us to formulate, clarify, and describe the construct or phenomenon we are interested in. Such descriptions and explanations provide better understanding of the abstract relationships that exist among hypothetical constructs as well as provide an understanding of the subtleties of the phenomenon (DeVellis, 1991).

If conceptual or theoretical frameworks are well written, they will provide theoretical or operational definitions of these major constructs. These definitions can provide empirical indicators that become the items in the instrument. They will also give us some insight into the problems we might encounter in measuring that construct. The more we know about the selected construct we wish to measure, the better able we are to develop reliable, valid, and usable instruments.

Constructs that are of interest in the health sciences often have several theoretical models that explain different aspects of that construct. *Anxiety* is an example of such a construct. Most contemporary conceptualizations of anxiety accept a stimulus-response model. There are many theories that can be developed from this model. Hoehn-Saric and McLeod (1993) describe the stimulus-response of anxiety from a physiological perspective, and Beck (1976) and Lazarus and Folkman (1991) describe anxiety from a behavioral response. They identify patterns of thoughts, feelings, and situations that are unique for the individual experiencing the anxiety.

If we were to develop an instrument that reflected individuals' concerns about genetic testing that was based on the theoretical frameworks related to anxiety, we might include four main categories of items: physiology, patterns of thoughts, feelings, and anxiety-producing situations. Because a large number of items could be derived for each category, the length of the instrument would render it impractical to administer. We might decide, therefore, to focus on only two categories of items such as patterns of thoughts and feelings. Some of the items that we might want to include under these two categories are the following:

- I worry about the future.
- I feel very uncertain about my ability to cope with a potentially life-threatening diagnosis.
- I worry about the financial outcomes of a potentially life-threatening diagnosis.

Conducting an Integrated Review of the Literature

After we have evaluated the conceptual or theoretical frameworks that are associated with our selected construct, we would need to undertake a literature search to determine if any empirical studies have been reported that either substantiate or refute parts of or even the entire framework. Conceptual or theoretical frameworks can be used either by themselves or in combination with other methods such as an integrated review of literature or concept analysis as described below. It is important for us to know as much about the construct as possible before embarking on developing the instrument.

If a body of literature exists for the construct of interest, it is useful to conduct an integrated review of literature to determine the empirical indicators of our construct. An integrated review of literature allows the researcher to gain an in-depth understanding of the construct by undertaking a rigorous, systematic review and analysis of the literature (Broome, 2000). This method also enables us to critically evaluate, organize, and synthesize findings from multiple sources regarding potential empirical indicators.

Five types of integrated reviews have been identified. These are abbreviated reviews, methodological reviews, theoretical reviews, critical reviews, and meta-analyses. Broome (2000) provides an excellent in-depth discussion of each of these approaches. Additional resources that discuss the process of an integrated review include Cooper (1989), Cooper and Hedges (1994), Kirkevold (1997), Lynn (1989), and Smith and Stullenbarger (1991, 1995). The following discussion is a brief overview of the process of conducting an integrated review of the literature.

Develop questions and evaluation criteria to guide the review. Most researchers start off broadly and narrow their focus as the review of literature proceeds. To help guide an integrated review of the literature, we may want to first develop some questions and criteria regarding the construct (Broome, 2000). For example, because we are interested in developing an instrument related to concerns about genetic testing, some of our questions might include the following:

- How is the construct defined conceptually and operationally in a published article?
- What kind of and how many concerns about genetic testing does the author identify?
- Were there specific empirical indicators listed in the article?
- Does that author cite other authors who have studied the construct?

These questions will help us to extract information needed to identify empirical indicators of our construct of interest.

Before the review process begins, criteria for critically evaluating the articles need to be established (Broome, 2000). Because this is not a linear process, analysis and synthesis of the information can occur simultaneously during the critique. There are a number of methods available that can facilitate the process of evaluating articles. Some resources that might be helpful are Barnum (1998), Burns and Grove (2001), Creswell (1994), Miller (1991), and Polit and Hungler (1999).

Develop a coding system to manage the information. Along with questions and criteria, a coding system needs to be developed to manage the information obtained from the review. Broome (2000) describes a two-step process for developing a codebook. The information that will be coded will depend on the purpose of the integrated review of literature. If we are interested in how the construct was defined and what kind of observed or empirical indicators were listed or described in the articles, we would want to record how the construct was measured in a given study. Was there an instrument used that was similar to the one that we want to develop? Can we build a case for constructing a new instrument? Definitions of the construct need to be recorded and possible empirical indicators listed. Because it is so easy to forget where we found that special bit of information, it is especially important to keep detailed records of obtained sources of information.

Examine the generated list of empirical indicators. After the researcher has critiqued and analyzed the articles that relate to the construct, the list of generated empirical indicators needs to be examined.

- Do the empirical indicators reflect the domain of the construct?
- Based on the knowledge obtained from this review of literature and the experience of the researcher, are there other possible empirical indicators that need to be added to the list?

At the end of this process, we should have a good basic knowledge of the construct and a list of possible empirical indicators that can be used as categories of items or items for our instrument.

Undertaking a Concept Analysis

The methods of concept analysis and integrative review of literature are very similar. Concept analysis is another method that can be used to determine the empirical indicators of the construct of interest. Concept analysis is a "strategy through which a set of attributes or characteristics essential to the connotative meaning or conceptual definition of a concept are identified" (Burns & Grove, 2001, p. 792). In order for this method to be successful, a body of literature should exist on the construct. The following steps, adapted from Walker and Avant (1995), could be used to determine the empirical indicators for instrument development:

- Determine the purpose of the concept analysis.
- Identify all of the uses of the concept that you can discover.
- Determine all possible attributes.
- Identify the antecedents and consequences if the construct is part of a process.
- Define the empirical indicators.

Determine the purpose of the concept analysis. The purpose of a concept analysis is to determine the attributes, including the antecedents and consequences of the selected construct. *Do not skip this step.* Stating the purpose helps us to focus our attention on the method. One purpose for development of the instrument Concerns About Genetic Testing might be to discover all of the possible observable or empirical indicators, including antecedents and consequences of this phenomenon.

If we have chosen a construct that has several related constructs, we may find ourselves questioning which construct we really want to measure. Referring back to the purpose will help you keep on track. Although we were doing a concept analysis on the construct of *needs,* we found ourselves trying to determine the difference between *needs* and the related constructs of *wishes, desires,* and *wants.* All four of these constructs have common attributes, but they also have some differing attributes that make each of them separate constructs in their own right. A well-stated purpose will save us time and energy when we attempt to determine specific empirical indicators that represent closely related abstract and complex constructs.

Identify all of the uses of the concept. It is important that we know as much about our construct of interest as possible. We should not limit ourselves initially to only one aspect of the construct. We might begin by examining a variety of dictionaries to determine all of the possible meanings of the construct. We could also use online resources, thesauruses, and encyclopedias to examine both the implicit and explicit meanings of the construct.

After we have determined as many meanings of the construct as possible, we would want to identify all literature that discusses or uses the construct in research. Do not limit yourself to the literature from your own discipline. Many of the constructs that we wish to measure in health care settings are not the province of a single discipline but rather have been the focus of interest of researchers from a variety of professions.

Determine all possible attributes, antecedents, and consequences. As we read the articles that relate to our selected construct, we need to keep in mind that we are seeking to identify definitions of the construct, observable or empirical indicators, and any instruments that have been developed to measure some aspect of our selected construct. For example, Jacobsen, Valdimarsdottir, Brown, and Offit (1997) report the results of a study, the purpose of which was to examine the relationship between women's interest in testing and their reasons for wanting or not wanting to be informed of their genetic susceptibility status for breast cancer. From this sample of 112 women, they identified 10 perceived pros of genetic testing and 11 perceived cons of genetic testing. Examples of the pros and cons identified in this study were these:

PROS

- My concerns about developing breast cancer would be reduced if I knew I did not carry the gene.

- My sense of uncertainty about the future would be reduced if I knew whether or not I carried the gene.
- Knowing that I carry the gene would help me decide whether to go for more frequent mammograms.

Cons

- Knowing that I carry the gene could cause me to worry more about other family members who could be carriers.
- My health insurance coverage would be jeopardized if it were found that I carried the gene.
- Knowing that I carry the gene would worsen my quality of life.

The list of pros and cons identified in this study are some of the attributes that we might want to consider as empirical indicators as we develop our instrument on concerns about genetic testing. All of the women in this study had a high familial risk for breast cancer. This would be considered an antecedent regarding their concerns about genetic testing. One of the identified consequences was that it might encourage women to increase their surveillance behavior for breast cancer.

We would continue our review of literature, looking for similar attributes that could be used to measure this phenomenon. After we have completed an exhaustive review of the literature regarding the construct, we will examine the list of attributes that we have identified from all of our resources, looking for clusters of attributes frequently associated with the construct. If there are not distinguishable clusters of attributes, we will try to identify those individual attributes that would be the most useful in helping us to determine the observable or empirical indicators of the selected construct.

Define the empirical indicators. Empirical indicators demonstrate the existence or presence of an actual phenomenon in the real world (Walker & Avant, 1995). In some instances, the attribute and the empirical indicator may be identical. We used some of the attributes reported in the Jacobsen et al. (1997) study as empirical indicators or items in our instrument on concerns about genetic testing. Table 2.1 gives some examples of the attributes listed in the article by Jacobsen and colleagues and the empirical indicators (items) as they appeared in the instrument.

Table 2.1   Examples of Attributes and Their Corresponding Empirical
Indicators of Concerns About Genetic Testing

Attributes	*Empirical Indicators (Items)*
My sense of uncertainty about the future could be reduced if I knew whether or not I carried the gene.	I hope that knowing the results will help reduce my uncertainty about the future.
Knowing that I carry the gene could help me decide whether to go for more frequent mammograms.	I need information to help me make decisions about future screening activities.
If I were found to carry the gene, it could jeopardize my insurance coverage or lead to problems with employers.	I want to know the financial and social implications of being identified as a carrier of the gene.

Additional resources for undertaking a concept analysis. We have given you a brief description of how one approach to concept analysis may be used to identify empirical indicators that could be used as items in instrument development. One of the best resources on the various approaches to concept analysis is the text by Rodgers and Knafl (2000). In each of the chapters of their book, the authors explain a different method and give examples of analyses using the specific approach. Additional resources regarding concept analysis are Chinn and Kramer (1999), Gift (1996), Hupcey, Morse, Lenz, and Tason (1996), Kissinger (1998), Norris (1982), Pedhazur and Schmelkin (1991), and Walker and Avant (1995).

USING QUALITATIVE RESEARCH METHODS
TO IDENTIFY EMPIRICAL INDICATORS

Qualitative research methods can also be used to study facts, observations, and experiences that can be used as empirical indicators when developing an instrument (Knapp, 1998). Three qualitative research methods that are useful for conceptualizing and operationalizing constructs are *phenomenology, naturalistic inquiry,* and *focus groups.*

Two basic assumptions underlie each of these three qualitative research methods. The first assumption is that multiple realities exist and these create meaning for the individual (Streubert & Carpenter,

1999). That is, individuals participate in numerous social actions and as a result come to know phenomena in different ways. For example, if we query two women who have a familial risk for breast cancer about their concerns for genetic testing, we might obtain very different responses. One woman's reality might be that she wants to know what her chances are of having this disease so that she can initiate and participate in various prevention activities. The other woman might not want to know if she is a carrier of the gene because of the potential effects this information could have on her family, job, or health and life insurance. It is important for us to understand this truth from each individual's perspective. The facts, observations, and experiences that are elicited from these women become the empirical indicators that can be used as items on an instrument that measures this phenomenon.

A second assumption is that data will be gathered within the natural context or setting where social actions occur (Hutchinson, 2001). Woods (1988) defines context as the larger domain or picture in which a phenomenon is experienced. Truths cannot be interpreted apart from the natural context in which they are developed. Subjects develop truth through their experiences in their physical environment, other people with whom they relate, the history of their past involvements, and all aspects of the social situation in which they participate (Miles & Huberman, 1994).

In our genetic testing example, the woman who wants to know if she is a carrier of the gene might have known several friends or relatives who were diagnosed with breast cancer. Because this was a part of her natural context, she knows enough about the disease and its trajectory that she wants to be able to participate in various screening activities to either prevent the disease or to have it diagnosed in its early stage. This information regarding her natural context would give us understanding about how her truths regarding concerns about genetic testing were formed.

Phenomenology

The purpose of phenomenology is to describe a particular phenomenon or construct as it is lived or experienced (Carpenter, 1999). *Phenomenology* is "the description of occurrences and events that are the focus of everyday life. It is that lived experience that gives meaning to each individual's perception of a particular phenomenon and is influenced by everything internal and external to the individual" (Carpenter, 1999, p. 44).

When using phenomenology to derive empirical indicators for an instrument (e.g., the Concerns About Genetic Testing Scale), the researcher seeks to remain as unbiased as possible. Therefore, the literature on this construct would not be reviewed until *after* the data are collected and analyzed. If researchers have some knowledge of this construct, then they would need to *bracket* that knowledge and experience (Denzin & Lincoln, 1998; Morse, 1994; Munhall, 1994). Bracketing is a methodological device that requires researchers to deliberately identify and suspend all judgments or ideas about the construct that they are about to study. The purpose of bracketing is to attempt to remove all preconceived ideas and knowledge so that one can hear the truth about the construct as the subject describes it. This is not an easy task if one has extensive knowledge of the research literature related to the construct or has extensive clinical experience with a given population.

Because our purpose is to identify empirical indicators for our instrument regarding concerns about genetic testing, our overarching question for the study needs to reflect this purpose. For example, we might ask, "What is it like to make a decision either to have or not to have genetic testing for breast cancer?" This question incorporates the assumptions of the method and indicates the focus of the study.

Because we want subjects who have experienced this construct, we would purposively select women at familial risk for breast cancer who have considered genetic testing. The researcher and subject would agree on an appropriate place for the interview. The interview would begin with the researcher asking the subject to tell her own story about what it was like to make the decision about having genetic testing for breast cancer. Throughout the interview, probing questions are used for clarification, elaboration, and elicitation of examples. The interviews are transcribed verbatim.

Several approaches to data analysis can be used with the phenomenology method (e.g., Colaizzi, 1978; Giorgi, 1985; Moustakas, 1994; Streubert, 1991; Streubert & Carpenter, 1999; van Kaam, 1959; van Manen, 1984). In this example, we will follow Colaizzi's (1978) method of analysis. Streubert and Carpenter (1999) present an excellent chart that summarizes this method.

First, each subject's description of the experience is reviewed. Next, the transcripts are reread and significant words, phrases, and statements regarding the women's concerns regarding genetic testing are extracted. Meanings are then derived for each word, phrase, or statement. These are then organized into either individual items or categories of items that identify a concern regarding genetic testing. The final list of categories and individual items are next given to approximately five subjects for confirmation. From this list, we would determine which categories and/or individual items within the categories would best measure women's concerns about genetic testing.

We have given you only a brief description of how phenomenology might be used to determine empirical indicators for a construct of interest. More information about phenomenology can be obtained from the following sources: Crabtree and Miller (1992), Denzin and Lincoln (1998), Maykut and Morehouse (1994), Moran (2000), Morse and Field (1995), Moustakas (1994), Munhall (1994), Sokolowski (2000), and Streubert and Carpenter (1999).

Naturalistic Inquiry

Naturalistic inquiry is a method that studies real-world situations as they unfold naturally (Patton, 1990). This unobtrusive approach to inquiry does not manipulate or control informational material and excludes predetermined constraints on the outcomes. The method is open to whatever emerges. Naturalistic inquiry involves the investigation of the construct or phenomenon through observation in its natural setting or "by listening to individuals describe their experience of the phenomenon as it occurs for them" (Streubert & Carpenter, 1999, p. 248). Lincoln and Guba (1985) list 14 characteristics that serve to describe this method: natural setting, human instrument, utilization of tacit knowledge, qualitative methods, purposive sampling, inductive data analysis, grounded theory, emergent design, negotiated outcomes, case study reporting mode, idiographic interpretation, tentative application, focus-determined boundaries, and special criteria for trustworthiness. It is these characteristics that provide the structure for the development of the study.

When using naturalistic inquiry, it is important to state specifically the purpose and research questions of the study. For example, we might state our purpose as follows: *The purpose of this naturalistic inquiry study is to explore women's concerns and knowledge about genetic testing.* Naturalistic inquiry would allow us to explore the women's experiences as told within the context of their own lives. Some appropriate research questions that would follow from our stated study purpose might be these:

- What concerns do women identify regarding genetic testing for breast cancer?
- Where did they get their knowledge of genetic testing?
- What process did the women go through in their decision to have or not have genetic testing?

Lincoln and Guba (1985) recommend purposive or theoretical sampling for naturalistic inquiry because it enhances the likelihood that the range of responses will be broad. In our study, such an approach would increase the chances that the women would express all concerns regarding genetic testing.

The instrument of data collection is the person conducting the interview. The focus of the questions for the open-ended interview might include the following:

- What concerns do you have about genetic testing for breast cancer?
- What do you know about genetic testing?
- Where did you learn about genetic testing?

Based on the women's responses, a more focused exploration could be conducted using probing questions to clarify information and context. The interviews need to be audiotaped and transcribed verbatim. Lincoln and Guba (1985) suggest a method of inductive data analysis with constant comparison, looking for items or clusters of items. These items would then become the empirical indicators that we would use as the items in our instrument.

This is a very brief overview of the naturalistic inquiry method. Other sources that describe this method are Erlandson, Harris, Skipper, and Allen (1993) and Guba (1978). More detailed information on the constant comparison method of data analysis can be obtained from Silverman (1997), Strauss (1987), and Streubert and Carpenter (1999).

Focus Groups

Focus groups are quite useful for identifying empirical indicators of a selected construct. This research method was originally developed in business and was used to obtain a range of opinions on products (Morse & Field, 1995). A focus group is "a semi-structured group session, moderated by a group leader, held in an informal setting with the purpose of collecting information on a designated topic" (Carry, 1994, p. 226). Because participation is enhanced in a group setting, the data regarding the perceptions and opinions are enriched through group interaction.

When using focus groups, the researcher should avoid assuming group leadership. Ideally, the leader should be an external person unknown to the researcher and one who has skills necessary for leading such a group. This will enhance the objectivity of the data collection (Carry, 1994). Even though each session will be tape-recorded, each group should have a recorder present to record those answers that might be missed by the tape recorder. If possible, the recorder should be the person who transcribes the tapes verbatim.

In planning a focus group, we would want to select a fairly homogeneous group because the purpose of this methodology is to encourage the group to share ideas and opinions regarding the topic to be discussed. In our example, because we are interested in collecting data regarding concerns about genetic testing, we might purposively select two different focus groups: one composed of women who do not carry the gene for breast cancer and a second consisting of women who are at risk for carrying the gene. Focus groups are generally composed of 7 to 10 subjects who are either knowledgeable about the selected topic or who have an opinion regarding the topic.

Before convening the focus group, a global question or several questions need to be developed to stimulate the discussion. For our focus group, one such global question might be, "What are your concerns about genetic testing for breast cancer?" This question should elicit responses that will identify specific concerns that could be used as items on our instrument.

Once the focus group is convened, the leader should introduce herself/himself, the members of the group, and the recorder. Next, the rules for the session are established. After the rules are agreed upon, the leader asks the global question and works to ensure that each member of the group has an equal opportunity to respond to the question. It is important that the leader remain neutral and not endorse or agree with the responses of the subjects (Carry, 1994).

After the data have been collected and the tapes transcribed verbatim, the analysis is very similar to other types of qualitative research studies. The global question can be used to identify the initial items that list the concerns regarding genetic testing. As with other qualitative methods, these items can be categorized and duplications deleted.

These categories of individual items can then be used in the instrument to measure the concerns about genetic testing.

Because the focus of this text is on what to do *after* the data have been collected on an instrument, we have limited ourselves to only a brief discussion of focus groups as a method for conceptualizing and operationalizing a construct of interest. To learn more about this qualitative research method, we recommend the following resources: Carry (1994), Crabtree and Miller (1992), and Morse and Field (1995).

ADDITIONAL QUALITATIVE APPROACHES TO IDENTIFYING EMPIRICAL INDICATORS

We have given you a brief introduction to three qualitative research methods that could be helpful in identifying empirical indicators of a construct of interest. Two additional approaches that could be used to elicit empirical indicators for instrument development are *ethnography* (Boyle, 1994; Leininger, 1985) and *case studies* (Stake, 1998). Moreover, the methods that have been described could also be used in combination (e.g., an integrated review of the literature with focus groups). Combinations of methods help to ensure that the domain of the construct has been explored in depth. Care should be taken, however, not to violate the rigor of the various methodologies.

DEVELOPMENT OF THE INSTRUMENT

Let us assume that you have been able to identify the empirical indicators or items that will measure your construct of interest. The next step is to arrange those items in a meaningful format that will allow the data to be collected effectively and efficiently. There are six common components of all instruments: (1) instrument format, (2) printed layout, (3) instructions to the subjects, (4) wording and structuring of the items, (5) response format, and (6) number of items.

Instrument Format

A number of strategies can be used to develop an instrument that seeks to measure a construct of interest. Our choice of strategy is important because it will influence the ultimate format of our items, their response categories, and the methods that we will use to evaluate the instruments (DeVellis, 1991; Kline, 2000a). Some of the more popular scaling approaches include Thurstone scaling, Guttman scaling, semantic differential scales, graphic rating scales, visual analog scales, and Likert scales.

Because the focus of this text is on factor analytic techniques used in instrument development and not on measurement techniques, we will confine our discussion to one of the most commonly used scaling techniques in psychosocial and health care research: the Likert scale. For those readers wishing additional information regarding other scaling methods, there are several excellent resources available. These resources include DeVellis (1991), Kline (2000a), McIver and Carmines (1981), Nunnally and Bernstein (1994), Pedhazur and Schmelkin (1991), Waltz et al. (1991), and Weisberg, Krosnick, and Bowen (1996).

Likert scales (Likert, 1932) are summated rating scales that can be used to measure opinions, beliefs, and attitudes. A summated rating scale is one that consists of a set of items that purports to measure a specific construct and that is typically summed across items to obtain a single score (Pedhazur & Schmelkin, 1991). Likert scales are composed of a number of positively or negatively worded declarative sentences followed by response options that indicate the extent to which the respondent agrees or disagrees with the statement. Examples of positive and negative declarative statements in the Concerns About Genetic Testing instrument are the following:

- I expect to be able to make better health and lifestyle choices as a result.
- Knowing that I carry the gene would cause me to worry more about other family members who could be carriers.

DeVellis (1991) suggests that the declarative statements should be strongly worded without ambiguity. Relatively mild statements may result in too much respondent agreement with little variability among the responses.

As we pointed out, when using a Likert scale, respondents are asked to indicate the extent to which they agree or disagree with a given favorable or unfavorable statement. The response options should be worded such that there are approximately equal intervals of agreement between them (DeVellis, 1991). Although Likert originally used a

5-point item response format (e.g., 1 = *strongly disapprove* to 5 = *strongly approve*), there are many variations to this approach, as we will see later in this discussion.

Printed Layout

Key criteria for determining a suitable print format that will be used for the instrument should be ease of handling and reading, clarity, and an organizational style that is easy to follow. Several additional issues also need to be addressed:

- Who are the respondents?
- Will the instrument be self-administered?
- Where will the instrument be administered?
- Will this instrument be administered alone or will it be given with other instruments?

If the respondents are the frail elderly in a nursing home, the format should be easy for them to handle and read. If the instrument is to be administered to acutely ill children in a clinical setting, it should be formatted in booklet form for easier handling and with a reading level suitable for that age group. If the instrument is to be administered along with other instruments, printing it on colored paper could be considered, as this will help to identify it quickly for future reference.

As the instrument is being developed, give special consideration to the font style and font size that will be used. A *sans serif* font, such as Arial, is one without *serifs*. That is, it does not have small horizontal strokes or lines at the top and bottom of the letters. This style of font makes each letter very distinct and easy to read (Zimmerman & Zimmerman, 1998). Times New Roman, on the other hand, is a *serif* font. It has fine lines embellishing the strokes of letters. Although Times New Roman is one of the most common font styles used for printing books, manuscripts, and newspapers, the embellishments associated with it makes the font more difficult to read for those with poor eyesight. You might consider changing the color of the font. The cost of printing, however, will be considerably more and photocopying may not reproduce the changes in color effectively.

Normal font size is either 10 or 12 point. If the instrument is to be given to children, frail elderly, or individuals who might have some degree of visual impairment, the size of the font should be increased to

Table 2.2   Examples of Font Styles in 12 Point

Type of Font Style	*Example of Font Style*
Arial, 12 point	This style is easy to read because of the distinctness of the letters. **If bolded, it could be administered to an elderly population or those with some visual impairment.**
Arial black, 12 point	**This style is not as easy to read as Arial 12 point. Although written in bold, the openings of the letters a, e, and s are too narrow, resulting in output that is blurred and difficult to read.**
Arial Rounded and bold, 12 point	**This style is not as easy to read as Arial 12 point but provides a bold style that is smaller and rounded in appearance.**
Times New Roman, 12 point	This style is the common style for printing books, manuscripts, and newspapers but is difficult to read for individuals with visual challenges.

14 point or larger. Table 2.2 gives examples of font styles in 12 point that you might consider using in the construction of an instrument.

The instrument should be printed in a format that is easy to handle and read. If the instrument is printed on both sides of the page and stapled in the upper left corner, the person completing the instrument often misses the questions on the back of the page. If the instrument is longer than one page, consider printing the instrument in booklet form. This helps to conserve paper, reduce printing cost, and decrease the chance of missing data because most people are familiar with booklets and know they are to read the back of each page. The booklet format also reduces the chance of pages of the instrument being misplaced.

Instructions to the Subjects

Instructions on how to complete the questionnaire have two basic goals: (1) to give the participants in the study directions for using the scale and (2) to give the participants a common frame of reference in regard to a specific construct (Spector, 1992). If the instrument is not complicated, the instructions can be included in a simple cover letter. If a self-report instrument is to be administered in a clinic or health care agency, it is best that the instructions be included on the instrument itself, preferably at the beginning of the first page. If possible, the first sentence of the instruction section should include the purpose of the instrument and what construct the instrument will be measuring. Instructions should follow this brief introduction.

The directions for the subjects need to be carefully, clearly, and concisely constructed. If the instrument contains several different types of formats, specific sets of instructions need to be provided with each change in format (Nieswiadomy, 2001). Consider the following issues before you start to write the directions:

- How will responses be recorded?
- Will subjects be familiar with the design format that has been selected?
- Will each sheet be optically scanned? If so, will subjects need to use special pencils or pens?
- What do we want the subjects to do with the instruments when they are completed?

Instructions should help the subjects understand the concept that is being examined. The instructions should be worded neutrally so that respondents are not led into providing either perceived socially acceptable responses or responses that reflect researcher bias. These instructions will provide a common frame of reference for all subjects without overfitting or generating leading responses. If subjects are not familiar with the given format, an example of an item, its response options, and a sample answer should also be included in these instructions.

For example, if we were going to administer our instrument Concerns About Genetic Testing to a group of women who are considering undergoing genetic testing for breast cancer, we might present them with the following instructions:

> The purpose of this study is to explore the concerns that individuals have as they consider the possibility of undergoing genetic testing for cancer and to develop a research tool that would accurately reflect these concerns. You are being invited to take part in this study because your health care provider has discussed with you the possibility of undergoing genetic testing for cancer. Approximately 1,000 individuals from throughout the United States will participate in this 3-year study.
>
> Your participation is completely voluntary. You are not required to fill out the attached questionnaire. Your decision whether or not to participate will have no effect whatsoever on the quality of care that you will receive from your health care provider. Your responses to the attached questions are completely confidential and will be identified only by the 4-digit ID at the top of the page. This ID number is being used only to help us with the coding and cleaning of data. Many of the questions may seem the same or redundant, but your response to each question is very important. Please answer each question to the best of your ability.
>
> By completing and returning this survey, you have indicated your willingness to participate in this research. The project has been approved by the [_____] Institutional Review Board. Should you have questions or concerns about this study, please do not hesitate to contact [_____].

Potential subjects often make the decision whether or not to complete the instrument after they have read the instructions. For this reason, instructions need to be pilot tested along with the rest of the instrument. One quick way of doing this is to ask an open-ended question(s) at the end of the instrument regarding the readability and clarity of the instructions. We also have found it helpful to ask respondents for suggestions for improving the readability and clarity of the instrument.

Wording and Structuring of the Items

A next step in developing the instrument is to determine how the items will be worded and structured when they are placed in the instrument. Development of items is not an easy task. There are many

Table 2.3   Some Suggested Guidelines for Developing Items
                 in an Instrument

Avoid statements referring to the past rather than the present unless your construct directly relates to the past.

Avoid factual statements.

Avoid statements likely to be endorsed by almost everyone or almost no one.

Avoid ambiguous pronoun references.

Select items that are believed to cover the entire range of responses concerning the construct of interest.

If personal or delicate content is included, word the item as inoffensively as possible.

Keep language simple, clear, and direct; avoid unnecessary wordiness.

Avoid ambiguous statements (i.e., those that could be interpreted in more than one way).

Use statements in the form of simple sentences rather than compound or complex sentences.

Avoid using words that might not be understood by those who are to be given the instrument.

Place sensitive questions as close as possible to the end of the instrument.

problems that can occur when wording items that can contribute to measurement error. To help decrease measurement error, items need to be stated as clearly and as unambiguously as possible. The researcher also wants to avoid items that are redundant, meaningless, or confusing. Items should be worded at an appropriate reading level for the respondents. It is also useful, if possible, to establish marker variables that will help with the later factor analysis. Table 2.3 presents a compilation of guidelines obtained from a number of difference sources (e.g., DeVellis, 1991; Mishel, 1998; Spector, 1992; Streiner & Norman, 1995; Sudman & Bradburn, 1982; Waltz et al., 1991; Ware, Snyder, McClure, & Jarett, 1972) that might help with the wording and structuring of items.

As indicated in Table 2.3, ambiguous pronoun references should be avoided. An example of an ambiguous pronoun reference is the following statement:

Women should carefully evaluate information about genetic testing that they get from the Internet, as it is often not scientifically based.

It is not clear from the wording if it is the information or the Internet that is not scientifically based. It is also not certain whether it is only women who should carefully evaluate information from the Internet. A clearer wording of this statement might be as follows:

Information obtained from the Internet about genetic testing is often not scientifically based and therefore should be evaluated carefully.

Duplication of statements should also be avoided. For the CGTS scale, for example, if the instrument contains two items, one asking about the need for information about chemotherapy and the other one asking for information about radiation, they could be combined into one item:

I need information regarding different types of breast cancer treatments.

Table 2.4 provides additional suggestions and examples of poorly and more clearly worded items.

Establish the reading level. The reading level of all items needs careful consideration. One approach is to use the reading difficulty level adopted by many community newspapers (i.e., about fifth- or sixth-grade reading level). Both semantic and syntactic factors should be considered when assessing reading difficulty. There are several methods that can be used to assess the reading level of a document. The *Fog Index* is a quick method for manually determining the reading level of the items. This method is described in detail in Burns and Grove (2001). Fry (1977) also lists steps that can be used to quantify the reading level.

We would encourage you to use the tools provided in your word processor. Microsoft Word, for example, provides information about the readability of a document in its *Tools ... Options ... Spelling and Grammar ...* window. By clicking on *Show Readability Statistics,* we can obtain the Flesch-Kincaid Grade Level score for a selected document. This approach rates text on a U.S. grade school level. A score of 6.0 on this scale means that a sixth grader can understand the document. It is recommended in Microsoft Word that, for most standard documents, a score of approximately 7.0 to 8.0 be obtained. Streiner and Norman (1995), however, suggest that unless the reading level is known, a scale

Table 2.4   Additional Guidelines and Some Examples for Writing Items

Guideline	Poor Example	Good Example
Each item should express only one idea.	I worry about being faced with an uncertain diagnosis, future, and insurance coverage.	I worry about being faced with an uncertain diagnosis.
Use positively and negatively worded items but not in the same item.	While genetic testing can help me plan for the future, it can result in decreased health insurance coverage.	(Positive) Genetic testing helps me plan for the future. (Negative) Genetic testing can be responsible for decreased health insurance coverage.
Avoid health care jargon, colloquialisms, and expressions.	I try to eat as many phytoestrogens as possible in my diet to prevent breast cancer.	I try to eat a healthy diet on a daily basis.
Avoid the use of negatives to reverse the wording of an item.	I am not worried about my future life.	I am at peace when I think about my future life.
Avoid exceptionally lengthy items.	I might be helped to make important future life decisions (e.g., getting married and having children) by knowing I carry the gene.	I might be helped to make important future life decisions by knowing I carry the gene.
Avoid multiple negatives.	I am not in favor of the federal government stopping funding for genetic research.	I am in favor of federal funding for genetic research.
Avoid double-barreled items.	I do not support genetic testing because the results could make me ineligible for health insurance.	I am worried about being able to maintain health and life insurance coverage.

(Continued)

Table 2.4 Continued

Guideline	Poor Example	Good Example
Avoid leading questions that suggest a particular kind of answer.	I agree that nurses play an indispensable role in genetic testing.	Nurses play an indispensable role in genetic testing.
Avoid value-laden, universal words, e.g., should, ought, always, none, and never.	Genetic testing should be required for all women who have a familial risk for breast cancer.	I would recommend that all women who have a familial risk for breast cancer have genetic testing.

should not require reading skills beyond that of a sixth grader (i.e., a 12-year-old).

Consider social desirability. As we are developing the instrument, we need to consider if the subjects will answer truthfully or will instead give socially desirable answers (Rosenthal & Rosnow, 1991; Waltz et al., 1991). Social desirability occurs when individuals seek to present themselves in a positive light and therefore respond to a question/item according to what they think is the socially correct answer rather than their true answer (Brink & Wood, 1998; Pedhazur & Schmelkin, 1991). Social desirability not only distorts the data that is collected but also affects the validity of the instrument.

Several social desirability measures have been developed that can be included in the instrument that is being developed. Three of these measures that could be used are the Edwards Social Desirability Scale (Edwards, 1970), Marlowe-Crowne Social Desirability Scale (Crowne & Marlowe, 1964), and the Multi-Dimensional Social Desirability Inventory (Jacobson, Brown, & Ariza, 1983). If the construct that is being measured has a social desirability component to it, we suggest that one or more of these measures be incorporated into the instrument. Streiner and Norman (1995) present an excellent discussion of response biases and approaches to recognizing and addressing the problem.

Develop marker variables. If it is suspected that there are several latent variables (or subscales) that make up the construct of interest, it is helpful to include items in your scale that represent *marker variables*

(Tabachnick & Fidell, 2001). *Marker variables* are thoroughly studied variables with well-known properties that are highly correlated with one and only one subscale (Nunnally & Bernstein, 1994). Therefore, the use of marker variables is restricted to those content areas in which considerable empirical work points to specific variables that could be included as markers in the measurement of a construct.

Marker variables are very useful in a factor analysis because they help to clearly define an extracted factor. It also means that fewer subjects per item will be required for the analysis. Unfortunately, in the initial development of a scale, marker variables are not easily identified. In our Concerns About Genetic Testing example, much of the prior research that has been undertaken in this area has been qualitative and exploratory. Although we may suspect that an *uncertainty about the future* variable may be a marker variable, we do not, as yet, have documented evidence that this item will load on a single factor.

Number of Response Categories

An important area of instrument development is determining the number of response categories our items will have. Issues to consider when determining a response option for the instrument include the following: the desired format of the items, need for variability of responses, number of response options desired, and reverse coding of some items.

Items usually consist of two parts, a stem and response option. The response option that accompanies each stem is generally a series of descriptors that allows the subjects to select their strength of agreement with the stem (DeVellis, 1991). These response options could be dichotomous (e.g., 1 = *yes*, 2 = *no*, 0 = *disagree,* 1 = *agree*) or they could be continuous (e.g., a 5-point Likert scale that ranges from 1 = *strongly agree* to 5 = *strongly disagree*).

There are anchors and scale steps associated with the response options (Mishel, 1998). *Anchors* define the scale steps and can be numbers, percentages, degrees of agreement or disagreement, adjectives, or actual behaviors (Waltz et al., 1991). *Scale steps* are those numbers that fall between the anchors. In Likert scales, most anchors represent degrees of agreement or disagreement with a statement and have numbers connected to them. The following example demonstrates one way that anchors and scale steps can be used in an instrument:

Strongly Agree   5   4   3   2   1   **Strongly Disagree**

In this example, *strongly agree* and *strongly disagree* are the anchors and the numbers, 5 to 1, are the scale steps. Five responses can also be arranged from *strongly disagree, disagree, undecided, agree,* and *strongly agree*, with numbers assigned to each of these words. The following is such an example taken from the Concerns About Genetic Testing instrument:

[Concerns About Genetic Testing Scale]

1	2	3	4	5
Not at all	Slightly	Moderately	Quite a bit	Extremely

In this example, the anchors are *Not at all* and *Extremely*. Although the more favorable responses might be assigned the highest scores and the least favorable responses the lowest scores, some items could be reverse coded to help reduce bias in responding (e.g., preventing subjects from habitually circling the same number), as you will see later in this section.

Item variability. We want the items on our instrument to have variability of responses. *Variability* is the extent to which the scores for an item deviate from the average score, such as the item mean. Two of the most commonly used measures of variability are the standard deviation and the variance. A sufficient range of responses is important in item development because without it, interitem correlations will be restricted and weak. An important source for obtaining variability of responses is the number of response options available to the subject.

Number of response options. When determining the appropriate number of response options, the researcher should consider the following:

- How many response options are needed to allow subjects to discriminate meaningfully?
- How fine a distinction can subjects make?
- How precise should subjects be in their responses?

Some of the factors that influence subjects' ability to discriminate are what is being measured, the specific wording or placement of the response options in the instrument, the clarity or ambiguity of the response options, or a combination of location of the response option on the page and the ambiguity of the response options. In determining the number of response options, the researchers need to consider how many values for the response options they are able and willing to record and analyze. This decision will also depend on the construct of interest being measured.

Another issue to be considered regarding response options is whether there should be an odd or even number of scale steps (DeVellis, 1991; Mishel, 1998; Rosenthal & Rosnow, 1991; Streiner & Norman, 1995; Waltz et al., 1991). For dichotomous response options (e.g., *yes/no* items), the number of scale steps is obviously two. For continuous scales such as the Likert scale, the number of scale steps generally recommended is from five to seven (Kirchhoff, 1999; Pedhazur & Schmelkin, 1991; Sudman & Bradburn, 1982).

An odd number allows for the middle scale step to be the neutral, or indifferent, point. Fewer choices of scale steps (e.g., two, three, or four) restrict the item's variance. Even numbers of scale steps (e.g., two, four, or six) force the subject to either agree or disagree to some extent. The problem is that the subject may, in reality, be undecided. Being forced to make a choice can lead to feelings of frustration on the part of the subject and ultimately a decision to not complete the instrument. As Streiner and Norman (1995) indicate, there is no hard-and-fast rule regarding the number of options; the decision rests with the researchers.

Choosing the numbering system. Do the numbers placed by the responses have an effect on response outcome? Does it matter, for example, whether the numbering of the response options ranges from 1 to 5 or –2 to +2? Interestingly, Streiner and Norman (1995) report that choice of numbering system does indeed affect subject responses.

The authors cite the research of Schwarz, Knauper, Hippler, Noelle-Neumann, and Clark (1991), who reported that, given two scales (0 to 10 vs. –5 to +5) for which extreme responses were similar (*not at all successful* and *extremely successful*), the tendency among respondents was to avoid negative numbers in favor of positive ones. When the 0-10 positive integer scale was used, 34% of the respondents chose the lower portion of the scale (0-5 = *relatively unsuccessful*) compared with only 13% of the respondents using the negative integer scale (5 to 0 = *relatively unsuccessful*). The result was a higher mean score for the negative integer scale (7.38) compared with the positive integer scale (5.96) (Streiner & Norman, 1995, p. 37). Our suggestion, therefore, is that unless you have a strong reason to do otherwise, you should follow the standard format of positive integer formatting.

Reverse coding of items. There are often items in an instrument for which correlations with other items are strongly negative (DeVellis, 1991). If that should happen, one of the items should be reverse scored. When items are constructed, we think of them as relating equally to the construct, but some may be written positively and some negatively. The statements *I feel cheerful* and *I feel downhearted and blue* both pertain to affect, yet they are opposites. If we want the high score to reflect positive affect, then we would assign the high value to *I feel cheerful* and a low value to *I feel downhearted and blue*. *I feel downhearted and blue* would then be reverse scored. The following are examples of such items:

1. I feel downhearted and blue.

1	2	3	4	5
Strongly agree	Agree	Unsure	Disagree	Strongly disagree

2. I feel cheerful.

5	4	3	2	1
Strongly agree	Agree	Unsure	Disagree	Strongly disagree

The reverse coding presented above can be very confusing to the subject because the response *Strongly agree* elicits a 1 for one item and a 5 in the other. The respondent may also fail to notice the change in scaling direction. Although an advantage to this type of error is that it is easily recognized, it also means that the data obtained may be rendered useless (Streiner & Norman, 1995).

A common solution to this problem is to maintain a similarity of response direction (e.g., 1 = *Strongly agree* to 5 = *Strongly disagree*) for all items in the questionnaire. Then, once the data have been entered into the statistical computer package, the variables are recoded to reflect the desired direction.

Number of Items

The number of items that should be included in an instrument is an often-debated topic. In determining the number of items initially to be included in the instrument, the researchers need to consider the item format, time availability of the subject, and characteristics of the population from which they will be collecting the data. In the health sciences, instruments are frequently administered to subjects whose state of health is compromised. Instruments that contain many items and have several response categories can be a burden for these subjects. Too few items will not capture the construct, however. Too many items will tire the subject, who will either not answer the items or not answer them carefully.

Ultimately, item analysis will determine the number of items that are needed to obtain an acceptable level of reliability. Remember that internal consistency reliability is a function not only of how strongly the items correlate with each other but also of how many items there are in the scale (DeVellis, 1991; Pedhazur & Schmelkin, 1991). Because we cannot predict, but only estimate, the size of the correlations among the items at this stage of instrument development, it is best to have a large pool of initial items.

There are no absolute guidelines as to how large is *large*. Nunnally (1978) has argued that "in order to discard items that work poorly, there should be at least one-and-a-half to twice as many items as will appear on the final test" (p. 261). He suggested that if dichotomous items are being used (e.g., *yes/no, true/false* responses), at least 30 final items are required in order to achieve a high reliability. That would mean that approximately 60 initial items are needed for a dichotomous scale. If, on the other hand, Likert scale items are used (e.g., the scale range is 1-5), 10 to 15 initial items per suspected subscale might be sufficient because reliability builds up quite rapidly with such items. If little is known about the construct or if the construct is known to be less internally consistent, we would need to increase the number of initial items to reflect this condition.

Other authors suggest larger pools of initial items. Allen and Yen (1979), for example, suggest developing 1.5 to 3 times as many items as the final version of the instrument will contain. DeVellis (1991) argues for an initial pool of items 3 to 4 times larger than the final instrument. All of these authors assume that the researcher has a preconceived idea of the number of items that the final instrument will contain. Unfortunately, this is rarely the case.

Nunnally and Bernstein (1994) present an alternative strategy for the generation of items. They suggest that a smaller number of items be constructed, such as 30, when it is thought that 40 will be required to obtain a coefficient alpha of .80.[2] These 30 items would then be pilot tested using a small sample of subjects. If either the total collection of items (30) or the most homogeneous subset has a coefficient alpha of less than .60, then the researcher would construct additional items, pilot-test the new group of items with another group of subjects, and repeat the item analysis. The researcher would continue to do this until a coefficient alpha of .80 is obtained. This strategy is labor intensive, but if the early results are not what the researcher wants them to be, then at any time during the process, the instrument can be abandoned, thus saving time, effort, and money.

SCORING THE INSTRUMENT

The purpose of administering an instrument is to distinguish the degree to which the subjects possess a given characteristic (McIver & Carmines, 1981; Mishel, 1998). Except when undertaking a factor analysis, researchers are rarely interested in the score of each separate item on the instrument; instead, they are ultimately interested in each subject's total score or in the subscale scores for the subset of items represented in the instrument. This composite score may consist of a simple summing of items, taking the average score of all of the items, or of transforming the scores in some way to produce standardized scores. In Chapter 7, we will discuss approaches to scoring an instrument in greater detail.

PILOT TESTING THE INSTRUMENT

No one can write a perfect instrument—even if that researcher has had years of experience in developing instruments. Pilot testing a new instrument is imperative (DeVellis, 1991; Kirchhoff, 1999; Nieswiadomy, 2001; Rosenthal & Rosnow, 1991). If resources are not available to pilot test an instrument, then the instrument development study should not be conducted (Sudman & Bradburn, 1982). Pilot testing an instrument before being used in a study allows the researcher to identify those items that are misunderstood or are not being answered in the way that the researcher desires. It also prevents the researcher from spending valuable resources on a study that uses an instrument that is not reliable and has no chance of obtaining construct validity.

Even before pilot testing, it is advisable to obtain peer evaluation of the original draft of the newly formed instrument (DeVellis, 1991). When an instrument is given to peers, they should be asked to respond to each item on the instrument as if they were actually participating in a study. As they go through this process, they should identify and mark those items that are confusing or ambiguous or do not appear to be related to the concept being studied. They should also be asked to critique the instructions and the instrument's appearance:

- Are the instructions clear and easy to follow?
- Are there parts of the instructions that need to be deleted?
- Should additional instructions be included?
- Would an example of how to answer an item help to clarify the instructions?
- Does the instrument's overall appearance look professionally designed?
- Is the instrument easy to read and answer? Is it easy to understand and mark the response items?
- Are the items too crowded on the page?

These questions can be listed and attached to the newly formed instrument, or they can be asked in an interview format. All of the concerns identified by such peers should be addressed and the instrument revised prior to undertaking the pilot testing.

Pilot testing a newly developed instrument should be undertaken with respondents selected from the same population from which the subjects in the proposed major study will be selected (Lackey & Wingate, 1998). Those individuals who participate in the pilot study should not be included in the major study. The sample size will depend on the overall size of the population, the amount of time the researcher has for the pilot study, and the resources available. It is recommended that the sample for a pilot study of an instrument be one tenth the size of the sample proposed for the major study.

Pilot testing can be used to determine the amount of time it takes to complete the instrument, establish if the instructions are clear, and identify if the participants found anything objectionable or inappropriate about the instrument (Wilson, 1985). It is wise to include some open-ended questions at the end of a newly developed instrument that ask the subjects to make any comments that they wish about the instrument.

DETERMINING THE NUMBER OF SUBJECTS

The number of subjects needed to undertake a factor analysis of an instrument will depend on the number of items that are initially included. There is, however, very little agreement among the authorities on factor analysis regarding sample size. Gorsuch (1983) argues that one needs "to have a sufficiently large sample so that anything that would be of interest for interpretation would be significant" (p. 209). He points out, however, that "no one has worked out what a safe ratio of the number of subjects to variable is" (p. 332). Nunnally (1978) suggests that, in order to reduce sampling error, a sample of at least 10 subjects per variable/item is needed. Comrey and Lee (1992) offer the following guidelines to assess the adequacy of the total sample size:

- 50—very poor
- 100—poor
- 200—fair
- 300—good
- 500—very good
- 1,000 or more—excellent (p. 217)

Tabachnick and Fidell (2001) indicate, "as a general rule of thumb, it is comforting to have at least 300 cases for factor analysis" (p. 588). They also point out that a smaller sample size is sufficient (e.g., $n > 150$) when there are several marker variables available with high loadings >.80.

Our suggestion is that there be at least 10 to 15 subjects per initial item, preferably aiming for a sample size that fits Comrey and Lee's *very good* to *excellent* category. Realistically, however, the number of available subjects may restrict that goal. For example, it would be a bit unrealistic to assume that we could easily identify and recruit 1,000 subjects who are considering undergoing genetic testing for cancer. This is an issue that is especially critical when the researcher is examining disease entities that occur in small numbers in the population.

SUMMARY

In this chapter, we have presented an overview of some of the critical issues to be considered in the development and initial testing of an instrument. It is impossible in the space of a single chapter to present this material in detail. Hopefully, the references that we have provided will give you additional sources of information on this important topic. Figure 2.1 summarizes the processes that we have discussed in this chapter. Now that you have successfully weathered the design and initial testing of your instrument, we assume you are ready to begin the descent into factor analysis. Let us move on, then, to Chapter 3, where we will introduce you to some of the matrices that are critical to factor analysis.

NOTES

1. *Levels of measurement* refer to Stevens' (1951, 1959, 1968) four-level classification of scale types. These four levels are based on the scales' ascending level of complexity and are defined as nominal, ordinal, interval, and ratio. For a review of the characteristics of these levels of measurement, please see Pedhazur & Schmelkin (1991), Pett (1997), or Stevens (1959).

2. Coefficient alpha is described in great detail in Chapter 6.

Figure 2.1   Developing and Administering the Instrument

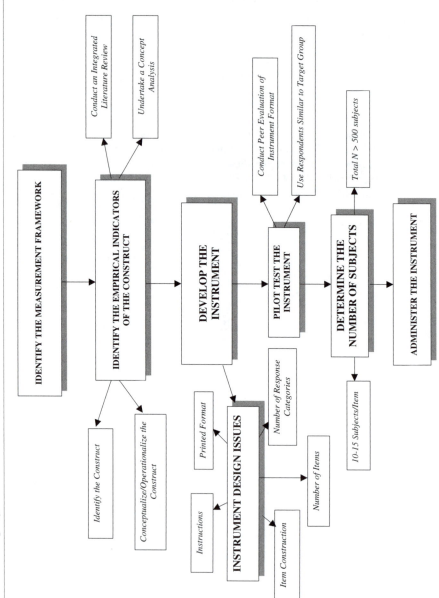

3

Assessing the Characteristics of Matrices

One of the most confusing areas in factor analysis for those of us who are mathematically challenged is this technique's generous use of matrices. In order to obtain an adequate understanding of the critical role that matrices play in factor analysis, the diligent researcher might want to take a course in matrix algebra. At the very least, an informed consumer should have an elementary understanding of what a matrix is, common types of matrices, determinants of matrices, and the various tests of matrices that are undertaken in factor analysis. These issues will be the focus of this chapter. For further information on these topics, we suggest that you examine Gorsuch (1983), Hays (1994), Pedhazur and Schmelkin (1991), Stevens (2001), and Tabachnick and Fidell (2001).

Appendix A presents the Concerns About Genetic Testing Scale (CGTS) that has been used to generate the matrices that are presented in this chapter. To obtain these matrices, 205 individuals were presented with a set of 20 items that people had indicated were concerns to them when making a decision about whether to undergo genetic testing for cancer. Next, they were asked to assess, on a five-point

Likert scale (1 = *not at all* to 5 = *extremely*), the extent to which a particular item (e.g., *being worried about being faced with an uncertain diagnosis*) was a concern to them. For each individual, then, we obtained responses to each of the 20 items. From these responses, we generated a set of matrices that are critical to the process of factor analysis.

Before discussing these matrices in detail, it is important that we review with you some elementary characteristics of matrices. We will supplement our discussion of these matrices with computer-generated examples obtained from two statistical computer packages: SPSS for Windows (v. 11.0) and the SAS System for Windows (SAS) (v. 8.2).

As we indicated in the Introduction, we have limited our presentation in the main body of the text to printouts obtained from SPSS for Windows, with the corresponding SAS examples given in Appendix B. References to SAS output will be cited in parentheses following the SPSS for Windows examples. When discussing this output, we will use a similar numbering system so that you can compare the SPSS and SAS results. Because of round-off differences, there may be slight discrepancies in the output generated by the two programs. If you are interested in learning more about SAS and its factor analysis programs, there are several excellent resources available. These include Cody and Smith (1997), Delwiche and Slaughter (1998), Der and Everitt (2002), and Hatcher (1994). Similar resources are available for SPSS for Windows. These include George and Mallery (2000), Green, Salkind, and Akey (2000), and Norusis (2000).

CHARACTERISTICS AND TYPES OF MATRICES

A matrix is a two-dimensional rectangular array of numbers or symbols. Typically, when graphically displayed, a matrix is enclosed by brackets ([ ]) and is summarized as a bold letter, for example, **A**:

$$\mathbf{A} = \begin{bmatrix} 4 & 1 \\ 2 & 7 \\ 7 & 2 \\ 5 & 9 \end{bmatrix}$$

The intent in presenting a matrix is to display a large amount of data in a succinct form. Simple arithmetic manipulations of matrices can be undertaken (e.g., addition, subtraction, multiplication, and division). Matrices also lend themselves readily to powerful mathematical manipulation and are used in computer operations to generate multivariate statistical analyses.

The number of rows and columns defines the *dimensions* of a matrix. The *elements* of a matrix are the numbers or symbols that appear in the matrix. A matrix that has four rows and two columns, such as that presented above, for example, is known as a 4×2 matrix. Because matrix **A** has more rows than columns, it is called a *vertical* matrix. A 2×4 matrix, such as **B** below, has more columns than rows and is therefore called a *horizontal matrix*:

$$\mathbf{B} = \begin{bmatrix} 4 & 2 & 7 & 5 \\ 1 & 7 & 2 & 9 \end{bmatrix}$$

There are a number of matrices that are critical to factor analysis. We will be examining several of these matrices in detail. These include the *data, correlation, covariance,* and *identity matrices*.

The Data Matrix

A matrix that usually has more rows than columns and therefore is *vertical* is the *data matrix*. The data matrix is typically identified with the bold letter **X**. In an exploratory factor analysis, **X** is the data matrix in which the columns are the scale items being considered in the factor analysis (e.g., Items 1-20 on the CGTS presented in Appendix A). The rows represent each subject's responses to these items. Thus, in a data matrix, there are as many rows as subjects and as many columns as variables.

In SPSS for Windows and SAS, the data matrix is represented by the spreadsheet created in either the Data Editor (SPSS) or the Table Editor (SAS). Figure 3.1 presents a portion of the spreadsheet that was generated in SPSS for Windows for the 205 individuals who completed the 20-item CGTS. A similar spreadsheet that was generated in SAS can be found in Appendix B, Figure B.3.1.

Subject 1, for example, assigned the value of '4' ("quite a bit") to the first five items of the CGTS. This vertical data matrix would be described as a 205×20 matrix because there are 205 respondents (rows) who answered all 20 items (columns). In Figure 3.1, the responses of the 205 subjects on the 20 items in the CGTS constitute the 4,100 $(205 \times 20 = 4,100)$ elements that make up this data matrix.

Figure 3.1 Data Matrix Generated From the Concerns About Genetic Testing Scale (CGTS), Appendix A

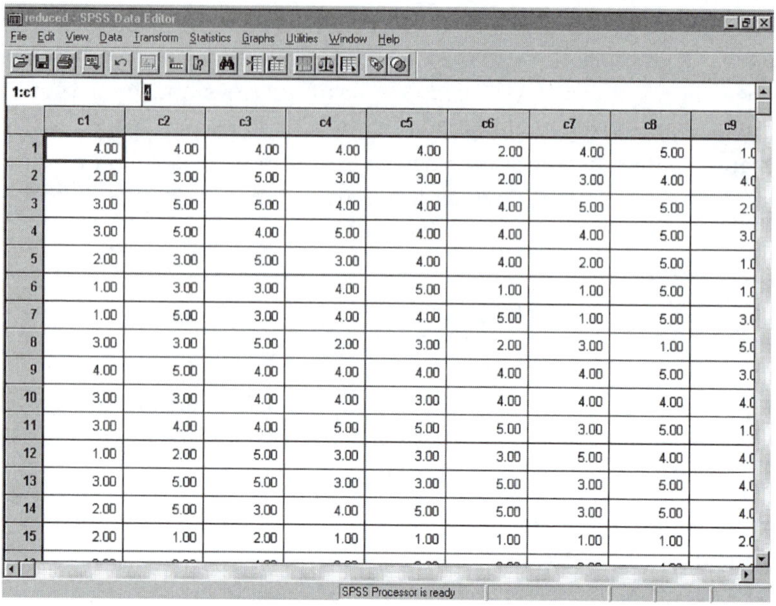

	c1	c2	c3	c4	c5	c6	c7	c8	c9
1	4.00	4.00	4.00	4.00	4.00	2.00	4.00	5.00	1.0
2	2.00	3.00	5.00	3.00	3.00	2.00	3.00	4.00	4.0
3	3.00	5.00	5.00	4.00	4.00	4.00	5.00	5.00	2.0
4	3.00	5.00	4.00	5.00	4.00	4.00	4.00	5.00	3.0
5	2.00	3.00	5.00	3.00	4.00	4.00	2.00	5.00	1.0
6	1.00	3.00	3.00	4.00	5.00	1.00	1.00	5.00	1.0
7	1.00	5.00	3.00	4.00	4.00	5.00	1.00	5.00	3.0
8	3.00	3.00	5.00	2.00	3.00	2.00	3.00	1.00	5.0
9	4.00	5.00	4.00	4.00	4.00	4.00	4.00	5.00	3.0
10	3.00	3.00	4.00	4.00	3.00	4.00	4.00	4.00	4.0
11	3.00	4.00	4.00	5.00	5.00	5.00	3.00	5.00	1.0
12	1.00	2.00	5.00	3.00	3.00	3.00	5.00	4.00	4.0
13	3.00	5.00	5.00	3.00	3.00	5.00	3.00	5.00	4.0
14	2.00	5.00	3.00	4.00	5.00	5.00	3.00	5.00	4.0
15	2.00	1.00	2.00	1.00	1.00	1.00	1.00	1.00	2.0

Square Versus Symmetric Matrices

As indicated, the data matrix in Figure 3.1 is vertical because it has more respondents (rows) than items (columns). A matrix that has the same number of rows and columns (e.g., 20 rows and 20 columns) is called a *square* matrix. The numbers that go from the top left-hand corner of the matrix to its bottom right-hand corner represent the principal or main *diagonal* of a square matrix. A *symmetric* matrix is a square matrix that has the same elements above its principal diagonal as below except that the numbers are transposed. One such symmetric matrix that is very important to factor analysis is the *correlation matrix* (**R**).

The Correlation Matrix

Appendix C (Table C3.1) presents the 20×20 correlation matrix for the 20 items in the CGTS. Because a 20×20 matrix would be too cumbersome to present in this chapter, the first eight items have been extracted for further discussion. This reduced 8×8 correlation matrix is presented in Figure 3.2.

Figure 3.2   The Full Correlation Matrix (**R**) for 8 of 20 Items in the CGTS

① Correlation of C1 with C2: $r = .07$.

② Correlation of C1 with C5: $r = -.04$.

	C1	C2	C3	C4	C5	C6	C7	C8
C1	1.00	.07	.34	.26	-.04	.17	.45	.10
C2	.07	1.00	.25	.56	.39	.51	.19	.28
C3	.34	.25	1.00	.24	.09	.38	.61	.21
C4	.26	.56	.24	1.00	.38	.39	.35	.25
C5	-.04	.39	.09	.38	1.00	.48	.06	.33
C6	.17	.51	.38	.39	.48	1.00	.36	.19
C7	.45	.19	.61	.35	.06	.36	1.00	.07
C8	.10	.28	.21	.25	.33	.19	.07	1.00

The correlation matrix in Figure 3.2 is both square and symmetric. It is a *square matrix* because it has as many rows as columns. It is *symmetric* because the principal diagonal of **R** is composed of 1's and the values below this diagonal are equal to those above the diagonal except that the numbers are transposed. For example, the numbers in row 1 (e.g., 1.00, .07, .34, and .26) are similar to column 1 (1.00, .07, .34, and .26). This is because the correlation between the row and column items is the same (e.g., C1 with C2 and C2 with C1). It is common, therefore, to avoid redundancy by presenting only the lower left or upper right triangle of the matrix as in Figure 3.3. When both triangles are presented (as in Figure 3.2), the matrix is called a *full matrix*.

Matrix data may be entered directly into the computer in both SPSS for Windows and SAS. SPSS for Windows uses the *Matrix Data . . .* command that is available in syntax mode (Figure 3.4). The subcommand *format* ① can then be used to specify the matrix format: upper or lower triangular, full, square, or rectangular, and whether there are values on the diagonal. The default format is a lower triangular matrix and, unless otherwise indicated, the contents are assumed to be a correlation matrix (SPSS, 1993). Matrix data may be input directly into SAS using DATA input statements. The DATA input statements for the eight-item CGTS (C1-C8) correlation matrix are presented in Appendix B (Figure B.3.2).

A correlation matrix summarizes the interrelationships among a set of variables or, as in our case, a set of items in a scale. The most

Figure 3.3 The Eight-Item Correlation Matrix, **R**, Presented as a Lower Triangular Matrix

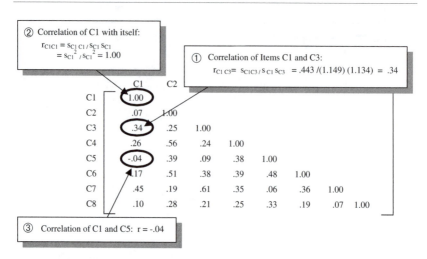

② Correlation of C1 with itself:

$$r_{C1C1} = s_{C1\,C1}/s_{C1}\,s_{C1}$$
$$= s_{C1}^{2}/s_{C1}^{2} = 1.00$$

① Correlation of Items C1 and C3:

$$r_{C1\,C3} = s_{C1C3}/s_{C1}\,s_{C3} = .443\,/(1.149)\,(1.134) = .34$$

	C1	C2						
C1	1.00							
C2	.07	1.00						
C3	.34	.25	1.00					
C4	.26	.56	.24	1.00				
C5	-.04	.39	.09	.38	1.00			
C6	.17	.51	.38	.39	.48	1.00		
C7	.45	.19	.61	.35	.06	.36	1.00	
C8	.10	.28	.21	.25	.33	.19	.07	1.00

③ Correlation of C1 and C5: $r = -.04$

common form of correlation matrix used in factor analysis is a matrix consisting of Pearson product moment correlations (also called *Pearson r* or r_{xy}). To understand how these correlations are obtained, we must first distinguish between the *variance* of a given item, its *standard deviation*, and the *covariance* between two items.

Variance, Standard Deviation, and Covariance

The *variance* (s_x^2) of a given item indicates the extent to which the individual scores for a particular item deviate from the item's mean. The variance represents the average of the squared deviations of each of the scores from the item's mean (Hays, 1994). The formula for the sample variance, s_x^2, is given as follows:

$$s_x^2 = \frac{\sum_{1}^{N}(x - \bar{x})^2}{N - 1}$$

where

$\sum$ = sum from the first to last observation

x = individual observation for Item X

$\bar{x}$ = mean for Item X

N = number of observations for Item X

Figure 3.4   Syntax Commands for Entering Matrix Data Into SPSS for Windows to Generate a Factor Analysis

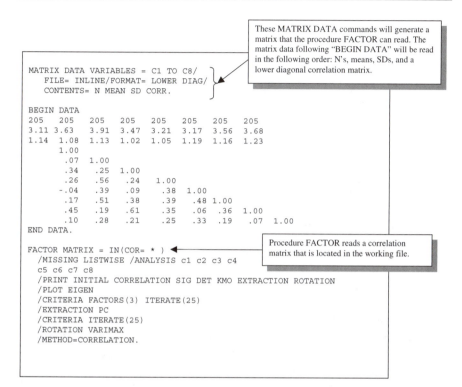

These MATRIX DATA commands will generate a matrix that the procedure FACTOR can read. The matrix data following "BEGIN DATA" will be read in the following order: N's, means, SDs, and a lower diagonal correlation matrix.

```
MATRIX DATA VARIABLES = C1 TO C8/
   FILE= INLINE/FORMAT= LOWER DIAG/
   CONTENTS= N MEAN SD CORR.

BEGIN DATA
205    205    205    205    205    205    205
3.11 3.63    3.91   3.47   3.21   3.17   3.56   3.68
1.14   1.08   1.13   1.02   1.05   1.19   1.16   1.23
       1.00
        .07   1.00
        .34    .25   1.00
        .26    .56    .24   1.00
       -.04    .39    .09    .38   1.00
        .17    .51    .38    .39    .48  1.00
        .45    .19    .61    .35    .06   .36  1.00
        .10    .28    .21    .25    .33   .19    .07  1.00
END DATA.

FACTOR MATRIX = IN(COR= * )
   /MISSING LISTWISE /ANALYSIS c1 c2 c3 c4
   c5 c6 c7 c8
   /PRINT INITIAL CORRELATION SIG DET KMO EXTRACTION ROTATION
   /PLOT EIGEN
   /CRITERIA FACTORS(3) ITERATE(25)
   /EXTRACTION PC
   /CRITERIA ITERATE(25)
   /ROTATION VARIMAX
   /METHOD=CORRELATION.
```

Procedure FACTOR reads a correlation matrix that is located in the working file.

Note that the formula for the sample variance, s_x^2, contains $(N - 1)$ in the denominator instead of (N). The reason for this is that the formula for the sample variance, s_x^2, that uses only (N) in the denominator is a *biased* estimator of the population variance (σ^2); it underestimates σ^2 by a factor of $N/(N - 1)$. To adjust for this underestimation, a corrected version of the variance, s_x^2, is used with $(N - 1)$ in the denominator. This unbiased version of the variance is what is generated in statistical computer packages and handheld calculators.

Although the variance is a useful measure of variability of a set of scores about its mean, it has the disadvantage of being represented in squared measurement units. By taking the positive square root of the variance, we obtain an index of variability of scores for an item in its original measurement units. This index is called the *standard deviation* and is

$$s_x = \sqrt{s_x^2}$$

The *covariance* of two items is a measure of two items' joint variability or degree of association (Rice, 1994). The sample covariance of two items, x and y, is defined as

$$s_{xy} = \frac{\sum_{1}^{N}(x - \bar{x})(y - \bar{y})}{N - 1}$$

where

x = individual observation for Item X

$\bar{x}$ = mean for Item X

y = individual observation for Item Y

$\bar{y}$ = mean for Item Y

N = number of paired observations for Items X and Y

The covariance is restricted in its use as a measure of association because its size is influenced by the unit(s) of measurement associated with the variables X and Y and is not standardized across all variables. For example, if our items on the CGTS were measured on a scale of 1 to 10 instead of 1 to 5 as presented in Appendix A, the covariance for the two variables C1 and C3 would be larger merely because of the difference in scale of measurement for the two variables. An alternative measure of association, the size of which does not depend on the scale of measurement, is the Pearson product moment correlation (r_{xy}).

Calculating the Pearson Product
Moment Correlation Coefficient

There are several ways to calculate the Pearson product moment correlation coefficient, r_{xy}. One approach is to define r_{xy} in terms of the covariance,

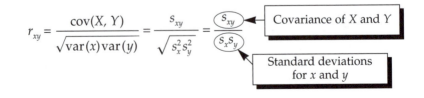

$$r_{xy} = \frac{\text{cov}(X, Y)}{\sqrt{\text{var}(x)\,\text{var}(y)}} = \frac{s_{xy}}{\sqrt{s_x^2 s_y^2}} = \frac{s_{xy}}{s_x s_y}$$

Covariance of X and Y

Standard deviations
for x and y

where

s_{xy} = sample covariance for Items X and Y, cov(X, Y)

s_x^2 = sample variance for Item X, var(X)

s_y^2 = sample variance for Item Y, var(Y)

$s_x = \sqrt{s_x^2}$ = the standard deviation for Item X

Note that by cross-multiplying the correlation coefficient, r_{xy}, by the two items' standard deviations, we are able to obtain the covariance, s_{xy}.

$$s_{xy} = (r_{xy})(s_x)(s_y)$$

The size of r_{xy} does not depend on specific units of measurement because the measurement units in the numerator and denominator cancel each other out. This dimensionless quality makes r_{xy} a preferable measure of association compared with the covariance s_{xy} because it can be used with and compared across different units of measurement.

The Pearson r (r_{xy}) ranges between −1.00 and +1.00, with higher absolute values indicating a stronger relationship between two variables or, in our case, two items in a scale. A *positive* value for r_{xy} indicates a direct relationship between two items. That is, subjects who rated a given item high tended to rate the comparison item also high. In Figure 3.2, for example, the correlation between Items C1 (*I might increase my sense of personal control over the condition after I receive the testing results*) and C7 (*I hope to be able to make better health and lifestyle choices as a result*) was .45. This means that respondents who scored high on C5 also scored high on C7.

A *negative* value for the Pearson r indicates an inverse relationship between two items: high scores on one item are associated with low scores on a second item. Unfortunately, the correlation matrix in Figure 3.2 does not present us with a strong negative correlation. One could imagine, for example, that there would be a negative correlation between such variables as stress and coping: as a person's perceived stress increases, that person's perceived ability to cope declines. A value for r_{xy} that is close to 0 indicates no relationship between two items. The correlation matrix in Figure 3.2 presents us

Table 3.1   Suggested Rule of Thumb for Evaluating the Strength
of the Pearson r

Absolute Value of rxy	R^2	Strength of Relationship
.00–.29	.00–.08	Weak
.30–.49	.09–.24	Low
.50–.69	.25–.48	Moderate
.70–.89	.49–.80	Strong
.90–1.00	.81–1.00	Very strong

with several near-zero correlations, e.g., C1 with C2 (.07) ① and C1 with C5 (−.04) ②.

Determining the Strength of Relationship Between Items

The coefficient of determination, r_{xy}^2, is used to assess the strength of relationship between the variables x and y. R_{xy}^2 represents the proportion of variance in variable X that is associated with variable Y. A suggested rule of thumb for evaluating the strength of the relationship is presented in Table 3.1 (Hinkle, Wiersma, & Jurs, 1998; Pett, 1997). For Items C5 and C7, for which the correlation is .45, $r_{xy}^2 = (.45)^2$. This means that the proportion of variance that the two items share is $(.45)^2$, or (.2025). According to Table 3.1, this is at best a *low* relationship.

Although Table 3.1 presents a reasonable rule of thumb for evaluating the strength of relationships among variables, these guidelines are not written in stone. The exploratory nature of the study and the theoretical maturity and content of the construct under study helps to determine the meaning of the strength of association among items.

Computing the Pearson Correlation Coefficient: An Example

Suppose we were interested in examining the degree of association between items C1 (variable X) and C3 (variable Y) on the CGTS (see Figure 3.3). To calculate the Pearson r for C1 and C3 by hand, we would first calculate the variances, standard deviations, and covariance for the two items. Given that there are 205 observations for C1 and C3, this would be a tedious task indeed! Luckily, all of these values are easily obtained from the descriptive statistics generated in SPSS for Windows using the commands *Analyze . . . Descriptive Statistics . . . Descriptives*. These results are presented in Table 3.2. PROC CORR in SAS will

Table 3.2 Descriptive Statistics for Items C1 to C8 of the Concerns About Genetic Testing Scale (CGTS)

Descriptive Statistics

	N	Minimum	Maximum	Mean	Std. Deviation
Increase of personal control	205	1.00	5.00	3.1122	1.14279
Worry about uncertain diagnosis	205	1.00	5.00	3.6341	1.08366
What to do to manage risk	205	1.00	5.00	3.9122	1.13418
Help reduce uncertainty about future	205	1.00	5.00	3.4732	1.02207
Fear ambiguity of results	205	1.00	5.00	3.2098	1.05250
Worry about diagnosis I can't do anything about	205	1.00	5.00	3.1707	1.19029
Hope to make better health, lifestyle choices	205	1.00	5.00	3.5610	1.15574
Worried about loss of health and life insurance coverage	205	1.00	5.00	3.6829	1.23350
Valid N (listwise)	205				

generate similar descriptive statistics as well as the correlation and covariance matrices (Appendix B, Figure B3.3)[1].

Having done that, we find that the sample variances, standard deviations, and covariance for Items C1 and C3 are as follows: $s_{C1}^2 = 1.32$, $s_{C1} = 1.149$, $s_{C3}^2 = 1.296$, $s_{C3} = 1.134$, and $s_{C1C3} = 0.443$. Using these values for C1 and C3, we can easily calculate the Pearson r that was presented to us in Figure 3.3 (Appendix B, Table B3.1A)① as

$$r_{xy} = \frac{\text{cov}(C1, C3)}{\sqrt{\text{var}(C1)\,\text{var}(C3)}} = \frac{s_{C1,C3}}{\sqrt{s_{C1}^2 s_{C3}^2}} = \frac{s_{C1,C3}}{s_{C1} s_{C3}} = \frac{0.443}{(1.149)(1.134)} = 0.34$$

The positive correlation of .34 between Items C1 and C3 indicates that subjects tended to rate these items in a similar direction. That is, higher scores on C1 were associated with higher scores on C3. The relationship between the two items is weak, however, because the correlation is only .34. Note that the values on the diagonal of the correlation matrix presented in Figure 3.3 are all equal to 1.00 ②. These diagonal values (1.00) represent the correlation of the items with themselves, that is, C1 with C1 and C3 with C3. Note also that the correlation between C1 and C5 is negative ($r = -.04$) ③ (Appendix B, Table B3.1B). Although the negative sign suggests an inverse correlation between C1 and C5, the fact that it is so close to 0 indicates that the association is nearly nonexistent.

The Covariance Matrix (C)

The covariance matrix (**C**), sometimes referred to as the *variance-covariance matrix*, is a critical matrix in factor analysis because it is used to generate the correlation matrix. The variances for each item are presented on the principal diagonal of the matrix, and the item covariances are on the off-diagonal. Figure 3.5 presents the covariance matrix for the first eight items of the CGTS (for the SAS output, see Appendix B, Table B3.1A).

Figure 3.5 (and Table B3.1A) indicates that the variance for Item 1, C1, is 1.32 ① and the covariance between Items C1 and C3 is .44 ②. These values can be readily obtained in SPSS for Windows when generating a correlation matrix using the commands *Analyze ... Correlate ... Bivariate ...*, selecting the items to be correlated (e.g., C1-C8) and, then,

Figure 3.5   Covariance Matrix (**C**) for 8 of 20 Items of the CGTS

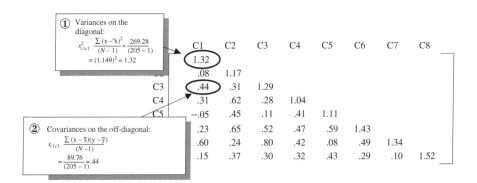

in the *Options . . .* menu, clicking on the *cross product deviations and covariance* box. Both the correlation and covariance matrices can also be obtained when generating a factor analysis solution (*Analyze . . . Data Reduction . . . Factor . . .*), as you will see in Chapter 4. The SAS PROC CORR commands for generating the covariance matrix are presented in Appendix B (Figure B.3.3).

Like the correlation matrix, the covariance matrix is both square and symmetric and is often presented as a triangular matrix (e.g., Figure 3.5). Such triangular matrices can also be saved to a disk to be directly entered into the computer for statistical analyses.

The Identity Matrix

A special case of the square matrix is the *identity matrix*, **I** (Figure 3.6). This is a matrix in which 1's appear on the diagonal and 0's on the off-diagonal. An example of such an identity matrix would be a correlation matrix in which all items on the off-diagonal are completely uncorrelated.

A correlation matrix that is an identity matrix is not a welcome sight in factor analysis because its presence would imply that there are no interrelationships among the items. As you will see when we examine tests of matrices later in this chapter, the presence of an identity matrix is what is being tested for in Bartlett's test of sphericity (Bartlett, 1950).

Figure 3.6   Example of a 3 × 3 Correlation Matrix That Is an Identity
Matrix

$$
\begin{bmatrix}
1.00 & .00 & .00 \\
.00 & 1.00 & .00 \\
.00 & .00 & 1.00
\end{bmatrix}
$$

Determinant of a Matrix

The *determinant* of a matrix is a unique numeric value that is
associated only with square matrices. It is denoted either by *Det(A)*
or by vertical lines on each side of the matrix symbol, e.g., |A|. |R|
represents the determinant for the correlation matrix and |C| is the
determinant for the covariance matrix.

The determinant is critical for solving simultaneous equations
using matrix algebra. The determinant "determines" whether or not a
given square matrix will have an *inverse* (Hays, 1994, p. 901), something that is essential to the undertaking of mathematical operations of
matrices, especially division. The inverse of a matrix is comparable
with the reciprocal of a number. For example, the reciprocal of 15 is 15^{-1},
or 1/15. If one were to multiply a number by its inverse, the resulting
value would be 1, that is, $(15)(15)^{-1} = 1$. The inverse of the correlation
matrix, **R**, is $\mathbf{R}^{-1}$. It is defined as that matrix $\mathbf{R}^{-1}$ such that $[\mathbf{R}][\mathbf{R}]^{-1} = \mathbf{I}$.
That is, an identity matrix (**I**) with 1's on the diagonal and 0's on the
off-diagonal is produced when a matrix is multiplied by its inverse
(Gorsuch, 1983; Hays, 1994).

Not all square matrices have inverses. To determine if a matrix has
an inverse, it is necessary to calculate the determinant of the matrix. If
the determinant is equal to 0, then there is no inverse associated with
the matrix and further mathematical manipulations of the matrix are
inadvisable. A square matrix that has no inverse is called a *singular*
matrix (Fraleigh, Beauregard, & Katz, 1994; Lawley & Maxwell, 1971).
This is not what we want in factor analysis.

Although determinants for 2 × 2 and 3 × 3 matrices are easily calculated by hand, it is quite cumbersome and time-consuming to calculate determinants for larger matrices. Luckily, computers perform these

Figure 3.7   Calculation of the Determinant of a 2 × 2 Matrix

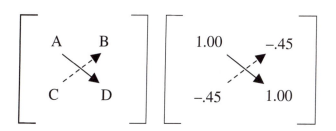

$$\text{Det} \, | \, \mathbf{A} \, | = AD - CB = (1.00)^2 - (-.45)^2$$

laborious operations quite easily. Nevertheless, to give you an idea of what a determinant is, we will calculate a determinant for both a 2 × 2 and a 3 × 3 correlation matrix. Later in this chapter, we will address the meaning of high or low values for the determinant.

Determinant of a 2 × 2 Matrix

The determinant of a 2 × 2 matrix is obtained by calculating the difference between the cross-products of the four cells. In Figure 3.7, for example, given the values in the four cells, A, B, C, and D, the determinant of that matrix is AD – CB:

$$\begin{aligned}
\text{Det}(\mathbf{R}) = | \, \mathbf{R} \, | &= AD - CB \\
&= (1.00)(1.00) - (-.45)(-.45) \\
&= 1.00 - .2025 = .7975
\end{aligned}$$

Determinant for a 3 × 3 Matrix

Calculating a determinant for a 3 × 3 matrix is somewhat similar though a bit more complicated than the 2 × 2 approach. It is still relatively easy to obtain if one uses the augmentation approach suggested by Hays (1994, pp. 950-951). Suppose, for example, we had a 3 × 3 correlation matrix such as that presented in Figure 3.8A.

According to Hays, we would first augment the correlation matrix by writing it again adjacent to the original matrix as in Figure 3.8B. Next, we would multiply across each of the three diagonals extending both downward (AEI, BFG, and CDH) and upward (GEC, HFA, and

Figure 3.8   Obtaining a Determinant for a 3×3 Correlation Matrix

A. The initial 3×3 matrix with nine cells, A-I

$$
\begin{bmatrix}
1.00 & -.45 & .30 \\
-.45 & 1.00 & .10 \\
.30 & .10 & 1.00
\end{bmatrix}
\text{ or }
\begin{bmatrix}
A & B & C \\
D & E & F \\
G & H & I
\end{bmatrix}
$$

B. Augmenting the 3×3 matrix

$$
\begin{bmatrix}
1.00 & -.45 & .30 & \vdots & 1.00 & -.45 & .30 \\
-.45 & 1.00 & .10 & \vdots & -.45 & 1.00 & .10 \\
.30 & .10 & 1.00 & \vdots & .30 & .10 & 1.00
\end{bmatrix}
$$

C. Multiplying across the downward and upward diagonals

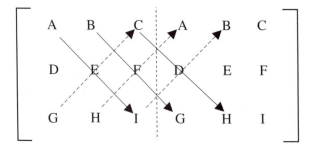

$$[AEI + BFG + CDH] - [GEC + HFA + IDB]$$

IDB), summing each of the results independently as in Figure 3.8C. Finally, we would subtract the upward sum [GEC + HFA + IDB] from the downward sum [AEI + BFG + CDH] to obtain the determinant, that is,

$$\text{Det}(\mathbf{R}) = |\mathbf{R}| = [AEI + BFG + CDH] - [GEC + HFA + IDB]$$

$$
\begin{aligned}
[AEI + BFG + CDH] &= [(1.00)(1.00)(1.00) + (-.45)(.10)(.30) \\
&\quad + (.30)(-.45)(.10)] \\
&= [(1.00) + (-.0135) + (-.0135)] \\
&= [.9730]
\end{aligned}
$$

$$
\begin{aligned}
[GEC + HFA + IDB] &= [(.30)(1.00)(.30) + (.10)(.10)(1.00) \\
&\quad + (1.00)(-.45)(-.45)] \\
&= [.09 + 0.1 + .2025] \\
&= [.3025]
\end{aligned}
$$

$$\text{Det }(\mathbf{R}) = |\mathbf{R}| = [.9730] - [.3025] = .6705$$

In general, the values for determinants of matrices can range between $-\infty$ and $+\infty$. Values for the determinant of a correlation matrix, however, range only between 0 and 1.00. When all of the off-diagonal elements in the correlation matrix are equal to 0, the determinant of that matrix will be equal to 1. That would mean that **R** is an identity matrix, **I**. If this should occur, it is unwise to continue with a factor analysis because there would be as many factors as there are items.

A value of 0 for a determinant indicates that there is at least one linear dependency in the matrix. That means that one or more columns (or rows) in the matrix can be obtained by linear transformations of other columns (or rows) or combinations of columns (or rows). An example of a linear transformation is when adding or subtracting two columns results in a third column and all three columns are included in the matrix to be analyzed.

Linear dependency could occur, for example, when one item is highly correlated with the other (e.g., $r > .80$) or when a total scale score is included in the matrix along with the subscales that made up the total scale. It could also occur when one person's answers are the exact replica or are a linear combination of another person's answers. The result is that the matrix is no longer square and has either more rows than columns or vice versa. When this occurs, SPSS for Windows issues the following warning:

Determinant = .0000
This Matrix Is Not Positive-Definite

When there are linear dependencies in the correlation matrix, SAS will issue the following message:

ERROR: CORRELATION MATRIX IS SINGULAR

As we indicated, a correlation matrix that is singular has no inverse and its determinant is equal to 0. Unfortunately, this SAS message only appears in the log file, not the output file, which means that an unwitting user may overlook this critically important message.

To state that a correlation matrix is not positive-definite implies that at least some of the eigenvalues associated with the correlation matrix are not positive. We will go into the meaning of this condition in greater detail when we discuss the relationship between determinants and eigenvalues in Chapter 4. For now, be aware that we have major problems with the correlation matrix if the determinant is equal to or very close to 0. It should also be noted that, even though SPSS for Windows issues this caution, the program may continue to produce output that is spurious, if not meaningless. Remember that *Garbage In Is Garbage Out (GIGO)*!

By clicking on the following commands in SPSS for Windows, the researcher can open the dialog boxes presented in Figure 3.9. These commands will generate the calculated determinant of the correlation matrix and significance levels for the items in a proposed scale:

Analyze . . . Data Reduction . . . Factor . . . Descriptives
   ✓ *Coefficients*
   ✓ *Significance levels*
   ✓ *Determinant*

Unfortunately, in SAS, a calculated value for the determinant is not available in either the PROC FACTOR program or any other SAS program.

Figure 3.9   SPSS Dialog Boxes Used to Generate the Correlation Matrix, Significance Levels, and Determinant for Items C1 to C8 of the CGTS

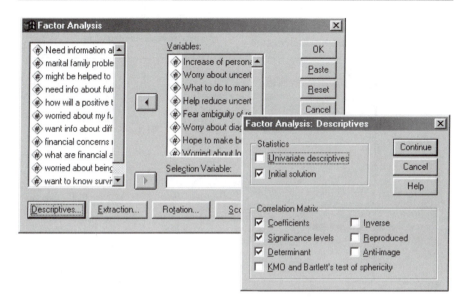

Table 3.3 presents the 8 × 8 correlation matrix for the first eight items in the CGTS that was generated from SPSS for Windows using the above-listed commands. The SAS output for the same correlation matrix is presented in Appendix B (Table B3.1B).

Notice that the upper half of Table 3.3 is a duplicate of the full 8 × 8 correlation matrix presented in Figure 3.2 with the correlation values being carried to three decimal places (Table 3.3, ①). The lower half of the figure presents the one-tailed significance levels (also known as p values) for the intercorrelations among the items ② and the calculated determinant of the correlation matrix ③. By default, the correlations in SAS are carried to five decimal places (Appendix B, Table B3.1B, ①) and the p values are two-tailed ②.

You may recall from statistical hypothesis testing that for correlations, the null hypothesis (H_0) of no association between two variables is rejected if the p value that is obtained is less than the alpha (α) level set prior to the study. According to Table 3.3, the correlation between Items C1 and C2 is .065 ④. If we had set our α = .05, we would *fail to*

Table 3.3   SPSS for Windows Generated Correlation Matrix, Significance
                    Levels, and Determinant

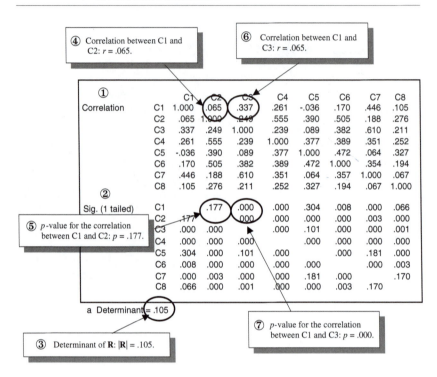

④ Correlation between C1 and
   C2: $r = .065$.

⑥ Correlation between C1 and
   C3: $r = .065$.

① Correlation

	C1	C2	C3	C4	C5	C6	C7	C8
C1	1.000	.065	.337	.261	-.036	.170	.446	.105
C2	.065	1.000	.249	.555	.390	.505	.188	.276
C3	.337	.249	1.000	.239	.089	.382	.610	.211
C4	.261	.555	.239	1.000	.377	.389	.351	.252
C5	-.036	.390	.089	.377	1.000	.472	.064	.327
C6	.170	.505	.382	.389	.472	1.000	.354	.194
C7	.446	.188	.610	.351	.064	.357	1.000	.067
C8	.105	.276	.211	.252	.327	.194	.067	1.000

② Sig. (1 tailed)

⑤ p-value for the correlation
  between C1 and C2: $p = .177$.

	C1	C2	C3	C4	C5	C6	C7	C8
C1		.177	.000	.000	.304	.008	.000	.066
C2	.177		.000	.000	.000	.000	.003	.000
C3	.000	.000		.000	.101	.000	.000	.001
C4	.000	.000	.000		.000	.000	.000	.000
C5	.304	.000	.101	.000		.000	.181	.000
C6	.008	.000	.000	.000	.000		.000	.003
C7	.000	.003	.000	.000	.181	.000		.170
C8	.066	.000	.001	.000	.000	.003	.170	

a Determinant = .105

③ Determinant of **R**: $|\mathbf{R}| = .105$.

⑦ p-value for the correlation
  between C1 and C3: $p = .000$.

reject the null hypothesis and conclude that there is no association
between C1 and C2 because the one-tailed p value (.177) is greater than
our α (.05) ⑤. In contrast, for Items C1 and C3, where $r = .337$ ⑥, we
would reject H_0 of no association because the obtained p value (.000) is
less than $\alpha = .05$ ⑦. Because SPSS for Windows goes to only three
decimal places, we should report this obtained one-tailed p value as
$p < .001$. In SAS, similar results for both sets of correlations are obtained
for the two-tailed p values (Appendix B, Table B3.1B).

Because we are unable to change the default in SPSS for Windows
from one-tailed to two-tailed p values using the *Analyze . . . Data
Reduction . . .* commands, to assess a two-tailed α (e.g., .05), we would
need to double the presented one-tailed p values and compare them to
our two-tailed α. In the test of association between C1 and C3, for

example, if our test had been nondirectional, α would be two-tailed. We would simply multiply our obtained p value by 2 (i.e., $p = (.000)(2) = .000$); .000 is still less than .05, meaning that the H_0 of no association between C1 and C3 would still be rejected, as indicated in the SAS output (Table B3.1B, ①).

Using the Correlation Matrix
to Identify Possible Item Clusters

The correlation matrix and significance table provides us with a beginning sense of which items might cluster in future factor analyses. In Table 3.3, the significant correlations among Items C1, C3, and C7 suggest that these three items might eventually combine in some fashion to form a subscale. The nonsignificant correlations of C5 and C8 with these three items indicate that C5 and C8 would probably not be included in such a subscale. It is also important to examine not only the p values but also the absolute size of the correlations because large sample sizes can contribute to small correlations being highly significant. This is a particular concern in factor analysis because we are usually dealing with large samples. This will be discussed in more detail in Chapter 4.

At the bottom of Table 3.3, the determinant of this 8×8 correlation matrix, $|\mathbf{R}|$, has been reported (.105) ③.[2] Because the determinant is not equal to zero, the correlation matrix under consideration is not singular. Therefore, there are no apparent linear dependencies in the data. It is interesting to note that the determinant for the 20×20 matrix for the full CGTS is 1.995E–05 (Appendix C, Table C4.1). This is math notation for 1.995×10^{-5}, indicating that the decimal point for this value is located five places to the left of 1.995, or .00001995. The fact that the determinant for the 20×20 correlation matrix in Appendix C is so close to 0 would suggest that there might be several items that are strongly correlated with one another. An examination of Table C4.1 in Appendix C indicates that there are several items for which intercorrelations are greater than .60, for example, C2 with C15 (.63) and C3 with C7 (.61). We will want to examine these items in greater detail to be certain that their wording and meaning are not redundant. We will discuss the management of potentially redundant items in Chapter 4.

Dealing With Ill-Conditioned or Singular Matrices

An *ill-conditioned* or *singular* matrix is a major problem for factor analysis. You will recall that a *singular* matrix is one that has no inverse. Its determinant, therefore, is equal to 0. An *ill-conditioned* matrix occurs when the matrix system being evaluated is unstable. Statistical computer packages have difficulty arriving at accurate solutions using ill-conditioned matrices because small round-off errors produced by the computer can result in large changes in the solution (Fraleigh, Beauregard, & Katz, 1994). This could result in very different and unstable factor solutions in factor analysis.

If SPSS for Windows or SAS should report an ill-conditioned or singular correlation matrix, the following steps are advised.

1. *Check the correlations of the items with each other.* If there are any items that have intercorrelations greater than .80, examine the items closely for their "clinical" usefulness and drop one or more of the items from the analysis.

2. *Examine the data for duplication of respondents.* No respondent should be entered more than once into the data matrix.

3. *Spot-check a selected number of items against respondents.* If there are similar response sets among subjects, you may need to drop one or more of the subjects from the analyses.

4. *Check to be certain that there are enough subjects per item.* Too few subjects per item (i.e., fewer than 10-15 subjects per item) can result in a correlation matrix being ill-conditioned.

TESTS OF MATRICES

During this exploratory phase of factor analysis, it is important to determine if there are sufficient numbers of significant correlations among the items to justify undertaking a factor analysis. If the correlations among the items are not significant, it will not be possible to obtain a parsimonious set of factors that represent the numerous items in the proposed scale. Rather, there could be as many factors as there are items.

There are several tests that can be undertaken by computer to ascertain whether it would be judicious to proceed with factor analysis.

These tests include *Bartlett's test of sphericity* and the *Kaiser-Meyer-Olkin test*. Let us first examine how these statistics are obtained mathematically, and then we will determine if and how they are generated in SPSS for Windows and SAS.

Bartlett's Test of Sphericity

Bartlett's test of sphericity (Bartlett, 1950) tests the null hypothesis that the correlation matrix is an identity matrix (i.e., that there is no relationship among the items). The null hypothesis states that there are all 1's on the diagonal of the matrix and 0's on the off-diagonal:

$$H_0: \mathbf{R} = \begin{bmatrix} 1 & 0 & 0 & 0 \\ 0 & 1 & 0 & 0 \\ 0 & 0 & 1 & 0 \\ 0 & 0 & 0 & 1 \end{bmatrix}$$

Larger values of Bartlett's test indicate greater likelihood that the correlation matrix is not an identity matrix and that the null hypothesis will be rejected.

Bartlett's test is a chi-square test that takes on the following form (Gorsuch, 1983; Pedhazur & Schmelkin, 1991):

$$\chi^2 = - \left[(N - 1) - \left(\frac{2k + 5}{6} \right) \right] \log_e |R|$$

where

χ^2 = calculated chi-square value for Bartlett's test

N = sample size

k = number of items or variables in the matrix

$\log_e$ = natural logarithm

$|\mathbf{R}|$ = determinant of the correlation matrix

The degrees of freedom (*df*) for this chi-square are $df = k(k - 1)/2$.

The degrees of freedom, df, represent the number of correlations above or below the principal diagonal of the correlation matrix. Notice, too, that Bartlett's test involves the determinant of the correlation matrix. If the value of this determinant is negative or 0, a value for Bartlett's test is indeterminant because it is not possible to take the natural logarithm of 0's or negative numbers.

For the 8×8 matrix presented in Table 3.3, we would obtain the following χ^2 value for Bartlett's test:

$$\chi^2 = -\left[(N-1) - \left(\frac{2k+5}{6}\right)\right]\log_e|R|$$

$$= -\left[(205-1) - \left(\frac{(2)(8)+5}{6}\right)\right]\log_e|.105|$$

$$= -[(204)-(3.5)](-2.254)$$

$$= -[200.5](-2.254)$$

$$= 451.92$$

The degrees of freedom for this χ^2 is $df = k(k-1)/2 = 8(8-1)/2 = 56/2 = 28$.

To determine whether we should reject the null hypothesis that the correlation matrix is an identity matrix, we need to compare our calculated χ^2 with an expected χ^2 value (given our df values and α level) under the null hypothesis. If the number of degrees of freedom is relatively small (e.g., $df \leq 30$), the expected value for the χ^2 can be easily obtained by examining a standard table containing the percentile points for the χ^2 distribution (e.g., Appendix D, Table D.1). We will reject the null hypothesis that the correlation matrix is an identity matrix if and only if the calculated χ^2 is greater than the tabled χ^2 value.

According to Table D.1, the critical value of the χ^2 with $df = 28$ and $\alpha = .05$ is 41.3372, a value that is considerably less than our calculated value of 451.92. We will, therefore, reject H_0 and conclude that the correlation matrix presented in Table 3.3 is not an identity matrix.

Using the Z Approximation
to the Chi-Square Distribution

The chi-square distribution quickly approximates a normal distribution as the degrees of freedom get large. Therefore, it is recommended that a standard normal distribution be used to assess the χ^2 for Bartlett's test when $df > 30$ (Gorsuch, 1983, p. 151; Pedhazur & Schmelkin, 1991, p. 795; Rice, 1994, p. 359):

$$z = \frac{\chi^2_{\text{calculated}} - (df)}{\sqrt{2(df)}}$$

where $(df) = k(k-1)/2 =$ the number of degrees of freedom for the calculated χ^2.

Notice that this z approximation takes on the typical form of a standard normal z statistic:

$$z = \frac{statistic - mean_{\text{statistic}}}{\sqrt{variance\ of\ the\ statistic}}$$

where the (df) for the first equation represents the mean and $2(df)$ equals the variance of the χ^2 statistic.

Using this alternative z formula, we would obtain the following value for the z approximation:

$$z = \frac{\chi^2_{\text{calculated}} - (df)}{\sqrt{2(df)}}$$

$$= \frac{451.92 - (28)}{\sqrt{2(28)}} = \frac{423.92}{\sqrt{56}} = 56.65$$

Our calculated z approximation, therefore, is 56.65. To determine if this z approximation is significant, we would compare our calculated z with the critical value of z given a prestated alpha level (e.g., $\alpha = .05$). These critical values can be easily determined using a table of cumulative probabilities for the standard normal distribution (e.g., Appendix D, Table D.2). The null hypothesis that the correlation matrix is an identity matrix is rejected if our calculated z is larger than the critical value of the z statistic at our prestated α level.

You will recall that a standard normal distribution is one for which scores can range from $-\infty$ to $+\infty$, with 99% of the scores being within ± 3 standard deviations. Also known as a z *distribution*, this distribution is symmetric, centered at 0, and has a variance of 1.0. As a result, the area under the curve that lies to the *right* of a given positive z score (e.g., $z = +1.96$) is equivalent to the area under the curve that lies to the *left* of the same negative value ($z = -1.96$). Table D.2 presents us with the area under the standard normal curve that lies to the left of z scores ≥ 0. Because this area represents $F(z)$, which is the cumulative probability for z, $[1 - F(z)]$ is the area that lies to the right of a given positive z score, as illustrated in the figure at the top of Table D.2.

To determine a two-tailed critical value for z at $\alpha = .05$, we need to distribute the .05 equally between the two tails of the z distribution. Therefore, we would locate that z score in Table D.2 such that $.05/2 = .025$ lies to the right of its positive value and .025 lies to the left of its negative value. According to Table D.2, at $z = +1.96$, $F(z) = .9750021$ and $[1\ F(z)] = 1 - .9750 = .0250$. The two-tailed critical value for z at $\alpha = .05$, therefore, would be ± 1.96. For a directional test, the one-tailed critical value for z at $\alpha = .05$ is either that value of z such that the area under the curve to the *left* of it is equal to .05 (i.e., $z = +1.64$) or that negative value of z whose area under the standard normal curve to the *right* of it is equal to .05 (i.e., $z = -1.64$). Our choice of critical value depends on the hypothesized direction of our alternative hypothesis.

Bartlett's test of sphericity is a one-tailed test because the generated χ^2 is always positive and we are interested only in rejecting large values of this distribution. Thus, our α level will be situated in one direction only and will lie in the upper tail of the standard normal curve. The one-tailed critical value for z if $\alpha = .05$ is $+1.64$ and $+2.33$ if $\alpha = .01$. Our calculated z, 56.65, is considerably larger than the critical value ($z = +1.64$) for a one-tailed z at $\alpha = .05$. Once again, we conclude that the correlation matrix is not an identity matrix and appears to be factorable.

A Cautionary Note

You mustn't get too excited when you see a significant χ^2 for Bartlett's test of sphericity. As can be seen from the formula for this χ^2, Bartlett's test is influenced by the sample size, N, with larger sample sizes resulting in larger values of Bartlett's test. Gorsuch (1983, p. 150) points out that with only 20 subjects and 10 items, all that is needed is an interitem average correlation of .36 for Bartlett's test to be significant. Because factor analysis most often involves large samples, this test will usually indicate, for even the most trivial correlations, that the correlation matrix is not an identity matrix. Pedhazur and Schmelkin (1991) suggest, therefore, that Bartlett's test be used only as a minimum standard for assessing the quality of the correlation matrix. That is, when Bartlett's test is not found to be significant (i.e., the resulting value is too small to reject the null hypothesis), the matrix should not be factor analyzed.

Kaiser-Meyer-Olkin Test (KMO)

A second indicator of the strength of the relationship among items is the partial correlation coefficient. These partial correlations represent the correlations between each pair of items after removing the linear effects of all other items. The *Kaiser-Meyer-Olkin test* (KMO) is a measure of sampling adequacy that compares the magnitudes of the calculated correlation coefficients to the magnitudes of the partial correlation coefficients and takes the following form:

$$KMO = \frac{\sum (correlations)^2}{\sum (correlations)^2 + \sum (partial\ correlations)^2}$$

If the items share common factors, then it would be reasonable to expect that the partial correlation coefficients between the pairs of items would be small when the linear effects of other items have been removed. The exact formula for the KMO is given as follows:

$$KMO = \frac{\sum_{i \neq j} \sum r_{ij}^2}{\sum_{i \neq j} \sum r_{ij}^2 + \sum_{i \neq j} \sum a_{ij}^2}$$

where

$\sum \sum$ = sum over all items in the matrix when Item $i \neq$ Item j

r_{ij} = Pearson correlation between Items i and j

a_{ij} = partial correlation coefficient between Items i and j

As can be seen from the formula for the KMO, if the sum of the squared partial correlation coefficients, a_{ij}^2, is small compared with the sum of the squared correlation coefficients, r_{ij}^2, the numerator and denominator for this test are similar and the KMO measure approaches 1. The KMO measure can range between 0 and 1, with smaller values indicating that r_{ij}^2 is small relative to a_{ij}^2 and therefore a factor analysis may be unwise.

Evaluating the size of the KMO. When evaluating the size of the overall KMO, Kaiser (1974, p. 35) suggests using the following criteria for these values:

- Above .90 is "marvelous"
- In the .80s is "meritorious"
- In the .70s is just "middling"
- Less than .60 is "mediocre," "miserable," or "unacceptable"

Calculating the KMO Measure

It is extremely tiresome to calculate a KMO statistic by hand for large correlation matrices. For the 8×8 correlation matrix in Table 3.3, we would first need to square the Pearson correlations for each of the 28 items on the off-diagonal of the triangular matrix and sum them[3]:

$$\sum_{i \neq j} \sum r_{ij}^2 = (.065)^2 + (.337)^2 + (.261)^2$$
$$+ \cdots + (.357)^2 + (.194)^2 + (.067)^2 = 2.9231$$

Next, we would need to square and sum the partial correlations of these eight items with each other having first controlled for their relationship with other items in the matrix. Although this would be a cumbersome task even for only eight items, these are given to us on the off-diagonal of the *anti-image correlation matrix* generated in SPSS for Windows (Table 3.5), which we will examine later in this chapter:

$$\sum_{i \neq j} \sum a_{ij}^2 = (.112)^2 + (-.0835)^2 + (-.182)^2$$
$$+ \cdots + (-.144)^2 + (.068)^2 + (.124)^2 = 1.1439$$

Finally, we would insert these two values into the KMO formula:

$$KMO = \frac{\sum_{i \neq j} \sum r_{ij}^2}{\sum_{i \neq j} \sum r_{ij}^2 + \sum_{i \neq j} \sum a_{ij}^2} = \frac{2.9231}{2.9231 + 1.1439} = .7187$$

The value of this KMO measure meets Kaiser's "middling" criteria.

Individual Measures of Sampling Adequacy (MSA)

In addition to the overall KMO, a *measure of sampling adequacy* (MSA) can be computed for each individual item using only the simple and partial correlation coefficients involving the particular item under consideration:

$$MSA_i = \frac{\sum\sum_{ij \neq i} r_{ij}^2}{\sum\sum_{ij \neq i} r_{ij}^2 + \sum\sum_{ij \neq i} a_{ij}^2}$$

The MSA for an individual item indicates how strongly that item is correlated with other items in the matrix. The same interpretation for standards of excellence outlined above for the KMO (Kaiser, 1974) can also be applied to the individual MSAs. That is, ideally, we would like to have individual MSAs that are greater than .70.

Calculating the individual MSAs. The approach to calculating the MSA for each individual item is similar to the overall KMO approach. Because our 8×8 matrix would require our calculating eight of these MSAs, we will only walk you through the MSA calculation for Item C1. That is, first, we would sum the seven squared Pearson correlations involving C1:

$$\sum_{i \neq j} r_{ij}^2 = (.065)^2 + (.337)^2 + \cdots + (.104)^2$$
$$= .4258$$

Next, we would sum the seven squared partial correlations involving C1 that we would obtain from the off-diagonal elements in Table 3.5:

$$\sum_{i \neq j} a_{ij}^2 = (.112)^2 + (-.0835)^2 + \cdots + (-.265)^2 + (-.8740)^2$$
$$= .1437$$

Finally, we would put the two values into the MSA equation and obtain a measure of sampling adequacy for Item C1:

$$MSA_i = \frac{\sum\sum_{ij \neq i} r_{ij}^2}{\sum\sum_{ij \neq i} r_{ij}^2 + \sum\sum_{ij \neq i} a_{ij}^2} = \frac{.4258}{.4258 + .1437} = .7187$$

If we use Kaiser's (1974) criteria for sampling adequacy, the MSA for Item C1 is "middling," which means that although it is sufficient for a factor analysis (i.e., MSA > .60), it is not a value to rave about.

Generating Tests of Matrices
in SPSS for Windows and SAS

Bartlett's test of sphericity and the two measures of sampling adequacy (KMO and MSA) are available in SPSS for Windows for both the overall scale and the individual items. Unfortunately, like the determinant, Bartlett's test of sphericity is not available in SAS. The KMO statistics, however, can be obtained using the MSA command in PROC FACTOR (Figure B3.4). The resulting output (Table B3.2) presents the partial correlations of the items with each other controlling all other variables, the individual measures of sampling adequacy (MSA), and Kaiser's overall measure of sampling adequacy.

These same statistics can be obtained in SPSS for Windows using the following commands:

Analyze . . . Data Reduction . . . Factor . . . Descriptives . . . Correlation Matrix . . .
    ✓ *KMO and Bartlett's test of sphericity*
    ✓ *Anti-image*

The results of these analyses are given as a single KMO value and in the form of an *anti-image correlation matrix* (AIC). The AIC reports the MSAs for each individual item on the diagonal. The negatives of the partial correlations between pairs of items (having first controlled for the effects of all other items) are presented on the off-diagonal. If the correlation matrix is factorable, the MSA values on the diagonal of the AIC should be large and the values of the negatives of the partial correlations should be small (Hair, Anderson, Tatham, & Black, 1995; Tabachnick & Fidell, 2001).

The KMO measure of sampling adequacy and Bartlett's test of sphericity that were generated in SPSS for Windows are presented in Table 3.4. The KMO statistic, .717, meets Kaiser's (1974) "middling" criteria. The KMO statistic for the 20-item correlation matrix (Appendix C, Table C3.2) was .763, not much better than our .717.

Table 3.4 also indicates that the significance level (*Sig*) for Bartlett's test of sphericity (452.512) for the eight-item correlation matrix is highly significant (*p* < .000). This highly significant value is probably due to the large sample size (205) relative to the number of items in the matrix (8). Interestingly, Bartlett's test for the 20-item matrix in Table C3.2, Appendix C is also highly significant ($\chi^2 = 2126.545$, $df = 190$, $p = .000$). We can conclude, therefore, that both the 8-item and 20-item CGTS correlation matrices are not identity matrices.

Table 3.4   KMO and Bartlett's Test of Sphericity for the Eight-Item Correlation Matrix Generated in SPSS for Windows

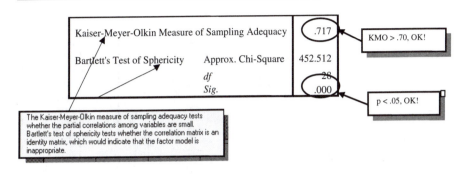

The output for the anti-image matrices is presented in Table 3.5. We are first given an *anti-image covariance matrix*. This matrix is used in SPSS for Windows to generate the anti-image correlation matrix (AIC), which is our primary focus of interest. Although it is generous of SPSS for Windows to provide us with this information, we can largely ignore the data in the anti-image covariance matrix and focus instead on the AIC, especially the MSAs that are presented on its diagonal.

According to Table 3.5, our MSAs range from .671 for Item C7 to .765 for Item C6①. Like the KMO statistic, the individual MSAs are "middling" according to Kaiser's (1974) criteria. Examining the off-diagonal elements of the AIC②, we find that, for 20 of the 28 possible pairs of items, the absolute values of the negatives of the partial correlations are ≤.191. These values range in absolute value from .00971 (for item pairs C4 and C6)[4] to .501 (for item pairs C3 and C7). Similar results were obtained using PROC FACTOR in SAS (Table B3.2) except that, instead of the anti-image correlation matrix, we are given the actual partial correlation matrix.

What do we conclude regarding our correlation matrix? Examining each of these statistics, our conclusions would be the following:

- According to Bartlett's test, the correlation matrix is not an identity matrix.
- The KMO statistic suggests that we have a sufficient sample size relative to the number of items in our scale.
- The MSA statistics indicate that the correlations among the individual items are strong enough to suggest that the correlation matrix is factorable.

Table 3.5   Anti-Image Covariance and Correlation Matrices Generated for the Eight-Item CGTS

	C1	C2	C3	C4	C5	C6	C7	C8
Anti-image Covariance								
C1	.754	7.30E-02	-5.43E-02	-.119	9.53E-02	-3.18E-02	-.164	-6.87E-02
C2	7.30E-02	.561	-5.400E-02	-.246	-2.90E-02	-.176	5.04E-02	-7.24E-02
C3	-5.42E-02	-5.40E-02	.560	5.53E-02	5.08E-02	-.101	-.268	-.129
C4	-.119	-.246	5.53E-02	.570	-.123	5.50E-03	-.126	-4.79E-02
C5	9.53E-02	-2.90E-02	5.537E-02	-.123	.647	-.225	3.36E-02	-.179
C6	-3.17E-02	-.176	5.085E-02	5.50E-03	-.225	.563	-7.73E-02	4.64E-02
C7	-.164	5.04E-02	-.101	-.126	3.36E-02	7.74E-02	.511	8.01E-02
C8	-6.87E-02	-7.24E-02	-.129	-4.79E-02	-.179	4.63E-02	8.01E-02	.821
Anti-image Correlation								
C1	.737[a]	.112	-8.35E-02	-.182	.136	4.87E-02	-.265	-8.74E-02
C2	.112	.729[a]	-9.62E-02	-.435	-4.82E-02	-.314	-9.41E-02	-.107
C3	-8.35E-02	-9.62E-02	.695[a]	9.79E-02	8.44E-02	-.180	-.501	-.191
C4	-.182	-.435	9.79E-02	.733[a]	-.202	9.71E-03	-.233	-7.01E-02
C5	.136	-4.82E-02	8.44E-02	-.202	.701[a]	-.372	5.84E-02	-.246
C6	4.87E-02	-.314	-.180	9.71E-03	-.372	.765[a]	-.144	6.83E-02
C7	-.265	-9.41E-02	-.501	-.233	5.84E-02	-.144	.671[a]	.124
C8	-8.74E-02	-.107	-.191	-7.01E-02	-.246	6.83E-02	.124	.710[a]

a Measures of Sampling Adequacy (MSA)

① The circled items are the measures of sampling adequacy (MSA) for the 8 individual items, C1 to C8. These values should be high, > .70.

② Off diagonal values are negatives of the partial correlations. Absolute values should be low. 6.82E-02 = .0682

Figure 3.10   Assessing the Characteristics of Matrices

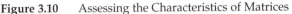

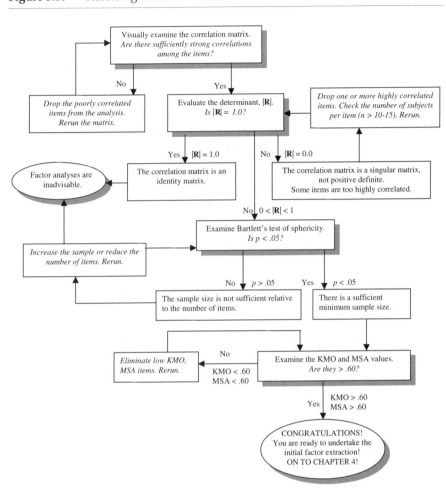

Dealing With Problem Items

What if several of the individual MSA coefficients are low and the resulting negative partial correlations high? If MSA coefficients for some individual items are mediocre (i.e., less than .60) and the partial correlations high, there may not be an underlying factor structure that can summarize the relationships among the items. To address this problem, the researcher should identify the item with the lowest MSA, remove it from the list of items to be analyzed, and rerun the tests of matrices. The process should be continued until the individual MSAs are within acceptable range. If this approach does not lead to an acceptable KMO or set of MSAs, the researcher should increase the sample size and rerun the analyses or reconsider the suitability of a factor analysis.

REVIEW OF THE PROCESS

In Chapter 3, we have introduced you to the various matrices that are important to factor analysis. You have also been presented with various tests of matrices that can be used to determine if the correlation matrix that you want to analyze is indeed factorable. The decision diagram outlined in Figure 3.10 summarizes our discussion of these tests of matrices. By following this process, you can determine whether, at least from an initial perspective, the correlation matrix appears to be factorable. With that task accomplished, you are ready to begin the initial rotation. This topic will be the focus of Chapter 4.

NOTES

1. You can run all of these statistics in SPSS for Windows using the data set CGTS.sav that is on the disk that is located on the back cover of this text. For SAS, you should use the CGTS20.SAS file. Remember, you will need these statistical packages loaded on your computer to do this.

2. Surprisingly, SAS does not present the value of the determinant in any of its programs. This is a distinct disadvantage to this otherwise excellent statistical package.

3. In math notation, '. . .' means to continue the process, for example, squaring and summing correlations.

4. Recall that 9.71E–03 means that you need to move 3 decimal places to the left of 9, that is, .00971.

4

Extracting the
Initial Factors

Y ou will recall from Chapter 1 that a major task for researchers
using factor analysis in scale development is to identify sets of
relationships among a large group of items. The challenge is to reduce
the number of items to smaller subsets that contain as much valuable
information from the initial items as possible. This process generally
involves two stages (Nunnally & Bernstein, 1994):

1. defining the number of initial factors, and

2. rotating the factors to improve interpretation.

In this chapter, we will discuss the data reduction methods that are
typically used in Stage 1 to determine the number of initial subsets or
factors that appear to represent the dimensions of the construct being
measured. Stage 2, rotating the factors to improve interpretation, will
be the focus of Chapter 5. To illustrate these processes, we will be
examining selected items of the Concerns About Genetic Testing Scale
(CGTS) presented in Appendix A.

Figure 4.1   The 8 × 8 Correlation Matrix (**R**) for Items C1 to C8 of the
CGTS Scale

	C1	C2	C3	C4	C5	C6	C7	C8
C1	1.00	.07	.34	.26	-.04	.17	.45	.10
C2	.07	1.00	.25	.56	.39	.51	.19	.28
C3	.34	.25	1.00	.24	.09	.38	.61	.21
C4	.26	.56	.24	1.00	.38	.39	.35	.25
C5	-.04	.39	.09	.38	1.00	.48	.06	.33
C6	.17	.51	.38	.39	.48	1.00	.36	.19
C7	.45	.19	.61	.35	.06	.36	1.00	.07
C8	.10	.28	.21	.25	.33	.19	.07	1.00

EVALUATING THE CORRELATION MATRIX

We typically begin a factor analysis with a correlation matrix that has been generated either from a data matrix or one that has been input directly into a factor analysis program. The example that we will use for this process is the 8 × 8 correlation matrix for Items C1 to C8 of the CGTS scale presented in Figure 4.1.[1]

Although it is also possible to use a variance-covariance matrix for factor analysis (both SPSS for Windows and SAS offer this option), few authors recommend this approach in exploratory factor analysis. Gorsuch (1983) cautions about inconsistency of results and the difficulty of interpreting certain matrices (e.g., the factor structure matrix) if the covariance matrix is used instead of the correlation matrix. Our recommendation is that you start your initial extraction process using a correlation matrix. This is the default option in SPSS for Windows.

Determining Whether the Matrix Is Factorable

In Chapter 3, we examined ways to evaluate the correlation matrix to determine if it is factorable. Key issues in this regard are Bartlett's test of sphericity, the Kaiser-Meyer-Olkin test, and the individual measures of sampling adequacy. We also recommend that you examine the correlation matrix closely for item consistency and to identify items that are either too highly correlated ($r \geq .80$) or not correlated sufficiently ($r < .30$) with one another. If items are too highly correlated, you have a problem with multicolinearity and will need to drop one or more of the highly correlated items from the analysis. If the items are not correlated strongly enough, there will not be much shared common variance, thus potentially yielding as many factors as items.

When we examined the 8×8 correlation matrix given in Figure 4.1 for its factorability, we concluded that, despite its small size, the correlation matrix was factorable and we could continue with the initial extraction process.[2] Our next step is to *condense* the variance that is shared among these items to determine the number of initial subsets or factors that appear to represent the dimensions of the construct being measured.

SOURCES OF VARIANCE IN FACTOR ANALYSIS MODELS

Variance condensation refers to the process by which the variance shared among a set of items or variables is compressed into (a) one or more factors reflecting the variance that the items share in common and (b) possible unique factors that represent the variance that items do not share with one another (Nunnally & Bernstein, 1994). This process is based on a multivariate linear model in which the sources of variance in scores on a set of items to be analyzed are broken down into three uncorrelated components: *common variance, specific variance,* and *error variance* (Kline, 1994).

Common variance, symbolized as h^2, represents the amount of variance that is shared among a set of items that can be explained by a set of common factors (Kline, 1994). Items that are highly correlated with one another will share a great deal of variance among themselves, and therefore a common set of factors that summarize the set of interrelationships among the variables can easily be identified. *Specific variance* is variance specific to a particular variable that is not shared with other items in the correlation matrix but that may be shared with other items that have been excluded from the analysis.

Error variance represents errors of measurement. Its impact on items can be evaluated by examining the items' internal consistency or *reliability* using the coefficient alpha (α) that we will discuss in Chapter 6. The more reliable the set of items, the lower are their errors of measurement. Suppose, for example, that a set of items has a coefficient alpha (α) of .80. Measurement error for this set of items would be $(1 - \alpha^2)$ or $(1 - .80^2 = 1 - .64 = .36)$. Multiplying $(1 - \alpha^2)$ by 100 (i.e., $[(1 - \alpha^2) \times 100]$) indicates the percent of variance in the items that could be attributed to measurement error. In this example, $[(.36) \times 100]$, or 36%, of the variance in the items can be attributed to measurement error.

The variance that the items share in common, h^2, is the major focus of interest in factor analysis. As you will soon see in this next section, factor extraction methods differ in their approaches to addressing the problem of what to do with specific and error variance in the factor analysis solution. These two sources of variance in combination—specific and error variance—are symbolized as $1 - h^2$ and have been described as *unique* variance (Kline, 1994).

DETERMINING THE
FACTOR EXTRACTION METHOD

The extraction process begins with providing an initial estimate of the total amount of variance in each individual item that is explained by the factors we are about to extract. This explained variance is referred to as the *communality* of an item. These communality estimates can range from 0 to 1.00, with higher values indicating that the extracted factors explain more of the variance of an individual item. A value of 0, for example, would indicate that none of the variance in a particular item is explained by the extracted factors. A value of 1.00 indicates that all of the variance in a given item is explained by the extracted factors.

Initially, these communalities are unknown; they cannot be identified until after a factor analysis has been run and we have extracted our factors. Yet, in order to begin the factor analysis solution, these initial communalities need to be placed on the diagonal of the matrix to be analyzed.[3] Pedhazur and Schmelkin (1991) describe this situation as the "Catch-22" of factor analysis (p. 600). The task, therefore, is to arrive at a reasonable estimate of these communalities based on preliminary information about the items.

There are two basic solutions to this dilemma. The first and easiest solution includes all three sources of variance (common, specific, and error) in the identification of factors or *components*. This solution operates from the perspective that each of the extracted components are *orthogonal* to one another (i.e., they are not correlated) and that they are linear combinations of the items included in the analysis. This approach assumes that the items included in the analysis can be perfectly calculated by the extracted components. Because each standardized item has a mean of 0 and variance of 1.00, the initial estimate of communality for each item is 1.00. This is what will be placed on the diagonal of the correlation matrix. This approach has been described as the full component model and is known as *principal component analysis* (PCA) (Gorsuch, 1983; Harman, 1976; Nunnally & Bernstein, 1994).

One drawback to PCA is that it accounts for all of the variance in the correlation matrix to which it is applied. The unique variance of a particular item, including its errors of measurement, is not factored out. A second, more classical factor analytic approach, *common factor analysis* (CFA), separates out the variance that the items share in common from this unique variance (Nunnally & Bernstein, 1994). According to CFA, variance in a given item is explained by a small number of underlying factors plus variation that is unique to the item, including error variance. The factors that we extract in CFA are not just mere linear combinations of the items being examined, as in PCA, but are instead hypothetical factors that are estimated from the items being examined. Because CFA focuses on the common variance shared among the items, the amount of variance extracted from the correlation matrix by these estimated factors is less than 100%. Therefore, initial communality values of less than 1.00 will appear on the diagonal of the correlation matrix.

A number of different approaches have been used in CFA to determine what reduced communality value should be placed initially on the diagonal. One popular solution is to use the squared multiple correlation (R^2) of each item with all of the other items included in the factor analysis. These squared multiple correlation coefficients (range: 0-1.00) provide an initial indication of the strength of the linear relationship among the items because higher values indicate stronger associations among the items. These are the values that initially appear on the diagonal of the correlation matrix from which the factors are to be extracted. This approach is known as *principal axis factoring* (PAF). Additional methods identified under the CFA umbrella (e.g., *alpha factoring, image factoring, unweighted and generalized least squares,* and *maximum likelihood* methods) use other approaches to obtaining their initial communality estimates. These alternative approaches will be briefly reviewed later in this chapter.

We are now ready to compare the PCA and CFA approaches in greater detail. For each approach, we will first present you with a general overview of the extraction process. All of the formulas that will be discussed may seem a little confusing to you initially. Hopefully, they will make more sense when we examine the computer printout obtained for each method when the 8×8 correlation matrix in Figure 4.1 was submitted to the factor analysis program in SPSS for Windows and SAS.[4]

To show you that these extraction procedures are not totally mystical, in Appendix E, we have walked you through the factor extraction process for PCA, generating the same factors *by hand*. Because the computational procedure is not difficult but is extremely labor intensive, we have limited the extraction process to the first two factors for the matrix. Hopefully, these presentations will facilitate your understanding of—and appreciation for—the factor extraction process. If you would like to read more on this subject, we refer you to the excellent materials offered by Bernstein (1988), Kline (1994), and Nunnally and Bernstein (1994).

PRINCIPAL COMPONENT ANALYSIS

Principal component analysis (PCA) was developed by Pearson (1901) and adapted for factor analysis by Hotelling (1933) (Harman, 1976). A goal for the user of PCA is to summarize the interrelationships among a set of original variables in terms of a smaller set of orthogonal (i.e., uncorrelated) principal components that are linear combinations of the original variables (Goddard & Kirby, 1976).

All three of the variance components (common, specific, and error variance) play an important role in the identification of the principal components. Because the method is so dependent on the total variance, PCA typically requires that the variables being examined be based on similar units of measurement. It is customary, therefore, to standardize the variables so that their means are equal to 0 and their variances equal to 1.00. In our example, Items C1 to C8 of the CGTS scale (Appendix A) have not been standardized using z scores and do not have means equal to 0 or variances equal to 1.00. However, each of the items has been measured on similar Likert scales of measurement (range: 1 = *not at all* to 5 = *extremely*). Thus, each item in the scale shares a similar or *standardized* scale of measurement.

Standardization has also been accomplished by using the matrix of correlation coefficients, which is a standardized representation of the relationships among the variables. This correlation matrix with 1.00s on the diagonal is then the focus of PCA. Because each standardized variable has a variance equal to 1.00, the total variance is equal to the number of original variables (i.e., the sum of the diagonal elements of the correlation matrix) (Harman, 1976).

Estimating the Initial Communalities

PCA assumes that there is as much variance to be analyzed as the number of observed variables and that *all* of the variance in an item can be explained by the extracted factors. PCA's initial estimate of the communality (i.e., the variance that the items and factors share in common) therefore is 1.00. These are the values that are placed initially on the diagonal of the correlation matrix when it is analyzed by PCA. In essence, there is no change in the correlation matrix.

Eigenvalues and Eigenvectors

PCA has been described as *eigenanalysis* or the seeking of the solution to the characteristic equation of the correlation matrix (Nunnally & Bernstein, 1994). To understand this process, you need at least a rudimentary understanding of the important role that *eigenvectors* and their associated *eigenvalues* play in factor analysis. For more detailed information about these constructs (which are sometimes called *characteristic vectors* and *characteristic values*), please refer to Appendix E. Additional resources are Kline (1994), Nunnally and Bernstein (1994), and Tabachnick and Fidell (2001).

Eigenvalues. An *eigenvalue*, denoted as λ, is a single value (a.k.a. *a scalar*); it represents the amount of variance in all of the items that can be explained by a given principal component or factor. Like many multivariate procedures, factor analysis uses eigenvalues and their corresponding eigenvectors to "consolidate the variance in a matrix (the *eigenvalue*) while providing the linear combination of variables (the *eigenvector*) to do it" (Tabachnick & Fidell, 2001, p. 915).

Conceivably, eigenvalues can be both negative and positive. However, in factor analysis, all eigenvalues need to be greater than

0 because they represent the amount of explained variance in the items that is associated with a given principal component. If this condition is met (i.e., that all of the eigenvalues associated with a given correlation matrix are greater than 0), the matrix being analyzed is said to be *positive-definite* and is therefore factorable.

In PCA, the maximum positive value that an eigenvalue can take on is the total amount of variance available for the items in the correlation matrix. In our example, we have eight items for which individual variances are equal to 1.00. Therefore, the maximum value for any eigenvalue in our example is 8.00.

Negative eigenvalues imply that the explained variance in the items is negative in value. This untenable situation means that the matrix is *ill-conditioned* and should not be factor analyzed. When eigenvalues closely approach 0, there is a strong possibility that multicollinearity or singularity exists among the variables[5] and the usefulness of factor analysis is questionable (Tabachnick & Fidell, 2001).

Eigenvectors. An *eigenvector* of a correlation matrix is a column of weights. Each of these weights is associated with an item in the matrix. If there are eight items in the matrix, there will be eight weights in that eigenvector. There are conceivably as many "nontrivial" eigenvectors (and associated eigenvalues) as there are items. For our 8×8 correlation matrix, therefore, we could generate as many as eight eigenvectors.

It is from these eigenvectors that the principal components of a correlation matrix are generated. To obtain a principal component, each of the weights of a given eigenvector is multiplied by the square root of the principal component's associated eigenvalue. These newly generated weights are called *factor loadings* and represent the correlation of each item with the given principal component. In our CGTS example, if we have eight nontrivial eigenvectors, we can generate eight principal components, each of which contains eight factor loadings.

The eigenvalue associated with a given principal component is equal to the sum of the squared factor loadings on that component (Pedhazur & Schmelkin, 1991). By our earlier definition, the sum of these squared factor loadings represents the amount of variance in the items that can be explained by that particular principal component. In PCA, the total amount of variance available is equal to the number of items; therefore, dividing the eigenvalue by the number of items gives the proportion of total item variance accounted for by the given principal component.

Extracting the Components

The aim of PCA is to duplicate the correlation matrix using a set of factors (also called *components*) that are fewer in number and are linear combinations of the original set of items. PCA assumes that there is as much variance to be analyzed as observed variables and that all of the variance in an item can be explained by the extracted factors. The amount of variance to be estimated in our example, therefore, is 8 (i.e., $8 \times s^2 = 8 \times 1.00 = 8.00$). There will be no change in the correlation matrix because 1s are placed initially on the diagonal of the correlation matrix when it is being analyzed using PCA.

Extracting principal components from a correlation matrix is an interactive procedure that consists of repeatedly refining the solution to finding a suitable *eigenvector* and associated *eigenvalue* from which the factor loadings for a principal component can be obtained. The process is designed such that the first component in PCA, PC_I, is a linear combination of the original variables that explains a maximum amount of the variance among the variables. The factor loadings on PC_I represent the correlation of each item in the correlation matrix with the first principal component. The eigenvalue for PC_I, λ_1, is the sum of squared factor loadings for that principal component and represents the amount of variance in the items that can be explained by PC_I.

The second principal component, PC_{II}, is obtained using an approach similar to that described for PC_I. The difference is that PC_{II} is obtained not from the original correlation matrix but from a residual matrix from which the effects of the first principal component have been removed. That is, PC_I's influence has been *partialed out* from the original matrix. Because PC_{II} is obtained from a residual matrix, it is uncorrelated with (i.e., it is *orthogonal* to) PC_I and accounts for the second greatest proportion of variance that is remaining among the items having factored out the influence of PC_I. Thus, the eigenvalue for PC_{II}, λ_2, is second only to λ_1 in size.

This process of extracting components is repeated on succeeding residual matrices until the elements in the residual variance-covariance matrix are reduced to random error (Nunnally & Bernstein, 1994). Each extracted principal component is orthogonal to the others and accounts for the greatest proportion of leftover variance after removing the influence of the previous components. In this way, the first extracted component accounts for the most variance and the last component accounts for the least variance.

There can be as many principal components in PCA as there are original variables, and the sum of the explained variance (i.e., the eigenvalues) among all of the components is equal to the sum of the variances of the original variables. When the number of variables is large, however, the majority of the variance is accounted for by a relatively small number of components (Goddard & Kirby, 1976). This would mean that the eigenvalues for the first few components would be large and the later eigenvalues would be relatively small.

Extracting the Initial Components in SPSS for Windows and SAS

In this section, we illustrate the process for extracting the initial factors from the 8×8 correlation matrix for Items C1 to C8 of the CGTS scale (Figure 4.1) using the PCA factor extraction methods in SPSS for Windows and SAS. We will first examine the PCA process in detail to arrive at a preliminary PCA solution and then later compare it with the solution generated by principal axis factoring (PAF) when the same number of factors is used. As we did in Chapter 3, we have limited our presentation in Chapter 4 to printouts obtained from SPSS for Windows. The corresponding SAS examples are given in Appendix B. References to SAS output will be cited in parentheses following the SPSS for Windows examples. When discussing this output, we will use a similar numbering system so that you can compare the SPSS and SAS results.

To obtain the PCA solution in SPSS for Windows, we clicked on *Analyze ... Data reduction ... Factor ... Extraction ... Descriptives ...* in the SPSS for Windows menus and indicated that the focus of our analysis was the correlation matrix. The dialog boxes that were opened to obtain the output are presented in Figure 4.2. The corresponding commands for SAS are presented in Appendix B (Figure B4.2).

In the Factor Analysis Extraction dialog box (Figure 4.2), we have requested an unrotated principal component solution and output for all eight principal components. This output will help us to determine the maximum number of components to retain in the final solution. Alternative extraction methods (e.g., PAF) can be selected by changing the desired extraction method (Figure 4.2, ①).

In the *Descriptives ...* dialog box (Figure 4.2), we have requested univariate descriptive statistics and various evaluation indices for the correlation matrix (e.g., the determinant, KMO test, and Bartlett's test of sphericity) ②. We have also requested printouts of additional matrices that will help us to evaluate the "goodness of fit" of our

Figure 4.2   SPSS for Windows Dialog Boxes Used to Generate the Initial Factors for the 8 × 8 CGTS Matrix

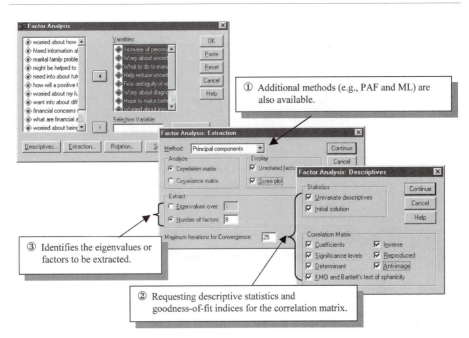

solution (e.g., the inverse, reproduced, and anti-image correlation matrices). In addition, for our initial analysis, we have requested that all eight factors be extracted ③.

Descriptive Statistics. In the printout generated from both SPSS for Windows and SAS, we are first presented with the descriptive statistics (means, standard deviations, and sample size) for the eight items in the correlation matrix (Table 4.1). Except for the number of decimals, this is similar to the SAS output in Table B4.1 (Appendix B).

Because the Likert scales for these eight items range from 1 to 5 (1 = *not at all a concern* to 5 = *extremely concerning*), it is apparent that the item means (range: 3.12–3.91) lie to the right of the midpoint of this distribution (3.0). This would suggest that the items are indeed a concern to the 205 respondents. The standard deviations (range: 1.02–1.23), however, suggest reasonable variation in the responses.

Generating the Correlation Matrix. Following the descriptive statistics, we are given the correlation matrix from Figure 4.1 that will be

Table 4.1   SPSS for Windows Computer-Generated Output for the Principal Components Analysis: Descriptive Statistics

		Mean	SD	Analysis N
C1	Increase of personal control	3.12	1.14	205
C2	Worry about uncertain diagnosis	3.63	1.08	205
C3	What to do to manage risk	3.91	1.13	205
C4	Help reduce uncertainty about future	3.47	1.02	205
C5	Fear ambiguity of results	3.21	1.05	205
C6	Worry about diagnosis I can't do anything about	3.17	1.19	205
C7	Hope to make better health, lifestyle choices	3.56	1.16	205
C8	Worried about loss of health, and life insurance coverage	3.68	1.23	205

Table 4.2   SPSS for Windows Computer-Generated Output for the Principal Component Analysis: Correlations and Significance Levels

① Pearson correlation, Item C1 with C3: $r = .337$.

Correlation		C1	C2	C3	C4	C5	C6	C7	C8
C1	Increase of personal control	1.00	.065	.337	.261	-.036	.170	.446	.105
C2	Worry about uncertain diagnosis	.065	1.00	.249	.555	.390	.505	.188	.276
C3	What to do to manage risk	.337	.249	1.00	.239	.089	.382	.610	.211
C4	Help reduce uncertainty about future	.261	.555	.239	1.00	.377	.389	.351	.252
C5	Fear ambiguity of results	-.036	.390	.089	.377	1.00	.472	.064	.327
C6	Worry about diagnosis I can't do anything about	.170	.505	.382	.389	.472	1.00	.354	.194
C7	Hope to make better health, lifestyle choices	.446	.188	.610	.351	.064	.354	1.00	.067
C8	Worried about loss of health, and life insurance coverage	.105	.276	.211	.252	.327	.194	.067	1.00
Sig. (1-tailed)									
C1	Increase of personal control		.177	.000	.000	.304	.008	.000	.066
C2	Worry about uncertain diagnosis	.177		.000	.000	.000	.000	.003	.000
C3	What to do to manage risk	.001	.000		.000	.101	.000	.000	.001
C4	Help reduce uncertainty about future	.001	.000	.000		.000	.000	.000	.000
C5	Fear ambiguity of results	.304	.000	.101	.000		.000	.181	.000
C6	Worry about diagnosis I can't do anything about	.008	.000	.000	.000	.000		.000	.003
C7	Hope to make better	.000	.003	.000	.000	.181	.000		.170
C8	Worried about loss o	.066	.000	.001	.000	.000	.003	.170	

② One-tailed significance level: C1 with C3: $p < .001$.

analyzed (Table 4.2). The significance levels, or p values, for each of the correlations are also presented. This is the same matrix that we obtained from the SAS PROC CORR (Table B3.1B).

For example, the correlation between Items C1 and C3 ($r = .337$) (Table 4.2,①) is significant at $p < .001$ ②. In SPSS for Windows, the significance levels are one-tailed by default and are taken to three decimal places. Unlike SAS (Table B3.1B), there is no available option to request two-tailed tests. We also suggest that when you are confronted with a p value of .000, you round up to $p < .001$. Note, too, that there are still 1.00s on the principal diagonal of the correlation matrix.

Table 4.3   SPSS for Windows Computer-Generated Output:
The Factor Loading Matrix

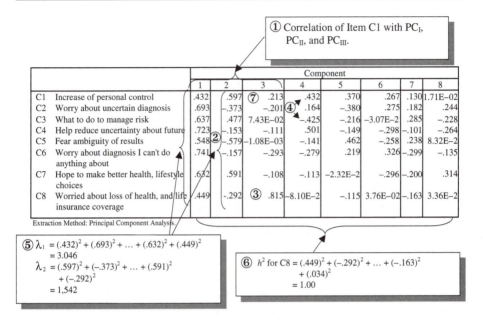

① Correlation of Item C1 with PC_I, PC_{II}, and PC_{III}.

		Component							
		1	2	3	4	5	6	7	8
C1	Increase of personal control	.432	.597	⑦ .213	.432	.370	.267	.130	1.71E–02
C2	Worry about uncertain diagnosis	.693	–.373	–.201	④ .164	–.380	.275	.182	.244
C3	What to do to manage risk	.637	.477	7.43E–02	–.425	–.216	–3.07E–2	.285	–.228
C4	Help reduce uncertainty about future	.723	–.153	–.111	.501	–.149	–.298	–.101	–.264
C5	Fear ambiguity of results	.548	② –.579	–1.08E–03	–.141	.462	–.258	.238	8.32E–2
C6	Worry about diagnosis I can't do anything about	.741	–.157	–.293	–.279	.219	.326	–.299	–.135
C7	Hope to make better health, lifestyle choices	.632	.591	–.108	–.113	–2.32E–2	–.296	–.200	.314
C8	Worried about loss of health, and life insurance coverage	.449	–.292	③ .815	–8.10E–2	–.115	3.76E–02	–.163	3.36E–2

Extraction Method: Principal Component Analysis.

⑤ $\lambda_1 = (.432)^2 + (.693)^2 + ... + (.632)^2 + (.449)^2$
$= 3.046$
$\lambda_2 = (.597)^2 + (-.373)^2 + ... + (.591)^2$
$+ (-.292)^2$
$= 1,542$

⑥ h^2 for C8 $= (.449)^2 + (-.292)^2 + ... + (-.163)^2$
$+ (.034)^2$
$= 1.00$

Recreating the Correlation Matrix

Table 4.3 presents the factor loadings for the eight items on the eight extracted principal components that were generated in SPSS for Windows using PCA. The loadings obtained from SAS are presented in Table B4.3 (Appendix B). These factor loadings represent the correlations of each of the items with the component. Item C1, for example, is correlated .432 with PC_I, .597 with PC_{II}, and .213 with PC_{III} (Table 4.3, ①). The loadings for C1 range from a low of .017 for PC_{VIII}[6] to a high of .597 for PC_{II}, suggesting that C1 may be associated more strongly with PC_{II} than with any of the other seven components.

We are also starting to see trends in the loadings. For example, Items C2, C3, C4, C6, and C7 load more strongly on PC_I than PC_{II}, and the reverse is true of Items C1 and C5. Notice, too, that we have some negative loadings (e.g., C5 with $PC_{II} = .579$ ②) and C8 is the only item that loads strongly on PC_{III} (.815) ③. Moreover, none of the items load greater than .46 on the last four components (their loadings range between –.380 and .462), suggesting that we may have no more than four components in our final solution.

In PCA, scores on an item are regarded to be a perfect function of the extracted factors. A standardized score for Item C1 on the CGTS, for example, can be defined in terms of its linear relationship to the uncorrelated extracted factors (Harman, 1976):

$$z_{C1} = a_{C1,I}PC_I + a_{C1,II}PC_{II} + \cdots + a_{C1,VIII}PC_{VIII}$$

where

$$z_{C1} = \text{standardized score for C1}$$

$$a_{C1,I} \cdots a_{C1,VIII} = \text{factor loadings of C1 on } PC_I \ldots PC_{VIII}$$

Using the loadings presented in Table 4.3, we would obtain the following result:

$$z_{C1} = .432PC_I + .597PC_{II} + \cdots + .017PC_{VIII}$$

In this way, each of the eight items that we are examining in the CGTS can be perfectly described in terms of eight new uncorrelated components.

The correlation between two items in the correlation matrix (e.g., C1 and C3) is the sum of the products of the factor loadings of the two variables vis-à-vis the extracted factors:

$$r_{C1,C3} = (a_{C1,I})(a_{C3,I}) + (a_{C1,II})(a_{C3,II})$$
$$+ (a_{C1,III})(a_{C3,III}) + \cdots + (a_{C1,VIII})(a_{C3,VIII})$$

where

$$r_{C1,C3} = \text{Pearson correlation between Items C1 and C3}$$
$$a_{C1,I} \cdots a_{C1,VIII} = \text{factor loadings of Item C1 on } PC_I \text{ through } PC_{VIII}$$
$$a_{C3,I} \cdots a_{C3,VIII} = \text{factor loadings of Item C3 on } PC_I \text{ through } PC_{VIII}$$

Items that are highly correlated with one another will display a similar pattern of high weights for some factors and low weights for others.

Using the information presented in Table 4.3, we would obtain the following correlation for Items C1 and C3:

$$r_{C1C3} = (.432)(.637) + (.597)(.477) + (.213)(.074)$$
$$+ \cdots + (.130)(.285) + (.017)(-.228) = .337$$

This is the same correlation with which we are presented in Table 4.2 ①. Note also that the factor loadings in Table 4.3 for Items C1 and C3 do not display a similar pattern of high weights for some components and low weights for others. In fact, there are some positive and negative factor loadings for the two items (e.g., .432 and −.425 on PC_{IV} ④). Therefore, we would not expect—nor did we obtain—a strong correlation between the two items.

Although all of the components are required to reproduce the correlations among the variables, realistically, only a few extracted components will likely be retained. Later in this chapter, we will review the criteria that are used to determine the number of retained factors.

Obtaining Eigenvalues for the Components

The columns in Table 4.3 (and Table B4.3 in Appendix B) represent the factor loadings of each item on all eight extracted principal components of the CGTS. Squaring these factor loadings and summing them down the column will generate the eigenvalue for each principal component. The eigenvalues for the first two principal components, PC_I and PC_{II}, would be given as follows ⑤:

$$\lambda_1 = (a_{C1,I})^2 + (a_{C2,I})^2 + \cdots + (a_{C7,I})^2 + (a_{C8,I})^2$$
$$= (.432)^2 + (.693)^2 + \cdots + (.632)^2 + (.449)^2 = 3.046$$
$$\lambda_2 = (a_{C1,II})^2 + (a_{C2,II})^2 + \cdots + (a_{C7,II})^2 + (a_{C8,II})^2$$
$$= (.597)^2 + (-.373)^2 + \cdots + (.591)^2 + (-.292)^2 = 1.542$$

where

$$\lambda_1 = \text{eigenvalue for } PC_I$$
$$a_{C1,I} \cdots a_{C8,I} = \text{factor loadings of Items C1 to C8 on } PC_I$$
$$\lambda_2 = \text{eigenvalue for } PC_{II}$$
$$a_{C1,II} \cdots a_{C8,II} = \text{factor loadings of Items C1 to C8 on } PC_{II}$$

Eigenvalues are direct indices of how much of the total item variance is accounted for by a particular component (Hair, Anderson, Tatham, & Black, 1995). The larger the eigenvalue, the more the variance in the items is explained by that component.

In PCA, dividing the eigenvalue, or the sum of the squared factor loadings, by the total number of variables (e.g., $\lambda_1/8$ for Items C1-C8) will give an indication of the proportion of variance in all of the variables that is explained by a given component. PC_I, for example, explains $3.046/8 = .3807$, or 38.07%, of the variance in the eight CGTS items. In contrast, $1.542/8 = .1928$; this means that 19.28% of the variance in those same items can be explained by PC_{II}.

Proportion of Variance in the Items Explained by the Components

Squaring a factor loading yields the proportion of variance in an individual item that is explained by a particular component. For Item C1, $(.432)^2 = .187$; therefore, 18.7% of the variance in Item C1 can be explained by PC_I (Table 4.3, ①). In contrast, $(.597)^2 = .356$, or 35.6%, of the variance in Item C1 can be explained by PC_{II}, and only $(.213)^2$, or 5.3%, of its variance is explained by PC_{III}.

The sum of the squared loadings across each row of Table 4.3 indicates the total amount of variance in each item that is explained by the extracted components. This is called the *item communality* (h^2). Because we initially requested all possible principal components (eight in this example) in PCA, the sum of these squared loadings across all eight components will be equal to 1.0 for all eight items. For Item C8, for example, we obtain the following communality value (Table 4.3, ⑥):

$$h_{C8}^2 = (.449)^2 + (-.292)^2 + (.815)^2 + \cdots + (-.163)^2 + (.034)^2 = 1.00$$

If we had requested a smaller number of components (e.g., two components), the sum of the squared loadings would be less than 1.00.

Table 4.4 presents the SPSS for Windows output reporting the total amount of variance in the items that is explained by the eight extracted factors. A similar type of table was obtained for SAS (Table B4.4, Appendix B). We are first presented with the initial eigenvalues for all eight components (e.g., 3.046 for PC_I and 1.542 for PC_{II}) in Column 2 (*Total*) (Table 4.4, ①). Notice that the total number of possible principal components is the same as the number of items in the correlation matrix being examined (8). Excluding round-off error, the total amount of variance in the items that can be explained by these eight principal components is also equal to the number of items in the correlation matrix ②:

$$3.046 + 1.542 + \cdots + .354 + .306 = 8.00$$

Dividing each of the eigenvalues by the total amount of variance ($s^2 = 8.00$) gives us the amount of variance in the items that is explained

Table 4.4 SPSS for Windows Computer-Generated Output for the Total Variance Explained in PCA

Explained in PCA

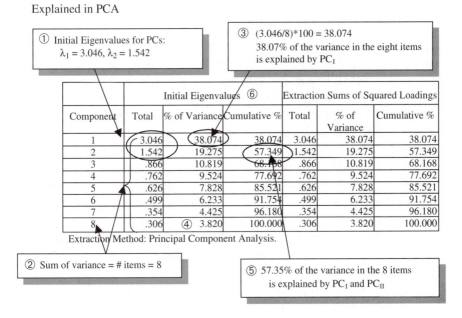

① Initial Eigenvalues for PCs:
$\lambda_1 = 3.046$, $\lambda_2 = 1.542$

③ $(3.046/8)*100 = 38.074$
38.07% of the variance in the eight items is explained by PC_I

Component	Total	Initial Eigenvalues ⑥		Extraction Sums of Squared Loadings		
		% of Variance	Cumulative %	Total	% of Variance	Cumulative %
1	3.046	38.074	38.074	3.046	38.074	38.074
2	1.542	19.275	57.349	1.542	19.275	57.349
3	.866	10.819	68.168	.866	10.819	68.168
4	.762	9.524	77.692	.762	9.524	77.692
5	.626	7.828	85.521	.626	7.828	85.521
6	.499	6.233	91.754	.499	6.233	91.754
7	.354	4.425	96.180	.354	4.425	96.180
8	.306	④ 3.820	100.000	.306	3.820	100.000

Extraction Method: Principal Component Analysis.

② Sum of variance = # items = 8

⑤ 57.35% of the variance in the 8 items is explained by PC_I and PC_{II}

by a particular component. These are summarized as percentages in Table 4.4, Column 3 (*% of Variance*). In Table 4.4, the first component, PC_I, explains the largest amount of variance (3.046/8.000 = .38074, or 38.074%) ③ and the last component, PC_{VIII}, explains the least amount of variance (.306/8.000 = .0382, or 3.820%) ④. This should not come as a surprise because this is exactly the intent of PCA: to extract explained variance in decreasing importance.

In the fourth column of Table 4.4, we are given the cumulative percent of variance that is extracted by each of the components (*Cumulative %*). The first two principal components, for example, extracted 57.349% of the variance in Items C1 to C8 ⑤. After the first two components, the increment in the amount of variance extracted by the remaining six components is relatively small (Table 4.4).

Table 4.4 also presents us with not only the initial eigenvalues but also the final eigenvalues after extraction (*Extraction Sums of Squared Loadings*) ⑥. Because we asked for all eight components to be extracted in this initial analysis, these two sets of values are exactly the same. Had we restricted our initial extraction request to fewer components (e.g., two), we would only be presented with the values for the extracted components, as you will see in Table 4.11.

Advantages and Disadvantages of PCA

Principal components analysis (PCA) is a straightforward, easily understood, and commonly used extraction technique in factor analysis. Its goal is to arrive at a succinct set of uncorrelated components that extract variance in descending order and that can empirically, parsimoniously, and effectively summarize the data set. PCA is especially useful when the researcher wants to summarize the relationships among a large number of variables with a smaller number of components (Tabachnick & Fidell, 2001).

Despite its usefulness, PCA has its problems. The biggest drawback is that PCA does not separate out errors of measurement from shared variance. Therefore, the extracted components tend to overestimate the linear patterns of relationships among sets of variables. Cattell (1965) strongly criticized PCA, saying, "The trick of putting ones in the diagonals, though comforting in accounting fully for the variance of variables, perpetrates a hoax, for actually it really drags in all the specific and error variance ... to inflate specious, incorrect common factors" (p. 201). Pedhazur and Schmelkin (1991) have argued, "unless the first few components extract a sizeable percentage of the total variance, there is little to be gained from the application of a PCA" (p. 598). *Sizeable* for these authors was 50% of the variance. They also questioned the usefulness of rotating principal components to arrive at more meaningful interpretation of them because the components are already independent of each other.

To counter these deficiencies, proponents of common factor analysis (CFA) (e.g., Cattell, 1978) have argued that factors should be extracted only from the variance that items share in common. Let us examine this approach in greater detail.

COMMON FACTOR ANALYSIS

All extraction techniques begin with the assumption that the initial components or factors to be extracted from the specified matrix are orthogonal or uncorrelated with one another. It is the criteria that are used to establish the solution that differ among the techniques.

Common factor analysis (CFA) starts with the assumption that the variance in a given variable can be explained by a small number of underlying common factors and by variance that is unique to the variable. Unlike PCA, factors in CFA are not completely defined as linear combinations of items but are instead hypothetical constructs that are estimated from those items. Because these hypothetical factors are generated from common variance, not total variance, all of the item communalities (h^2) that are initially placed on the diagonal of the correlation matrix are less than 1.00. As a result, there will be fewer extracted factors than there are items.

The challenge in CFA is to determine what values for the communality estimates should be initially placed on this diagonal. This issue is extremely important because the choice of these values affects the solution, especially the number of factors that can be extracted (Kline, 1994).

Several methods have been developed to obtain the initial communality estimates to insert in the diagonal of the correlation matrix. Guttman (1956) argued that the lower bound for this estimate is the square of the multiple correlation coefficient (R^2) resulting from the regression of each item on all other items in the matrix. This classic factor analytic approach has several names: the *principal factor method* (Harman, 1976) and, more commonly, *principal axis factoring* (PAF) (Gorsuch, 1983). Its name, principal axis factoring, reflects the fact that this method uses the same decomposition strategies as PCA to determine its factor solution (Kim & Mueller, 1978). This is the term (PAF) that we will use in this text.

Extracting the Factors Using Principal Axis Factoring

Thurstone (1935, 1947) developed the iterative approach to estimating the communalities and subsequently extracting the factors in principal axis factoring (PAF) (Kline, 1994). First, the initial estimates based on the squared multiple correlation coefficient (R^2) are inserted in the diagonal of the correlation matrix and then the analysis is undertaken in the same way as that outlined for PCA. These R^2 values are used to estimate the new communalities that will replace the old communality estimates on the diagonal of the correlation matrix. This iteration process continues until a satisfactory convergence of the two sets of input and output communalities is achieved (Nunnally & Bernstein, 1994).

The default convergence criterion in SPSS for Windows is a maximum of 25 iterations or until the difference between the input and output communality over all variables is less than .001. Sometimes in PAF, this convergence is not achieved and the factor analytic solution is not obtained. When this occurs, you may want to use PCA during the initial analyses, at least until some of the items have been discarded.

Like PCA, PAF factors are extracted successively and therefore are orthogonal to one another. The first factor is extracted such that it accounts for the maximum amount of common variance. The second factor is extracted from the residual correlation matrix after having factored out the influence of the first factor. This process continues until a sufficient number of factors have been extracted. When should we terminate the extraction process? As we have promised, we will review the criteria used to determine the number of factors later in this chapter.

Recreating the Correlation Matrix in PAF

In PAF, scores on an item are no longer perfect functions of the extracted factors as in PCA. Rather, each of the items being considered in the correlation matrix can be described linearly in terms of m factors that are less than the number of items (n) plus a unique factor that takes into account both specific and error variance (Harman, 1976). The formula for a standardized score for Item C1 on the CGTS, for example, would be given as follows:

$$z_{C1} = a_{C1,I}F_I + a_{C1,II}F_{II} + \cdots + a_{C1,m}F_m + u_{C1}Y_{C1}$$

where

$$z_{C1} = \text{standardized score for Item C1}$$
$$a_{C1,I} \cdots a_{C1,m} = \text{factor loadings of Item C1 on the } m \text{ extracted}$$
$$\text{factors } F_I \dots F_m$$
$$u_{C1}Y_{C1} = \text{factor loading of C1 on its unique factor } Y_{C1}$$

The coefficients $a_{C1,I} \cdots a_{C1,m}$ are the factor loadings that are being estimated in PAF. If the factors being extracted are uncorrelated, the correlation between two items in the correlation matrix (e.g., C1 and C3) can be estimated from the sum of the products of these factor loadings of the two variables vis-à-vis the extracted factors:

$$\hat{r}_{C1C3} = (a_{C1,I})(a_{C3,I}) + (a_{C1,II})(a_{C3,II}) + (a_{C1,III})(a_{C3,III}) + \cdots + (a_{C1,m})(a_{C3,m})$$

Table 4.5   Factor Matrix Generated in SPSS for Windows Using Principal Axis Factoring

① Size ranking: PCA and PAF.

② Squaring and summing the factor loadings for an item produces its communality:
$(.374)^2 + (.428)^2 + \ldots (.243)^2 + (.005)^2 = .459$

Factor Matrix[a]

PCA				Factor					
		1	2	3	4	5	6	7
.432	C1 Increase of personal control	**8**	.374	.428	−.184	.134	.157	.243	5.227E−03
.693	C2 Worry about uncertain diagnosis	**3**	.662	−.353	−.159	−.153	−.294	2.572E−02	6.007E−02
.637	C3 What to do to manage risk	**5**	.607	.448	.236	9.645E−02	−.219	−676E−02	−8.51E−02
.723	C4 Help reduce uncertainty about future	**2**	.691	−.160	−.432	−.140E−02	7.999E−02	−801E−02	−7.37E−02
.548	C5 Fear ambiguity of results	**6**	.512	−.512	.204	.106	.264	−.105	−2.84E−03
.741	C6 Worry about diagnosis I can't do anything about	**1**	.712	−.152	.283	−.254	6.443E−02	.181	−1.18E−02
.632	C7 Hope to make better health, lifestyle choices	**4**	.622	.577	8.445E−03	−7.94E−02	.112	−.165	8.777E−02
.449	C8 Worried about loss of health, and life insurance coverage	**7**	.378	−.202	4.709E−02	.471	−995E−02	4.382E−02	4.240E−02

Extraction Method: Principal Axis Factoring.

a. 7 factors extracted. 21 iterations required.

where

$$\hat{r}_{C1C3} = \text{estimated Pearson correlation between}$$
$$\text{Items C1 and C3}$$
$$a_{C1,I} \cdots a_{C1,m} = \text{factor loadings of Item C1 on } F_I \text{ through } F_m$$
$$a_{C3,I} \cdots a_{C3,m} = \text{factor loadings of Item C3 on } F_I \text{ through } F_m$$

Unlike PCA, the estimated correlation coefficient in PAF will not replicate *r* exactly because the factors are generated from only common variance, not total variance.

Table 4.5 presents the factor-loading matrix generated in SPSS for Windows using PAF. This output was obtained by opening the same dialog boxes presented in Figure 4.2 but indicating instead that the factor extraction method is PAF, not principal components (Figure 4.2, ①). The PAF output that was generated in SAS is presented in Table B4.5, Appendix B.

In PAF, only seven factors were extracted in SPSS for Windows. When we requested eight factors, the following warning appeared:

Warnings

> You cannot request as many factors as variables with any extraction method except PC. The number of factors will be reduced by one.

There are fewer factors extracted in PAF than numbers of items. The final factor represents variance that is unique to the item.

Notice that although the factor loadings for PAF are consistently smaller than those for PCA, their size rankings are similar (Table 4.5, ①). Item C1's loading on the first factor ranks eighth in size for both the PCA and PAF extraction methods, although Item C5 ranks first among the eight-item loadings on Factor 1 ①.

Interestingly, when we requested the same seven factors in SAS, we were presented with the following error message:

```
ERROR: Maximum iterations exceeded.
NOTE: 4 factors will be retained by the MINEIGEN criterion.
```

As Table B4.5 in Appendix B indicates, four of the initial extracted eigenvalues were negative. Hatcher (1994) indicates that negative eigenvalues may occur in a SAS factor analysis because the cumulative proportion of explained variance sometimes exceeds 1.00 in the initial stages of PAF. Because this is unacceptable in a factor analysis (the minimum acceptable eigenvalue is 0), only the four factors with positive eigenvalues were retained in SAS. Few differences were found in the sizes of the loadings on these four factors when the results from SPSS for Windows and SAS were compared (Table B4.6, Appendix B).

Obtaining Item Communalities in PAF

In PAF, the item communalities, or the total amount of variance in the item that can be explained by the extracted factors, are no longer equal to 1.00, as was the case for PCA when all eight factors were extracted. You will recall from our earlier discussion that squaring and summing the item's factor loadings across all of the extracted factors will generate an item's communality. For Item C1, for example, the following item communality is obtained from Table 4.5 ②:

$$h_{C1}^2 = (.374)^2 + (.428)^2 + (-.184)^2 + \cdots + (.243)^2 + (5.277E{-}03)^2 = .459$$

This means that .459, or 45.9%, of the common variance that Item C1 shares with the other seven items can be explained by the seven extracted factors. The remaining variance $(1 - .459 = .541)$, or 54.1%, represents the variance that is unique to the item and includes both specific and error variance.

In PAF, we can no longer perfectly recreate the correlation matrix because a unique factor is involved. The estimated correlation between Items C1 and C3, for example, is as follows:

$$
\begin{aligned}
\hat{r}_{C1C3} =\ & (a_{C1,I})(a_{C3,I}) + (a_{C1,II})(a_{C3,II}) + (a_{C1,III})(a_{C3,III}) \\
& + \cdots + (a_{C1,VII})(a_{C3,VII}) \\
=\ & (.374)(.607) + (.428)(.448) + (-.184)(.236) \\
& + \cdots + (.00522)(-.0851) = .337
\end{aligned}
$$

Although this correlation may appear to be exactly equal to the correlation presented in the matrix in Table 4.2, it is only exact to three decimal places.

The reproduced correlation and residual matrices that were generated in SPSS for Windows using PAF is presented in Table 4.6. The reproduced correlation matrix in PAF is presented in the upper half of the table (Table 4.6, ①) and the residual matrix is presented in the lower half of the table ②. Interestingly, SAS does not provide a reproduced correlation matrix but does present the residual correlation matrix if the RESIDUALS or ALL subcommand is used. The residual correlation matrix for the four extracted factors obtained in SAS is presented in Table B4.7a-b, Appendix B.

These residuals represent the differences between the estimated and observed correlations between pairs of variables. If the reproduced correlations estimate the actual correlations precisely, there will be 0s on the off-diagonal of the residual matrix. As indicated in Table 4.6, when we used all seven factors in PAF, the estimated correlation between Items C1 and C3 is similar to that presented in Table 4.2 (i.e., .337 ③). There is, however, some residual correlation remaining, $-3.795E{-}04$, or $-.0003795$ ④, indicating that the seven extracted factors in PAF do not perfectly reproduce the correlation matrix.

The values in the residual matrix serve as indicators of how well our extracted factors reproduce the correlation matrix. If there have been a sufficient number of factors extracted, these residuals will be small. The presence of moderate (.05–.10) or large residuals (> .10) suggests that there may be more factors remaining to be extracted (Tabachnick & Fidell, 2001).

The item communalities are presented on the diagonal of the reproduced correlation matrix.[7] For Item C1, for example, the item communality that we calculated earlier (.459) is on the diagonal ⑤. Item C7 had the largest communality (.774) ⑥, indicating that 77.4% of the common variance in Item C7 could be explained by the seven extracted factors in PAF.

Obtaining the Eigenvectors and Eigenvalues in PAF

As in PCA, the eigenvector for a given common factor in PAF is a $1 \times n$ column vector, containing a value or weight for each of the n items in the correlation matrix. As we saw in Table 4.5, the weights in the eigenvector for PAF will generally be smaller than those for PCA but will demonstrate a similar pattern of large to small loadings.

Similar to PCA, the eigenvalue for each of the factors in PAF is obtained by summing the squared column factor loadings for each item being considered in the analysis. Unlike PCA, eigenvalues in PAF are not estimates of total variance but are estimates of the amount of

Table 4.6 Reproduced Correlations and Residual Matrix Generated in SPSS for Windows Using Principal Axis Factoring

Reproduced Correlations

		C1 Increase of personal control	C2 Worry about uncertain diagnosis	C3 What to do to manage risk	C4 Help reduce uncertainty about future	C5 Fear ambiguity of results	C6 Worry about diagnosis I can't do anything about	C7 Hope to make better health, lifestyle choices	C8 Worried about loss of health, and life insurance coverage
Reproduced Correlation ①	C1 Increase of personal control	⑤ .459[b]	6.563E-02	③ .337	.260	-3.515E-02	.169	.445	.105
	C2 Worry about uncertain diagnosis	6.563E-02	.703[b]	.249	.555	.391	.504	.188	.275
	C3 What to do to manage risk	.337	.249	.694[b]	.239	8.986E-02	.381	.610	.211
	C4 Help reduce uncertainty about future	.260	.555	.239	.708[b]	.376	.389	.351	.252
	C5 Fear ambiguity of results	-3.515E-02	.391	8.986E-02	.376	.659[b]	.471	6.365E-02	.326
	C6 Worry about diagnosis I can't do anything about	.169	.504	.381	.389	.471	.711[b]	.354	.195
	C7 Hope to make better health, lifestyle choices	.445	.188	.610	.351	6.365E-02	.354	⑥ .774[b]	6.722E-02
	C8 Worried about loss of health, and life insurance coverage	.105	.275	.211	.252	.326	.195	6.722E-02	.422[b]
Residual[a] ②	C1 Increase of personal control		-6.554E-04	④ -3.795E-04	5.232E-04	-8.162E-04	7.498E-04	2.888E-04	7.190E-04
	C2 Worry about uncertain diagnosis	-6.554E-04		-3.519E-04	4.851E-04	-7.568E-04	6.952E-04	2.678E-04	6.667E-04
	C3 What to do to manage risk	-3.795E-04	-3.519E-04		2.809E-04	-4.382E-04	4.026E-04	1.551E-04	3.861E-04
	C4 Help reduce uncertainty about future	5.232E-04	4.851E-04	2.809E-04		6.041E-04	-5.550E-04	-2.138E-04	-5.322E-04
	C5 Fear ambiguity of results	-8.162E-04	-7.568E-04	-4.382E-04	6.041E-04		8.658E-04	3.335E-04	8.303E-04
	C6 Worry about diagnosis I can't do anything about	7.498E-04	6.952E-04	4.026E-04	-5.550E-04	8.658E-04		-3.064E-04	-7.627E-04
	C7 Hope to make better health, lifestyle choices	2.888E-04	2.678E-04	1.551E-04	-2.138E-04	3.335E-04	-3.064E-04		-2.938E-04
	C8 Worried about loss of health, and life insurance coverage	7.190E-04	6.667E-04	3.861E-04	-5.322E-04	8.303E-04	-7.627E-04	-2.938E-04	

Extraction Method: Principal Axis Factoring.

a. Residuals are computed between observed and reproduced correlations. There are 0 (.0%) nonredundant residuals with absolute values > 0.05.

b. Reproduced communalities

109

common variance among the items that is explained by the particular common factor. The larger the eigenvalue, the more total common variance in the items that is explained by that factor. Like PCA, PAF also maximizes the extracted common variance in decreasing order so that F_I will account for the most common variance and F_m the least variance.

Table 4.7 presents the seven extracted eigenvalues that were generated in SPSS for Windows using PAF. In SPSS for Windows, the initial estimates for the eigenvalues are similar to those of PCA (Table 4.7, ①). After extraction, however, the estimated eigenvalues for the PAF solution are considerably smaller because they reflect common variance rather than total variance ②. Like PCA, the sum of the eigenvalues in PAF equals the sum of the elements that were placed on the diagonal of the correlation matrix. Unlike PCA, however, the sum of these eigenvalues will be less than the number of variables (Nunnally & Bernstein, 1994). In our example, the sum of the extracted eigenvalues is 5.129, which is less than 8.00 ③.

Table B4.8 in Appendix B presents the output from both SPSS for Windows and SAS with regard to the total variance explained by the principal axis factoring solution with four extracted factors.

Advantages and Disadvantages of PAF

As with any factor extraction method, there are advantages and disadvantages associated with PAF. An advantage of PAF is that the squared multiple correlations are easy to obtain from the correlation matrix. The values are unique and intuitively make sense. Nunnally and Bernstein (1994) argue that a PAF solution that contains the same number of factors as PCA will provide a better estimate of the correlations because PCA solutions include errors of measurement. In PAF, the leftover or residual correlations will be smaller in absolute value and, as a result, will produce a smaller *root mean square error* (RMS) (Nunnally & Bernstein, 1994). *Root mean square error* is the square root of the average squared discrepancies between the estimated correlation matrix ($\hat{\mathbf{R}}$) and the actual correlation matrix ($\mathbf{R}$) excluding the diagonal elements. RMS is used to evaluate how well a given model *fits* the data. Because lower values of RMS indicate a better fit of the model to the data, PAF may be a superior solution to PCA (Nunnally & Bernstein, 1994).

There are a number of difficulties with PAF, however (Nunnally & Bernstein, 1994). First, the squared multiple correlation for each item,

Table 4.7   Total Variance Explained by the Principal Axis Factoring
Solution

Total Variance Explained

Factor	① Initial Eigenvalues			② Extraction Sums of Squared Loadings		
	Total	% of Variance	Cumulative %	Total	% of Variance	Cumulative %
1	3.046	38.074	38.074	2.725	34.057	34.057
2	1.542	19.275	57.349	1.193	14.911	48.968
3	.866	10.819	68.168	.425	5.318	54.286
4	.762	9.524	77.692	.355	4.437	58.723
5	.626	7.828	85.521	.262	3.272	61.995
6	.499	6.233	91.754	.144	1.795	63.790
7	.354	4.425	96.180	2.595E-02	.324	64.114
8	.306	3.820	100.000			

Extraction Method: Principal Axis Factoring.

③   2.725 + 1.193 + ... + .144 + .0259 = 5.129

R^2, that is initially placed on the diagonal of the correlation matrix is not quite the same as common variance. Common variance (h^2) refers to how much the items share with the factors. In contrast, R^2 values relate to how much variance the items share with each other. As a result, the R^2 values are sample specific, can change from study to study, and tend to increase spuriously with the number of variables. Computer simulations have also indicated that R^2 values do not necessarily reproduce the actual communalities generated from a known structure. The R^2 values in PAF may also be too low as communality estimates because most algorithms that are used to obtain R^2 will not work when the R^2 values that are placed on the diagonal approach 1.0. This is the value used by PCA and could potentially be a valid R^2 value (Nunnally & Bernstein, 1994).

Sometimes the iterative methods used in PAF can lead to final communalities greater than 1.00 (Kline, 1994). This would not make sense because it would imply that *more* than the total shared variance is explained by a given factor. A situation in which a final communality equals 1 is referred to as a *Heywood case*, and if communality is greater than 1, it is called an *ultra-Heywood case* (SAS Institute, Inc., 1985). A serious problem exists when the communality of a variable is greater than 1 because it implies that some unique factor has a negative variance. The result is that the factor solution in this situation is invalid. SAS writers suggest that possible contributors to this situation are poor initial communality estimates, too many or too few common factors, not enough data to provide stable estimates, or an inappropriate common factor model (SAS Institute, Inc., 1985).

Other Extraction Methods in Common Factor Analysis

Although PAF is the most commonly used method in CFA, there are five additional factor extraction methods available in both SPSS for Windows and SAS. Three of these common factor approaches, maximum likelihood methods (ML), unweighted least squares (ULS), and generalized least squares (GLS), attempt to maximize an expected relationship between a sample and a population. The two additional approaches, alpha and image factoring, use slightly different approaches to estimate communalities. A sixth approach, the minimum residual method, uses only the off-diagonal elements of the correlation matrix and therefore does not require initial estimates of communality (Comrey & Lee, 1992). Unfortunately, this factor extraction technique is not available in either SAS or SPSS for Windows and therefore will not be reviewed here.

Maximum Likelihood Methods. The maximum likelihood method of estimation (ML) (Bentler & Bonett, 1980; Jöreskog & Sorbom, 1989) is a favorite among statisticians because of its desirable asymptotic properties (Bickel & Doksum, 1977). Because of its hypothesis-testing capabilities, this method is used in confirmatory factor analysis (e.g., structural equation modeling). ML methods are based on the assumption that the distribution for each item is normal and that the correlation matrix is positive-definite (i.e., all eigenvalues > 0).[8]

ML methods generate parameter estimates that are most likely to have produced the observed correlation matrix if the sample were from a multivariate normal distribution. In ML, starting values are input into a matrix-generating equation to obtain a reproduced correlation matrix. This reproduced matrix is then compared with the actual correlation matrix to see how closely the initial estimates reproduce the observed values. Through a computationally demanding iterative process, old estimates are replaced by new estimates until a satisfactory convergence between the reproduced and actual correlation matrix has been achieved. Like all common factor models, the generated ML communality estimates are less than 1.0.

There are several different versions of ML, which may not all reach the same solution (Nunnally & Bernstein, 1994). Moreover, unlike PCA, convergence to a satisfactory factor analytic solution is not always forthcoming and, at the very least, takes considerably longer to run than either PCA or PAF. ML methods will also not run if the correlation matrix is singular (i.e., it is a matrix that does not have an inverse). These methods are also extremely susceptible to creating Heywood cases in which communalities are ≥ 1 (Cureton & D'Agostino, 1983). The reason for this is that during the ML iteration process, more emphasis is placed on variables with high communality values; this increases their weights, which, in turn, increases their communality values (SAS Institute, Inc., 1985).

Unweighted Least Squares. Unweighted least squares (ULS) is a factor extraction method that minimizes the sum of the squared differences between the observed and reproduced correlation matrices, ignoring the values on the diagonals. Although PCA also attempts to minimize these squared differences, PCA is restricted to analyses in which there are 1.0s on the diagonal of the correlation matrix. As a common factor technique, ULS provides solutions in which the communalities are less than 1.0. Like ML, ULS is most often used in confirmatory factor analysis.

Because a ULS solution is scale dependent, different solutions to the minimum value for the fitting function will be obtained depending on the matrix to be analyzed (i.e., covariance vs. correlation matrix) (Jöreskog, 1977). For this reason, it has been recommended that ULS be restricted to the correlation matrix (Comrey & Lee, 1992). Moreover, the number of factors to be extracted must be specified. An advantage to ULS over ML methods is that ULS will still run if the correlation matrix is not positive-definite (i.e., some eigenvalues are negative) (Jöreskog, 1977). ULS is especially useful when the item distributions are non-normal (Nunnally & Bernstein, 1994).

Generalized Least Squares. Like ULS, generalized least squares (GLS) is a factor extraction method that minimizes the sum of the squared differences between the observed and reproduced correlation matrices. One of the differences between the two methods is that in GLS, the correlations are weighted by the inverse of their uniqueness. This means that those variables that are more highly correlated with other items and therefore have higher squared multiple correlations (R^2) are given more weight than those with lower R^2 values.

Like ML methods (and unlike ULS), GLS solutions to the minimum value for the fitting function are not scale dependent (Jöreskog, 1977).

This means that the same solution can be obtained using either the correlation or covariance matrix (Comrey & Lee, 1992). Although GLS is available in SPSS for Windows, this factor extraction method is not available in SAS.

Alpha Factoring. Alpha factoring is an extraction method that uses Cronbach's (1951) alpha or the intercorrelations among the items to obtain a measure of internal consistency of the extracted factors. More homogeneous scales have higher alpha coefficients. The factor with the highest alpha coefficient is extracted first; subsequent factors are removed sequentially until no more factors with positive alphas remain (Comrey & Lee, 1992). Alpha factoring is available in both SPSS for Windows and SAS but has not been a popular extraction tool, possibly because the approach yields too few extracted factors (Cattell, 1978; Comrey & Lee, 1992).

Image Factoring. Image factoring is an extraction technique developed by Guttman (1953) that has been touted as an alternative model to common factor analysis. Based on image theory, the common variance in a given variable is defined as its linear regression on remaining variables in the correlation matrix rather than a function of hypothetical factors as in CFA. The part of the variable that can be predicted by the other variables is called the *image* and the part that cannot be predicted is called the *anti-image* (Comrey & Lee, 1992; Kaiser, 1963). The resulting R^2 values are placed on the diagonal of the correlation matrix and the off-diagonal elements are adjusted to assure no negative eigenvalues.

Although it is available in both SPSS for Windows and SAS, image factoring is not a widely used extraction technique in the research literature. Comrey and Lee (1992) argue that there is little advantage to image factoring over PAF because both use R^2 values as initial estimates.

DETERMINING WHICH
EXTRACTION APPROACH TO USE

With six or seven factor extraction techniques available in SAS and SPSS for Windows, it is no wonder that the researcher might be confused about which technique is best to use in given circumstances. Each approach has its own proponents and critics. Our suggestion is that for an exploratory factor analysis, you start with a PCA solution, solve the problems associated with it (e.g., items with too high or too low intercorrelations), and come up with a preliminary solution. Then compare these results with a PAF solution on the same matrix and pick the one that is the best fit and that makes the most intuitive sense.

SELECTING THE NUMBER OF FACTORS TO RETAIN

You will recall that a task of the beginning extraction process is to determine the number of initial subsets or factors that appear to represent the dimensions of the construct being measured. Using all eight components to determine the domains of the eight items of the CGTS scale clearly would not be a parsimonious solution to this challenge. We would like instead to reduce the number of factors or components such that we would maximize the amount of variance explained with the fewest number of factors or components.

Although the goal is simple, there is no precise solution to determining the number of factors to extract. Given the same data set, a team of researchers might arrive at very different solutions. There are, however, several guidelines that can be used to help determine when to stop extracting factors.

Eigenvalues > 1

One approach to determining the number of initial factors is to select only those factors for which the eigenvalues are greater than 1.00. This would mean that these factors would account for more than their share of the total variance in the items. This is known as the Kaiser-Guttman rule (Comrey & Lee, 1992; Guttman, 1954; Kaiser, 1960, 1970; Nunnally & Bernstein, 1994) and is the default criterion in SPSS, although other minimum eigenvalues can be specified in SPSS for Windows using the *Factor Analysis . . . Extract . . . Eigenvalues over . . .* dialog box (Figure 4.2, ③). In SAS, the number of eigenvalues exceeding a given value can be specified using the PROC FACTOR: MINEIGEN = p option where p represents the smallest eigenvalue for which a factor is retained (e.g., 1.0) (Figure B4.4, Appendix B ①).

Comrey and Lee (1992) caution that the *Eigenvalue >1* criterion should only be used when 1.0s have been inserted on the diagonal as the initial communality values (e.g., PCA). They argue that, even with this criterion, the researcher may over- or underestimate the correct number of factors. For example, if there are large numbers of items in the instrument development pool, there will also be large numbers of eigenvalues that meet this criterion. It would be most unreasonable, for example, to create an instrument that contains 30 factors.

Gorsuch (1983) reviewed a number of studies that examined the accuracy of this criterion. He suggests that, in general, this criterion is most accurate when there are fewer than 40 variables, the sample size is large, and the number of factors is expected to be between [n of variables/5] and [n of variables/3]. In our eight-item CGTS example, using the *Eigenvalue > 1* criterion, we have fewer than 40 variables ($n = 8$) and a reasonable sample size ($n = 205$). We could, therefore, expect to end up with two (rounding off 8/5 = 1.6) to three (rounding off 8/3 = 2.67) factors. If we used the total scale of 20 items, we would expect between four (20/5 = 4) and seven (rounding off 20/3 = 6.67).

Interestingly, when we compared the PCA and PAF final solutions for our eight-item CGTS example in SPSS for Windows (Table 4.8), we found that, regardless of factor extraction method, only two extracted factors meet the *Eigenvalue > 1* criterion ①. In SAS, the same 2-factor results were obtained using both PCA (Table B4.4, Appendix B) and PAF (Table B4.8).

For the 20-item scale, five extracted factors in SPSS for Windows met the *Eigenvalue > 1* criterion for both PCA and PAF solutions (Table C4.2, Appendix C). In SAS, the same analysis yielded the same five extracted factors for PCA but only four factors for PAF.

Percent of Variance Extracted

A second criterion for determining the number of factors is the cumulative percentage of variance extracted by successive factors. That is, the researcher terminates the factor extraction process when a threshold for maximum variance extracted (e.g., 75-80%) has been achieved. An advantage of this approach is that it would ensure practical significance of the factors.

There are, however, no definitive guidelines for what that threshold should be for either PCA or PAF. Hair and colleagues (1995) suggest that in the natural sciences, factor extraction should be continued until all extracted factors account for at least 90% of the explained variance or until the last factor accounts for only a small portion of the

Table 4.8   Comparison of the Principal Component Analysis (PCA) and Principal Axis Factoring (PAF) Solutions for the Eight-Item CGTS

Factoring (PAF) Solutions for the Eight-Item CGTS

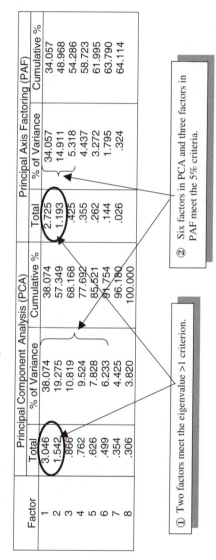

Factor	Principal Component Analysis (PCA)			Principal Axis Factoring (PAF)		
	Total	% of Variance	Cumulative %	Total	% of Variance	Cumulative %
1	3.046	38.074	38.074	2.725	34.057	34.057
2	1.542	19.275	57.349	1.193	14.911	48.968
3	.866	10.819	68.168	.425	5.318	54.286
4	.762	9.524	77.692	.355	4.437	58.723
5	.626	7.828	85.521	.262	3.272	61.995
6	.499	6.233	91.754	.144	1.795	63.790
7	.354	4.425	96.180	.026	.324	64.114
8	.306	3.820	100.000			

① Two factors meet the eigenvalue >1 criterion.

② Six factors in PCA and three factors in PAF meet the 5% criteria.

117

explained variance (less than 5%). Unfortunately, these criteria do not readily apply in the less precise social sciences, where extracted factors could account for less explained variance (e.g., 50-60%). Given that PAF only addresses common variance, it is also reasonable to expect that these threshold criteria would be considerably lower for PAF than for PCA.

The SPSS for Windows output presented in Table 4.8 indicates that, for eight items, there are six PCA components, PC_I to PC_{VI}, that meet the 5% criteria, with percents of explained variance ranging from 6.23 to 38.074% (Table 4.8, ②). Although the total cumulative variance explained by these six components is 91.754%, using so many components to explain an eight-item scale is hardly a parsimonious solution. The PAF solution indicates that only three factors meet the 5% criteria and that these factors account for 54.286% of the common variance in the items ②.

For the 20-item correlation matrix, there are five PCA components in SPSS for Windows that meet the 5% criteria (range of explained variance: 5.274-33.490%), with a cumulative percent equal to 67.326% (Appendix C, Table C4.2 ①). The PAF solution in SPSS for Windows, on the other hand, indicates that only four factors meet the 5% criteria. These four factors account for 53.5047% of the common variance in the 20 items (Table C4.2 ②).

The SAS output for the PCA analysis (Table B4.4, Appendix B) presents the same results as that of SPSS for Windows. However, for our PAF analyses in SAS (Table B4.8, Appendix B), the results are very different and could be potentially misleading (e.g., for Factor I, 33.7% explained variance in SPSS for Windows vs. 56.3% explained variance in SAS). The reason for such different values is that both the proportion and cumulative values are based on *all* the eigenvalues, including the negative values that were obtained in SAS. Our advice, therefore, is that you carefully examine your output to be sure that you are correctly interpreting the results.

Examining the Scree Plot

A third method for determining the number of factors is to plot the extracted factors against their eigenvalues in descending order of magnitude to identify distinct breaks in the slope of the plot. This method, called the *scree plot*, was first offered by Cattell (1966) as a way to identify distinct breaks between the steep slope of the larger eigenvalues

Figure 4.3   Scree Plot Generated in SPSS for Windows of the Eigenvalues
Plotted Against Their Principal Components

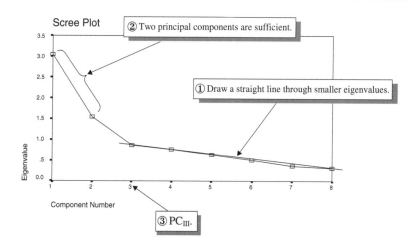

and the trailing off of the smaller ones. Cattell referred to this gradual
trailing off as the *scree* because it is akin to the rubble that ends up at
the foot of a mountain. To determine where the break occurs, a straight
line is drawn with a ruler through the lower values of the plotted
eigenvalues. That point where the factors curve above the straight line
drawn through the smaller eigenvalues identifies the number of factors
(Cattell & Jaspars, 1967; Gorsuch, 1983).

Figure 4.3 presents the scree plot that was generated in SPSS for
Windows for the eight items of the CGTS scale using PCA. This scree
plot is similar to one that would have been generated in SAS. To determine how many factors to retain, a ruler was laid across the lower
eigenvalues to determine where they formed a straight line. This
occurred for those eigenvalues associated with Factors 3 through 8
(Figure 4.3, ①).

Using the Cattell criteria for this output, only two factors remain
above that line that account for the maximum amount of variance in
the eight items ②. This is also what we learned when we examined the
criterion *Eigenvalues > 1* in Table 4.8. Because these two components
only explain 57.3% of the variance in the items, the question arises as
to whether we should extract a third component to increase the amount

of explained variance in the items to 68.2% (Table 4.8). To answer this question, we need to examine the loadings of the items on the factors to determine which solution makes the most theoretical and intuitive sense.

Although the scree plot presented in Figure 4.3 is relatively easy to interpret, other scree plots can be more difficult to assess. For example, several breaks in the plotted values may result in several straight lines that could be drawn through the plotted eigenvalues. A second possibility is that there might not be an obvious break in the plotted values. It is also not entirely clear from the literature where the cutoff should be. Cattell (1966) originally suggested that the first factor on the straight line (e.g., PC_{III} in Figure 4.3, ③) be the cut-off factor. He later revised this rule to be the numbers of factors that appear prior to the beginning of the straight line (Cattell & Jaspars, 1967). Still others (Tabachnick & Fidell, 2001) suggest that the researcher identify that point where the line drawn through the plotted eigenvalues changes direction or slope.

It is often necessary to use subjective judgment to determine where the discontinuity of the eigenvalues occurs. Several authors (Gorsuch, 1983; Tabachnick & Fidell, 2001) suggest that if the cutoff for the number of factors is unclear, the researcher might find it useful to undertake several factor analyses with different numbers of specified factors. By examining the results of extracting different numbers of factors, the researcher can more easily arrive at that parsimonious set of factors that makes the most intuitive sense given the problem area. In the statistical package BMDP, it is possible to request several factor analyses to be conducted simultaneously (e.g., two, three, or four). In both SPSS for Windows and SAS, these analyses cannot be done in a single run. It is possible, however, to specify different numbers of factors to be extracted.

Gorsuch (1983) recommends scree plots over the *Eigenvalue > 1* criterion. Unlike the *Eigenvalue > 1* criterion, scree plots can be used when communalities replace 1s on the diagonal of the correlation matrix as in PAF. The size breaks in the eigenvalues for both PCA components and PAF factors also appear to be at the same place (Gorsuch, 1983; Tucker, Koopman, & Linn, 1969). Scree plots are most reliable when sample sizes are large, communality values are high, and the ratio of variables to factors is at least three to one (Gorsuch, 1983).

Statistical Significance of the Extracted Factors

Examining the Chi-Square Values. Some factor extraction methods (e.g., ML and GLS) provide significance tests to help determine whether the number of extracted factors is sufficient. Both ML and GLS methods, for example, provide a large-sample chi-square (χ^2) goodness-of-fit test. This statistic tests the null hypothesis, which states that, compared with a one-factor model (i.e., all of the items load on a single factor), the fit of the data with the number of factors chosen (k) is adequate. In this test, the researcher is looking for the minimum number of factors that would result in a nonsignificant χ^2 value. An assumption of this test is multivariate normality: each item in the correlation matrix needs to be distributed normally both individually and in combination with other items.

Kim and Mueller (1978) suggest that, in exploratory factor analysis, the researcher start with a one-factor model and add additional factors until the significance test indicates that a given factor model does not significantly deviate from the observed data. Although these authors do not identify what represents a *nonsignificant* χ^2 value, they do warn that if the sample size is large (e.g., 800-1,000), the researcher can end up with too many common factors. Even minor misfits between the data and factors can result in additional significant, though trivial, factors.

Cureton and D'Agostino (1983) suggest that, because the researcher terminates with acceptance rather than rejection of a null hypothesis, $p > .20$ rather than $p > .05$ be used to guard against the Type II error of rejecting a factor when in fact the factor is significant. The problem with this more conservative p value, however, is that it will more likely result in more factors being extracted. Indeed, this problem arises with our eight-item CGTS data.

Using the ML extraction method in SPSS for Windows, we compared the χ^2 results for two, three, and four extracted factors (Table 4.9). As p values from Table 4.9 indicate, both the two- and three-factor solutions resulted in significant χ^2 values ①, indicating that these solutions did not sufficiently describe our data. If we had kept our alpha at $p > .05$ rather than $p > .20$, the four-factor solution would have resulted in an insignificant χ^2 value $(p = .058)$ ②. This indicates that, statistically, a four-factor model did not significantly deviate from our observed data.

Table 4.9   Comparison of α^2 Goodness-of-Fit Tests in SPSS for Windows: Two, Three, and Four Factors Extracted

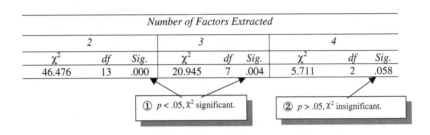

	Number of Factors Extracted							
2			3			4		
χ^2	df	Sig.	χ^2	df	Sig.	χ^2	df	Sig.
46.476	13	.000	20.945	7	.004	5.711	2	.058

① $p < .05, \chi^2$ significant.   ② $p > .05, \chi^2$ insignificant.

It is interesting to note that when we attempted to extract five factors in SPSS for Windows in order to arrive at the more stringent $p > .20$ criterion suggested by Cureton and D'Agostino (1983), we received the following two error messages:

> **Warnings**
>
> The number of degrees of freedom (−2) is not positive. Factor analysis may not be appropriate.

> **Factor Matrix[a]**
>
> [a] Attempted to extract 5 factors. In iteration 25, the Hessian was not positive definite. Extraction was terminated.

These two error messages indicate that it was not possible to extract five factors from the eight-item CGTS correlation matrix using ML methods. Even when we increased the number of CGTS items in the correlation matrix to 20, we could not arrive at a solution such that $p > .20$. This would suggest that this statistical criterion ($p > .20$) might not provide a parsimonious and practical solution to determining the number of extracted factors.

When the same χ^2 values were generated using maximum likelihood methods in SAS, we obtained similar results for the two-factor solution as in SPSS ($\chi^2 = 46.476$ Table B4.9, Appendix B ①). When three- and four-factor solutions were sought, however, the following error message was obtained:

```
ERROR: Communality greater than 1.0.
```

SAS Institute, Inc. (1985) indicates that ML methods are especially prone to Heywood cases where communalities (i.e., the explained variance) are greater than 1.0. By default, the iteration process will stop and the offending factors will be set to 0. The HEYWOOD option in PROC FACTOR will set to 1.0 any communality greater than 1, allowing the iterations to proceed. When this was done, the output presented in Table B4.9B in Appendix B was obtained ②. These are the same values obtained in SPSS for Windows for three and four factors (Table 4.9).

Examining the Residuals. Although no χ^2 goodness-of-fit tests are available for PCA or PAF, the researcher can perform a somewhat similar function by examining the residual correlation matrix that is formed by subtracting the reproduced correlation matrix generated by the factors from the actual correlation matrix. The reproduced correlation and residual matrices that were generated in SPSS for Windows using a two-factor PCA solution for the eight-item CGTS correlation matrix is presented in Table 4.10. As we saw with Table 4.5, the reproduced correlations using two principal components is presented in the upper half of the table (Table 4.10, ①); the differences between the actual correlations and the reproduced correlations among the items (i.e., the *residuals*) are presented in the lower half of the table ②.

If there have been a sufficient number of factors extracted, the residuals will be small. The presence of moderate (.05–.10) or large residuals (> .10) suggests that there may be more factors remaining to be extracted (Tabachnick & Fidell, 2001). For example, the estimated correlation between Items C1 and C3 based on the two factors is .560 ③. The difference between the reproduced correlation and the actual correlation ($r = .337$) between the items (i.e., their *residual*) is −.223 ([.337 − .560] = −.223) ④. This value, −.223, is higher than our designated *moderate* cutoff (.05).

It is apparent that we have a number of residuals that exceed the .05 cutoff. The footnote in Table 4.10 indicates that for the two-factor solution in PCA, there were 17, or 60.0%, of the nonredundant residuals

Table 4.10   Reproduced Correlation and Residual Matrices Generated Using a Two-Factor Solution in SPSS for Windows

⑥ Communality for Item C1

		C1	C2	C3	C4	C5	C6	C7	C8
① Reproduced Correlation	C1	.542(b)	7.66E-02	.560	.221	-.109	.226	.626	1.95E-02
	C2	7.66E-02	.620(b)	.264	.558	.596	.573	.217	.420
	C3	.560	.264	.633(b)	.387	7.26E-02	.397	.684	.147
	C4	.221	.558	.387	.546(b)	.485	.560	.366	.369
	C5	-.109	.596	7.26E-02	.485	.636(b)	.498	3.59E-03	.415
	C6	.226	.573	.397	.560	.498	.574(b)	.375	.379
	C7	.626	.217	.684	.366	3.59E-03	.375	.749(b)	.111
	C8	1.95E-02	.420	.147	.369	.415	.379	.111	.287(b)
② Residual	C1		-1.16E-02	-.223	4.01E-02	7.33E-02	-5.63E-03	-.180	8.59E-02
	C2	-1.16E-02		1.46E-02	-3.08E-03	-.206	-6.81E-02	-2.92E-02	-.145
	C3	-.223	1.46E-02		-.148	1.68E-02	-1.54E-02	-7.45E-02	6.46E-02
	C4	4.01E-02	-3.08E-03	-.148		-.108	-.171	-1.52E-02	-.118
	C5	7.33E-02	-.206	1.68E-02	-.108		-2.55E-02	6.04E-02	-8.83E-02
	C6	-5.63E-03	-6.81E-02	-1.54E-02	-.171	-2.55E-02		-2.11E-02	-.185
	C7	-.180	-2.92E-02	-7.45E-02	-1.52E-02	6.04E-02	-2.11E-02		-4.40E-02
	C8	-8.59E-02	-.145	6.47E-02	-.118	-8.83E-02	-.185	-4.40E-02	

③ Reproduced Correlation between C1 and C3: $\hat{r} = .560$

④ Residual for items C1 and C3: [.337 − .560 = −.223]

⑤ Extraction Method: Principal Component Analysis.

A. Residuals are computed between observed and reproduced correlations.
    There are 17 (60.0%) nonredundant residuals with absolute values > 0.05.
B. Reproduced communalities

with absolute values greater than .05 ⑤. These findings suggest that two extracted factors may not represent a good fit for our data. Yet even when we ran a three-factor solution for these data, we still had 16 (57.0%) residuals with absolute values greater than .05, 7 (21.9%) of which were greater than the moderate cutoff of |.10|.

The item communalities are presented on the diagonal of this matrix. You will recall that *item communality* represents the amount of variance in the item that can be explained by the extracted factors. For Item C1, for example, .542, or 54.2%, of its variance can be explained by the two extracted factors ⑥.

Factor Interpretability and Usefulness

How many factors should we extract . . . two . . . three . . . four? There is no easy solution to this decision. Nunnally and Bernstein (1994) caution the researcher against using rigid guidelines for determining the ultimate number of factors to extract. Whatever solution we arrive at should not be solely based on statistical criteria; it also needs to make theoretical sense. The ultimate criteria for determining the number of factors are factor interpretability and usefulness both during the initial extraction procedures and after the factors have been rotated to achieve more clarity.

Gorsuch (1983) suggests that if there is doubt concerning the correct number of factors, the researcher should err on the side of selecting too many rather than too few factors. There is a cost associated with that recommendation, however. Extracting too many factors can dilute the structure of the factors once they are rotated (Nunnally & Bernstein, 1994). Too many factors may also reduce the number of salient items (i.e., items that load strongly on a factor) available to a factor, thus making the rotated factors difficult to interpret. Nunnally and Bernstein (1994) also argue that if the extracted factors serve to describe characteristics that variables have in common, then, by definition, there need to be at least two items for each extracted factor.

Our suggestion is that you examine several solutions to your factor solution. Look at the eigenvalues, explained variance, and scree plot; decide on the range of possible factors to extract; run the different solutions; and examine the loadings on the factors. There may be some items that will need to be dropped. There may also be some factors that do not have sufficient items loading on them to contribute meaningfully to the solution. Critically examine your obtained results from

Table 4.11   SPSS for Windows Computer-Generated Output for the
Principal Components Analysis (PCA) and Principal Axis Factoring
(PAF) Solutions

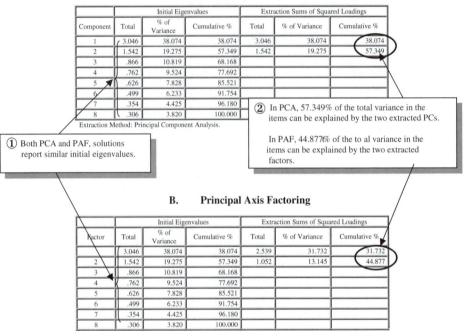

A.   Principal Components Analysis

Component	Initial Eigenvalues			Extraction Sums of Squared Loadings		
	Total	% of Variance	Cumulative %	Total	% of Variance	Cumulative %
1	3.046	38.074	38.074	3.046	38.074	38.074
2	1.542	19.275	57.349	1.542	19.275	57.349
3	.866	10.819	68.168			
4	.762	9.524	77.692			
5	.626	7.828	85.521			
6	.499	6.233	91.754			
7	.354	4.425	96.180			
8	.306	3.820	100.000			

Extraction Method: Principal Component Analysis.

② In PCA, 57.349% of the total variance in the items can be explained by the two extracted PCs.

In PAF, 44.877% of the to al variance in the items can be explained by the two extracted factors.

① Both PCA and PAF, solutions report similar initial eigenvalues.

B.   Principal Axis Factoring

Factor	Initial Eigenvalues			Extraction Sums of Squared Loadings		
	Total	% of Variance	Cumulative %	Total	% of Variance	Cumulative %
1	3.046	38.074	38.074	2.539	31.732	31.732
2	1.542	19.275	57.349	1.052	13.145	44.877
3	.866	10.819	68.168			
4	.762	9.524	77.692			
5	.626	7.828	85.521			
6	.499	6.233	91.754			
7	.354	4.425	96.180			
8	.306	3.820	100.000			

Extraction Method: Principal Axis Factoring.

PCA and PAF and decide which of the initial solutions appears to make the most sense theoretically and intuitively.

COMPARING THE TWO-FACTOR SOLUTION USING PCA AND PAF

To conclude this chapter, we will compare the two-factor PCA and PAF solutions for the eight-item CGTS using SPSS for Windows. Table 4.11 presents the initial eigenvalues and extracted sums of squared loadings for the two factors generated in SPSS for Windows for both PCA (Table 4.11A) and PAF (Table 4.11B). As we indicated earlier in this chapter, in SPSS, both the PCA and PAF solutions report the same initial eigenvalues, 3.046 for PC_I to .306 for PC_{VIII} ①. After extraction, the

Table 4.12   Initial and Extracted Communalities Generated
                   in PCA and PAF

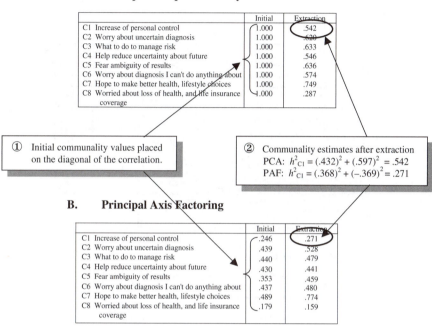

A.   Principal Component Analysis

	Initial	Extraction
C1 Increase of personal control	1.000	.542
C2 Worry about uncertain diagnosis	1.000	.620
C3 What to do to manage risk	1.000	.633
C4 Help reduce uncertainty about future	1.000	.546
C5 Fear ambiguity of results	1.000	.636
C6 Worry about diagnosis I can't do anything about	1.000	.574
C7 Hope to make better health, lifestyle choices	1.000	.749
C8 Worried about loss of health, and life insurance coverage	1.000	.287

① Initial communality values placed on the diagonal of the correlation.

② Communality estimates after extraction
PCA: $h^2_{C1} = (.432)^2 + (.597)^2 = .542$
PAF: $h^2_{C1} = (.368)^2 + (-.369)^2 = .271$

B.   Principal Axis Factoring

	Initial	Extraction
C1 Increase of personal control	.246	.271
C2 Worry about uncertain diagnosis	.439	.528
C3 What to do to manage risk	.440	.479
C4 Help reduce uncertainty about future	.430	.441
C5 Fear ambiguity of results	.353	.459
C6 Worry about diagnosis I can't do anything about	.437	.480
C7 Hope to make better health, lifestyle choices	.489	.774
C8 Worried about loss of health, and life insurance coverage	.179	.159

amount of explained variance is lower in PAF (44.877%) than in PCA (57.349%) ②, reflecting PAF's emphasis on shared variance rather than total variance.

Table 4.12 presents the initial and extracted communalities generated in PCA (Table 4.12A) and PAF (Table 4.12B). PCA's initial estimates of the communalities are the 1s that appear on the diagonal of the correlation matrix. In contrast, the initial communalities for PAF are the R^2 values, or the amount of variance in one item (e.g., C1) that is explained by the remaining items (e.g., C2-C8) (Table 4.12, ①). The final extracted values represent the amount of variance, or communality, in the items that is explained by the factors. They are the sum of the squared loadings of the items on the two extracted factors, as we will see in Table 4.13.

Table 4.13 summarizes the loadings for the two-factor solution in PCA and PAF. For Item C1 in PCA, $(.432)^2 + (.597)^2 = .542$. That is, 54.2% of the variance in Item C1 can be explained by the two principal components (Table 4.13, ①). In contrast, in PAF, .271, or 27.1%, of the common variance in C1 can be explained by the two extracted factors ①.

Table 4.13   Generating the Factor Matrix in SPSS for Windows

A.   Principal Component Analysis

Item	Content Area	Component 1	Component 2
C1	Increase of personal control	.432	.597
C2	Worry about uncertain diagnosis	.693	−.373
C3	What to do to manage risk	.637	.477
C4	Help reduce uncertainty about future	.723	−.153
C5	Fear ambiguity of results	.548	−.579
	...thing about	.741	−.157
	...choices	.632	.591
C8	Worried about loss of health, life insurance coverage	.449	−.292

② Σ column loadings = Eigenvalue = total variance explained by PCA components:
$$\lambda_1 = (.432)^2 + (.693)^2 + \ldots + (.632)^2 + (.449)^2 = 3.046$$
$$\lambda_1 = (.597)^2 + (-.373)^2 + \ldots + (.591)^2 + (-.292)^2 = 1.542$$

① Same communality estimates as in Table 4.12:
PCA: $h^2_{C1} = (.432)^2 + (.597)^2 = .542$
PAF: $h^2_{C1} = (.368)^2 + (-.369)^2 = .271$

B.   Principal Axis Factoring

Item	Content Area	Factor 1	Factor 2
C1	Increase of personal control	.368	−.369
C2	Worry about uncertain diagnosis	.635	.354
C3	What to do to manage risk	.588	−.365
C4	Help reduce uncertainty about future	.644	.161
		.483	.475
	...g about	.673	.164
	...ces	.658	−.585
C8	Worried about loss of health, life insurance coverage	.350	.191

③ Eigenvalue = amount of common variance explained by the PAF factor:
$$\lambda_1 = (.368)^2 + (.635)^2 + \ldots + (.658)^2 + (.350)^2 = 2.539$$
$$\lambda_2 = (-.369)^2 + (.354)^2 + \ldots + (-.585)^2 + (.191)^2 = 1.052$$

It is also possible to determine from the factor matrix in Table 4.13 where the eigenvalues presented in Table 4.11 were obtained. That is, summing the column loadings produces the eigenvalues that represent the total amount of variance in the items that are explained by the factors. For PCA, the amount of total variance is 3.046 for PC_I and 1.542 for PC_{II} ②; for PAF, the amount of common variance is 2.539 and 1.052, respectively ③.

Figure 4.4 Extracting the Initial Factors

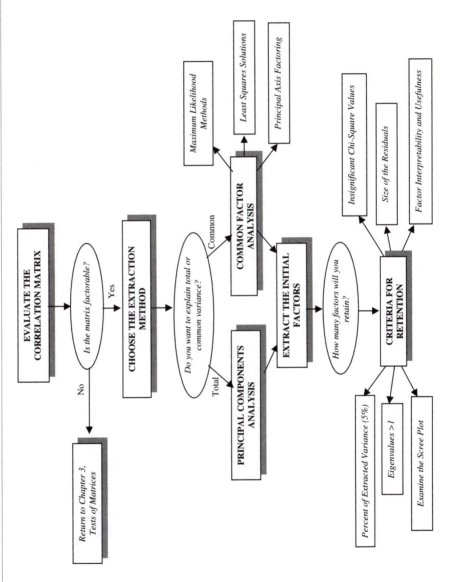

SUMMARY

In this chapter, we have presented you with the various issues about which you need to be concerned when extracting the initial factors from your correlation matrix. These considerations are summarized in Figure 4.4. Once you have identified the number of factors that you will retain, the next step is to rotate those factors in order to produce greater clarity. Factor rotation will be the focus of Chapters 5 and 6.

NOTES

1. Because of space limitations, we are continuing to use a smaller 8×8 correlation matrix for illustrative purposes. Ordinarily, we would use a correlation matrix containing all of the items in question.

2. See Chapter 3 for details.

3. As we indicated earlier, the initial matrix to be analyzed is most often the correlation matrix.

4. The output for the 8×8 correlation matrix is presented in the body of this chapter. To view the output for the full 20×20 matrix, please see Appendix A.

5. See Chapter 3 for a discussion of multicollinearity, singularity, and positive-definite and ill-conditioned matrices.

6. Remember that $1.71E{-}02 = (1.71)(10^{-2}) = .0171$.

7. In SAS, the final communality estimates are located above the residual correlation matrix, as illustrated in Table B4.7, Appendix B.

8. Some writers argue that normality of distributions is less an issue when the ML method is used as a descriptive technique as in exploratory factor analysis (SAS Institute, Inc., 1985).

5

Rotating the Factors

In Chapter 4, we examined various approaches to obtaining unrotated factor solutions to the number of factors that best summarize the information contained in a set of given items or variables. As we pointed out in that chapter, unrotated factors are usually extracted in order of their importance. The first unrotated factor is most often a general factor on which most items load significantly. It also accounts for the largest amount of explained variance among the items. Each additional factor that is extracted accounts for the remaining amount of variance in successively smaller proportions.

A problem with unrotated factor solutions is that they often do not provide meaningful and easily interpretable clusters of items. There is also the unfortunate temptation to conclude that a 'general' factor is present in the data when, in fact, such a general factor is an artifact of the unrotated factor solution (Kline, 1994; Nunnally & Bernstein, 1994). Most researchers, therefore, rely on rotation to improve the meaningfulness and interpretation of the generated factors.

ACHIEVING A SIMPLE STRUCTURE

Factor rotation is the process of turning the reference axes of the factors about their origin to achieve a *simple structure* and theoretically more meaningful factor solution (Hair, Anderson, Tatham, & Black, 1995). The factor matrix that is the focus of evaluating this simple structure is the *factor-loading* matrix.[1]

The criteria of *simple structure* was originally proposed by Thurstone (1947), who reasoned that this simple structure could be achieved if the following criteria were met (Harman, 1976, p. 98):

- Each row of the factor matrix should contain at least one zero;
- If there are *m* common factors, each column of the factor matrix should have at least *m* zeros. For example, if there are two common factors, each column should have at least two zeros;
- For every pair of columns of the factor matrix, there should be several variables for which entries approach zero in one column but not in the other;
- For every pair of columns of the factor matrix, a large proportion of the variables should have entries approaching zero in both columns when there are four or more factors;
- For every pair of columns of the factor matrix, there should be only a small number of variables with nonzero entries in both columns.

Table 5.1 presents a hypothetical 10-item rotated factor matrix that meets the criteria of simple structure. As you can see from the circled values in Table 5.1, each row of this hypothetical factor matrix has at least one loading that is near zero. Given that there are three common factors, each column of the factor matrix has at least three near-zero loadings (Table 5.1, ①). For each pair of factors (e.g., Factors I vs. II, Factors I vs. III, and Factors II vs. III), there are several items for which loadings approach zero in one column but not in the other. In addition, for each pair of factors, there are only a small number of items (e.g., Items 6 and 7 on Factors II and III ②) with nonzero entries in both columns.

Pedhazur and Schmelkin (1991) summarize an ideal factor rotation as one that results in a simple structure such that

- each [item] has a high, or meaningful, loading on one factor only and

Table 5.1   An Example of a Hypothetical Rotated Solution Having Simple Structure

Structure

| | ② These two items have non-zero loadings on both Factors II and III. | | |

		Factor	
Item	*I*	*II*	*III*
1	.74	(−.02)	.21
2	.78	.12	(.07)
3	.56	(.05)	−.14
4	−.13	.85	(−.03)
5	.27	.49	(−.008)
6	(.09)	.65	−.31 ⎤
7	(.004)	−.27	.54 ⎬
8	(−.05)	.16	.63 ⎦
9	−.21	(.04)	.59
10	(.002)	−.19	.72

① **A Rotated 3-Factor Matrix With Simple Structure**
- Every row has at least one near zero loading.
- Given 3 factors, every column has at least 3 near zero loadings.
- For every pair of columns (e.g., I vs. II, I vs. III), there are several items with near zero loadings in one column but not the other.
- For every pair of columns, there are only a small number of items with non-zero loadings in both columns.

- each factor has high, or meaningful, loadings for only some of the [items]. (p. 612)

Later in this chapter, we will examine the extent to which our rotated solutions for the CGTS scale meet these same criteria for simple structure.

TYPES OF ROTATIONS

There are two broad classes of rotation, *orthogonal* and *oblique*, which have different underlying assumptions but which share the common goal of simple structure. In an orthogonal rotation, it is assumed that the generated factors are independent of each other (i.e., they are uncorrelated). In contrast, in an oblique rotation, the supposition is made that the factors are not independent of one another. Rather, there is some correlation among two or more of the factors being rotated.

Because an orthogonal rotation results in uncorrelated factors, the factor-loading matrix represents not only the simple correlations of the items with the factors but are also standardized regression-like beta weights that can be used to estimate the unique contribution of each factor to the explained variance of an item (Tabachnick & Fidell, 2001). Therefore, when evaluating simple structure in an orthogonal rotation, there is really only one factor matrix with which to contend: the *factor-loading matrix*. In SPSS for Windows, this factor-loading matrix is called the *component matrix*. An example of a component matrix will be presented later in this chapter (Table 5.3).

In contrast, in an oblique rotation, the resulting rotated factors are correlated and two different factor-loading matrices are generated: a *factor pattern matrix* (a matrix of loadings that are like *partial* standardized regression coefficients) and a *factor structure matrix* (a matrix of simple correlations of the items with the factors). It is the factor pattern matrix in an oblique rotation that is used to determine the extent to which simple structure has been achieved.

The processes of orthogonal and oblique factor rotations can be confusing and difficult to follow. A geometric interpretation of these procedures may facilitate your understanding. This next section, therefore, introduces you to the process of mapping factors in geometric space. Hopefully, this presentation will clarify what happens when factors are rotated. Then, in subsequent sections, specific approaches to orthogonal and oblique solutions are described in greater detail and their results compared. In the concluding section of this chapter, we discuss considerations to be made when deciding on which approach provides the most adequate simple solution for your data set.

MAPPING FACTORS IN GEOMETRIC SPACE

Although factors are mathematical descriptors that summarize the relationships among a set of items, they can also be represented as vectors in a geometric space that contains as many dimensions as factors. A two-factor solution, for example, can be represented in

Figure 5.1   Mapping Data Points in Two-Dimensional Space

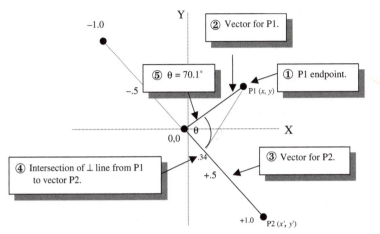

A. A Positive Correlation (*r* = .34) Between Two Items

B. A Negative Correlation (*r* = −.34) Between Two Items

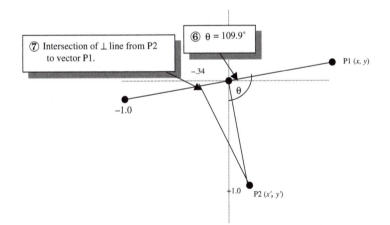

two-dimensional space, a three-factor solution in three-dimensional space, and a four-factor solution in four-dimensional space.

In this geometric space, a variable can be represented as either an endpoint with coordinates (e.g., *x, y*) or as a line segment (a.k.a. *vector*) that extends from the point of origin (0, 0) to the coordinates of the vari-able. There are as many coordinates for a given endpoint as there are dimensions in this space. Endpoints in two-dimensional space have two coordinates (e.g., x, y), and endpoints in three-dimensional space have three coordinates (x, y, z).

In Figure 5.1A, for example, point P1 has two coordinates, x and y, that define the point in space where item P1 resides ①. That is, P1 is that point that is formed by moving x units along the horizontal X axis and y units along the vertical Y axis. The vector for P1 is the line segment that starts at point (0, 0) and extends to the endpoint (x, y) ②. The point P2 occupies the endpoint position (x', y') and can also be expressed as a vector that extends from point (0, 0) to (x', y') ③. In this way, every point can be mapped in geometric space.

Assessing the Correlation Between Two Items

Not only do the two vectors for P1 and P2 share a common origin (0, 0), the vectors have also been set to be of a standardized unit length equal to 1 on both sides of that origin (Figure 5.1A). Nunnally and Bernstein (1994) describe these unit vectors as "correlation yardsticks" (p. 461) with values ranging from −1.0 to +1.0 plotted along their line segments. The correlation between two variables in geometric space can be determined by drawing a perpendicular line from either vector to the endpoint of the other or by using a hand calculator or statistical computer program to calculate the cosine of the angle that is formed by the intersection of the two vectors at point (0, 0) (Nunnally & Bernstein, 1994). We will call this angle *theta*, or θ.[2]

In Figure 5.1A, the line that is drawn at right angles from the vector for P2 to the endpoint of P1 intersects the line segment for P2 at the point .34 ④. The correlation between these two variables, therefore, is .34. Similarly, if we did not know the correlation but knew the value for the angle θ formed by the intersection of the two vectors for P1 and P2, we could use the cosine of θ to determine their correlation. In our example, if $\theta = 70.1°$, then the correlation between P1 and P2 is .34 because the cosine of 70.1° is .34 ⑤.

If two variables are located very close to one another such that their vectors nearly overlap, the angle θ will be very small and the cosine of the angle θ will be close to 1.00. That would mean that there is a nearly perfect positive correlation between the two variables (Figure 5.2A). Angles between 0° and 90° represent positive correlations because their cosines are positive. The cosine for an angle of 90° is 0, indicating that the two variables whose line segments are at right angles to one

Figure 5.2   Examples of Strongly Correlated and Uncorrelated Items
Mapped in Two-Dimensional Space

A. Items Having a Very Strong Correlation

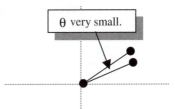

B. Uncorrelated Items

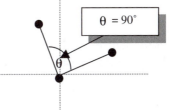

C. Items With a Strong Negative Correlation

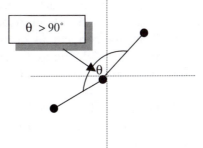

another are uncorrelated (Figure 5.2B). Angles between 90° and 180° have negative cosines and therefore represent negative correlations between two variables (Figure 5.2C) (Nunnally & Bernstein, 1994).

If we know the value of the correlation between two variables, we can also use our knowledge of trigonometry and a hand calculator to determine the angle θ. First, we would let omega (Ω) equal the correlation between the two variables and θ be the angle between the vectors of these two variables. Then, by definition, cosine(θ) = Ω and the arc or inverse cosine of Ω (symbolized as $\cos^{-1}\Omega$) is equal to θ (i.e., $\cos^{-1}\Omega = \theta$).

For a more concrete example, let us return to Figure 5.1A. To determine the angle that would be formed by two intersecting vectors whose variables are correlated +.34, let Ω = +.34. Because $\cos^{-1}\Omega$ = $\cos^{-1}(+.34) = 70.1$, the angle θ formed by the two intersecting vectors for P1 and P2 is 70.1° (Table 5.1A, ⑤). In contrast, a negative correlation of −.34 between P1 and P2 would indicate that θ = 109.9° because the $\cos^{-1}$ $\Omega = \cos^{-1}(-.34) = 109.9$ (Figure 5.1B, ⑥) Similarly, if θ = 109.9°, then the perpendicular line drawn from P2 to P1 intersects that vector at −.34 because cos(109.9) = −.34 ⑦ .

Using the Unrotated Factor
Loadings to Map Points in Space

Table 5.2 presents the unrotated factor loadings for Items C1 to C8 of the CGTS scale for the two unrotated principal components, PC_I and PC_{II}, that were generated in SPSS for Windows. The two columns presented in Table 5.2 represent the principal components, PC_I and PC_{II} ① . The rows in the table represent the loadings of each item on these two factors ② . These loadings not only indicate the extent to which these items correlate with the two factors, they also can be used to plot the items in a two-dimensional space, as in Figure 5.3.

In Figure 5.3, the x and y axes have scales of values that range from −1.00 to +1.00 and represent the orthogonal factors, PC_I and PC_{II}. The factor loadings are the correlations of the items with the factors and define the coordinates of the items. Given that the two principal components form right angles (90°) to one another, they are uncorrelated because the cosine of 90° = 0.

From Table 5.2, we can see that Item C1 loads .432 on PC_I and .597 on PC_{II} (Table 5.2, ③). As per our earlier discussion about correlations, that would mean that a line drawn from the endpoint of C1 to meet the principal components at right angles would intersect PC_I at .432 and

Table 5.2   Factor Loadings of the Eight Items From the CGTS Scale
on the Two Unrotated Principal Components

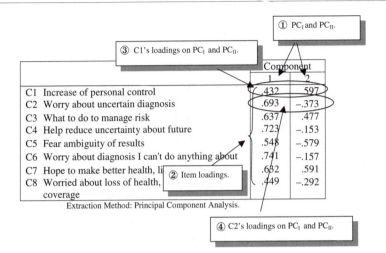

	Component	
	1	2
C1 Increase of personal control	.432	.597
C2 Worry about uncertain diagnosis	.693	−.373
C3 What to do to manage risk	.637	.477
C4 Help reduce uncertainty about future	.723	−.153
C5 Fear ambiguity of results	.548	−.579
C6 Worry about diagnosis I can't do anything about	.741	−.157
C7 Hope to make better health, li...	.632	.591
C8 Worried about loss of health, coverage	.449	−.292

① PC$_I$ and PC$_{II}$.

③ C1's loadings on PC$_I$ and PC$_{II}$.

② Item loadings.

Extraction Method: Principal Component Analysis.

④ C2's loadings on PC$_I$ and PC$_{II}$.

Figure 5.3   Plot of the Unrotated Two-Factor Principal Component Solution for Items
C1 to C2

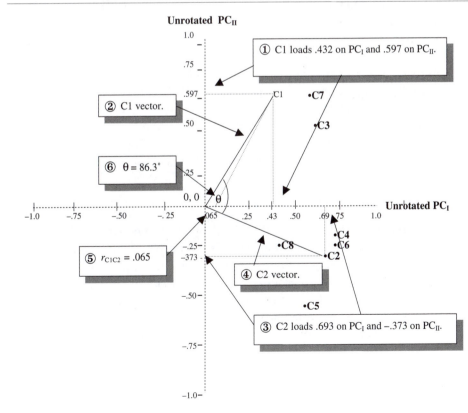

① C1 loads .432 on PC$_I$ and .597 on PC$_{II}$.

② C1 vector.

⑥ θ = 86.3°

⑤ r_{C1C2} = .065

④ C2 vector.

③ C2 loads .693 on PC$_I$ and −.373 on PC$_{II}$.

PC_{II} at .597 (Figure 5.3, ②). In two-dimensional space, therefore, Item C1 is located at point (.432, .597), or .432 units in the positive direction along PC_I and .597 units in the positive direction along PC_{II}. The line segment, or vector, for C1 is the straight line drawn from the point of origin (0, 0) to the point (.432, .597) ②.

In contrast, Item C2 loads .693 on PC_I and −.373 on PC_{II} (Table 5.2, ④). Item C2's position in two-dimensional space, then, is (.693, −.373). That is, Item C2 is located .693 units in the positive direction along PC_I and −.373 units in the negative direction on PC_{II} (Figure 5.3, ③). The vector for C2 is the straight line drawn from the point of origin (0, 0) to the point (.693, −.373) ④.

The correlation between Items C1 and C2 can be determined either by locating the intersection of a line drawn at right angles from one item's vector (e.g., vector C2) to the endpoint of the other item (e.g., C1) or by determining the cosine of the angle θ that is formed by the two item vectors. To determine the angle θ, we would need either a protractor or the correlation coefficient. Fortunately, the correlation matrix in Chapter 4 (Table 4.2) has provided us with the information that Items C1 and C2 correlate .065. Therefore, the line drawn from C1 perpendicular to the vector C2 intersects C2's line segment at .065 ⑤, and the angle θ formed by the two item vectors must be 86.3° because $\cos^{-1}\Omega = \cos^{-1}(+.065) = 86.3$ (Figure 5.3, ⑥).

Notice in Figure 5.3 that there are four quadrants formed by the two orthogonal vectors that represent unrotated factors PC_I and PC_{II}. In our example, all eight items are plotted in either the first or second quadrant; however, items can fall in any of those four quadrants. For example, one item might load negatively on both components although a second item might load negatively on PC_I but positively on PC_{II}. These items would then be plotted in the third and fourth quadrants, respectively.

Rotating Factors in Geometric Space

The data from Table 5.2 indicate that our unrotated factor solution does not meet the simple solution criteria put forth by Thurstone (1947) that we described above. None of the loadings in the two columns or eight rows are smaller in absolute value than .153. It is clear that if we are to achieve a simple solution that contains values closer to zero, we will need to rotate these factors.

Factor rotation involves turning the reference axes of the factors about their origin in order to achieve a simpler and theoretically more meaningful factor solution than is produced by the unrotated factor solution. To achieve this, the positions of the items are fixed in geometric space while the factor axes are rotated through specified angles. In these next two sections, we will examine the differences in solutions that occur when we undertake orthogonal and oblique rotations of the factors.

ORTHOGONAL ROTATIONS

As we indicated earlier, an assumption underlying an orthogonal rotation is that the subscales formed from the factors are independent of each other (i.e., they are uncorrelated). If the two factors are uncorrelated, the cosine of the angle θ that is formed by the two factors is equal to 0 and the corresponding angle is equal to 90°. In an orthogonal rotation, therefore, the factors are fixed at right angles (90°) to one another and rotated as a pair through an angle θ to obtain an optimal fit with the distribution of the variables in space, as you will soon see in Figure 5.5. Because they are maintained at right angles to one another, these newly rotated factors are also uncorrelated. As a result, the standardized regression-like beta weights presented in the factor pattern matrix are equivalent to the simple correlations of the items with the factors presented in the factor structure matrix.

There are three major approaches to orthogonal rotation: *Varimax, Quartimax,* and *Equamax.* All of these approaches are available in SPSS for Windows and SAS. Each approach has a slightly different goal for achieving an orthogonal solution and for determining the angle of rotation for the orthogonal factors.

The Varimax Rotation

Varimax (Kaiser, 1958, 1959) is the default option in both SPSS for Windows and SAS and is the most commonly used orthogonal rotation. Among some writers (e.g., Nunnally & Bernstein, 1994), it is the definitive orthogonal solution. For these reasons, we will focus most of our discussion of orthogonal solutions on the Varimax rotation.

The goal of Varimax is to simplify the columns of the unrotated factor-loading matrix. To accomplish this goal, Varimax maximizes the variances of the loadings within the factors while also maximizing differences between the high and low loadings on a particular factor (hence the name Varimax). In essence, higher loadings on a factor are made higher and lower loadings are made lower (Tabachnick & Fidell, 2001).

This orthogonal solution is achieved by multiplying the unrotated factor-loading matrix by one of two transformation matrices, the choice of which depends on the direction of rotation. These matrices consist of sines and cosines of the angle of rotation (θ) for each factor (Comrey & Lee, 1992; Harman, 1976). The size of the transformation matrix depends on the number of factors to be analyzed (e.g., a four-factor matrix uses a 4×4 transformation matrix). For a two-factor matrix, the following transformation matrices are used:

$$\text{Transformation matrix } 1 = \begin{bmatrix} \cos\theta & -\sin\theta \\ \sin\theta & \cos\theta \end{bmatrix} \text{ or}$$

$$\text{Transformation matrix } 2 = \begin{bmatrix} \cos\theta & \sin\theta \\ -\sin\theta & \cos\theta \end{bmatrix}$$

This will generate a newly rotated factor matrix as follows:

$$[\text{newly rotated factor matrix}] = [\text{unrotated factor matrix}] \begin{bmatrix} \cos\theta & -\sin\theta \\ \sin\theta & \cos\theta \end{bmatrix}$$

This newly rotated factor matrix is both a factor pattern matrix (consisting of regression-like beta weights) and a factor structure matrix (consisting of simple correlations of items and factors) because, in orthogonal rotations, the two are numerically equivalent.

Notice that the only difference between the two transformation matrices that are being used is the switch in positive and negative values for $\sin\theta$. Because determining the direction of axis rotation and therefore the transformation matrix of choice is most often a computer program decision, we will not discuss these issues in depth. The interested reader is referred to Comrey and Lee (1992), who present an excellent in-depth discussion of these transformation matrices.

Advantages and Disadvantages of Varimax

A Varimax solution is easily interpreted and provides relatively clear information about which items correlate most strongly with a given factor. Varimax provides us, therefore, with a good picture of our ability to reach a *simple structure.* Factor scores generated for each individual are also more interpretable because the explained variances among the factors do not overlap and are therefore independent of each other.

A disadvantage of Varimax is that it tends to split up the variances of the major factors among the less important factors, thus reducing the possibility of identifying an overall general factor. A Varimax solution, therefore, may not be appropriate if the researcher suspects that the construct being studied contains a general overall factor. Nunnally and Bernstein (1994) also warn against prematurely concluding that, based on a Varimax solution, a general factor is absent because Varimax is designed to eliminate general factors (Gorsuch, 1983).

Comrey and Lee (1992) suggest that the researcher avoid including too many factors in a Varimax rotation solution because it tends to overinflate the importance of lesser factors. Although the authors do not indicate how many factors are *too many,* they point out that trial and error is the only way to arrive at the appropriate number of factors.

Quartimax and Equamax Rotations

Quartimax and Equamax rotations are not as popular as the more widely used Varimax rotation. Quartimax (Carroll, 1953; Neuhaus & Wrigley, 1954; Saunders, 1960) focuses on simplifying the rows of the factor-loading matrix. That is, it rotates the factors in such a way as to maximize the squared loadings for each variable so as to enable each item to load most strongly on a single factor. The result is that Quartimax tends to produce a single general factor with which most of the items are strongly correlated (Hair et al., 1995). This method, therefore, would be particularly useful if a general factor is suspected.

Equamax (Saunders, 1962) is a combination of the Varimax and Quartimax solutions. It simultaneously simplifies the factors (columns) and the items (rows). As a hybrid, Equamax behaves somewhat erratically and should be used only when the number of factors has been clearly identified (Tabachnick & Fidell, 2001).

An Example of a Varimax Orthogonal Rotation

An orthogonal Varimax rotation was undertaken in SPSS for Windows for the two-factor principal components solution for Items

Figure 5.4 The SPSS for Windows Dialog Boxes for Generating a Varimax Rotation of a Principal Components Solution for Items C1 to C8 of the CGTS Scale

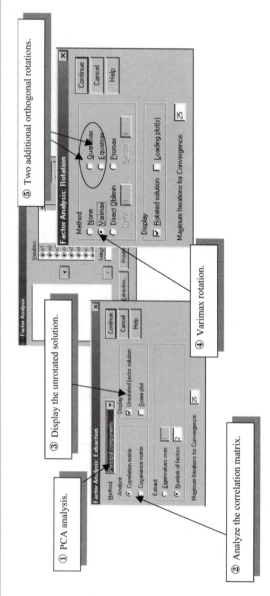

C1 to C8 of the CGTS scale. This rotation was obtained in SPSS for Windows by highlighting the SPSS commands *Analyze . . . Data Reduction . . . Factor . . . .* These commands enabled us to open the *Extraction . . .* and *Rotation . . .* dialog boxes (Figure 5.4). The SAS commands used to generate a similar Varimax rotation using PROC FACTOR are given in Figure B5.4 (Appendix B).

In the extraction window, we indicated that our method of extraction was principal components (Figure 5.4, ①) and that we were analyzing a correlation matrix ②. We also indicated that we wanted to display the unrotated factor solution ③. In the *Rotation . . .* window, we requested the Varimax rotation ④ along with a display of the rotated solution. Note that two additional orthogonal rotations, Quartimax and Equamax, are available in SPSS ⑤.

To hand calculate the factor loadings for this newly rotated factor solution for which the angle of rotation $\theta = 37.34°$, we would multiply the unrotated factor loadings by one of the two transformation matrices (in our case, Transformation matrix 2) consisting of the cosine and sine of $37.34°$ to obtain the following transformation matrix:

$$\begin{bmatrix} \cos \theta & \sin \theta \\ -\sin \theta & \cos \theta \end{bmatrix} = \begin{bmatrix} \cos (37.34) & \sin (37.34) \\ -\sin (37.34) & \cos (37.34) \end{bmatrix} = \begin{bmatrix} .795 & .607 \\ -.607 & .795 \end{bmatrix}$$

Substituting these values into our equation for a rotated factor-loading matrix, we obtain the following results:

$$\begin{bmatrix} .432 & .597 \\ .693 & -.373 \\ .637 & .477 \\ .723 & -.153 \\ .548 & -.579 \\ .741 & -.157 \\ .632 & .591 \\ .449 & -.292 \end{bmatrix} \begin{bmatrix} .795 & .607 \\ -.607 & .795 \end{bmatrix} = \begin{bmatrix} -.019 & .736 \\ .778 & .124 \\ .216 & .766 \\ .668 & .317 \\ .787 & -.128 \\ .685 & .325 \\ .143 & .854 \\ .534 & .040 \end{bmatrix}$$

As we indicated earlier, because the Varimax solution is orthogonal, this newly rotated factor-loading matrix for the orthogonal solution represents not only the simple correlations between the items and the factors but is also a matrix of regression-like beta weights that can

Figure 5.5   Plot of Rotated Varimax Solution for Two-Factor Principal
Component Solution, Items C1 to C8

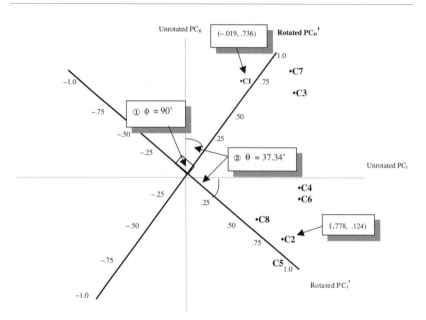

be used to estimate the unique contribution of each factor to the explained variance of an item (Tabachnick & Fidell, 2001).

Figure 5.5 presents the SPSS-generated plot of this rotated Varimax solution. Notice that the factors have maintained their right-angle relationship to one another because phi(Φ) = 90° (Figure 5.5, ①) but have been rotated, as a fixed pair, through an angle θ of 37.34° to generate the rotated factors PC$_\mathrm{I}$′ and PC$_\mathrm{II}$′ ②. *Why 37.34°?* It was at this angle of rotation that the computer satisfied the requirements of the Varimax solution: to maximize the variance of the loadings on the two factors while also maximizing differences between the high and low loadings on a particular factor.

The SAS plot of the rotated Varimax solution is presented in Figure B5.5 (Appendix B). This plot is a lot more confusing to read because SAS assigns letters to the items (e.g., 'A' for Item C1). Nevertheless, its results are similar to those obtained in SPSS for Windows.

No Change in Correlations

Notice in Figure 5.5 that the positions and configuration of Items C1 to C8 in the two-dimensional geometric space are not altered. This

Table 5.3   Generated Output From SPSS for Windows: Varimax Rotation of the Two Principal Components for the Eight Items of the CGTS Scale

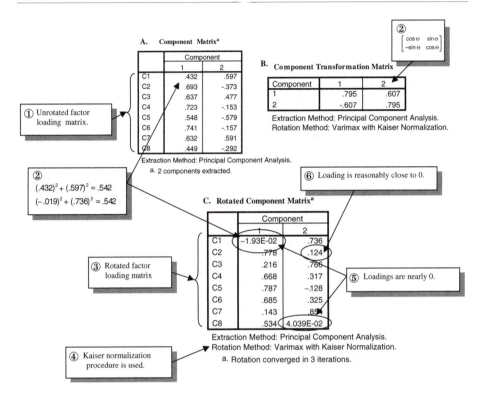

A. Component Matrix[a]

	Component 1	2
C1	.432	.597
C2	.693	-.373
C3	.637	.477
C4	.723	-.153
C5	.548	-.579
C6	.741	-.157
C7	.632	.591
C8	.449	-.292

Extraction Method: Principal Component Analysis.
a. 2 components extracted.

① Unrotated factor loading matrix.

② $[\begin{smallmatrix} \cos\theta & \sin\theta \\ -\sin\theta & \cos\theta \end{smallmatrix}]$

B. Component Transformation Matrix

Component	1	2
1	.795	.607
2	-.607	.795

Extraction Method: Principal Component Analysis.
Rotation Method: Varimax with Kaiser Normalization.

②
$(.432)^2 + (.597)^2 = .542$
$(-.019)^2 + (.736)^2 = .542$

⑥ Loading is reasonably close to 0.

C. Rotated Component Matrix[a]

	Component 1	2
C1	-1.93E-02	.736
C2	.778	.124
C3	.216	.766
C4	.668	.317
C5	.787	-.128
C6	.685	.325
C7	.143	.854
C8	.534	4.039E-02

③ Rotated factor loading matrix

⑤ Loadings are nearly 0.

Extraction Method: Principal Component Analysis.
Rotation Method: Varimax with Kaiser Normalization.
a. Rotation converged in 3 iterations.

④ Kaiser normalization procedure is used.

means that the correlations among the items have not changed because the angles that are formed by the intersection of the item vectors at point (0, 0) remain the same. Through our use of a transformation matrix, we have changed the loadings of the items on the newly rotated orthogonal factors. The high loadings are substantially higher and the low loadings are considerably lower.

Table 5.3 presents the SPSS for Windows output for both the unrotated and Varimax rotated factor loadings for the two principal components, PC_I and PC_{II}, for Items C1 to C8 of the CGTS scale. Similar output obtained from SAS is presented in Table B5.3 (Appendix B).

The first 'component' matrix[3] (Table 5.3A, ①) summarizes the unrotated factor loadings for the items on the two principal components. Next, we are presented with the component transformation matrix (Table 5.3B, ②) that was used to generate the rotated component matrix given to us in Table 5.3C ③. Each item now loads most strongly on a single factor: Items C2, C4, C5, C6, and C8 load on the rotated factor PC$_I$′ and Items C1, C3, and C7 load on PC$_{II}$′.

The *Kaiser normalization* procedure referred to in the footnotes for Table 5.3 ④ was developed by Kaiser (1958, 1959) in an effort to obtain relative stability of solutions across samples (Comrey & Lee, 1992). Before undertaking the Varimax rotation, the factors are first scaled to unit length by dividing each item's loading by the square root of its individual communality (h^2). Then, after rotation, the item loadings on the factors are rescaled to proper size by multiplying the generated item loading by its communality. In this way, equal weight is given to all items in determining the rotations. Comrey and Lee (1992) point out that, although this procedure tends to inflate the influence of items for which communalities are particularly low, it is a reasonable approach if items in a data set have high communalities. The default in SAS for normalization is NORM = KAISER. If the option NORM = NONE or NORM = RAW is specified, normalization is not performed.

Examining the Varimax solution in Table 5.3C for its simple structure (Thurstone, 1947), we can see that there is at least one item for each principal component (C1 for PC$_I$′ and C8 for PC$_{II}$′) for which the loadings are very close to zero ⑤. There are three additional items (e.g., C2 on PC$_{II}$′) for which loadings are now within what Harman (1976) has described as being reasonably close to 0: a 0 or 1 in the first decimal place of the factor loading ⑥.

No Change in Communalities

Despite the changes in the factor loadings as a result of the orthogonal rotation, the item communalities, or the proportion of variance in the items explained by the factors, remain the same. You will recall from Chapter 4 that the communality for an item is the sum of its squared factor loadings on the extracted factors. For example, from Table 5.3 (A and C), we can determine that Item C1 has a communality (h^2) of .542 for both the unrotated and rotated solutions ⑦:

$$h^2_{\text{unrotated}} = (.432)^2 + (.597)^2 = .542$$

$$h^2_{\text{rotated}} = (-.019)^2 + (.736)^2 = .542$$

This means that, regardless of rotation, 54.2% of the explained variance in Item C1 can be explained by the two extracted orthogonal factors.

No Change in Estimated Correlations

In Chapter 4, we indicated that the test of a successful factor analysis is the extent to which it can reproduce the original correlation matrix (Kline, 1994). The correlation between two items, C1 and C2, for example, can be estimated as follows:

$$\hat{r}_{C1C2} = (a_{C1,I})(a_{C2,I}) + (a_{C1,II})(a_{C2,II})$$

where

$\hat{r}_{C1C2}$ = stimated Pearson correlation between Items C1 and C2

$a_{C1,I}, a_{C1,II}$ = factor loadings of Item C1 on PC_I and PC_{II}

$a_{C2,I}, a_{C2,II}$ = factor loadings of Item C2 on PC_I and PC_{II}

Plugging in the loadings from Table 5.3 (A and C) into this formula, we can see that the estimated correlation between Items C1 and C2 for the unrotated and rotated orthogonal solutions is exactly the same:

$$\text{unrotated: } \hat{r}_{C1C2} = (.432)(.693) + (.597)(-.373) = .076$$
$$\text{rotated: } \hat{r}_{C1C2} = (-.019)(.778) + (.736)(.124) = .076$$

Thus, these unrotated and rotated solutions do equally well—or badly—at reproducing the correlation matrix.

OBLIQUE ROTATIONS

Although orthogonal rotations often produce attractively simple solutions, these rotations rest on the critical assumption that the factors, or subscales of interest, are uncorrelated with one another. This assumption is rarely met in health care research. For this reason, Pedhazur and Schmelkin (1991) argue that orthogonal factor solutions are "in most instances, naïve, unrealistic portrayals of sociobehavioral phenomena" (p. 615).

That factors might be correlated is a reasonable assumption in the health sciences because we are often dealing with conceptually different but nevertheless correlated dimensions of a construct. The dimensions of general health, for example, might be broken down into physical and emotional health. These are two factors that, although separated, are also correlated to some extent (i.e., a person who perceives his/her physical health to be positive will also tend to rate his/her emotional health to be positive as well).

Approach to Oblique Rotations

An oblique rotation follows the same rotation principles as an orthogonal rotation. Like the orthogonal rotation, for example, there is no change in the interitem correlations because the position of the scale items relative to each other do not change. The difference is that, in an oblique rotation, the assumption is made that there is some correlation among two or more of the factors being rotated. Because the factors are not independent, a 90° angle of rotation is not fixed between the axes. Instead, each original factor is rotated separately by different amounts.

Because the resulting factors are correlated, the regression-like beta weights that estimate the unique contribution that each factor con-tributes to the explained variance in a given item are no longer equal to the simple correlations between the items and the factors as in the orthogonal solution. For this reason, three factor matrices are gener-ated in the oblique solution: (1) a *factor pattern matrix*, (2) a *factor struc-ture matrix*, and (3) a *factor correlation matrix*.

The *factor pattern matrix* contains loadings that are similar to partial standardized regression coefficients in a multiple regression analysis. That is, these loadings indicate the effect of a given factor on a given item while controlling for other factors. The simple zero-order correla-tions of the items with the factors are presented in the *factor structure matrix*. The information presented in the structure matrix can be useful in interpreting and naming the factors. The *factor correlation matrix* is a matrix of intercorrelations among the factors.

Factor Pattern Versus Factor Structure Loadings

Nunnally and Bernstein (1994) present an excellent visual explana-tion of the differences that result in the factor loadings for the factor pattern and factor structure matrices in an oblique rotation. These differences are illustrated in Figure 5.6.

To obtain the factor pattern loading for an item (e.g., C1) on a rotated factor (e.g., PC_I'), a line is drawn from that item *parallel* to the other rotated factors (e.g., PC_{II}'). The point at which the parallel line intersects the rotated factor represents the factor pattern loading for that item on the given rotated factor (e.g., PC_I') (Figure 5.6, ①). In

Figure 5.6   Example of the Differences Between Factor Pattern and Factor Structure Loadings: A. More Highly Correlated Factors. B. Less Highly Correlated Factors

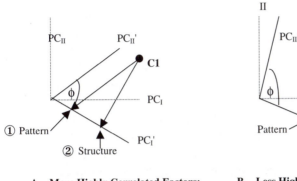

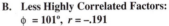

A. **More Highly Correlated Factors:**
   $\phi = 64°$, $r = .43$

B. **Less Highly Correlated Factors:**
   $\phi = 101°$, $r = -.191$

contrast, the factor structure loading, or simple correlation of the item with the factor, is obtained by drawing a line from the given item *perpendicular* to the rotated factor (Figure 5.6, ②).

The more correlated the factors, the greater the difference between the factor pattern and structure loadings and the more difficult it is to interpret the factor structure loadings. In Figure 5.6A, for example, the correlation between the factors was set at .43 and $\Phi = 64°$. As a result, the factor pattern and structure loadings are relatively far apart. In Figure 5.6B, the factors are less correlated ($r = -.19$, $\Phi = 101°$). Consequently, the resulting factor pattern and structure loadings begin to converge. When the factors are orthogonal (i.e., they are uncorrelated and $\Phi = 90°$), the factor pattern and structure loadings are equivalent. Nunnally and Bernstein (1994) argue that factor pattern loadings are affected by the size of the correlation between the factors although factor structure loadings remain the same.

Because they represent simple correlations between the items and the factors, values for elements in the factor structure matrix cannot exceed 1.00 because zero-order correlations only range between −1.00 and +1.00. When factors are correlated, however, elements in the factor pattern matrix not only can exceed 1.00, they can also be of opposite sign to their factor structure counterparts (Pedhazur & Schmelkin, 1991).

Given the lack of equivalence of the two matrices in an oblique rotation, there is some confusion as to which matrix, factor pattern or factor structure, should be the focus of analysis. Several authors (e.g., Harman, 1976; Kline, 1994; Nunnally & Bernstein, 1994) argue that the each of the loadings in the factor structure matrix represents the simple correlation of an item with a factor (ignoring the influence of the other factors); therefore, these loadings are equivalent to the factor loadings given in the unrotated matrix. Because the factor structure matrix is more stable, in that it is unaffected by changing the size of the correlation among the factors, it should be the focus of factor interpretation. In contrast, the partial correlations represented by the loadings in the factor pattern matrix are affected by the size of the correlations among the factors. Therefore, it would be useful for determining factor scores, or the scores of the participants on the factors, and for reproducing the correlation matrix.

Hair and colleagues (1995) take the opposite position. They maintain that, because the factor structure matrix does not control for correlations among the factors in an oblique rotation, it is more difficult to use the factor structure matrix to determine which items load uniquely on each factor; therefore, the factor pattern matrix should be the focus of factor interpretation, especially when the factors are highly correlated. Tabachnick and Fidell (2001) support this position, arguing that interpretation of the factor pattern matrix is easier than the factor structure matrix and that the difference between the high and low loadings in the factor pattern matrix is more apparent than in the structure matrix.

Despite these reasonable arguments, we would support the first authors. That is, when undertaking an oblique rotation, the factor structure matrix should be the focus of factor identification and interpretation. The factor pattern matrix would be used for obtaining factor scores and for reproducing the correlation matrix. In reporting the results of the analyses, both matrices should be reported, especially if there are strong correlations among the factors.

Determining the Angle of Rotation for Oblique Rotations

Although oblique rotations are more flexible than orthogonal rotations, they are also more complex because the direction and strength of the correlation between the factors is often not known initially. Yet,

Figure 5.7   Rotating Two Correlated Factors for Which the Correlation Is Fixed Through Different Angles of Rotation

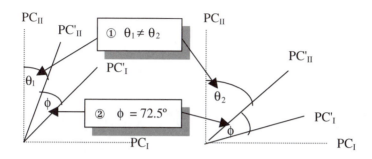

for some approaches to oblique rotations, this relationship must be specified from a range of possibilities prior to undertaking an oblique rotation. In addition, the angle between the unrotated and rotated factor (e.g., θ) must also be determined because a given set of fixed factors that are correlated could be rotated through a variety of different angles (i.e., $\theta_1 \neq \theta_2$; Figure 5.7, ①).

As we saw earlier in this chapter, the estimated correlation between the factors determines the size of their fixed angle of rotation (e.g., Φ; Figure 5.6) because the cosine of Φ represents their correlation. For example, suppose we had estimated the correlation between PC_I and PC_{II} to be +.30. If Ω equals the correlation between the two factors (e.g., .30), the arc, or inverse cosine, of Ω ($\cos^{-1}\Omega$) represents the angle Φ between the two correlated factors. In our example, if $r = .30$, the angle Φ between PC_I' and PC_{II}' would be 72.5° because $\cos^{-1}\Omega = \cos^{-1}$ (+.30) = 72.5° (Figure 5.7, ②).

Because the two factors that form the angle Φ could be located in a variety of places in geometric space, we want to position those correlated factors such that the solution obtained is a simple one according to Thurstone's (1947) criteria: each rotated factor has a few high loadings on the factor pattern matrix with most other loadings approaching zero.

Figure 5.8 illustrates an oblique rotation of the two factors, PC_I and PC_{II}, in geometric space that was undertaken in SPSS for Windows. Because this is an oblique rotation, the factors are correlated, Φ no longer equals 90° (Figure 5.8, ①), and the two angles of rotation, θ_1 and θ_2, are not necessarily equal ②. Let us now examine the various approaches to oblique solutions in greater detail.

Figure 5.8   Plot of an Oblique Rotation Two-Factor Principal Component
Solution for Items C1 to C8

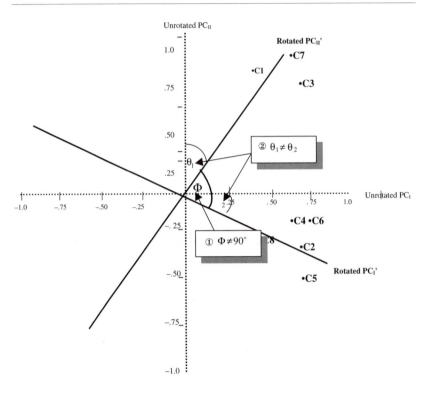

Types of Oblique Rotations

There are a number of approaches that have been used to achieve
simple structure in an oblique solution. Thurstone (1935, 1947) and his
colleagues, for example, developed the concept of a *reference vector
structure* that was designed to obtain oblique solutions when rotating
factors by hand. With the advent of high-speed computer technology,
it became possible to go directly from the unrotated factor matrix to the
rotated factor pattern matrix without the need for intermediate reference vector structures (Comrey & Lee, 1992). As a result, the use of
these vectors in factor analysis has become nearly obsolete. For this
reason, reference vector structures will not be discussed here.[4] Rather,
we will focus on approaches to achieving a simple oblique solution that
are available in the SPSS for Windows and SAS computer packages.

Although there are numerous approaches to oblique rotations (Gorsuch, 1983), only two oblique procedures are available in SPSS for Windows: *Direct Oblimin* and *Promax*. In SAS, there are many choices for oblique rotation, including the Oblimin, Promax, Orthoblique, and Procrustes solutions. Each of these methods of rotation uses a slightly different approach to achieving an oblique solution. Because Oblimin and Promax are two of the most popular oblique rotations, we will examine the process and output generated from these two rotational methods in greater depth and will only briefly discuss the Orthoblique and Procrustes solutions.

Direct Oblimin

Direct Oblimin (Jennrich & Sampson, 1966) attempts to satisfy the principles of *simple structure* with regard to the factor pattern matrix through a parameter that is used to control the degree of obliqueness, or correlation, allowed between the factors.[5] In SPSS for Windows and SAS, this parameter is referred to as *delta* (δ); other statistical packages (e.g., BMDP) label this parameter as *gamma* (Comrey & Lee, 1992; Jennrich & Sampson, 1966). For clarity, we will refer to this parameter as delta (δ).

Values for δ can range from negative to positive. Larger negative values of δ decrease the magnitude of the correlations among the factors, making them more orthogonal. Larger positive values for δ will increase the magnitude of the correlation among the factors. When δ is set at 0, this rotation has been referred to as the *Direct Quartimin* method (Comrey & Lee, 1992; Jennrich & Sampson, 1966).

Harman recommends that for practical purposes, the range of values for δ be restricted to 0 or negative values because values greater than $\delta = +.80$ produce extremely high correlations among the factors that, in turn, cause problems for the Direct Oblimin solution. It also does not make sense to have highly correlated factors because they would then be indistinguishable from one another. It is not surprising, therefore, that in SPSS for Windows, the default value for δ is 0 and the maximum value allowed for δ is .80.

There is no simple relationship between a specific value for δ and a resulting correlation among the factors because the number of variables and factors influences this relationship. There is also no clearly defined negative value for δ that would result in a completely orthogonal solution. Although Tabachnick and Fidell (2001) suggest that a δ

of about −4.0 results in an orthogonal solution, such a high negative value can also lead to a failure of the factor solution to converge.

There does not appear to be any definite opinion in the literature as to how large in absolute value δ should be. Rather, determining the absolute size of δ (e.g., choosing 0 rather than −.5) is a trial-and-error technique. Our experience suggests that if the researcher suspects that the resulting correlation among the factors is approximately .30, values of δ between −.5 and +.5 generally achieve this.

Promax

Promax (Hendrickson & White, 1964) is an oblique rotation that begins with an orthogonal rotation, usually Varimax. The orthogonal loadings are first raised to a stated power, *kappa* (κ). This value is usually κ = 2, 4, or 6. The default value in SPSS for Windows is 4, and in SAS it is 3. Then the solution is rotated to allow for correlations among the factors (Comrey & Lee, 1992; Tabachnick & Fidell, 2001).

Raising the loadings to powers results in values for the smaller loadings that are close to 0, but the larger loadings, although reduced, remain substantial. Higher powers result in higher correlations among the factors. The goal is to obtain a solution that provides the best structure using the lowest possible power loadings and therefore with the lowest correlation among the factors.

Promax has the advantage of reaching a solution more quickly than Direct Oblimin. In the past, therefore, when computers were not quite as powerful as they are now, Promax was extremely useful for larger data sets.

Orthoblique

The *Orthoblique* rotation method (Harris & Kaiser, 1964) is only available in SAS. Like Promax, this method begins with an orthogonal solution, generally Varimax. A diagonal matrix is then created, of which the diagonal elements are equal to the eigenvalues obtained during the factor extraction process (Comrey & Lee, 1992). This diagonal matrix is raised to a power, *p*, and then, through a series of manipulations of matrices, the factor structure and pattern matrices are obtained.

The value for *p* controls the obliqueness of the rotated solution. Harris and Kaiser (1964) recommend *p* = .5, indicating that *p* = 1.0 would result in an orthogonal solution. Comrey and Lee (1992) point out that the challenge with this method is determining the value at which p should be set.

Procrustes

Although *Procrustes* is generally an oblique rotation, it can also be used as an orthogonal rotation. It is available in SAS and is most often used in confirmatory rather than exploratory factor analyses. Procrustes is part of a family of forced rotations in which, using a least-squares method, a transformation matrix is sought that will force the factors to rotate to a specified target pattern that has been hypothesized by the researcher.

Gorsuch (1983) indicated that the term *Procrustes* was borrowed by Hurley and Cattell (1962) from Greek mythology. Procrustes, whose name means *he who stretches,* was an innkeeper/robber who preyed on travelers along the road to Athens. He would offer his victims hospitality on a magical bed guaranteed to fit any guest. His *one-size-fits-all* solution was to stretch on a rack those guests who were too short and to cut off the limbs of those too tall to make them fit perfectly into the bed. The authors used this analogy to point out that the resulting solution looked—but was not necessarily—a good fit for the hypothesized solution.

The Procrustes approach has declined in use since the development of maximum likelihood methods and with the increasing availability of multiple group programs (Gorsuch, 1983). For the interested reader, there are several good discussions about the advantages and limitations of this approach. These include Cramer (1974), Gorsuch (1983), Guilford (1977), Harman (1976), Horn (1967), Hurley and Cattell (1962), and Nunnally and Bernstein (1994).

Examples of an Oblique Rotation

Two separate oblique rotations, Oblimin and Promax, were undertaken in both SPSS for Windows and SAS for the two-factor principal components solution for Items C1 to C8 of the CGTS scale. To do this in SPSS for Windows, we highlighted the SPSS commands *Analyze . . . Data Reduction . . . Factor . . . Extraction . . .* and opened the *Rotation . . .* dialog box (Figure 5.9). The Oblimin and Promax rotations can be easily obtained by clicking on one of these two methods. For both the Oblimin and Promax solutions, we chose as the default values

Figure 5.9   The Rotation Dialog Box in SPSS for Windows

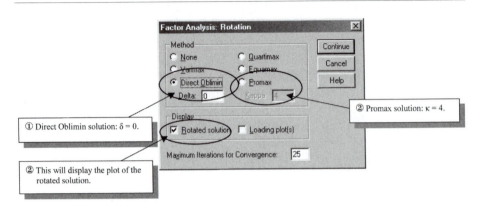

① Direct Oblimin solution: δ = 0.

② This will display the plot of the rotated solution.

② Promax solution: κ = 4.

in SPSS for Windows δ = 0 (for Oblimin) (Figure 5.9, ①) and κ = 4 for Promax ②. Clicking on the *Display . . . rotated solution . . .* ③ will produce a plot of the rotated solution as in Figure 5.10. Remember, each solution needs to be run separately.

The commands that were used to generate the SAS output for the Oblimin and Promax solutions are presented in Figure B5.5 (Appendix B). The PROC FACTOR subcommand, ROTATE=OBLIMIN(p) specifies p as the delta value to be used.

The Oblimin Solution

Table 5.4 (A-C) presents the SPSS for Windows output using PCA and the Direct Oblimin solution for the two rotated principal components, PC'_I and PC'_{II}. The SAS output is presented in Table B5.4, Appendix B.

The first 'component' matrix (Table 5.4A) summarizes the factor pattern factor loadings for the items on the two principal components. These loadings are like standardized partialized beta weights that indicate the effect of a particular factor on an item having controlled for the effects of the other correlated extracted factors ①.

The squares of the item loadings in the factor pattern matrix represent the unique contribution of the factor to the variance in the item, excluding the overlap between the correlated factors. Factor 1, for example, uniquely contributes $(-.104)^2$, or 1.08%, to the variance in Item C1 and $(.782)^2$, or 61.15%, to the variance in Item C2. In contrast,

Table 5.4   Generated Output From SPSS for Windows: PCA With Oblimin Rotation of the Two Principal Components for the Eight Items of the CGTS Scale

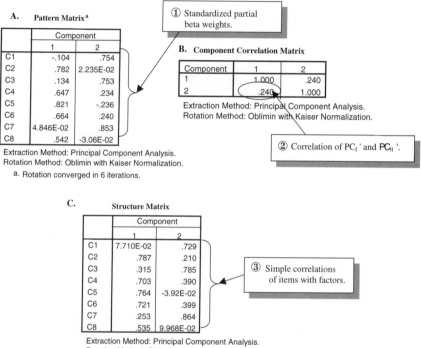

A.   Pattern Matrix[a]

	Component	
	1	2
C1	-.104	.754
C2	.782	2.235E-02
C3	.134	.753
C4	.647	.234
C5	.821	-.236
C6	.664	.240
C7	4.846E-02	.853
C8	.542	-3.06E-02

Extraction Method: Principal Component Analysis.
Rotation Method: Oblimin with Kaiser Normalization.
a. Rotation converged in 6 iterations.

① Standardized partial beta weights.

B.   Component Correlation Matrix

Component	1	2
1	1.000	.240
2	.240	1.000

Extraction Method: Principal Component Analysis.
Rotation Method: Oblimin with Kaiser Normalization.

② Correlation of PC_I' and PC_{II}'.

C.   Structure Matrix

	Component	
	1	2
C1	7.710E-02	.729
C2	.787	.210
C3	.315	.785
C4	.703	.390
C5	.764	-3.92E-02
C6	.721	.399
C7	.253	.864
C8	.535	9.968E-02

Extraction Method: Principal Component Analysis.
Rotation Method: Oblimin with Kaiser Normalization.

③ Simple correlations of items with factors.

Factor 2 explains $(.754)^2$, or 56.9%, of the variance in Item C1 and only $(.022)^2$, or .05%, of the variance in Item C2.

In Table 5.4B, we are presented with the factor correlation matrix that was generated as a result of setting $\delta = 0$. Notice that the correlation between the two factors for this setting is .24 ②. If we thought the resulting correlation were too high, we could set δ lower, for example, $\delta = -.5$. For our data set, this would result in a factor correlation equal to .204 (see Table 5.6). A higher δ (e.g., $\delta = +.5$) would have resulted in a factor correlation equal to .410 (Table 5.6).

The factor structure matrix in Table 5.4C contains the simple correlations of C1 to C8 with the two newly rotated principal components ③.

This structure matrix is the product of both the factor pattern (Table 5.4A) and the factor correlation matrices (Table 5.4B):

$$
\begin{vmatrix}
-.104 & .754 \\
.782 & .022 \\
.134 & .753 \\
.647 & .234 \\
.821 & -.236 \\
.664 & .240 \\
.048 & .853 \\
.542 & -.031
\end{vmatrix}
\begin{vmatrix}
1.000 & .240 \\
.240 & 1.000
\end{vmatrix}
=
\begin{vmatrix}
.077 & .729 \\
.787 & .210 \\
.315 & .785 \\
.703 & .390 \\
.764 & -.039 \\
.721 & .399 \\
.253 & .864 \\
.535 & .099
\end{vmatrix}
$$

As with the orthogonal solution in Table 5.3, each item in this structure matrix loads most strongly on a single factor: Items C2, C4, C5, C6, and C8 on the rotated factor PC_I and Items C1, C3, and C7 on PC_{II}.

Figure 5.10 presents a plot for the Oblimin solution produced in SPSS for Windows. Unfortunately, the plot produced in SPSS is a deceptive version of that presented to you in Figure 5.7. Because of the apparent 90° angle between the two components, the solution looks like it is orthogonal. It is not. An advantage of the SAS output for the same plot (Figure B5.10, Appendix B) is that, although it is difficult to read (A = Item C1) and still looks like there is a 90° angle between the two components, it also presents us with the angle of rotation for the two components (103.9°).

Promax Solution

Table 5.5 presents the SPSS output for the Promax solution using κ = 4. The SAS output for the same solution is presented in Table B5.5 (Appendix B).

Table 5.5 indicates that, although the factor structure and pattern loadings are different from those presented in Tables 5.3 and 5.4, the pattern of high and low loadings is similar. The component correlation matrix in Table 5.5B indicates that the correlation between the factors is .322. The SAS output (Table B5.5, Appendix B) presents similar results.

Figure 5.10   A Plot of the PCA Rotated Oblimin Solution Generated in
SPSS for Windows

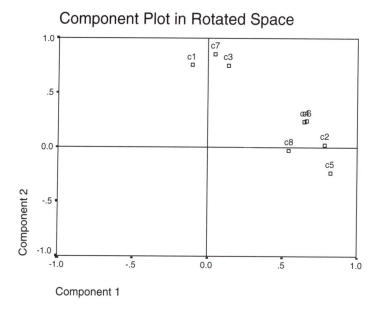

Component Plot in Rotated Space

COMPARING THE ORTHOGONAL
AND OBLIQUE SOLUTIONS

Table 5.6 compares the results obtained from three rotated two-factor orthogonal (Varimax) and oblique (Direct Oblimin and Promax) solutions generated in both SPSS for Windows and SAS using principal components analysis. For the Oblimin solution, delta (δ) was set at $-.5$, 0, and $+.5$ to compare the resulting correlations and factor loadings. The generated correlations among the factors ranged from 0 (for the Varimax rotation) to .410 for the oblique Oblimin solution ($\delta = +.5$). The angles of rotation ranged from 65.8° for the Oblimin solution (when $\delta = +5$) to 90° for the orthogonal Varimax solution.

The results that are reported in Table 5.6 suggest that, for the eight items on the CGTS, correlating the factors did not add measurably to the simplicity of the rotated factor solution. Of the five rotated solutions, the orthogonal Varimax solution generated the greatest number of highest and lowest factor loadings. This would lead us to conclude that, for our eight-item CGTS, the simplest solution would be the orthogonal rotation.

Table 5.5   Generated Output From SPSS for Windows: Promax Rotation of the Two Principal Components for the Eight Items of the CGTS Scale

A. **Pattern Matrix**[a]

	Component	
	1	2
C1	-.146	.770
C2	.789	-5.83E-03
C3	9.481E-02	.760
C4	.642	.214
C5	.843	-.270
C6	.658	.219
C7	3.254E-03	.864
C8	.550	-5.09E-02

B. **Component Correlation Matrix**

Component	1	2
1	1.000	.322
2	.322	1.000

Extraction Method: Principal Component Analysis.
Rotation Method: Promax with Kaiser Normalization.

Extraction Method: Principal Component Analysis.
Rotation Method: Promax with Kaiser Normalization.

a. Rotation converged in 3 iterations.

C.   **Structure Matrix**

	Component	
	1	2
C1	.102	.723
C2	.787	.249
C3	.340	.791
C4	.711	.421
C5	.755	1.308E-03
C6	.729	.431
C7	.282	.865
C8	.534	.126

Extraction Method: Principal Component Analysis.
Rotation Method: Promax with Kaiser Normalization.

ADVANTAGES AND DISADVANTAGES OF THE OBLIQUE SOLUTION

There are advantages and concomitant disadvantages of the oblique rotation solution. One distinct advantage is that the factor axes can be rotated to any position without changing the correlations among the items or their shared communalities. Kline (1994) argues that correlated axes reflect the real world and that it is rare that factors are truly orthogonal. Using an oblique rotation also does not exclude the

Table 5.6 Comparison Between the Orthogonal and Oblique Rotated Factor Structure Loadings on PC_I and PC_{II}

	Type of Rotation								
	Orthogonal		Oblique						
Method	Varimax		Direct Oblimin						Promax
			$\delta = -.5$		$\delta = 0$		$\delta = +.5$		$\kappa = 4$
$\angle\Phi^a$	90°		78.2°		76.1°		65.8°		71.2°
$r_{PC1,PCII}^b$:	0		.204		.240		.410		.322
Item	I	II	I	II	I	II	I	II	I	II
C1	−.019	.736	.073	.732	.077	.729	.131	.715	.102	.723
C2	.778	.124	.787	.186	.787	.210	.787	.289	.787	.249
C3	.216	.766	.310	.780	.315	.785	.368	.794	.340	.791
C4	.668	.317	.702	.369	.703	.390	.718	.454	.711	.421
C5	.787	−.128	.765	−.065	.764	−.039	.745	.045	.755	.001
C6	.685	.325	.720	.378	.721	.399	.736	.465	.729	.431
C7	.143	.854	.249	.862	.253	.864	.314	.864	.282	.865
C8	.534	.040	.535	.083	.535	.099	.531	.155	.534	.126

a. Angle of rotation for the two principal components, PC_I' and PC_{II}'.

b. Resulting correlation between PC_I' and PC_{II}'.

possibility that an orthogonal rotation will be obtained. If it is found after oblique rotation that the factors are indeed orthogonal, the researcher can be confident that the result is not an artifact of the choice of rotation (Kline, 1994).

Despite their attractiveness, there are also disadvantages of oblique rotations. For example, in oblique rotations, the sum of the squared loadings in any *row* will equal h^2 only by chance. The sum of the squares of the factor loadings in the *columns* for each factor will also not equal the total variance in the matrix except by chance. In addition, the original correlations between the variables cannot be completely reproduced from the cross products of the factor loadings.

Most authorities on factor analysis agree that care must be taken not to set the correlations among the factors too high or too low (Nunnally & Bernstein, 1994). Kline (1994) warns that if the factors are too highly correlated, the factor structure matrix (the matrix of the simple correlations of the items with the factors) may not share the same simple structure as the pattern matrix. Unfortunately, there is little agreement on what the value of *too high* or *too low* should be. Nunnally and Bernstein (1994) suggest maintaining factor correlations around .30. These authors suggest that if the correlations among the factors are low, then the results from the orthogonal rotation be retained, interpreted, and reported regardless of the underlying assumptions about the subcategories of the concept under study. Factors with correlations that are too high should be rejected because they are undoubtedly measuring the same construct.

CHOOSING BETWEEN ORTHOGONAL AND OBLIQUE ROTATIONS

Historically, orthogonal solutions were preferred because they were easier to obtain without a computer and provided more ease of interpretation. An examination of reports of instrument development in the health care literature indicates that researchers tend to use orthogonal rotations in their instrument development. Perhaps this is because orthogonal rotations are easier to apply and interpret. Like Pedhazur and Schmelkin (1991), we question whether orthogonal rotation is appropriate for use in the development of instruments that measure physiological or psychological constructs because most of these constructs have subcategories that are naturally correlated to some degree.

We suggest that the researcher peruse the construct to be measured. If, after such study, the researcher believes that some degree of correlation exists between the subcategories of the construct, then it would make cognitive sense to apply oblique rotations to the data. An even better alternative is to apply both orthogonal and oblique rotations to the data and then to interpret, compare, and report both solutions.

SUMMARY OF THE PROCESS OF ROTATIONS

Throughout this chapter, we have attempted to provide you with an overview of the process of factor rotation and the issues that you need to consider when choosing between orthogonal and oblique rotations. Figure 5.11 summarizes these issues for you and walks you through the

Figure 5.11   Decision Tree for Rotating the Factors

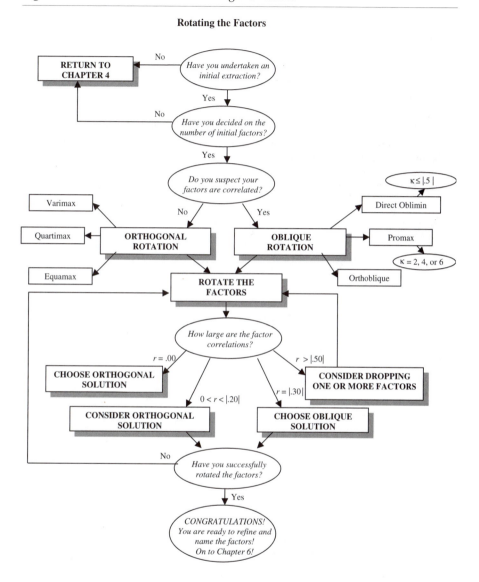

Rotating the Factors

decisions that are involved in factor rotation. In Chapter 6, we begin
the process of refining and interpreting our generated factors.
Remember that factor analysis is not only a statistical procedure but
also an art; it is the *artful* part of factor analysis in which we are about
to engage.

NOTES

1. You will recall from Chapter 3 that a factor-loading matrix is a matrix of which the columns represent the factors and its rows are the factor loadings for a given variable or item on the factors.

2. Because we will be using these letters quite often in this text, be aware that the Greek letter *theta* is symbolized as θ, *omega* = Ω, *phi* = Φ, and *delta* = δ.

3. Recall that in a principal components analysis, factors are referred to as 'components.'

4. The interested reader is referred to some excellent discussions of the development of reference vectors in Comrey and Lee (1992), Kline (1994), and Nunnally and Bernstein (1994).

5. Harman (1976) presents a clearly written mathematical description of the Direct Oblimin method.

6

Evaluating and Refining the Factors

In test construction, the researcher begins with a conceptual set of beliefs about the domain to be explored that is based on theory, previous research, and clinical experience. Although factor analysis can help clarify and make specific the structure of this domain, oftentimes, the number of factors generated from factor analysis is not the number that will eventually be used.

The decision as to the number of factors to be retained should be based on an artful combination of the outcomes obtained from the statistical indicators discussed in Chapter 5, the factors' theoretical coherence, a desire for simplicity, and the original goals of the factor analysis project. If the main purpose of this project is to identify sets of homogeneous items for the construction of scales, then the constraints of using the test (e.g., the test length and number of subscales) should be important considerations. In health care research, for example, an extended battery of tests administered to an acutely ill person would clearly be counterproductive. The challenge, therefore, is to construct a set of scales that are few in number and as short as possible while meeting the requirements of scale reliability.

In this chapter, we will continue to examine approaches to evaluating and refining the factors that have been produced from a factor analysis. Because our decision to retain factors is based in part on how well the items that load on a particular factor fit together, we will also address methods for assessing the internal consistency of factors.

EVALUATING AND REFINING THE FACTORS

Most instruments that are developed in the health sciences do not address a single phenomenon but rather measure several aspects of a construct. Therefore, several factors will likely emerge as potential descriptors of a given set of items. Ideally, each item will load strongly on a single factor following factor rotation. In reality, even with factor rotation, items will sometimes demonstrate weak loadings on all factors or will load strongly on several factors.

One of the first steps in evaluating and refining a set of factors is to examine the rotated factor matrices for high or low loadings. As we indicated in Chapter 5, two factor matrices are generated as a result of factor rotation: the *factor pattern matrix* and the *factor structure matrix*. In an uncorrelated orthogonal rotation (e.g., Varimax), these matrices are identical. In an oblique rotation (e.g., Oblimin), the factors are correlated; as a result, the two factor matrices are different.

In an oblique rotation, the *factor pattern matrix* contains the loadings that represent the unique relationship of each item to a factor having first controlled for the correlation among the factors (Hair, Anderson, Tatham, & Black, 1995). Because they are like partial regression coefficients, the magnitudes of these loadings are influenced by the strength of the correlations among the factors. In contrast, the loadings in the *factor structure matrix* are simple zero-order correlations of the items with the factors. Because they do not control for the between-factor correlations, the sizes of these loadings are not influenced by the strength of the correlations among the factors.

As we indicated in Chapter 5, there is some disagreement in the factor analysis literature as to which matrix, factor pattern or factor structure, should be the focus of evaluation when the factors are correlated. We suggest that you focus first on the factor structure matrix for factor interpretability and then compare your decisions with what you observe in the factor pattern matrix. You can also use the factor pattern matrix to determine factor scores. When writing up the results of an oblique rotation, include both of these matrices in your report.

Evaluating the Loadings
in the Factor Structure Matrix

To begin the process of evaluating the factor loadings, it is best to simplify the presentation so that the patterns of item-to-factor correlations in the factor structure matrix are more distinct. In SPSS for Windows, this is achieved by directing the computer to suppress absolute values in the factor structure matrix that are less than a specified value (e.g., < .40) using the commands *Analyze . . . Data Reduction . . . Factor . . . Options . . .* and clicking on the box *Suppress absolute values less than* .40.

Table 6.1A-B presents the results of this process for the 20-item CGTS scale. This output was generated using a four-factor principal axis factoring solution with a Direct Oblimin rotation (delta = 0).[1]

SAS (v. 8.2) provides options for suppressing loadings that are less than a specified value using the FUZZ subcommand in PROC FACTOR. The subcommand, FUZZ = .4, for example, will suppress factor loadings that are less than .40. Unfortunately, these options were not supported in recent versions of SAS (e.g., v. 8.0 and v. 8.1). For those versions of SAS, it will be more difficult and time-consuming to identify significant loadings, especially in large data sets. That is a strong argument for updating to v. 8.2.

Whichever version of SAS is used, it is possible to reorder the loadings using the REORDER subcommand in PROC FACTOR. Items with the highest absolute loading on the first factor are displayed first, from largest to smallest loading, followed by items with their highest absolute loading on the second factor, and so on. (SAS, 2000). These SAS results (along with the suppressed loadings less than .40) are presented in Table B6.1A–B (Appendix B).

Output Generated in SPSS for Windows

Table 6.1A is the rotated factor structure matrix generated in SPSS for Windows that includes all of the item-to-factor correlations. This unsuppressed factor structure matrix can be quite overwhelming to evaluate, especially if there are large numbers of items in the matrix. Many of these values are also not worth noting. Item C1, for example, is correlated very weakly with Factor 2 (9.868E02 = .0987) and Factor 4 (−.489E03 = .00489) ①. Item C20, on the other hand, is correlated relatively strongly with Factor 1 (.715) and Factor 3 (.569) ②. Because there are so many factor loadings ($n = 80$) presented in Table 6.1A (and

Table 6.1   Evaluating the Factor Structure Matrix for High and Low Item-Factor Correlations

A. Factor Structure Matrix—All Loadings

Structure Matrix

	Factor			
	1	2	3	4
C1 Increase of personal control	.514	9.868E-02	.251	-4.89E-03
C2 Worry about uncertain diagnosis	.268	.753	.201	.274
C3 What to do to manage risk	.784	.268	.276	.209
C4 Help reduce uncertainty about future	.369	.658	.276	1.014E-02
C5 Fear ambiguity of results	5.271E-02	.662		
C6 Worry about diagnosis I can't do anything about	.448	.611	.264	.383
C7 Hope to make better health, lifestyle choices	.735	.208	.170	.117
C8 Worried about loss of health, and life insurance coverage	.130	.363	.584	-6.42E-02
C9 worried about how family will react	.106	.233	9.858E-02	.722
C10 Need information about types of cancer at risk for	.729	.252	.320	.170
C11 marital family problems that might occur	6.851E-02	.195	8.204E-02	.617
C12 might be helped to make future life decisions	.633	.122	.269	.220
C13 need info about future screening activities	.752	.336	.370	.321
C14 how will a positive test affect children and other family members	.416	.251	.284	.677
C15 worried about my future life	.378	.741	.235	.377
C16 want info about difference between diagnosis and getting cancer	.650	.328	.225	.137
C17 financial concerns related to screening	.485	.153	.582	.320
C18 what are financial and social implications of being identified	.367	.186	.807	.186
C19 worried about being targeted as carrier	.369	.254	.859	.231
C20 want to know survival prospects	.715	.254	.569	9.146E-02

Extraction Method: Principal Axis Factoring.
Rotation Method: Oblimin with Kaiser Normalization.

① C1 correlates weakly with Factors 2 and 4.

② C20 is strongly correlated with Factors 1 and 3.

Table B6.1A, Appendix B), it is very difficult to discern the patterns of high and low loadings.

By directing SPSS for Windows and SAS to suppress absolute values less than .40, we obtain the result presented in Table 6.1B (and Table B6.1B in Appendix B). It should be noted that, by suppressing the loadings, we do not delete any of the item-to-factor correlations. They are still lurking in the background and are included in calculations of item communalities and percent of variance explained by the factors.

Table 6.1 Continued

B. Factor Structure Matrix—Only Loadings > .40

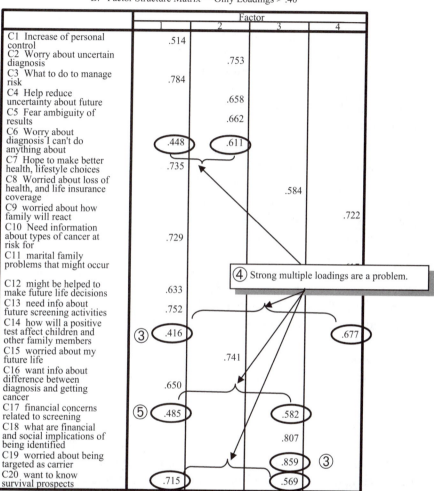

	Factor			
	1	2	3	4
C1 Increase of personal control	.514			
C2 Worry about uncertain diagnosis		.753		
C3 What to do to manage risk	.784			
C4 Help reduce uncertainty about future		.658		
C5 Fear ambiguity of results		.662		
C6 Worry about diagnosis I can't do anything about	.448	.611		
C7 Hope to make better health, lifestyle choices	.735			
C8 Worried about loss of health, and life insurance coverage			.584	
C9 worried about how family will react				.722
C10 Need information about types of cancer at risk for	.729			
C11 marital family problems that might occur				
C12 might be helped to make future life decisions	.633			
C13 need info about future screening activities	.752			
C14 how will a positive test affect children and other family members	.416			.677
C15 worried about my future life		.741		
C16 want info about difference between diagnosis and getting cancer	.650			
C17 financial concerns related to screening	.485		.582	
C18 what are financial and social implications of being identified			.807	
C19 worried about being targeted as carrier			.859	
C20 want to know survival prospects	.715		.569	

④ Strong multiple loadings are a problem.

Extraction Method: Principal Axis Factoring.
Rotation Method: Oblimin with Kaiser Normalization.

Their absence from the table just makes it easier for us to view the patterns of factor loadings.

In Table 6.1B (and Table B6.1B), for example, it is more obvious that 11 items load on the first factor, 5 items load on the second and third factors, and 3 items load on the fourth factor. Given that we have suppressed loadings less than .40, the loadings that remain in view are strong, ranging in value from .416 for Item C14 on Factor 1 to .859 for Item C19 on Factor 3 ③.

The suppression of the loadings reveals an additional problem with multiple factor loadings. Although Item C6 loads most strongly on Factor 2 (.611), it also loads nearly as strongly (.448) on Factor 1 ④. Multiple loadings are also problems for Items C14, C17, and C20 ④. The challenge will be to determine where best to place these items.

Items With Weak Loadings on All Factors

In Chapters 3 and 4, we examined approaches to determining the factorability of the correlation matrix. We indicated that a correlation matrix in which items are weakly correlated with one another would not produce a satisfactory factor analysis solution because there could potentially be as many factors as items. We suggested examining the correlation matrix carefully and eliminating items that were insufficiently correlated with all of the other items in the matrix (i.e., < .30).

Despite this careful initial screening, there may still remain items that load weakly on the identified rotated factors. From a practical standpoint, *weak loadings* are those that are less than |.30| (Hair et al., 1995). Hair and colleagues suggest two solutions to weak factor loadings:

- Drop items that do not load reasonably on any factor.
- Evaluate the weak loading item's communality and its unique contribution to the instrument.

If an item has low communality (i.e., the proportion of explained variance in the item by the factors is low) or its contribution to the overall instrument is of little importance (e.g., its meaning relative to the other items is unclear), the item should be eliminated. A new factor solution that excludes the eliminated items should then be undertaken and the results reevaluated.

Luckily, the factor structure matrix in Table 6.1A (and Table B6.1A, Appendix B) does not have problems with low item-to-factor correlations. All of the items load ≥ .40 on at least one factor.

Items That Are Important but Rarely Checked

Sometimes items will fail to load significantly (e.g., their loadings are < .30) on any of the factors and yet these weak-loading items are such important contributors to the content of a scale that they should not be eliminated. In their development of a College Student Hassles Scale, for example, Pett and Johnson (2002) found that because of low within-item variance, several potential hassles related to gender (e.g., *Not taken seriously because of my gender*) and race/ethnicity bias (e.g., *Perceptions others have about me based on race/ethnic stereotypes*) failed to load significantly (> .30) on any of the authors' identified factors. The major reason for these poor loadings was that most of the 965 students in this university sample did not experience hassles-related gender or race/ethnicity bias. Yet when the hassle did occur, it was of much importance to the respondent. For that reason, the authors decided to retain the problem items in the scale to be analyzed as subscales separate from the identified factors.

If you should encounter this situation in a factor analysis, our suggestion is that you examine the problem items closely for their relevance to your construct. If the poor loading items are of much importance to a subset of your respondents, you may want to retain these items as potential subscales. Be sure to note this decision in your write-up.

Items With Strong Loadings on Multiple Factors

Ideally, the researcher would like an item to load significantly on a single factor. This would provide the *simple structure solution* (Thurstone, 1947) that we discussed in Chapter 5. However, as we saw with the factor structure matrix in Table 6.1B, it is quite common for items to load significantly on multiple factors (e.g., loadings > .30), especially with an oblique rotation that assumes that the factors are correlated.

There is some disagreement in the factor analysis literature as to what to do about the multiple-loading problem. Kline (2000a) suggests eliminating high multiple-loading items because of the difficulty in interpreting the meaning of the resulting scales. Hair and colleagues (1995) agree that the presence of items with moderate-sized loadings on multiple factors makes interpretation of the factors more difficult, but they are less inclined to drop the offending item(s). They argue that the meaning of an item must be taken into account when assigning labels to each of the factors on which the item loads. An additional challenge is to decide on which factor to ultimately place that item.

We suggest placing the item with the factor that it is most closely related to conceptually. As we indicate in the next section, the *Reliability* programs in both SPSS for Windows and SAS will generate a set of

Cronbach's alphas for the group of items that load on a given factor. These alphas can be used to evaluate the factor's internal consistency and to decide where to best place an item with strong loadings on several factors.

In Table 6.1B, for example, Item C17 has multiple loadings on Factor 1 and Factor 3 ⑤. It appears, however, that Item C17 (*Financial concerns related to screening*) fits better with Item C18 (*What are the financial and social implications of being identified*), which loads on Factor 3, than it does with Item C16 (*Want information about the differences between diagnosis and getting cancer*), which loads on Factor 1. We might want to place C17 on Factor 3 and assess the two factors' interitem reliability with and without C17.

ASSESSING THE RELIABILITY OF AN INSTRUMENT

All instruments, specifically those that examine behaviors, are subject to measurement error. The *reliability* of an instrument refers to the extent to which scores on an instrument are free from this measurement error (American Psychological Association, 1985; Pedhazur & Schmelkin, 1991). Two types of measurement error have been identified in the test construction literature: *systematic* and *random* (Nunnally & Bernstein, 1994; Pedhazur & Schmelkin, 1991).

Error that is *systematic*, or nonrandom, consistently reoccurs on repeated measures of the same instrument even when it is assumed that the person being rated has not changed on the construct of interest. Systematic error can either affect all observations equally or it can affect some subsets of observations but not others. It is often the result of miscalibration of an instrument or problems with the underlying construct being measured, e.g., failure to differentiate between the selected construct and a closely related one. Although systematic error may contribute to the reliability of an instrument, its strongest negative effect is on the *validity* of an instrument. That is, it impacts the extent to which the instrument truly measures what it purports to measure (Nunnally & Bernstein, 1994; Pedhazur & Schmelkin, 1991).

Random error, on the other hand, is inconsistent and not predictable given similar repeated measurements of an instrument under the same respondent conditions. This type of error can come from numerous sources (Kline, 2000a, 2000b; Nunnally & Bernstein, 1994; Polit & Hungler, 1999):

- Situational contaminants (e.g., environmental factors of the data-gathering facility, friendliness of the researchers)
- Transitory personal factors (e.g., alertness, hunger, anxiety, or mood of the subject)
- Response-set biases (e.g., social desirability and acquiescence)
- Administration variations (e.g., inconsistencies in test-taking instructions)
- Instrument clarity (e.g., unclear directions)
- Item sampling (e.g., insufficient number of items)
- Instrument format (e.g., confusing format, the ordering of questions on the page)

Random error affects the *reliability* of an instrument: The lower the random error, the higher the instrument's reliability (Kline, 2000a; Mishel, 1998).

Reliability in the test construction arena focuses on three aspects of the instrument: *internal consistency, stability,* and *equivalence.* At this stage of instrument development, our primary concern is to evaluate the *internal consistency* of each of our derived factors. Although internal consistency will be the main focus of our discussion of reliability in this chapter, we will also briefly address issues related to stability and equivalence. For excellent in-depth discussions of all three dimensions of reliability, the interested reader is referred to Burns and Grove (2001), Kline (2000a, 2000b), Nunnally and Bernstein (1994), and Pedhazur and Schmelkin (1991).

EVALUATING THE INTERNAL CONSISTENCY OF AN INSTRUMENT

The *internal consistency* of an instrument refers to how well the items that make up an instrument or one of its subscales fit together. If a given set of items were relatively homogeneous, it would be expected that the correlations among the items that make up the set would be high. The instrument or subscale that contains these items would then be said to have high *internal consistency.* In a moment, we will look at what an acceptable level of internal consistency might be. First, however, let us examine some statistical approaches that have been developed to determine the internal consistency of an instrument or its subscales.[2] These include the *split-half technique* and *Cronbach's alpha.*

We will use both approaches to internal consistency to evaluate the internal consistency of the 11 items that loaded ≥ .40 on Factor 1 presented in Table 6.1B.

Split-Half Reliability

Historically, a commonly used and easily calculated method for determining internal consistency has been the *split-half technique* (Pedhazur & Schmelkin, 1991). This approach involves administering an existing instrument or set of subscales to a group of subjects. The set of items contained within the instrument (or subscale) is then split in half and the resulting scores on the two forms are correlated. Strong correlations between the two halves of the instrument (or subscale) imply that the scale being examined is internally consistent. To determine the internal consistency for Factor 1 using the split-half technique, for example, we would split the 11-item subscale into two parts of 6 and 5 items each and evaluate the correlation between these two halves.

To estimate this internal consistency, the Spearman-Brown formula is applied to the obtained split-half correlation as follows (Pedhazur & Schmelkin, 1991):

$$r_{xx} = \frac{2r_{1/2\,1/2}}{1 + r_{1/2\,1/2}}$$

where

r_{xx} = split-half reliability of a measure

$r_{1/2\,1/2}$ = correlation between the two halves of a scale

Suppose, for example, that the correlation between the respondents' scores of two halves of our 11-item CGTS scale were .70. Then according to the Spearman-Brown formula given above, the instrument's reliability for this 11-item subscale would be

$$r_{xx} = \frac{2r_{1/2\,1/2}}{1 + r_{1/2\,1/2}} = \frac{2(.70)}{1 + (.70)} = .82$$

Although the split-half technique is convenient and relatively straightforward statistically, there are distinct limitations to this approach. First, it is necessary to determine how the split will take place (e.g., a random selection of items, first and second halves of the test, or odd vs. even items). This is not necessarily an easy decision because the number of possible split halves that are available in a given set of items is

$$number\ of\ possible\ split\text{-}halves = \frac{k!}{2(k_1!)\ (k_2!)}$$

where

k = total number of items in the subscale
k_1 = number of items contained in the first half
k_2 = number of items contained in the second half
! = symbol for the factorial

For the 11-item subscale that represents Factor 1, for example, there are 231 different ways that we could split this scale into two halves of 6 and 5 items:

$$number\ of\ possible\ split\text{-}halves = \frac{k!}{2(k_1!)\ (k_2!)} = \frac{11!}{2(6!)\ (5!)} = 231$$

Given these 231 different ways to split an odd-numbered set of 11 items, it is not surprising that quite different Spearman-Brown values may be obtained depending on the particular split selected.

A second problem with the split-half reliability coefficient is that estimation of the reliability of a total scale (e.g., our 11-item Factor 1) is based on two scales that are approximately half the original size (e.g., 6 and 5 items). Because reliability is positively related to test length (i.e., increased test length will result in increased reliability) (Kline, 2000a), the split-half reliability obtained from a shorter set of scales (e.g., 6 and 5 items) will underestimate the reliability of the larger scale (e.g., 11 items).

To correct for this test-length deficiency in the split-half technique, the Spearman-Brown prophecy formula was introduced (Kline, 2000a; Nunnally & Bernstein, 1994; Pedhazur & Schmelkin, 1991):

$$\hat{r}_{kk} = \frac{k\,\bar{r}_{ij}}{1 + (k-1)\,\bar{r}_{ij}}$$

where

k = total number of items in the scale being considered

$\hat{r}_{kk}$ = estimated reliability of an instrument with k items

$\bar{r}_{ij}$ = average correlation among the items

Suppose, for example, that the average correlation among the items on our 11-item subscale that represents Factor 1 was .30. The estimated reliability for the subscale would be as follows:

$$\hat{r}_{kk} = \frac{k\bar{r}_{ij}}{1 + (k-1)\bar{r}_{ij}} = \frac{(11)(.30)}{1 + (11-1).30} = \frac{3.3}{4.0} = .825$$

Note that, despite a low average correlation among the items (.30), it is possible to obtain a respectable estimate of the instrument's reliability (.825) with only an 11-item pool.

An assumption of these Spearman-Brown formulas is that the two scales generated from the split halves are strictly parallel. That is, they have identical true scores and equal error variances and, as a result, have equal means and variances (Pedhazur & Schmelkin, 1991). If this rather stringent assumption is not met, then the reliability estimate for the entire scale will be biased upward. This issue would be of particular concern, for example, if the instrument being constructed had items that were of increasing difficulty for the respondent. One could reasonably expect that some splits of the items (e.g., first half, second half) would not result in parallel forms.

Evaluating Split-Half
Reliability Using SPSS for Windows

To obtain a split-half reliability analysis in SPSS for Windows, click on the commands *Analyze . . . Scales . . . Reliability Analysis*. This will open the SPSS dialog box in Figure 6.1. For this analysis, the *Model . . .* that we will select is *Split-half* ①. This *Split-half* technique will split the scale into two parts and examine the correlation between the two halves. Additional models that might be of interest in this analysis are the *Parallel* and *Strict Parallel* models. The *Parallel* and *Strict Parallel* models assume that all items have equal variances and, when replicated, equal error variances. The strict parallel model makes the

Figure 6.1   Reliability Dialog Box Generated in SPSS for Windows

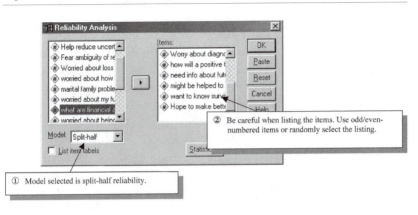

① Model selected is split-half reliability.

② Be careful when listing the items. Use odd/even-numbered items or randomly select the listing.

additional assumption that the means across all items are equal. Another optional model, *Alpha,* is one that we will examine in depth when we discuss Cronbach's coefficient alpha.

Next, highlight and bring over the scale items that will be evaluated. Because SPSS computes a split-half coefficient between the first and second half of the items listed in the reliability analysis, the choice of listing of the items is very important because it will influence the size of the correlation between the two halves of the instrument (Green, Salkind, & Akey, 2000). Because there are 231 ways to split a set of 11 items, many researchers choose to use the odd/even-numbered items to split the set. For our 11 items that load on Factor 1, that would mean that the odd-numbered items (i.e., C1, C3, C7, C13, and C17) would be listed first, followed by the even-numbered items (i.e., C6, C10, C12, C14, C16, and C20). Although this is common practice, we suggest that you also consider randomly selecting the order of the items that you want to include in your split-half analysis. You can either use a table of random numbers or generate a random variable in SPSS using the commands *Transform . . . Compute . . . Randnum = RV.UNIFORM (1,20).*

Using these commands, we created a random variable called *Randnum,* which assigned to each case in our data set a random value from a uniform distribution with a specified minimum (1) and maximum (20). By rounding the generated values to whole numbers and going down the list of cases, we obtained the following random order of items to be selected for our analysis and entered into the item list: C1, C16, C10, C17, C3, C6, C14, C13, C12, C20, and C7 (Figure 6.1, ②).

Reliability Commands in SAS

A reliability analysis using Cronbach's coefficient alpha can be obtained in SAS using the PROC CORR commands given in Figure B6.1 in Appendix B. Unfortunately, there is no simple, straightforward strategy to request a split-half reliability analysis in SAS. One approach might be to create two separate scales, each representing a split half of randomly selected scale items, and then run a correlation between the two forms using PROC CORR.

Split-Half Reliability Output Generated in SPSS for Windows

Table 6.2 presents the results of the split-half reliability analysis for the 11 items that loaded $\geq .40$ on Factor 1. We are first presented with the descriptive statistics: means, variances, standard deviations, and interitem correlations for both halves of the scale as well as the average interitem correlation, $\bar{r}_{ij}$ (.4060), for the entire scale (Table 6.2, ①).

The *correlation between forms*, .8414 ②, is the correlation between the two halves of the scale, $r_{1/2,1/2}$, and is obtained using the following formula (SPSS, Inc., 1999):

$$r_{1/2\,1/2} = \frac{\frac{1}{2}\,(S_p^2 - S_{p1}^2 - S_{p2}^2)}{S_{p1}S_{p2}} = \frac{\frac{1}{2}\,(73.3961 - 20.9284 - 18.9525)}{(4.5748)\,(4.3534)}$$

$$= \frac{16.7576}{19.9159} = .8414$$

where

S_p^2 = variance for the entire scale, 73.3961 ③

S_{p1}^2 = variance for the first half of the scale, 20.9284 ③

S_{p2}^2 = variance for the second half of the scale, 18.9525 ③

S_{p1} = standard deviation for the first half of the scale, 4.5748 ③

S_{p2} = standard deviation for the second half of the scale, 4.3534 ③

This correlation, $r_{1/2\,1/2}$, is what we used to obtain the Spearman-Brown reliability coefficient presented in Table 6.2 ④:

$$r_{xx} = \frac{2r_{1/2\,1/2}}{1 + r_{1/2\,1/2}} = \frac{2(.8414)}{1 + (.8414)} = .9139$$

Table 6.2   Results of Split-Half Reliability Analysis Generated in SPSS for Windows

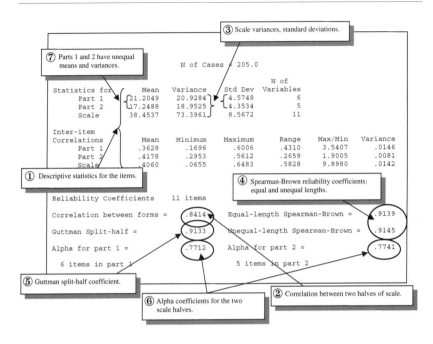

③ Scale variances, standard deviations.

⑦ Parts 1 and 2 have unequal means and variances.

① Descriptive statistics for the items.

④ Spearman-Brown reliability coefficients: equal and unequal lengths.

⑤ Guttman split-half coefficient.

⑥ Alpha coefficients for the two scale halves.

② Correlation between two halves of scale.

```
                                        N of Cases =   205.0

                                                       N of
Statistics for      Mean     Variance  Std Dev  Variables
       Part 1     21.2049   20.9284    4.5748         6
       Part 2     17.2488   18.9525    4.3534         5
       Scale      38.4537   73.3961    8.5672        11

Inter-item
Correlations     Mean    Minimum   Maximum   Range    Max/Min   Variance
     Part 1     .3628     .1696     .6006    .4310     3.5407     .0146
     Part 2     .4178     .2953     .5612    .2659     1.9005     .0081
     Scale      .4060     .0655     .6483    .5828     9.8980     .0142

Reliability Coefficients   11 items

Correlation between forms =     .8414    Equal-length Spearman-Brown =     .9139

Guttman Split-half =            .9133    Unequal-length Spearman-Brown =   .9145

Alpha for part 1 =              .7712    Alpha for part 2 =                .7741

    6 items in part 1                        5 items in part 2
```

Spearman-Brown Results

There is also a Spearman-Brown result presented for unequal lengths (.9145) ④. If the two halves of our CGTS scale had been of equal length (e.g., six items each), the two Spearman-Brown results would have been the same (.9139). Because we had an odd number of items in Factor 1 (i.e., 11 items), the two halves of the scale are of unequal length. This Spearman-Brown formula is given as follows (SPSS, Inc., 1999):

$$\text{unequal length } r_{xx} = \frac{-r^2_{1/2\,1/2} + \sqrt{r^4_{1/2\,1/2} + (4r^2_{1/2\,1/2}(1 - r^2_{1/2\,1/2})k_1k_2/k^2)}}{2(1 - r^2_{1/2\,1/2})k_1k_2/k^2}$$

where

$r^2_{1/2\,1/2}$ = square of the correlation between the split-halves = $(.8414)^2$

k_1 = number of items in the first half = 6

k_2 = number of items in the second half = 5

k = total number of test items = 11

If it had been necessary to calculate the Spearman-Brown coefficient using this somewhat unwieldy formula with a pocket calculator, we would have obtained the following results:

$$r_{xx} = \frac{-r_{1/2\,1/2}^2 + \sqrt{r_{1/2\,1/2}^4 + \left[4r_{1/2\,1/2}^2(1 - r_{1/2\,1/2}^2)k_1k_2/k^2\right]}}{2(1 - r_{1/2\,1/2}^2)k_1k_2/k^2}$$

$$= \frac{-(.8414)^2 + \sqrt{(.8414)^4 + \left[4(.8414)^2(1 - (.8414)^2)(6)(5)/11^2\right]}}{2(1 - (.8414)^2)(6)(5)/11^2}$$

$$= \frac{-.7080 + \sqrt{.5012 + \left[24.8067/121\right]}}{17.52/121} = \frac{.1324}{.1448} = .9145$$

Luckily, thanks to statistical computer packages, it is no longer necessary to compute this rather unwieldy formula by hand; the result is given to us in Table 6.2 ④. This is the Spearman-Brown split-half reliability result that we would report since we have an uneven number of items.

Guttman Split-Half Coefficient

The *Guttman split-half* presented in Table 6.2 ⑤ is a second split-half reliability coefficient that is less widely used than the Spearman-Brown coefficient. In format, the equation closely resembles the correlation between the split halves (SPSS, Inc., 1999):

$$G = \frac{2(S_p^2 - S_{p1}^2 - S_{p2}^2)}{S_p^2} = \frac{2(73.3961 - 20.9284 - 18.9525)}{73.3961} = .9133$$

The final values we are given in the results for Table 6.2 are the alpha coefficients for both halves of the CGTS scale ⑥. For now, we will withhold our discussion of these coefficients because we will be addressing their meaning in detail in the next section.

To summarize the results of Table 6.2, both the Spearman-Brown and Guttman split-half results for our 11-item Factor 1 subscale are above .90. This would suggest that the estimate of reliability for the total scale is quite high despite the somewhat middling average interitem correlation (.4060). Of concern are the unequal means and variances for the two halves of the scale ⑦ because an assumption of the Spearman-Brown test is that the two halves are strictly parallel with equal means and variances.

ESTIMATING THE EFFECTS ON RELIABILITY OF INCREASING OR DECREASING ITEMS

Pedhazur and Schmelkin (1991) present a useful approach that can be used to estimate changes in the reliability of a given instrument should the number of items be increased or decreased. The formula that is used is a modified Spearman-Brown formula:

$$\hat{r}_{kk} = \frac{k\,r_{xx}}{1 + (k-1)\,r_{xx}}$$

where

k = factor by which the number of items is increased or decreased

r_{xx} = calculated reliability of the existing instrument

$\hat{r}_{kk}$ = estimated reliability of the instrument that is k times longer (or shorter) than the existing instrument

Suppose, for example, we wanted to estimate the reliability of a scale that is twice as long as our 11-item set that loaded $\geq$ .40 on Factor 1 for which the estimated unequal-length Spearman-Brown reliability was .9145 (Table 6.2, ④). For this example, $k = 2$, $r_{xx} = .9145$, and the estimated reliability for this 22-item scale would be

$$\hat{r}_{kk} = \frac{k\,r_{xx}}{1 + (k-1)\,r_{xx}} = \frac{(2)(.9145)}{1 + (2-1)(.9145)} = \frac{1.829}{1.9145} = .9553$$

Using this same formula, we could also estimate the scale's reliability if the number of items were decreased. Suppose, for example, we wanted to estimate the reliability of this same scale if we reduced the number of items from 11 to 7. In this instance, $k = .6434$ (7/11 = .6364) and $r_{xx} = .9145$. Our estimated reliability for this newly created seven-item scale would be

$$r_{kk} = \frac{k\,r_{xx}}{1 + (k-1)\,r_{xx}} = \frac{(.6434)(.9145)}{1 + (.6434 - 1)(.9145)} = \frac{.5820}{.6675} = .8719$$

Notice that there is a point of diminishing returns as a result of increasing the number of items in an instrument (Pedhazur & Schmelkin, 1991). Doubling the number of items in our subscale from 11 to 22 did not double its reliability. We only increased the estimated reliability .0408 over our original estimated reliability of .9145. Also, by decreasing our items from 11 to 7, we only decreased this scale's estimated reliability by .0426, from .9145 to .8719.

Obtaining a Desired Scale Reliability

By solving for k, this Spearman-Brown formula can also be used to estimate the increased or decreased number of items that would be needed to obtain a desired scale reliability (Pedhazur & Schmelkin, 1991). For example, suppose we wanted to know by what factor we could reduce our 11-item scale and still maintain a desired reliability of at least .80. How many items could we drop (assuming, of course, the interitem correlations remain the same)? Solving for k in the above formula (with $r_{xx} = .9145$ and $r_{kk} = .80$), we obtain the following equation:

$$k = \frac{r_{kk}(1 - r_{xx})}{r_{xx}(1 - r_{kk})} = \frac{(.80)(1 - .9145)}{(.9145)(1 - .80)} = \frac{(.80)(.0855)}{(.9145)(.20)} = \frac{.0684}{.1829} = .3740$$

According to the Spearman-Brown formula, we could decrease the number of items by a factor of .3740 and still maintain a reliability of .80. This translates into decreasing the number of items from 11 to 5 [(.3740)(11) = 4.114, rounding up to 5]. In health care research, given the fatigue factor for many patients, there is a clear advantage to maximizing reliability with the fewest number of items.

It is hopefully apparent from this discussion that, although an instrument that is internally consistent will generally have items that are highly correlated, reliability also depends on the number of items contained in the instrument. As we saw from the Spearman-Brown formula, the greater the number of items, the higher the estimated reliability. However, doubling or tripling the number of items in a scale will not necessarily enhance the scale's reliability. It also should be noted that, given a sufficient number of items in the scale, it is possible to obtain a very respectable level of reliability with low average interitem correlations.

Limited Use of Split-Half Reliability

Because of the inherent drawbacks of the split-half technique, the use of the Spearman-Brown approach has declined with the advent of advanced computer technology. Today, Cronbach's coefficient alpha (Cronbach, 1951) is the preferred approach to the estimate of internal consistency. Let us look, therefore, at the uses of this second measure of internal consistency.

CRONBACH'S COEFFICIENT ALPHA (α)

An important and widely used measure for assessing the internal consistency of a set of items is *Cronbach's coefficient alpha* (α) (Cronbach, 1951, 1984). This measure of reliability represents the proportion of total variance in a given scale that can be attributed to a common source (DeVellis, 1991). It is also defined as the estimated correlation of the given scale with another scale of the same length from the universe of possible items (Kline, 1986). The square root of coefficient alpha represents the estimated correlation of the obtained scores with the true scores (Nunnally & Bernstein, 1994).

Coefficient alpha has the advantage over split-half reliability in that it is not a single estimate of a scale's reliability but rather the *average* of all possible split-half reliability coefficients that can be obtained from a given set of items in a scale (Cronbach, 1951; Pedhazur & Schmelkin, 1991). Coefficient alpha can be derived from the Spearman-Brown prophecy formula, and its formula is given as follows:

$$\alpha = \frac{k}{k-1}\left(1 - \frac{\sum \sigma_i^2}{\sigma_x^2}\right)$$

where

α = coefficient alpha

k = number of items in the scale

$\sum \sigma_i^2$ = sum of the variances of the items

σ_x^2 = variance of the scale's composite score

Pedhazur and Schmelkin (1991) show that the variance of the composite score for a set of items, σ_x^2, is equal to the sum of the variances of those items, $\sum \sigma_i^2$, plus two times the sum of the covariances of all possible pairs of items, $2\sigma_{ij}$ (where $i \neq j$). Thus, a practical formula for the coefficient alpha is as follows:

$$\alpha = \frac{k}{k-1}\left(1 - \frac{\sum \sigma_i^2}{\sum \sigma_i^2 + 2\sum \sigma_{ij}}\right)$$

If there is little correlation among the items, the sum of the covariances among the pairs of items, $2\sum \sigma_{ij}$, will be close to 0; therefore, the ratio of the two variance expressions will be equal to 1, and α will equal 0. The higher the correlation among the items, the larger will be the expression $2\sum \sigma_{ij}$, with a resulting higher value of α. Values for α should range between 0 and 1, with higher values indicating greater reliability among the items in the set. Green and colleagues (2000) warn, however, that coefficient alpha can fall outside the range of these values if there are a number of negative correlations among the items being considered.

Limitations of the Alpha Coefficient

Although coefficient alpha has avoided many of the pitfalls inherent in split-half reliability, the size of coefficient alpha continues to be influenced not only by the size of the correlation among the items but also by the number of items in the set. Pedhazur and Schmelkin (1991) demonstrate that increasing the number of items (k) in the set dramatically increases the number of covariances in the set. As a result, the expression in the denominator, $\sum \sigma_i^2 + 2\sum \sigma_{ij}$, increases at a faster rate relative to the numerator, $\sum \sigma_i^2$. Therefore, as we saw with the Spearman-Brown formulas, increasing the number of items in an instrument will increase the size of coefficient alpha even when the correlations among the items are small. When the variances of the items are all equal, the formula for standardized coefficient α is given as follows (Pedhazur & Schmelkin, 1991):

$$\alpha = \frac{k\bar{r}_{ij}}{1 + (k-1)\bar{r}_{ij}}$$

where

k = number of items

$\bar{r}_{ij}$ = average correlation among the k items

Kuder-Richardson Coefficient

Cronbach's coefficient alpha is intended for use with items that are scored on a continuum, i.e., ordinal level of measurement (e.g., 1-5 or 1-7). When the items in the instrument are scored dichotomously with values 0 and 1 (e.g., 1 = *true* vs. 0 = *false*; 1 = *yes* vs. 0 = *no*), the Kuder-Richardson 20 formula (KR-20) (Kuder & Richardson, 1937) is used instead. This formula merely substitutes the variance for a binary item ($\sigma_i^2 = p_i q_i$) into the formula for α:

$$\alpha = \frac{k}{k-1}\left(1 - \frac{\sum p_i q_i}{\sigma_x^2}\right)$$

where

p = proportion of respondents who have a score of 1 on item i

q = proportion of respondents who have a score of 0 on item i

σ_x^2 = variance of the scale's composite score

ASSESSING RELIABILITY USING CRONBACH'S ALPHA: A COMPUTER EXAMPLE

Both SAS and SPSS for Windows will generate a set of Cronbach's alphas for the group of items that load on a given factor. These alphas can be used to evaluate a factor's internal consistency and to help determine where items best fit when they load on multiple factors.

In Table 6.1B, we present the rotated factor structure matrix for the 20-item CGTS scale that was generated using the factor analysis program in SPSS for Windows. In this example, we used principal axis factoring with Oblimin rotation that we discussed in detail in Chapters 4 and 5.[3] The commands used to generate this analysis were *Analyze . . . Data Reduction . . . Factor*. A four-factor solution was selected and loadings less than the absolute value of .40 were suppressed. The same information generated in SAS is presented in Table B6.1B, Appendix B. As we indicated earlier, Cronbach's alphas can be generated in SAS using the PROC CORR commands presented in Figure B6.1, Appendix B.

The number of items with significant loadings ($\geq .40$) on the four rotated factors presented in Table 6.1B ranged from 3 items (for Factor 4) to 11 items (for Factor 1). Four items, C6, C14, C17, and C20, loaded $> .40$ on multiple factors. To evaluate the internal consistency of each of these four factors, we would generate coefficient alphas for each of the factors independently, looking especially closely at what happens to coefficient alpha when the items are removed from consideration. As an example, we will run this analysis on the 11 items in the CGTS scale that loaded $\geq .40$ on Factor 1.

As with split-half reliability, coefficient alpha is generated in SPSS for Windows using the commands *Analysis . . . Scale . . . Reliability Analysis . . . .* These commands will open the *Reliability Analysis* Window in Figure 6.2. The 11 items that loaded $\geq .40$ on Factor 1 have been chosen for analysis. Notice that the *Alpha Model* has been selected (Figure 6.2, ①). This will generate Cronbach's coefficient alpha. If the items have dichotomous responses, this analysis is the same as the Kuder-Richardson 20 (KR-20) coefficient.

By clicking on *Statistics . . .* , the Statistics dialog box is opened and we have our choice of descriptive statistics, summaries, interitem matrices, ANOVA table, as well as other statistics both for the scales and the items contained within the scales (Figure 6.2). For this analysis, we will examine the descriptive statistics, summaries, interitem correlations, and the ANOVA table ②. These analyses will help identify problems with the data (e.g., undetected coding errors or unexpected negative correlations that may require the rescaling of items) and determine whether we meet the assumption of equality of means for parallel tests. It should be emphasized that a reliability analysis should not be interpreted until all errors have been corrected or rescaling of items has been undertaken. Remember the well-documented truth: *GIGO* (*Garbage In Is Garbage Out*)!

Recoding Negative Correlations

Suppose, for example, that we found that an item (e.g., Item C3) was negatively correlated with the other items in the correlation matrix. Negative correlations can drastically affect the value of coefficient alpha (even to the point of producing out-of-range alpha coefficients) and can lead to misinterpretation of the coefficient. To change

Figure 6.2   Reliability Analysis Dialog Boxes Opened in SPSS for Windows

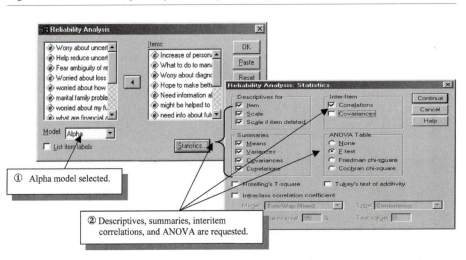

① Alpha model selected.

② Descriptives, summaries, interitem correlations, and ANOVA are requested.

these negative signs into positive correlations of equal magnitude, we would reverse-code these items. This can be accomplished in SPSS for Windows through the *Recode . . . Into a Different Variable . . .* command. The recoded item (e.g., C3) would be assigned a new variable name (e.g., RC3) and the old values for C3 (e.g., 1) recoded into new values (e.g., 5). This newly created variable, RC3, would then be substituted for C3 in subsequent reliability analyses.

Additional Potential Analyses

Three sets of analyses have *not* been requested in this analysis: *Hotelling's T square, Tukey's test of additivity,* and the *intraclass correlation coefficient. Hotelling's T square* is a multivariate test of equality of means and gives similar information on the multivariate level to univariate F tests in ANOVA. *Tukey's test of [non]additivity* produces a test of the assumption that there is no evidence of multiplicative interaction among the items in the scale (SPSS, Inc., 1999). The *intraclass correlation coefficient* produces a measure of consistency or agreement of values of the items within the respondents. It is commonly used when assessing interrater agreement. Because this is not an issue here, we will not be discussing this procedure.

Table 6.3 (A-D) presents the results of the coefficient alpha reliability analysis of the first factor of the CGTS scale that was generated

Table 6.3   Results of the Reliability Analysis for Factor 1 of the 20-Item CGTS Scale Generated in SPSS for Windows

A.   Descriptive Statistics

		Mean	Std Dev	Cases
1.	C1	3.1122	1.1428	205.0
2.	C3	3.9122	1.1342	205.0
3.	C6	3.1707	1.1903	205.0
4.	C7	3.5610	1.1557	205.0
5.	C10	3.8341	1.0534	205.0
6.	C12	3.0780	1.3769	205.0
7.	C13	3.2146	1.1258	205.0
8.	C14	3.7220	1.2702	205.0
9.	C16	3.8293	1.1004	205.0
10.	C17	3.3463	1.0719	205.0
11.	C20	3.6732	1.0504	205.0

① Item summary statistics.

B.   Correlation Matrix

R E L I A B I L I T Y   A N A L Y S I S - S C A L E   (A L P H A)

Correlation Matrix

② Lowest and highest correlated items.

	C1	C3	C6	C7	C10
C1	1.0000				
C3	.3367	1.0000			
C6	.1696	.3815	1.0000		
C7	.4457	.6099	.3541	1.0000	
C10	.3413	.4924	.3198	.4956	1.0000
C12	.4119	.4470	.3208	.4190	.5835
C13	.3384	.6483	.3713	.5362	.6171
C14	.0655	.4423	.4303	.3171	.3061
C16	.2063	.6006	.4116	.4727	.5168
C17	.1722	.4001	.2915	.2420	.3811
C20	.4309	.5806	.3781	.5111	.4735

Correlation Matrix

	C12	C13	C14	C16	C17
C12	1.0000				
C13	.4034	1.0000			
C14	.3320	.3813	1.0000		
C16	.3130	.4650	.2499	1.0000	
C17	.3469	.4662	.3519	.4202	1.0000
C20	.4210	.5612	.2953	.5197	.4319

	C20
C20	1.0000

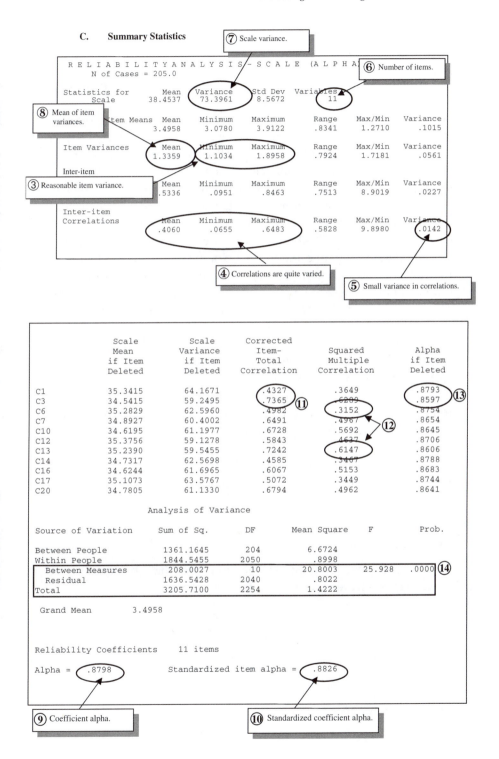

C.   Summary Statistics

⑦ Scale variance.

R E L I A B I L I T Y A N A L Y S I S — S C A L E (A L P H A)
      N of Cases = 205.0

⑥ Number of items.

Statistics for Scale	Mean 38.4537	Variance 73.3961	Std Dev 8.5672	Variables 11		

⑧ Mean of item variances.

Item Means	Mean 3.4958	Minimum 3.0780	Maximum 3.9122	Range .8341	Max/Min 1.2710	Variance .1015
Item Variances	Mean 1.3359	Minimum 1.1034	Maximum 1.8958	Range .7924	Max/Min 1.7181	Variance .0561

Inter-item

③ Reasonable item variance.

	Mean .5336	Minimum .0951	Maximum .8463	Range .7513	Max/Min 8.9019	Variance .0227
Inter-item Correlations	Mean .4060	Minimum .0655	Maximum .6483	Range .5828	Max/Min 9.8980	Variance .0142

④ Correlations are quite varied.

⑤ Small variance in correlations.

	Scale Mean if Item Deleted	Scale Variance if Item Deleted	Corrected Item-Total Correlation	Squared Multiple Correlation	Alpha if Item Deleted
C1	35.3415	64.1671	.4327	.3649	.8793
C3	34.5415	59.2495	.7365	.6209	.8597
C6	35.2829	62.5960	.4982	.3152	.8754
C7	34.8927	60.4002	.6491	.4967	.8654
C10	34.6195	61.1977	.6728	.5692	.8645
C12	35.3756	59.1278	.5843	.4637	.8706
C13	35.2390	59.5455	.7242	.6147	.8606
C14	34.7317	62.5698	.4585	.3467	.8788
C16	34.6244	61.6965	.6067	.5153	.8683
C17	35.1073	63.5767	.5072	.3449	.8744
C20	34.7805	61.1330	.6794	.4962	.8641

⑪ ⑫ ⑬

Analysis of Variance

Source of Variation	Sum of Sq.	DF	Mean Square	F	Prob.
Between People	1361.1645	204	6.6724		
Within People	1844.5455	2050	.8998		
Between Measures	208.0027	10	20.8003	25.928	.0000
Residual	1636.5428	2040	.8022		
Total	3205.7100	2254	1.4222		

⑭

Grand Mean   3.4958

Reliability Coefficients   11 items

Alpha = .8798   Standardized item alpha = .8826

⑨ Coefficient alpha.

⑩ Standardized coefficient alpha.

using the SPSS for Windows commands presented in Figure 6.2. The reliability analysis generated in SAS is presented in Table B6.3 in Appendix B.

Table 6.3A presents the descriptive statistics that were requested. Given that the scale range for the items was 1 to 5, all of the means are in the middle to high range (range of means: 3.0-3.9) ①. Of possible concern would be the higher means for Items C3, C10, and C16. Despite their respectable standard deviations (all were greater than 1.0), these items should be examined more closely for possible ceiling effects (i.e., having too many respondents strongly agree with these statements).

The interitem correlations presented in the matrix of Table 6.3B range from a low of .0655 between Items C1 and C14 to a high of .6483 between C3 and C13 ②. Although there are some items that have very low correlations with one another, none of the interitem correlations in the matrix are so high (e.g., > .80) as to suggest that items are duplicates of one another. There are also no negative correlations in the matrix. This means that we can proceed with our item analysis and interpretation of the reliability analyses presented in Table 6.3.

The statistics presented in Table 6.3C summarize the scale and item statistics (e.g., means, variances, covariances, and average interitem correlations) for the 11 items that loaded $\geq$ .40 on the first factor of the 20-item CGTS scale. The item variances seem reasonable, with a minimum of 1.1034 to a maximum of 1.8958 (Table 6.3C, ③). The interitem correlations, however, are quite varied, ranging from .0655 to .6483 ④, with an average interitem correlation of .4060. Notice, however, that the variance for the interitem correlations is small (.0142) ⑤. The closer this variance value is to 0, the more consistency there is among the interitem correlations.

Coefficient alpha

You will recall from our earlier discussion that one equation for Cronbach's coefficient alpha was given as follows:

$$r_{kk} = \frac{k}{k-1}\left(1 - \frac{\sum \sigma_i^2}{\sigma_x^2}\right)$$

where

r_{kk} = coefficient alpha

k = number of items in the scale

$\sum \sigma_i^2$ = sum of the variances of the individual items

σ_x^2 = variance for the composite scale

Table 6.3C gives us all of these values. The number of items, k, is 11, the number of items loading on Factor 1 ⑥. σ_x^2 is the variance of the composite scale, 73.3961 ⑦. $\sum \sigma_i^2$, the sum of the variances for the individual items, can be derived for the definition of the mean of the item variances (1.3359) ⑧ and solving for $\sum \sigma_i^2$:

$$\bar{x}_{\sigma_i^2} = \frac{\sum \sigma_i^2}{k} = 1.3359$$

$$\sum \sigma_i^2 = \bar{x}_{\sigma_i^2} k = (1.3359)(11) = 14.6949$$

Given this information, the coefficient alpha that is presented to us in Table 6.3D (.8798) ⑨ can be obtained as follows:

$$r_{kk} = \frac{k}{k-1}\left(1 - \frac{\sum \sigma_i^2}{\sigma_x^2}\right) = \frac{11}{11-1}\left(1 - \frac{14.6949}{73.3961}\right) = (1.1)(1 - .2002) = .8798$$

The standardized item alpha, .8826, which is also presented in Table 6.3D ⑩, is derived from the average interitem correlation, .4060, given in Table 6.3C ④, as

$$\alpha = \frac{k\bar{r}_{ij}}{1 + (k-1)\bar{r}_{ij}} = \frac{(11)(.4060)}{1 + (11-1)(.4060)} = \frac{4.466}{5.06} = .8826$$

The standardized alpha is reported when a scale score has been computed by summing items that have been either standardized like z scores to have uniform means and standard deviations or when the item means and standard deviations are equal. Because we do not have items that have been standardized or equal means and standard deviations, we would report the unstandardized coefficient alpha.

Our conclusion is that our coefficient alpha is strong: .8798, or 87.98%, of the variance of the total scores on this subscale can be attributed to reliable, or systematic, variance. As we discussed earlier, a possible concern with this level of reliability is that the subscale that is represented by Factor 1 may have too narrow a focus. Let us now examine the items that loaded strongly on Factor 1 in greater depth.

Undertaking an Item Analysis of Factor 1

Now we are ready to determine which items we might want to exclude from Factor 1. As we have indicated throughout this text, our decisions should be based not only on our statistical findings but also on our knowledge about how the items fit together both rationally and theoretically.

Table 6.3D presents the scale analysis for the 11 items that loaded $\geq .40$ on Factor 1 of the CGTS scale. These results include the scale means, variances, corrected item-total correlation with the item deleted, the squared multiple correlation, and the coefficient alpha if the item had been deleted. The *scale means if item deleted* (i.e., the sum of the items without the targeted item) and *the scale variance if item deleted* presented in the first two columns of Table 6.3D appear to be fairly consistent across items.

The *corrected item-total correlation* presented in Column 3 is the correlation between the given item and the total scale score, having removed the given item from the total score. If Factor 1 is internally consistent, the items that load on it will demonstrate strong positive correlations with the total scale score. A negative item-total correlation would suggest that the given item is measuring a different construct from the other items, and values close to zero imply no relationship between the given item and other items loading on the factor. The item-total correlations for our 11 items that loaded on Factor 1 range from .4327 for Item C1 to .7365 for Item C3 ①. These relatively high item-total correlations are not surprising because we had excluded items that loaded < .40 on Factor 1.

In the fourth column, we are presented with squared multiple correlations (R^2) for each of the items. These R^2 values represent the proportion of variance in a given item that is shared with the other items. R^2 values can range between 0 and 1.00, with higher values indicating greater consistency among the items. Our R^2 values ranged from .3152 to .6289. For Item C6, for example, only 31.52% of its variance ($.3152 \times 100 = 31.52$) is shared with the other items that loaded $\geq .40$ on Factor 1. In contrast, 62.89% of the variance in Item C13 is shared variance with the other items ②.

Coefficient Alpha if Item Deleted

The final column in Table 6.3D presents information regarding what would happen to the coefficient alpha for Factor 1 if the given item were to be deleted. This information will help us decide whether to retain an item on a factor and, when faced with multiple loadings, on which factor the multiple-loading item should be placed. We would not want to remove an item from a factor if it seriously lowers the value of coefficient alpha when deleted. However, there might be something to be gained by removing an item from a factor if its removal increases coefficient alpha. We would also want to place a multiple-loading item on the factor where it makes the most positive contribution to the size of coefficient alpha.

The results presented in Table 6.3D indicate that our unstandardized coefficient alpha is .8798 ⑨. All of the *alphas, when deleted,* that are presented in the last column of this table are lower than .8798, ranging from .8597 (C3) to .8793 (C1) ⑬. Although this finding would indicate that all of the items are contributing to high reliability, it is also apparent that none of the items seriously reduces the value of coefficient alpha by being removed from the factor.

Nevertheless, coefficient alpha would be most affected by dropping C3 and least affected by dropping C1. Additional items that could be deleted without seriously affecting coefficient alpha are C6, C14, and C17. Notice that these are also the same items that have the lowest corrected item-total correlation (.4327-.5072). These last three items are also among the four items on Factor 1 that have multiple loadings with other factors (Table 6.1B). In a moment, we will evaluate these multiple loadings to determine where best to place the four items. First, however, let us look at the results that are presented in the ANOVA table (Table 6.3D).

The Analysis of Variance (ANOVA) Table

The 11 items that loaded significantly on Factor 1 were all measured using a 5-point Likert scale. Given that the item responses for the 11 items were similar, it is not unreasonable to expect that, if Factor 1 is internally consistent, the means for all these 11 items will be equal. This is, in fact, one of the assumptions of the strictly parallel form of split-half reliability that we discussed earlier in this chapter. The *analysis of variance (ANOVA)* table that is presented in Table 6.3D will help us to determine whether, indeed, we have equality of item means.

The part of the ANOVA table that will provide us with information regarding the equality of item means is the *Within People . . . Between Measures* source of variation ⑭. This between-measures variation

ifferences among the k item means. Because there are
$k - 1 = 10$ ($11 - 1 = 10$) between-measures degrees of
tween-measures variation will be compared to the
sidual source of variation with $(N - 1)(k - 1) = (205 - 1)$
u_j. The resulting F ratio, 25.9288, is obtained by dividing
the mean square between measures by the mean square residual
(error):

$$F = \frac{MS_{\text{between measures}}}{MS_{\text{residuals}}} = \frac{SS_{\text{between measures}}/df_{\text{between measures}}}{SS_{\text{residuals}}/df_{\text{residuals}}}$$

$$= \frac{208.0027/10}{1636.5428/2040} = \frac{20.8003}{.8022} = 25.928$$

This F ratio is significant at $p = .0000$ ⑭, indicating that the null
hypothesis of equality of item means is rejected. There is significant
variation in item means. Although this discrepancy in item means
would be of concern had we been trying to create strictly parallel forms
of the same scale, this is not a serious problem in our preliminary item
analysis, especially when the scale means, if the item were deleted, do
not indicate any serious differences.

Deciding Where to Place
Items With Multiple Loadings

As we indicated earlier, there are four items in the factor structure
matrix (C6, C14, C17, and C20) that load $\geq .40$ on multiple factors.
Although none of these items would seriously reduce the coefficient
alpha for Factor 1 if they were removed, some of their content areas
may fit better with one factor than another. If, however, Cronbach's
alpha for each of the factors to which the item could be potentially
assigned would be higher without the item and the item does not help
to increase the interpretability of the factor, then the item should be
eliminated completely from the instrument.

Table 6.4 presents the items, their content area, and the factors on
which the items loaded. The goal is to group items together so that the
factor on which they are placed represents a consistent content area.
The content area of Item C6 (*worry about diagnosis*), for example, has a
better fit with the items that load on Factor 2, e.g., Item C2 (*uncertain
diagnosis*) and Item C4 (*reduce uncertainty*), than those that load on

Table 6.4   Content Areas and Factors on Which the 20 CGTS Items Loaded

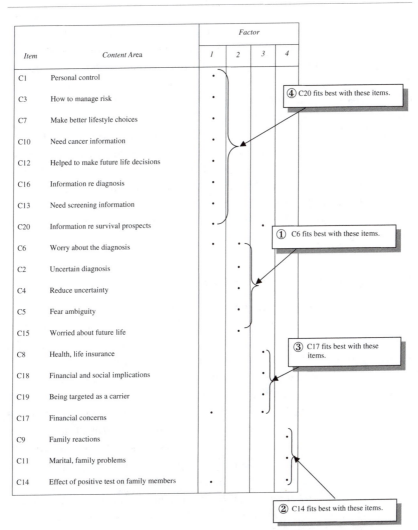

Item	Content Area	Factor 1	2	3	4
C1	Personal control	•			
C3	How to manage risk	•			
C7	Make better lifestyle choices	•			
C10	Need cancer information	•			
C12	Helped to make future life decisions	•			
C16	Information re diagnosis	•			
C13	Need screening information	•			
C20	Information re survival prospects	•		•	
C6	Worry about the diagnosis	•	•		
C2	Uncertain diagnosis		•		
C4	Reduce uncertainty		•		
C5	Fear ambiguity		•		
C15	Worried about future life		•		
C8	Health, life insurance			•	
C18	Financial and social implications			•	
C19	Being targeted as a carrier			•	
C17	Financial concerns	•		•	
C9	Family reactions				•
C11	Marital, family problems				•
C14	Effect of positive test on family members	•			•

④ C20 fits best with these items.

① C6 fits best with these items.

③ C17 fits best with these items.

② C14 fits best with these items.

Factor 1, e.g., Item C1 (*personal control*) and Item C13 (*need screening information*) (Table 6.4, ①). Similarly, Items C14 (*family member issues*) ② and C17 (*financial concerns*) ③ fit better with those items that loaded on Factor 4 (e.g., C9, *family reactions*) and Factor 3 (e.g., C19, *being targeted as a* carrier), respectively, than they did with the items on Factor 1. Item C20 (*information re survival prospects*) is most consistent with the items that loaded singularly on Factor 1, e.g., C16 (*information re diagnosis*) and therefore will be retained on Factor 1 ④.

Table 6.4 also reveals that there may be two main content themes running through the eight items that best load on Factor 1: *information-seeking* (four items) and *desire for personal control* (four items). Although it might be argued that *seeking information* may satisfy a *desire for personal control,* these eight items may need to be isolated and a new factor analysis undertaken on just those items to determine if there are multiple factors residing within this single factor.

Table 6.5 summarizes the changes in the coefficient alpha for the four factors before and after the multiple-loading items were placed on the most appropriate factor. Factor 1 did not appear to lose much as a result of reducing the number of items from 11 to 8; its coefficient alpha only declined .0043, from .8798 to .8755. The other three factors, however, gained in reliability, confirming that the assignment choices were appropriate.

Refining Factors Through Item Reduction

As indicated earlier, factors can be refined through successive factoring of a set of items within a single factor. We could, for example, choose to factor analyze Factor 1 a second time to determine if the eight items represent a single factor or several smaller factors.

A second approach to successive factoring is through item reduction. To illustrate, when the first author initially analyzed the 60-item College Student Hassles Scale (CSHS), she found that 26 items from the CSHS loaded > .40 on Factor 1. Coefficient alpha for this 26-item factor was .9182. Should all 26 items be retained on this factor, or, as we indicated earlier in our discussion of the Spearman-Brown prophecy formula, is there some *point of diminishing returns* at which the scale's reliability is no longer significantly increased by the addition of items?

This is a critical issue for researchers because, as we saw earlier, the reliability of a scale based on a factor depends in part on both the length of the scale and the format of the item responses. The more items in a scale and the greater the number of response categories, the higher will be the scale's reliability. A reasonable goal is to derive a highly reliable subscale that has 10 to 15 items. This task is relatively easy to accomplish if the responses to the items are in Likert-scale format (e.g., on a 5-point scale) but more difficult to achieve if the items have been scored with dichotomous *yes/no* responses.

Table 6.5   Reliability Results from Reassigning Multiple-Loading Items

Factor	Before		After		Gain in α
	N	α	N	α	
1	11	.8798	8	.8755	−.0043
2	4	.7951	5	.8214	+.0263
3	3	.7716	4	.7918	+.0202
4	2	.6250	3	.7103	+.0853

The following procedure was used to determine the best cutoff for achieving the maximum reliability with the fewest number of items. First, the four items that loaded highest on Factor 1 were identified and that four-item scale's coefficient alpha was calculated. Then the two next-highest-loading items were added to the initial four items, and this six-item scale's coefficient alpha was calculated. This process of adding the two next-highest-loading items to the previous smaller set of items continued until the total of 26 items was reached. In each instance, the scales' reliabilities were calculated using the *Reliability* program in SPSS for Windows. Pett found this easiest to achieve using the syntax commands in Figure 6.3.

The items in the variable list are listed according to the size of their loadings on Factor 1 ①. That is, H8 had the highest loading on Factor 1 and H26 had the lowest loading. This made it easier to add the next-highest-loadings to the reliability analysis. An alpha coefficient was first obtained for the top four highest-loading items ② followed by the top six items ③.

The coefficient alphas for the different scale compositions (i.e., four items, six items, eight items, etc.) can then be plotted against the size of the scale to determine if the addition of a two-item set results in substantially higher alphas. This can be ascertained by observing the slope of the curve of the plots. Where the scale's reliability plot

Figure 6.3   SPSS Syntax Commands for Generating Alpha Coefficients

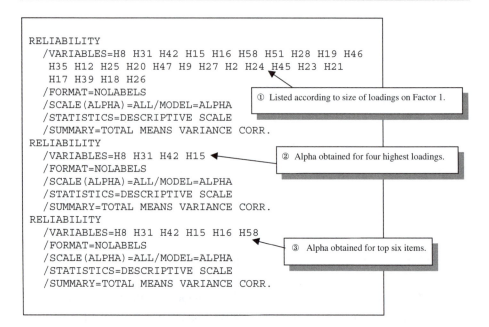

```
RELIABILITY
  /VARIABLES=H8 H31 H42 H15 H16 H58 H51 H28 H19 H46
  H35 H12 H25 H20 H47 H9 H27 H2 H24 H45 H23 H21
  H17 H39 H18 H26
  /FORMAT=NOLABELS
  /SCALE(ALPHA)=ALL/MODEL=ALPHA
  /STATISTICS=DESCRIPTIVE SCALE
  /SUMMARY=TOTAL MEANS VARIANCE CORR.
RELIABILITY
  /VARIABLES=H8 H31 H42 H15
  /FORMAT=NOLABELS
  /SCALE(ALPHA)=ALL/MODEL=ALPHA
  /STATISTICS=DESCRIPTIVE SCALE
  /SUMMARY=TOTAL MEANS VARIANCE CORR.
RELIABILITY
  /VARIABLES=H8 H31 H42 H15 H16 H58
  /FORMAT=NOLABELS
  /SCALE(ALPHA)=ALL/MODEL=ALPHA
  /STATISTICS=DESCRIPTIVE SCALE
  /SUMMARY=TOTAL MEANS VARIANCE CORR.
```

① Listed according to size of loadings on Factor 1.

② Alpha obtained for four highest loadings.

③ Alpha obtained for top six items.

appears to level off is the point at which it may no longer be useful to add items.

This scatterplot can be generated in SPSS for Windows by first creating a new data file consisting of two variables: the number of items in the set and the resulting coefficient alpha for that number of items. Then the commands *Graphs . . . Interactive . . . Scatterplot . . .* are highlighted and the variables that represent the alpha coefficients and sample size as coordinates are added.

Figure 6.4 presents the plot that was obtained for the 26 items that loaded on Factor 1 when the College Student Hassles Scale was submitted for analysis. Through successive reliability analyses, this subscale was reduced from 26 items to 12 based on the examination of the plot in Figure 6.4. At 16 items, the increase in coefficient alpha appeared to level off (Figure 6.4, ①). By reducing the number of items loading on Factor 1 from 26 items to 12 items, Cronbach's alpha was reduced from .9182 (26 items) to .8624 (12 items), a reduction of .0558. Twelve items were considered to be superior to a 16-item subscale (alpha = .8921) ② because of concern for the length of the test.

Is this item reduction procedure an art, good science, or manipulation? It is our opinion that refining factors is a good measurement

Figure 6.4   Plot of Coefficient Alpha Against the Number of Items

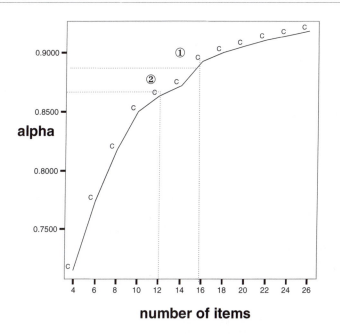

construction technique that will, hopefully, be based on good science. In test construction, the researcher wishes to add items to a scale that are similar and delete items that do not contribute substantially to internal consistency. The refinement of the item set and therefore the factor ensures that the scale fits the model of measurement better by adding only those items that are from the same (small) domain.

A warning, however, is in order: reliability goes hand-in-hand with validity. Although plotting item reliability against number of items may help the researcher to visualize the *diminishing* returns of reliability, the focus of item analysis should not only be on maximizing reliability with the minimum number of items but also on evaluating how well items fit together and represent our potential construct of interest.

TWO ADDITIONAL RELIABILITY ESTIMATES: TEMPORAL STABILITY AND EQUIVALENCE

At the beginning of our discussion of scale reliability, we indicated that there were three dimensions of reliability: internal consistency, temporal stability, and equivalence. Because it is so critical to our use of factor analysis in scale development, our discussion of reliability has mainly focused on internal consistency. Before we conclude this discussion, we need to address, however briefly, two additional dimensions of reliability: *temporal stability* and *equivalence*. For further information concerning these two issues, we refer you to Crocker and Algina (1986), Kline (2000a), Nunnally and Bernstein (1994), and Streiner and Norman (1995).

Assessing Temporal Stability

Temporal stability of an instrument is concerned with the consistency of repeated measures of the same construct using the same instrument and is often referred to as *test-retest reliability* (Burns & Grove, 2001; Kline, 1986, 2000a; Polit & Hungler, 1999). The assumption underlying this type of reliability measure is that, assuming that the person being rated does not change, the construct of interest remains the same at any testing time and that change is the result of random error.

To establish test-retest reliability, the researcher administers the instrument to a specific group of subjects and then, after a specified period of time, readministers the same instrument to the same group of subjects under the same conditions as the first administration. Several methods are available to evaluate the comparability of the two sets of scores from the two time periods. Most simply, the two sets of scores can be correlated using a simple correlation (e.g., Pearson product moment correlation or Spearman rho). This correlation is then taken to be an assessment of the temporal stability of the instrument. Values of the correlation coefficient can range between -1.0 and $+1.0$. The closer the test-retest correlation is to 1.0, the greater the stability of the instrument.

A more complex but much more informative method of evaluation is the application of generalizability theory to assess the dependability of a particular scale (Cronbach, Gleser, Nanda, & Rajaratnam, 1972; Shavelson & Webb, 1991). This approach uses various ANOVA models to simultaneously evaluate the simple and interactive effects of multiple sources of measurement error (e.g., person, time, and person × time interaction) on the variability of item scores. To describe this rather complicated approach in any detail is not the intention of this text. Rather, we refer you to the Shavelson and Webb (1991) text, which provides an excellent overview of the logic and application of generalizability theory.

Factors That Influence Test-Retest Reliability

There are a number of factors that can affect temporal stability and, as a consequence, potentially lead to inflated estimates of test-retest reliability (Kline, 2000a). These include characteristics of the sample, respondent maturity, changes in respondent emotional states, differences in the testing situation, recollection of previous answers, difficulty of the items, sample size, and the construct being tested (e.g., state vs. trait).

A particular concern when undertaking an assessment of temporal stability is the time to be allotted between test and retest. If the time period between the two testing periods is too short, the subjects may remember their answers and repeat them. This can lead to inflated estimates of reliability (Pedhazur & Schmelkin, 1991). Conversely, longer time periods between administrations create their own problems (e.g., subjects undergoing true changes with regard to a given construct), with resulting underestimates of reliability. The challenge is to select a time period that would maximize the potential for an accurate estimate of the stability of a measure.

It is generally suggested that the time period between the testing times be short, e.g., 1 to 2 weeks (Nunnally & Bernstein, 1994; Pedhazur & Schmelkin, 1991). If the researcher wants to assess the stability of the scores over a longer period of time, Nunnally and Bernstein (1994) suggest that the time period could be extended to 6 months or more. These authors also warn against overreliance on test-retest reliability evaluation because items on measures with poor internal consistency may in fact be highly correlated with themselves in a test-retest situation.

Equivalence of an Instrument

In an effort to avoid the problems encountered with temporal stability, some researchers have turned to examining the correlation between the scores of two equivalent forms. *Equivalence* compares the difference between two versions or *parallel forms* of the same instrument (Burns & Grove, 2001; Pedhazur & Schmelkin, 1991; Polit & Hungler, 1999). According to this model, two parallel measures of the construct in question are administered to the same group of subjects. The correlation between the two forms (sometimes called the *coefficient of equivalence*) is then used as an estimate of both scales' reliability.

Evaluating equivalence has many of the same difficulties as split-half reliability, especially with regard to effectively creating equivalent parallel forms. There are also not a lot of guidelines regarding timing of administration of these parallel forms or acceptable levels of reliability. This absence may be due primarily to the fact that there are very restrictive assumptions underlying the concept of parallel forms (Pedhazur & Schmelkin, 1991). It is also a drain on limited resources to develop two exact forms of the same instrument. Nunnally and Bernstein (1994), however, do suggest comparing the results of administering these parallel forms on the same day with that obtained from a 2-week delay. Kline (2000a) indicates that the correlation between two parallel forms should be at least .9 because, with anything lower, it would be difficult to assume that the two instruments are indeed parallel. With strictly parallel forms, it is also assumed that the means, standard deviations, and distributions of scores are also equal (Kline, 2000a).

SUMMARY

Throughout this rather lengthy chapter, we have attempted to provide you with guidelines for refining the factors generated in a factor analysis. We have also outlined for you approaches to assessing the internal consistency of the generated factors. The factor analysis example that we used to introduce you to factor refining and internal consistency was the 20-item Concerns About Genetic Testing Scale (CGTS) provided for you in Appendix A. Figure 6.5 summarizes the steps of refining a set of factors generated in a factor analysis and of examining those generated factors for their internal consistency. In Chapter 7, we will examine approaches to the interpretation and naming of factors as well as the utility of generating factor scores.

Figure 6.5 A Suggested Approach to Refining the Factor and Evaluating Its Internal Consistency

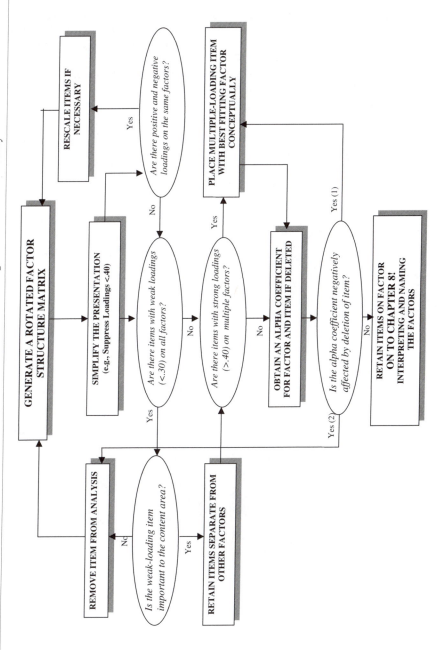

NOTES

1. See Chapter 5 for an in-depth discussion of the meaning of this rotation.

2. Please note that the term *subscale* is being used to describe the set of items that load on a given factor, for example, the 11 items with loadings =.40 on Factor 1 of the CGTS Scale.

3. Principal components analysis with Varimax rotation generated the same four factors with similar item loadings.

7

Interpreting Factors and Generating Factor Scores

In Chapter 6, we examined approaches to evaluating and refining the factors as well as assessing their internal consistency. Let us assume that you have identified the items that best load on given factors and are ready to interpret the meaning of these factors and to assign them names. Once these factors have been named, you might also want to generate factor scores for the persons who completed the instrument. These factor scores could then be used to examine the relationships between scores received on the named factors and other variables of interest (e.g., age, gender, and ethnicity of the respondent). These issues will be the focus of Chapter 7.

INTERPRETING THE FACTORS

Interpretation and naming of factors "should be a natural outgrowth of the theoretical considerations that have led to the definition of the construct" (Pedhazur & Schmelkin, 1991, p. 622). Did the items that were selected as representing similar aspects of the phenomenon share high loadings on the same factors? Did those items that were selected to represent different aspects of the phenomenon have high loadings on different factors (Pedhazur & Schmelkin, 1991)?

The researcher begins this process by closely examining the loadings of the items with the factors not only to determine the strength of the loadings but also to ascertain whether the item loadings are consistent with the original conceptualizations before the factor analysis began. One convenient way to examine these loadings is to sort the factor pattern matrix so that items with high loadings on a factor will be placed together. It is also possible to suppress items for which loadings are very low. Sorting and suppressing item loadings can be accomplished in the SPSS for Windows factor analysis program (*Analyze . . . Data Reduction . . . Factor*) by opening the *Options . . .* dialog box and in the *Coefficient Display Format . . .* indicating the following:

- Sorted by size
- Suppress absolute values less than . . . [.40]

A similar sorting process can be undertaken in SAS PROC FACTOR using the subcommand REORDER (Figure B7.1, Appendix B). This option reorders the factor loadings for the items on the output. Items with the highest absolute loading on the first factor are displayed first, from largest to smallest loading, followed by items with the highest absolute loading on the second factor, and so on. Using the FUZZ = .40 subcommand in SAS (v 8.2), loadings less than .40 can be suppressed. This output is presented in Table B6.1B, Appendix B.

During the interpretative process, it is important to decide how high a factor loading needs to be if that item is to be regarded as an important contributor to the interpretation of that factor. Items that load strongest on a given factor are considered to be most "like" the construct that the factor represents and those items that have weak loadings are least "like" the potential construct. Unlike structure equation modeling, which generates t tests to help evaluate the sufficiency of loadings on a latent variable, there are no definitive statistical tests in factor analysis to indicate whether an item is *significant* for the purposes of factor interpretation.

Comrey and Lee (1992) offer some guidelines for evaluating factor loadings. They suggest that in an orthogonal rotation, no item that loads < .30 should be part of defining a factor because less than 9% ($.30^2$) of that item's variance is shared with the factor. These authors also provide the following guidelines for item-to-factor loadings in orthogonal solutions to help determine if an item should be included among those defining the factor:

.45 (20% shared variance): fair

.55 (30% shared variance): good

.63 (40% shared variance): very good

.71 (50% shared variance): excellent

In oblique solutions, the loadings in both the factor pattern and factor structure matrices must be considered because these loadings are not equivalent. Comrey and Lee (1992) suggest that the simple item-to-factor correlations that are presented in the factor structure matrix be subjected to the same guidelines outlined above to determine if an item facilitates the interpretation of the factor. Regardless of the solution, orthogonal or oblique, the researcher can be more confident in having achieved a more definitive interpretation of the factor if there are several items for which loadings on a specific factor can be classified as *very good* or *excellent* (Comrey & Lee, 1992). Like Pedhazur and Schmelkin (1991), the authors further warn against merely using statistical criteria to name a factor. Rather, the researcher needs to consider the breadth and complexity of the factor as well as its relationship to the initial conceptualization.

Comrey and Lee (1992) identify three conditions that facilitate the process of interpreting the factors:

- The higher the factor loadings, the greater is the degree of overlapping true variance between the [item] and the factor and the more the factor is like the [item] in question. (p. 241)
- The greater the number of [items] with a substantial loading on the factor, other things being equal, the easier it is to isolate what the factor probably represents. (p. 241)

Ideally, we would like to base our interpretation and naming of a factor on several high-loading items. Comrey and Lee warn, however, that if the sample of items is biased in some way (e.g., the content pool of the items is insufficient), even a large number of items may fail to represent the important characteristics of a factor.

- The more factor pure an [item] is that defines a factor, the easier it is to make inferences regarding the nature of the factor. (p. 241)

Items that are complex in structure may not be useful in increasing the factor's interpretability because of the difficulty in determining which of the many parts of the item's structure contribute to the meaning of the factor. This is one reason why it is unwise to use multiple-loading items as major descriptors of a factor.

NAMING THE FACTORS

Naming factors is a poetic, theoretical, and inductive leap. Usually three or four items with the highest loadings on a factor are selected and studied. Is there a theme or common element that these three or four items tend to suggest? If so, then a descriptive name should be selected that would be representative of all the items loaded on that factor. The item with the highest loading should provide a strong clue, particularly if the loading is $\geq$.90. When the highest loadings on a factor are lower (e.g., less than .60), the researcher is faced with potentially weak interpretations.

In selecting a name for the factor, it is best that the interpretation remain simple but at the same time suggestive as to what dimension that factor represents. Being too clever, imprudent, or indifferent in the naming of factors in an instrument is unwise. Once a factor has been given a name, the identity of the items is often lost and the given name of the factor is what is communicated to those who are interested either in using the instrument for other research or in applying the results of studies that have used the instrument (Kachigan, 1986).

If the items for the factor analysis were derived from theory or from a conceptualization, then the researcher should return to the original theory or conceptualization to name the factors. Are there items that were originally classified together that loaded together? If so, the name given that classification might be the name selected for that particular factor (Pedhazur & Schmelkin, 1991).

Hair, Anderson, Tatham, and Black (1995) suggest that situations might arise especially in exploratory phases of instrument development in which the researcher elects not to assign a specific name to a factor. The factor is then labeled as *undefined* and could be classified as

Factor I or *Factor A*. If the researcher is having difficulty naming factors that are less meaningful or less congruent, perhaps those factors might best be considered for elimination.

INTERPRETING AND NAMING THE FOUR FACTORS ON THE CGTS SCALE

Table 7.1 presents the rotated factor structure matrix for the Concerns About Genetic Testing Scale (CGTS). Included in the table are the items, their content, and the identification of which of the four factors that the item most strongly loaded (>.40). Following the decisions made in Chapter 6, the four multiple-loading items (C6, C14, C17, and C20) were placed with those items that had content area they most closely resembled.

The eight items that loaded on Factor 1 (Table 7.1) appear to have several themes running through their content area. Five of the eight items (C3, C10, C13, C16, and C20) reflect *information-seeking* related to cancer risk, screening activities, and survival prospects. The three remaining items with lower loadings (C1, C7, and C12) reflect the respondents' need for *personal control* over lifestyle choices. As we indicated in Chapter 6, although *information-seeking* may be strongly linked to *personal control*, we may want to separate out these two constructs and examine them more closely in future studies. We might also want to more closely examine the relationship of the construct *information-seeking* to *concerns about genetic testing*. Does *information-seeking* reflect a *concern* or does it represent a closely related construct, e.g., the *needs* of a person seeking genetic testing for cancer?

Factor 2 seems to represent the respondents' general *worry, uncertainty,* and *anxiety* about the future. The content area for the items on Factor 3 reflects respondent concerns about *finances, stigmatization,* and *potential discrimination*. Finally, the items on Factor 4 relate to concerns about the impact of the results of genetic testing on important *family relationships*.

Because our factor analytic solution assumed that the factors were correlated, we should also examine the factor pattern matrix to determine if our identified themes were supported in that matrix. You will recall from Chapter 6 that, for an oblique (i.e., correlated) factor analysis solution, the loadings in the factor structure matrix represent simple correlations of the items with the factors and the loadings in the factor

Table 7.1 The Loadings of the 20 CGTS Items on the Rotated Factor Structure Matrix

	Factor			
	1	2	3	4
C1 Increase of personal control	.514			
C2 Worry about uncertain diagnosis		.753		
C3 What to do to manage risk	.784			
C4 Help reduce uncertainty about future		.658		
C5 Fear ambiguity of results		.662		
C6 Worry about diagnosis I can't do anything about		.611		
C7 Hope to make better health, lifestyle choices	.735			
C8 Worried about loss of health, and life insurance coverage			.584	
C9 worried about how family will react				.722
C10 Need information about types of cancer at risk for	.729			
C11 marital family problems that might occur				.617
C12 might be helped to make future life decisions	.633			
C13 need info about future screening activities	.752			
C14 how will a positive test affect children and other family members				.677
C15 worried about my future life		.741		
C16 want info about difference between diagnosis and getting cancer	.650			
C17 financial concerns related to screening			.582	
C18 what are financial and social implications of being identified			.807	
C19 worried about being targeted as carrier			.859	
C20 want to know survival prospects	.715			

Extraction Method: Principal Axis Factoring.
Rotation Method: Oblimin with Kaiser Normalization.

pattern matrix represent the unique relationship of the item with the factor. Because these loadings are like partial regression coefficients, the differences between high and low loadings on a factor are a little more apparent (Tabachnick & Fidell, 2001).

The factor pattern matrix for the 20 CGTS items is presented in Table 7.2. The factor loadings of this matrix have been sorted by size and loadings less than .40 have been suppressed. Indeed, the pattern of these identified themes is even more obvious when we examine this factor pattern matrix (Table 7.2).

Should we accept these descriptors as *names* for the factors? Are these content areas consistent with our original conceptualization concerning the dimensions of the general construct, *Concerns About Genetic Testing*? The content areas for the four rotated factors on the CGTS are consistent with research in this area (e.g., Jacobsen, Valdimarsdottir, Brown, & Offitt, 1997; Lerman & Croyle, 1994). However, given the uncertainty about the content structure of Factor 1 and the small number of loadings on the remaining three factors, it is premature at this early stage of development of the CGTS to assign names to these factors.

Clearly, the task of interpreting and naming a factor is not a simple one. Rather, a thorough investigation of the content of a factor is necessary in order to provide the researcher with important interpretive information (Comrey & Lee, 1992). How useful is the factor? Is the content too broad to be of use or is it too specific and limited in scope? How does this identified construct fit with other identified taxonomies in the field? What is missing from this construct? In what areas do we need to direct our future factor analysis activities? As Comrey and Lee lament, "All too often, the report of a factor analysis presents a list of factors with the data variables that are highly loaded on the factors together with factor names but not a great deal else in the way of factor interpretation" (p. 244). In assigning names to the factors that have been generated in a factor analysis, we need to be extremely careful not to succumb to this temptation.

DETERMINING COMPOSITE FACTOR SCORES

Once the number of factors has been determined, it may be useful to generate a score for a particular respondent on each identified factor. These scores could be used in subsequent analyses (Kim & Mueller, 1978). For example, having identified several dimensions of a particular construct, the researcher could use the generated composite scores to represent values for the factors and to examine their relationship to demographic and psychosocial characteristics of the sample that have been measured on a continuous scale (e.g., age and level of anxiety of the respondent) or to examine differences between selected subgroups

Table 7.2   Factor Pattern Matrix for the 20-Item CGTS

Pattern Matrix[a]

	Factor			
	1	2	3	4
C7 Hope to make better health, lifestyle choices	.776			
C3 What to do to manage risk	.770			
C10 Need information about types of cancer at risk for	.695			
C13 need info about future screening activities	.665			
C16 want info about difference between diagnosis and getting cancer	.625			
C12 might be helped to make future life decisions	.615			
C20 want to know survival prospects	.597			
C1 Increase of personal control	.515			
C2 Worry about uncertain diagnosis		.720		
C5 Fear ambiguity of results		.665		
C15 worried about my future life		.658		
C4 Help reduce uncertainty about future		.628		
C6 Worry about diagnosis I can't do anything about		.487		
C19 worried about being targeted as carrier			.829	
C18 what are financial and social implications of being identified			.784	
C8 Worried about loss of health, and life insurance coverage			.578	
C17 financial concerns related to screening			.472	
C9 worried about how family will react				.716
C11 marital family problems that might occur				.616
C14 how will a positive test affect children and other family members				.608

Extraction Method: Principal Axis Factoring.
Rotation Method: Oblimin with Kaiser Normalization.
   a. Rotation converged in 7 iterations.

of respondents (e.g., gender and ethnicity). These generated factor scores could also be used as predictor variables in other studies. Plots of factor scores for pairs of factors are also useful for detecting unusual observations in the data set.

There are two basic approaches to arriving at such composite scores: calculation of factor scores and construction of factor-based scales (Pedhazur & Schmelkin, 1991). Each of these approaches has advantages and disadvantages.

Calculation of Factor Scores

A *factor score* for an individual can be estimated using a linear combination of the items that load on the factor of interest. To estimate a respondent's score on a particular factor, all of the individuals' scores on the items in the instrument pool are standardized, weighted by a generated factor score coefficient for the factor under consideration, and then summed across all items. Except for the principal components model in factor analysis, exact factor scores cannot be obtained but rather must be estimated. This is because it is only in principal components analysis (PCA) that it is assumed that all of the variance in the items can be accounted for by the factors.[1]

Factor Score Indeterminancy

Because it is assumed in PCA that all of the variance in the items can be predicted by the generated principal components, or factors, the factors are exact linear combinations of the items included in the analysis. This means that the multiple correlations that are obtained from predicting factor scores from items are equal to 1.00 and the elements in the factor score coefficient matrix (W_{jk}) are unique values (Nunnally & Bernstein, 1994). As a result, there is a unique solution to generating factor scores in PCA. The problem is, however, that the solution is unique only to the sample being studied.

In common factor analysis (of which principal axis factoring is one approach), the only variance that is considered in generating factors is shared variance. Factors, therefore, are not exact linear combinations of the items, and the multiple correlations between the items and the factors are less than 1.0. This means that an infinite number of factor score coefficient matrices can be used to create factor scores. Thus, in common factor analysis, there is no unique solution to generating factor scores, a situation known as *factor score indeterminacy.*

Should we be worried about factor score indeterminacy? There appears to be some disagreement in the factor analysis literature about the seriousness of this condition (McDonald & Mulaik, 1979; Nunnally & Bernstein, 1994; Schönemann & Wang, 1972). Nunnally and Bernstein (1994) indicate that, because of factor score indeterminacy, estimation of the matrix of factor score coefficients will vary from study to study and from approach to approach.

Several different approaches to estimating factor scores have been proposed (Comrey & Lee, 1992; Harman, 1976; Kim & Mueller, 1978; Tucker, 1971). Each approach has different properties and the resulting scores are different. Both the topic and the mathematics involved can be complicated, particularly when item loadings on a factor are not equal and an oblique rotation is used. Because there is no single correct method, there are no strong guidelines in the literature as to the preferred method of factor score estimation.

Comrey and Lee (1992), Harman (1976), and Kim and Mueller (1978) offer clear descriptions of the different types of methods used to estimate these factor scores. Some methods use all of the items in the factor and weigh each item equally, and others weigh items differentially depending on the size of their loadings. Still others use only those items that load above a certain cut-off value (e.g., .40). Although ideally one would like a consistent score, in reality, different factor scores will be produced for the same factor depending on the approach used.

Three factor score methods are offered in SPSS for Windows: regression, Bartlett, and Anderson-Rubin. All of these methods produce factor scores with a mean equal to 0; however, given their different approaches to calculating the values, the resulting factor scores and variances are different. To obtain these scores in SPSS, click on *Analyze . . . Data Reduction . . . Factor.* After selecting the items to be analyzed and the factor analysis approach to be used, click on *Factor Scores . . . .* This will open the dialog box in Figure 7.1.

In SAS, standardized factor coefficients can be generated in PROC FACTOR using the subcommand SCORE (Figure B7.1, Appendix B). In addition, the OUT = option creates a data set containing all the data from the DATA = data set plus variables called Factor 1, Factor 2, and so on. These new variables contain the estimated factor scores for each individual. To obtain this new file, the DATA = data set must contain multivariate data, not correlations or covariances. The NFACTORS = option must also be specified in order to determine the number of factor scores to be generated.

Figure 7.1   Generating Factor Scores in SPSS for Windows

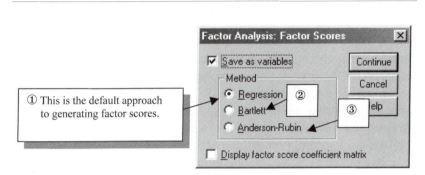

Multiple Regression Approach

In SPSS for Windows, the first factor score estimation method, *Regression,* represents the default multiple regression approach used for estimating factor score coefficients (Figure 7.1①). This popular approach produces standardized scores that will be saved at the end of the SPSS data file. This is the same default approach that is used in SAS. These scores will have a mean equal to 0 and a variance equal to the squared multiple correlation between the estimated factor scores and the true factor values. A drawback to this approach is that the estimated factor scores may be correlated even when the factors are assumed to be orthogonal, as in principal components analysis.

In the multiple regression approach, factor score coefficients (W_{jk}) are generated from the product of the inverse of the interitem correlation matrix ($\mathbf{R}^{-1}$) and the factor-loading matrix (e.g., the orthogonal factor loadings or factor structure coefficients if an oblique solution is being used) and are similar to regression coefficients (βs) obtained in multiple regression. That is, for respondent *i,* the estimated standardized score that would be received on factor *j* would be as follows (Comrey & Lee, 1992; SPSS, Inc., 1993):

$$\hat{F}_{ij} = \sum_{k=1}^{p} W_{jk} z_{jk}$$

where

$\hat{F}_{ij}$ = estimated standardized score for respondent *i* on
Factor *j*

W_{jk} = factor score coefficient for Item *k* on Factor *j*

z_{ik} = standardized score for respondent i on Item k
p = number of items in the correlation matrix

We will now illustrate how the computer arrives at estimated factor scores using regression. First, Table 7.3A presents the standardized scores on the 20 items for one respondent on the CGTS that were generated in SPSS for Windows and SAS. Then Table 7.3B presents the factor score coefficient matrix (W_{jk}) generated in SPSS for Windows. The SAS output for the same matrix is presented in Table B7.3, Appendix B.

Using the formula for estimated factor scores and the information provided in Table 7.3, we can obtain Respondent 1's estimated score for Factor 1:

$$\hat{F}_{11} = \sum_{k=1}^{20} W_{jk}\, z_{1k} = (.062)(.777) + (-.027)(.338)$$
$$+ (.217)(.077) + \cdots + (-.007)(-1.574)$$
$$+ (.002)(-1.756)+(.167)(-.641) = -.520$$

Similarly, Respondent 1's estimated standardized score for Factor 2 would be

$$\hat{F}_{12} = \sum_{k=1}^{20} W_{jk}\, z_{1k} = (-.018)\,(.777) + (.293)(.338)$$
$$+ (-.014)(.077) + \cdots + (-.033)(-1.574)$$
$$+ (.000)(-1.756) + (.003)(-.641) = .722$$

If requested, these estimated factor scores can be saved as new variables (e.g., fac1_1, fac2_1, etc., in SPSS or Factor 1, Factor 2, etc., in SAS) at the end of the data file to be used in future analyses.

Bartlett Method

A second method for estimating factor score coefficients is the Bartlett method (Figure 7.1, ②). The scores produced by this method also have a mean of 0, but the sum of squares of the unique factors over the range of variables is minimized (Harman, 1976). The result is that

Table 7.3   Standardized Scores for Respondent 1 and Factor Score
Coefficients for the Factors on the 20-Item CGTS Scale

A. Standardized Scores for Respondent 1

Item	Standardized Scores (z_{ik}) Respondent 1
C1	.777
C2	.338
C3	.077
C4	.515
C5	.751
C6	−.984
C7	.380
C8	1.078
C9	−1.598
C10	−.792
C11	−.560
C12	−1.509
C13	−1.079
C14	−2.143
C15	.494
C16	1.064
C17	−1.256
C18	−1.574
C19	−1.756
C20	−.641

B. Factor Score Coefficient Matrix (W_{jk})

	Factor			
	1	2	3	4
C1	.062	−.018	−.004	−.036
C2	−.027	.293	.027	.015
C3	.217	−.014	.009	−.001
C4	.036	.202	.009	−.111
C5	−.070	.225	.051	.003
C6	.048	.155	−.032	.083
C7	.195	.012	−.034	−.053
C8	−.047	.101	.129	−.101
C9	−.024	−.003	−.073	.380
C10	.176	−.017	−.031	−.013
C11	−.021	−.001	.000	.223
C12	.111	−.059	−.018	.034

(Continued)

Table 7.3 Continued

C13	.155	.014	.021	.091
C14	.021	−.018	.024	.323
C15	.111	.285	−.041	.097
C16	.085	.032	−.009	−.015
C17	.049	−.040	.087	.073
C18	−.007	−.033	.315	.022
C19	.002	.000	.510	.028
C20	.167	.003	.103	−.096

variables that have lower loadings on the factor are given less weight than those with higher loadings in the calculation of the factor score.

Anderson-Rubin Method

Finally, there is the Anderson-Rubin approach (Anderson & Rubin, 1956) (Figure 7.1 ③), which is a modification of the Bartlett method but has the constraint that the created scales are orthogonal to one another (Harman, 1976). The scores produced by this method always have a mean of 0 and a standard deviation equal to 1 and the factor scores are uncorrelated.

Choosing the Best Approach

Choosing which method is the best approach to generating factor scores can be confusing. Several authors (e.g., Gorsuch, 1983; Harman, 1976; McDonald & Burr, 1967; Nunnally & Bernstein, 1994) have outlined some desired properties for a *good* factor scoring estimation procedure:

- The correlation between the estimated factor scores and the factor they represent should be high. That is, the method generates scores that are highly valid.
- If factors are orthogonal, the factor scores estimated from one factor should be uncorrelated with all other factors. This is known as *univocality*.
- If factors are orthogonal, their estimated factor scores should also be uncorrelated with one another.
- If factors are oblique, the correlations among the estimated factor scores should be correlated to the extent of the correlation among the associated factors.

This means that if Factor 1 and Factor 2 are uncorrelated, their estimated factor scores should be as well. If, on the other hand, the two factors have a correlation of .30, then the correlation of the estimated factor scores for Factor 1 should be correlated no more than .30 with the estimated factor scores for Factor 2. As Gorsuch (1983) has indicated, "When factors are allowed to be correlated, the correlations among factor scores should reproduce those correlations" (p. 266).

Kim and Mueller (1978) discuss the choice of approach issue in great detail. They point out that, because most underlying factors are not completely orthogonal, the choice is usually between the regression and Bartlett approaches. They also indicate that, for most projects, the factor scores generated by the three approaches are highly correlated; therefore, choice of approach may be purely academic. Indeed, when we ran all three approaches to generating factor scales for our 20-item CGTS scale in SPSS for Windows, the average correlation among the generated factor scores was .838. The interscale correlations ranged from .645 (for the regression and Bartlett approaches on Factor 2) to 1.00 (for all of the Bartlett and Anderson-Rubin comparisons).

Generating Factor-Based Scales

In test construction, the tendency has been to avoid using factor scores, choosing instead to generate factor-based scales. Estimated factor scores can be clumsy because they are usually generated from all of the items in the item pool. Even items that load very low on a factor (e.g., <.30) could be included in factor score estimations.

In general, scores on factor-based scales are obtained by summing the scores for only those individual items that have been selected for inclusion on a given factor. Those items that did not load satisfactorily on a given factor or that had been moved to another factor would be excluded from the calculations. Scores on each factor would then be obtained by summing across items or by obtaining an average score for a respondent on the factor.

This is the approach preferred by Pedhazur and Schmelkin (1991), who argue that it is better to use scales that have been constructed from the factors to obtain scale reliabilities and intercorrelations and to correlate demographic and psychosocial measures with these subscale scores than to use estimated factor scores.

Figure 7.2   Creating Factor-Based Scales in SPSS for Windows

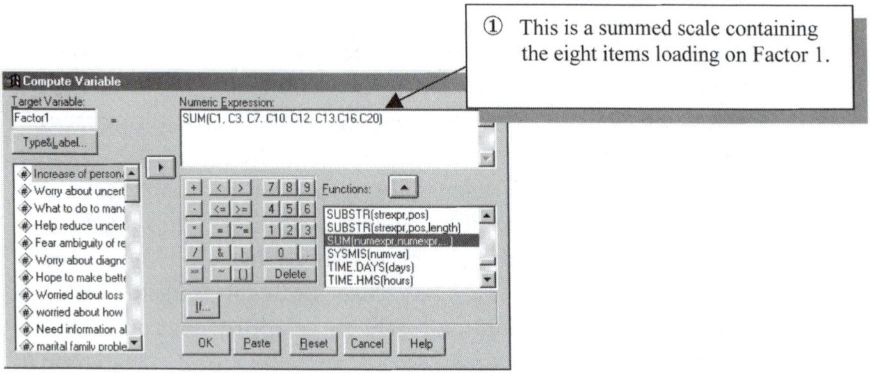

① This is a summed scale containing the eight items loading on Factor 1.

Generating Factor-Based Scales in SPSS for Windows

Factor-based scales can be generated in SPSS for Windows using the *Transform . . . Compute . . .* command. This will open the *Compute Variable . . .* dialog box (Figure 7.2). The composite score, *Factor 1,* will be the newly created variable that appears at the end of our data file. By selecting the *Sum . . .* command in the *Functions . . .* window, Factor 1 will be a composite scale that represents the sum of the unstandardized scores that each subject received on the items of interest. In this example, we are creating a summed scale for Factor 1 using the eight unstandardized items that loaded >.40 on Factor 1 (Figure 7.2, ①). Because these items all have a 5-point Likert scale format, the possible range of scores for this newly created scale (*Factor 1*) will be from 8 to 40. Had we elected to, we could also have used the *Mean . . .* command in the *Function* box to create a scale for which the range would be 1.00 to 5.00.

Generating Factor-Based Scales in SAS

Factor-based scales can be generated in SAS using a method similar to SPSS for Windows. That is, a new variable (e.g., *Factor 1*) can be computed using the commands presented in Figure B7.2 (Appendix B). You can use either the PROC MEANS or PROC UNIVARIATE commands (Figure B7.2, Appendix B) in SAS to generate descriptive statistics and request normal probability plots to evaluate the shape of the distribution of the newly created scale.

Table 7.4   Intercorrelations of the Factor-Based Scales Among Themselves and With the Estimated Factor Scores

| Factor-Based Scales | Intercorrelations: Factor-Based Scales | | | | Estimated Factor Scores | | |
	F1	F2	F3	F4	Regression ⑤	Bartlett's	Anderson-Rubin ⑥
Factor 1	1.00	.43	.46 ②	.26	④ .989	.887	.886
Factor 2		1.00	.36	.37	.983	③ .597	.598
Factor 3			1.00	.25 ①	.970	.688	.693
Factor 4				1.00	.969	.711	.710

Advantages and Drawbacks to Factor-Based Scales

An advantage to using a factor-based scale approach to generating factor scores is that these scores are more easily interpreted than estimated factor scores and can also be compared from one study to another. The correlations between estimated factor scores and factor-based scales are also high. Table 7.4 summarizes the correlations of the factor-based scales both among themselves and with the three approaches to estimating factor scores for the 20-item CGTS scale that were generated in SPSS for Windows.

The correlations among the factor-based scales ranged from .25 (between the scale scores for Factors 3 and 4) (Table 7.4, ①) to .46 (Factor 1 and Factor 3) ②. The correlations of the factor-based scales with the estimated factor scores ranged from .597 (Factor 2 with the Bartlett approach ③) to .989 (Factor 1 with the multiple-regression approach ④). It is also apparent that there is not much difference between the results obtained from factor-based scales and the estimated factor scores based on multiple regression because all four correlations were higher than .969 ⑤. The lower correlations between our factor-based scales generated from an oblique solution (using principal axis factoring with a Direct Oblimin rotation) that assumes that the factors are correlated and the Anderson Rubin approach ⑥ is not surprising because the Anderson-Rubin approach generates estimated factor scores that are uncorrelated.

A disadvantage of the factor-based scale approach is that the item loadings on a factor are generally not considered when calculating scores. This means that items with lower factor loadings are given the same weight as items with higher factor loadings. Pedhazur and Schmelkin (1991) have also observed that too often researchers are tempted to calculate total scale scores even when the factor analysis results indicate otherwise. This would occur, for example, if we reported a total scale score for our 20-item CGTS when in fact our factor analysis indicated that there were four factors, or subscales, that best described the 20 items.

Relating Factor-Based Scores to Other Variables

However they are created, factor-based scores and scales are extremely valuable and necessary outcomes to a factor analysis. They can be useful for assessing differences among groups of subjects, comparing scores on the factors against a criterion, and evaluating the effects of controlled experiments/interventions. In our CGTS study, for example, we could examine the relationship of the scores that the respondents obtained on the generated factor-based scales to a number of different demographic variables, e.g., age, ethnicity, educational level, socioeconomic status, marital status, possession of health insurance, and number of first-degree relatives who have developed breast cancer. These comparisons not only would give us information about how persons of different backgrounds react to the issues contained in the subscales but also would give us information about the generalizability of our findings.

SUMMARY

Throughout this chapter, we have provided you with some suggested guidelines for interpreting and naming the factors that have been identified in your factor analysis study. We have also presented you with potentially useful approaches to generating estimated factor scores and factor-based scales. Figure 7.3 summarizes our discussion with regard to interpreting and naming the factors. In Chapter 8, we will examine approaches that you could use to present the findings of your factor analysis both visually and in words.

Figure 7.3   Some Guidelines for Interpreting and Naming the Factors

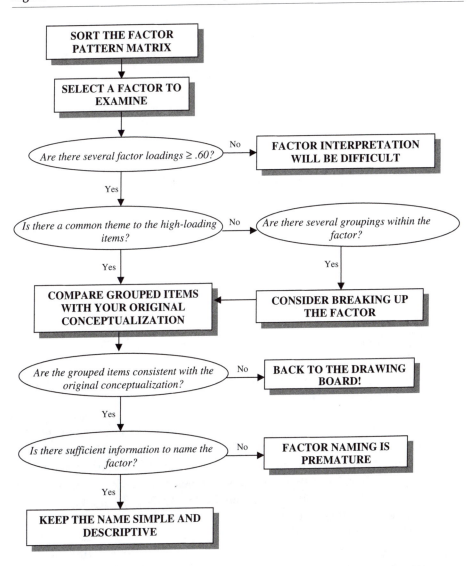

NOTE

1. Please see Chapter 3 for more detail on variance estimation in the different factor analysis models.

8

Reporting and Replicating the Results

N ow that you have developed your instrument, pilot tested it, used it in a research study, identified and named subscales, and assessed their reliability, you want to share it with the world. But you are in a quandary regarding just what to report. How much of the development of the instrument do you describe? What parts of the factor analysis that you undertook do you include in your report? Who is the targeted audience to whom you will be reporting the results?

Unfortunately, although there are many excellent texts available on approaches to instrument development (e.g., DeVellis, 1991; Nunnally & Bernstein, 1994), there are not many comprehensive strategies offered with regard to what phase of instrument development one should publish or what to report when writing up the results (exceptions being Comrey & Lee, 1992; Norbeck, 1985; Pedhazur & Schmelkin, 1991). The main focus of this chapter, therefore, will be to address what should be reported in a journal article that describes the development of an instrument and, specifically, the results of a factor analysis. We will conclude this chapter—and this book—with a brief examination of strategies to use when seeking to replicate the obtained results.

WHEN TO REPORT THE RESULTS

An instrument is ready for reporting when the developer can clearly state the conceptual bases for the instrument, how it was constructed, the minimal reliability and validity that have been established, and the type of subjects and research situations in which the instrument can be used (Norbeck, 1985). Reports of *minimal reliability and validity* should include the instrument's content validity, test-retest reliability, internal consistency reliability, and at least one type of criterion-related or construct validity. If testing fails to produce acceptable standards of reliability and validity, then the instrument should be modified before its development is reported. Reports of instrument development that do not include this information are of limited value to the reader (Norbeck, 1985).

In her position as an editor of *Research in Nursing and Health,* Oberst (1994) observed that manuscripts that report the results of an instrument development are often rejected because the instrument is not *cooked enough* (p. 399). She suggested that at least three studies be completed before a report of the instrument development is submitted for publication consideration. The first study should include how the items were developed and content validity established. Subscales should be listed and representative items for each subscale identified. The experts who helped establish content validity should also be described.

The second study should involve the field testing of the items, response format, and instructions. The outcome of this study would be the initial reliabilities of both the instrument as a whole and the subscales if appropriate. The third study should establish construct validity of the instrument. If any of this information regarding the newly developed instrument is unacceptable, then the instrument should be modified and retested before its development is reported.

WHAT TO INCLUDE IN THE REPORT

The target audience to whom the author will be reporting the findings of the factor analysis is most likely other researchers who are either interested in the specialty area or in approaches to instrument development (Norbeck, 1985). Therefore, the content of this report should be directed toward these individuals and should contain sufficient information to

Table 8.1   Suggested Items to Be Included in a Report of a Factor
                   Analysis Study

A REPORT OF A FACTOR ANALYSIS SHOULD INCLUDE

- The theoretical rationale for the use of factor analysis
- Detailed descriptions of the sampling methods and participants
- Descriptions of the items, including means and standard deviations
- An evaluation of the assumptions of factor analysis
- A justification for the choice of factor extraction and rotation methods
- Evaluation of the correlation matrix: Bartlett's test of sphericity, Kaiser-Meyer-Olkin test
- Criteria for extracting the factors: the scree test, eigenvalues, percent of variance extracted
- Cutoffs for meaningful factor loadings
- The structure matrix for orthogonally rotated solutions; the structure and pattern matrices and interfactor correlations for obliquely rotated solutions
- Descriptions and interpretation of the factors
- Internal consistency of the identified factors (e.g., Cronbach's alpha)
- Approach to calculation of factor-based scores
- Assessment of the study limitations and suggestions for future research directions

---

allow the results of the analysis to be assessed independently (Comrey & Lee, 1992). It is the responsibility of both the author and journal editors to ensure that sufficient information is provided so that the analyses can be approximated in other studies (Gorsuch, 1983).

Both Comrey and Lee (1992) and Pedhazur and Schmelkin (1991) offer general guidelines for what should be included in the report of a factor analysis study. These guidelines, along with our own recommendations, are summarized in Table 8.1. Hopefully, this table can serve as a checklist for you when evaluating the content of a published report of a factor analysis or when organizing your own report.

It is important to remember that factor analysis is but one dimension that needs to be included in a report of the development of an instrument. Additional elements that need to be included focus more specifically on the various phases of instrument development. The following is a brief discussion of these elements.

Design and Administration of the Instrument

The reader of a report of a factor analysis that was used in the development of an instrument should be told what construct is being measured and how it was conceptualized and operationalized. The methods that were used to generate, develop, and refine the items need to be described. If the construct is multidimensional, these dimensions should be identified, theoretically defined, and examples of items for each dimension included. How was content validity established? If a panel of experts was used in this process, the group should be described and the method used to establish content validity explained.

The approach used to pilot-test the newly developed instrument needs to be described and the results reported. Explain any refinement of the instrument as the result of this pilot testing. The final design of the instrument along with the rationale for its selection needs to be stated. How was the order of the items established? Were the items randomly placed in the instrument? Instructions for either administering or self-administration should be included.

Include a selection of items along with the response options in the report. Norbeck (1985) cautions, however, against publishing the instrument in its totality in an article. When an article is published, the author gives the copyright to the publisher. If the entire instrument is included in the article, the publisher has a copyright to it. This means that if the developer of the instrument wishes to refine the instrument, permission would have to be sought from the publisher before changes could be made to the instrument.

You should also present detailed descriptions of the demographic characteristics of the subjects who took part in the instrument development phase and outline the characteristics of those for whom the instrument is intended. Additional information could include issues related to the protection of human subjects, the specific instructions for administration, recommended scoring procedures, and the possible range of scores for the instrument.

Report of the Factor Analysis

As indicated in Table 8.1, the content and suitability of the inter-item correlation matrix and item-total correlations should be evaluated and the results of both Bartlett's test of sphericity and the Kaiser-Meyer-Olkin test reported and interpreted. Comrey and Lee (1992) suggest that if the correlation matrix is too large to be printed in the body of the report, its content, along with the means and standard deviations for the items, be made available to the interested reader upon request. Items that were eliminated because of redundancy or lack of homogeneity with the construct should be identified along with the reliability analyses that were undertaken (e.g., Cronbach's alpha and test-retest measures).

Next, the methods used for extraction of the factors should be discussed. Which factor analytic approach was used? What was the rationale for selecting this approach? What were the acceptable levels of the eigenvalues and what percent of variance was extracted by each factor? The results of the scree plot need to be interpreted and reported. Also, the differences between the observed and estimated correlation coefficients and goodness of fit of the factor solution need to be examined and discussed.

The type of factor rotation that was undertaken and the criteria used to determine its selection need to be addressed. It is not uncommon for researchers to run both the Varimax and Oblimin solutions on the data and report the results of both. Attention should also be given to how the factors were refined and interpreted. Included in this discussion should be an examination of the item-to-factor loadings. As we indicate in the next section, this information may be best displayed in a table format.

Included in the report should be a discussion of construct validity. How were the names of the factors derived and how was the conceptualization of the construct of interest supported by the data? Recommendations for future studies to further support construct validity need to be presented. Based on this evaluation of the new instrument, how would the researcher suggest this instrument be used in future research? What other types of testing will be needed to further refine the instrument?

Types of Tables to Include in the Report of a Factor Analysis

A variety of tables could be included in a report of a factor analysis. These tables should be clearly and simply presented and be able to stand on their own. Brief summary interpretations of the tables should also be included in the text.

Demographic Profile of the Respondents

One of the first tables should be a presentation of the demographic profile of the respondents. An example of such a table is given in Table 8.2.[1] This table describes the subjects who took part in the instrument development study, e.g., their ages, gender, ethnicity, marital status, and educational level. Additional demographic characteristics that are important to the given study could also be included. For example, in the development of the Concerns About Genetic Testing Scale (CGTS), we might also report health insurance status and number of first-degree relatives diagnosed with breast cancer. This table should be accompanied by a summary description of the respondents.

For Table 8.2, for example, we might present the following description:

A demographic profile of the 205 respondents is presented in Table 8.2. The women ranged in age from 21 to 64 (mean age = 40.7 years). They were predominantly Caucasian (79.0%) and married (50.2%). The women were mostly well educated, with 75.1% of the sample reporting having at least some college education. Nearly three quarters of the women (74.1%) reported having health insurance.

Correlation Matrix

A second table might contain the correlation matrix along with the means and standard deviations for the items included in the final form of the instrument (e.g., Table 8.3).

As we indicated, this information will allow a researcher to replicate the results if desired. If such a table is too cumbersome to be included in the manuscript, then the author should offer to make the data available to interested researchers. When describing the table in the text, attention should be given to the range of size of the correlations, the acceptability of the means, and the outcome of Bartlett's test of sphericity and the KMO statistic. For example, regarding Table 8.3, the following summary might be offered in the text:

The item means, standard deviations, and interitem correlation matrix are presented in Table 8.3. On a 5-point scale, where 1 = *not at all* to 5 = *extremely*, the means ranged from 2.7 (Item 11: *Worried about marital and family problems that might occur*) to 3.9

Table 8.2   Demographic Characteristics of the Sample ($N = 205$)

Variable	N	%
Age (years)[a]	41.0 ± 10.3	
21-30	39	19.0
31-39	61	29.8
40-49	73	35.6
50-59	20	9.8
60 and over	12	5.9
Ethnicity		
White/Caucasian	162	79.0
Black/African American	19	9.3
Hispanic-Latina	16	7.8
Native American/Alaskan Native	5	2.4
Other	3	1.5
Marital status		
Married	103	50.2
Single	70	34.1
Divorced	26	12.7
Widowed	4	2.0
Other	2	1.0
Educational level		
Less than high school	13	6.3
High school graduate	38	18.5
Some college	96	46.8
College graduate	52	25.4
Graduate/professional school	6	2.9
Health insurance		
Yes	152	74.1
No	53	25.9

a. Mean ± SD.

(Item 3: *What to do to manage the risk*). Examination of the correlation matrix indicated that all items correlated $\geq |.30|$ with at least three other items in the matrix (range: 3–14). Twelve of the 20 items (60%) had 9 or more shared correlations that exceeded $\geq |.30|$. No interitem correlation exceeded $r = .68$, thus indicating no problems with multicollinearity.

Bartlett's test of sphericity and the Kaiser-Meyer-Olkin (KMO) measure of sampling adequacy were used to evaluate the strength of the linear association among the 20 items in the correlation matrix. Bartlett's test of sphericity was significant ($\chi^2 = 2126.545$,

Table 8.3 Correlation Matrix, Means, and Standard Deviations for the 20-Item Concerns About Genetic Testing Scale (CGTS)

Item	1	2	3	4	5	6	7	8	9	10	11	12	13	14	15	16	17	18	19	20	$\bar{X}$	SD
1	1.0																				3.1	1.1
2	.07	1.0																			3.6	1.1
3	.34	.25	1.0																		3.9	1.1
4	.26	.56	.24	1.0																	3.5	1.0
5	-.04	.39	.09	.38	1.0																3.2	1.1
6	.17	.51	.38	.39	.47	1.0															3.2	1.2
7	.45	.19	.61	.35	.06	.35	1.0														3.6	1.2
8	.11	.28	.21	.25	.33	.19	.07	1.0													3.7	1.2
9	.004	.32	.08	-.009	.26	.31	.17	-.07	1.0												3.0	1.3
10	.34	.33	.49	.29	.03	.32	.50	.10	.04	1.0											3.8	1.1
11	.04	.20	.07	.08	.14	.18	-.05	-.03	.46	.08	1.0										2.7	1.2
12	.41	.20	.45	.21	-.10	.32	.42	.01	.08	.58	.12	1.0									3.1	1.4
13	.44	.28	.65	.34	.21	.37	.54	.15	.20	.62	.25	.40	1.0								3.2	1.1
14	.07	.20	.44	.14	.18	.43	.32	.12	.48	.31	.42	.33	.38	1.0							3.7	1.3
15	.17	.63	.34	.52	.48	.49	.15	.19	.22	.33	.32	.30	.42	.37	1.0						3.5	1.1
16	.21	.23	.60	.26	.19	.41	.47	.09	.08	.52	-.01	.31	.47	.25	.40	1.0					3.8	1.1
17	.17	.11	.40	.15	.09	.29	.24	.26	.21	.38	.15	.35	.47	.35	.26	.42	1.0				3.3	1.1
18	.22	.21	.27	.27	.13	.15	.21	.45	.11	.33	.14	.28	.37	.35	.17	.16	.51	1.0			3.7	1.1
19	.29	.19	.21	.23	.19	.34	.15	.47	.22	.35	.11	.33	.34	.27	.27	.23	.58	.68	1.0		3.2	1.2
20	.43	.18	.58	.32	.14	.38	.51	.30	.08	.47	.004	.42	.56	.30	.25	.52	.43	.52	.52	1.0	3.7	1.1

233

Table 8.4   Total Variance Explained by the Four Extracted Factors of the CGTS Scale

Factor	Initial Eigenvalues			Extracted Sums of Squares Loadings		
	Total	% Variance	Cumulative %	Total	% Variance	Cumulative %
I	6.70	33.49	33.49	6.25	31.26	31.26
II	2.29	11.47	44.96	1.81	9.03	40.29
III	1.76	8.82	53.78	1.36	6.82	47.11
IV	1.66	8.27	62.05	1.15	5.76	52.87

$p = .000$), which indicated that the correlation matrix was not an identity matrix. The KMO statistic (.76), which is an index that compares the magnitude of the observed correlations with the magnitude of the partial correlation coefficients, was just "middling" according to Kaiser's (1974) criteria. These results suggest that, although a factor analysis was appropriate and could be expected to yield common factors, there was some concern for the few number of items ($N = 20$) in the correlation matrix.

The item-to-total scale correlations ranged from .25 (Item 11: *Worried about marital and family problems that might occur*) to .70 (Item 13: *Need information about future screening activities*). This range of item-total correlations was considered to be acceptable (Nunnally & Bernstein, 1992). No items were eliminated because of redundancy or lack of homogeneity with the construct. Cronbach's alpha for the total 20-item scale was .89.

Total Variance Explained

A table that would be useful for the reader would be one that summarizes the total amount of variance in the items that is explained by the extracted factors. An example of such a table is presented in Table 8.4. In this example, the sums of squared loadings cannot be added to obtain a total variance because the factors were correlated.

Factor Structure and Pattern Matrices

Two additional tables that are important to a report of the findings of a factor analysis are the factor loadings from the rotated factor structure matrix (e.g., Table 8.5) and, if an oblique (correlated) solution was used, the factor pattern matrix (e.g., Table 8.6).

Table 8.5   Factor Loadings From the Rotated Factor Structure Matrix for the Concerns About Genetic Testing Scale: Principal Axis Factoring With Oblimin Rotation

CGTS Items	Factors			
	1	2	3	4
1. Information seeking				
What to do to manage risk	.78	.27	.28	.21
Need information about future screening activities	.75	.34	.37	.32
Hope to make better lifestyle choices	.74	.21	.17	.12
Need information about types of cancer at risk for	.73	.25	.32	.17
Want to know survival prospects	.72	.25	.57	.09
Information about the difference between diagnosis and getting cancer	.65	.33	.23	.14
Might be helped to make future life decisions	.63	.12	.27	.22
Increase of personal control	.51	.09	.25	−.005
2. Uncertainty				
Worry about uncertain diagnosis	.27	.75	.20	.27
Worried about my future life	.38	.74	.24	.38
Fear ambiguity of results	.05	.66	.22	.22
Help reduce uncertainty about future	.37	.65	.28	.01
Worry about a diagnosis I cannot do anything about	.45	.61	.26	.38
3. Financial, social stigma				
Being targeted as a carrier	.37	.25	.86	.23
Financial and social implications of being identified	.37	.19	.81	.19
Loss of health and life insurance coverage	.13	.36	.58	−.06
Financial concerns related to the screening	.49	.15	.58	.32
4. Family relationships				
How will family react	.11	.23	.10	.72
How will a positive test affect children, other family members	.42	.25	.28	.68
Marital and family problems that might occur	.07	.20	.08	.62

Note: Underlined values indicate a double loading on two factors. Loadings highlighted in bold indicate the factor on which the item was placed.

Table 8.6   Rotated Factor Pattern Matrix for the 20-Item CGTS: Principal Axis Factoring With Oblimin Rotation

	Factors			
CGTS Items	1	2	3	4
1. Information seeking				
What to do to manage risk	.77	.06	−.27	−.34
Need information about future screening activities	.77	.06	−.26	.04
Hope to make better lifestyle choices	.78	.04	−.12	−.03
Need information about types of cancer at risk for	.70	.05	.05	.01
Want to know survival prospects	.60	.02	.36	−.08
Want information about the difference between diagnosis and getting cancer	.63	.18	−.05	−.03
Might be helped to make future life decisions	.62	−.08	.05	.11
Increase of personal control	.52	−.04	.08	−.11
2. Uncertainty				
Worry about uncertain diagnosis	.06	.72	−.03	.10
Worried about my future life	.17	.66	−.03	.19
Fear ambiguity of results	−.18	.67	.10	.09
Help reduce uncertainty about future	.22	.63	.05	−.19
Worry about a diagnosis I cannot do anything about	.27	.49	.007	.21
3. Financial, social stigma				
Being targeted as a carrier	.04	−.004	.83	.11
Financial and social implications of being identified	.08	−.06	.78	.08
Loss of health and life insurance coverage	−.12	.28	.58	−.18
Financial concerns related to the screening	.29	−.10	.47	.22
4. Family relationships				
How will family react	−.06	.08	.004	.72
How will a positive test affect children and other family members	.25	.01	.11	.61
Worried about marital and family problems that might occur	−.08	.07	.01	.62

Note: Underlined values indicate a double loading on two factors. Loadings highlighted in bold indicate the factor on which the item was placed.

Table 8.7   Factor Correlations and Factor Alpha Coefficients for the
CGTS Scale (N = 205)

Factor	M^a	SD	1	2	3	4
1. Information seeking (n = 8)	3.53	0.84	(.88)			
2. Uncertainty (n = 5)	3.89	0.83	.272	(.82)		
3. Financial, social stigma (n = 4)	3.47	0.91	.366	.266	(.79)	
4. Family relationships (n = 3)	3.15	1.00	.204	.231	.134	(.71)
Total scale (n = 20)	3.42	0.65				(.89)

a. Range: 1.00 to 5.00.
Note: Reliability estimates appear in the parentheses on the diagonal.

A final table that is useful in a report of the development of a scale using factor analysis is one that reports the factor correlations and alpha coefficients for the subscales. Hatcher (1994) suggests including simple descriptive statistics (e.g., means and standard deviations) along with the correlations and coefficient alpha reliability estimates. Table 8.7 presents the means, standard deviations, factor correlations, and alpha coefficients for the CGTS scale.

In the text, the data presented in Table 8.7 could be summarized as follows:

Table 8.7 presents the descriptive statistics, between-factor correlations, and alpha coefficients for the four generated subscales of the CGTS. The correlations between the subscales ranged from .134 (for the two subscales Financial, Social Stigma and Family Relationships) to .366 (for Information Seeking and Financial, Social Stigma). The reliability estimates presented in parentheses on the diagonal of Table 8.7 ranged from .71 to .88 with a total scale coefficient alpha equal to .89.

AN EXEMPLAR OF A PUBLISHED REPORT

We reviewed a number of published reports of newly developed instruments and found varying amounts of information presented. An exemplar of a published report on the development of an instrument was that written by Leske (1991), in which she described the internal psychometric properties of the Critical Care Family Needs Inventory (CCFNI).

In her report, Leske described the conceptualization of the construct of family needs and how the 45 items were generated, refined, and randomly placed in the instrument self-report Likert-type format. She then proceeded to describe the study that established the psychometrics of this instrument. The sample size for this study was 677 family members of 552 critically ill patients. This number of subjects exceeded the recommended number of 10 subjects per item. She described the demographic characteristics of both the family members and the patients. Procedures for this study were well delineated.

In the data analysis section, Leske began by describing the item analysis. Item means, standard deviations, interitem correlation matrix, and item-total correlations were computed for each item. She reported the highest and lowest mean scores and the range of item-total correlations. Values for corrected item-total correlations were stated along with the overall Cronbach's alpha.

Next, Leske (1991) described the methods of factor analysis that were used in the development of her instrument. In this discussion, she reported the results of Bartlett's test of sphericity and Kaiser-Meyer-Olkin measure of sampling adequacy. She indicated that a principal components analysis with both Varimax and Oblimin rotations were undertaken and gave her rationale for selecting these two analyses. Factors with eigenvalues greater than 1.0 were included in her next level of analysis. The results of a scree plot were reported along with an evaluation of goodness of fit. Next, she included a detailed discussion of the factor rotation including the criteria used. The rationale was given for the selection of the rotation type.

In the factor interpretation and labeling section, Leske described the factor loadings, the number of items loading above .30 on each of the five extracted factors, the themes of each factor, and the names or labels she assigned to each of the factors. She then reported her examination of factor independence and scale reliability. Reliabilities for the five established factors were reported. In the discussion section, she discussed the strengths and weaknesses of the psychometric evaluation. In general, this was an excellent report.

REPLICATING THE FACTORS IN OTHER STUDIES

Are we through now with instrument development and factor analysis? No, we are not. One must not assume that all of the items that define a factor have been delineated in a single study. At this stage in instrument development, one must embark on interpretation with caution and trepidation. Many studies must be undertaken in order to determine if all items of the factor have been derived and correctly interpreted. Although factor analysis provides the researcher with methods to evaluate the *goodness of fit* of items within an instrument's subscales, it does not enable the researcher to assess the *goodness* of the instrument as a whole (i.e., its reliability and validity) except in terms of establishing beginning construct validity. That is, it helps the researcher to begin to answer the question, "Does my instrument measure what it was constructed to measure?"

Construct validity is a never-ending, ongoing, complex process that is determined over a series of studies in a number of different ways. Hopefully, through this text, you have become aware that, in the initial phase of instrument development, exploratory factor analysis helps to define the internal structure for a set of items and to group the items into factors. In subsequent phases of instrument development, confirmatory factor analysis needs to be used to establish construct validity.

Basically, a *good* instrument has to have two conditions to survive. First, a good instrument is stringently operationally defined. The derivation of items and procedures used in the construction of the instrument must be clearly delineated and reported in the literature. In the final chapter of this text, we have reviewed with you what you would want to include in a report of the results of a factor analysis study that focused on instrument development. Second, a good instrument must also be significant. If an instrument that has been developed has no significance in the health care sciences, what use can be made of it? The *goodness* of an instrument depends on what it predicts, how well it predicts it, and its usefulness in the practice of health care.

CONCLUSIONS

The above suggestions for information that needs to be reported about a newly developed instrument are the ideal. Unfortunately, the amount of information reported is often limited by the space constraints of the journal. If the researcher is restricted regarding the amount of information allowed in a report, a note can be included in the report that further information regarding the development of the instrument can be obtained directly from the author. It has been our experience that once the article regarding the newly developed instrument is published, there will be many requests for the use of the instrument. We would highly suggest that the researcher have the instrument ready for distribution before the article is published. Unfortunately, the initial psychometric evaluation of a newly developed instrument it not the end—it is just the beginning. We look forward to the many published research articles that you will present to us with regard to your instrument development.

NOTE

1. Please note that the numbers presented in the tables are fictitious (as is the entire CGTS data set) and are given merely for purposes of illustration.

APPENDIX A

Concerns About
Genetic Testing Scale

THESE ARE SOME ISSUES THAT PEOPLE HAVE INDICATED ARE CONCERNS WHEN MAKING THEIR DECISION ABOUT GENETIC TESTING	IS THIS A CONCERN FOR YOU?				
	1	2	3	4	5
	Not at all	Slightly	Moderately	Quite a bit	Extremely
1. I might increase my sense of personal control over the condition after I receive the testing results	□	□	□	□	□
2. I worry about being faced with an uncertain diagnosis	□	□	□	□	□
3. I want to know what I should do to manage my risk for cancer.	□	□	□	□	□
4. I hope that knowing the results will help reduce my uncertainty about the future.	□	□	□	□	□
5. I fear being faced with the ambiguity of the results	□	□	□	□	□
6. I worry about being faced with a diagnosis I don't know what to do about	□	□	□	□	□
7. I hope to be able to make better health and lifestyle choices as a result.	□	□	□	□	□
8. I am worried about being able to maintain health and life insurance coverage.	□	□	□	□	□
9. I am worried about how my family will react to the testing information.	□	□	□	□	□
10. I need information about the types of cancers I am at risk for.	□	□	□	□	□
11. I am concerned about marital/family problems that might occur from obtaining the test results.	□	□	□	□	□
12. I might be helped to make important future life decisions by knowing I carry the gene, e.g., getting married, having children.	□	□	□	□	□
13. I need information about participation in future screening activities.	□	□	□	□	□
14. I want to know how a positive test will affect my children and other family members.	□	□	□	□	□
15. I am worried about my future life.	□	□	□	□	□
16. I want information about the difference between the diagnosis of having the gene and getting cancer.	□	□	□	□	□
17. I have financial concerns related to the screening.	□	□	□	□	□
18. I want to know the financial and social implications	□	□	□	□	□
19. I worry about being targeted as a carrier. of being identified as a carrier.	□	□	□	□	□
20. I want to know my survival prospects.	□	□	□	□	□

APPENDIX B

SAS Commands and Generated Output

Figure B.3.1 SAS Data Table Generated for the Concerns About Genetic Testing Scale (CGTS)

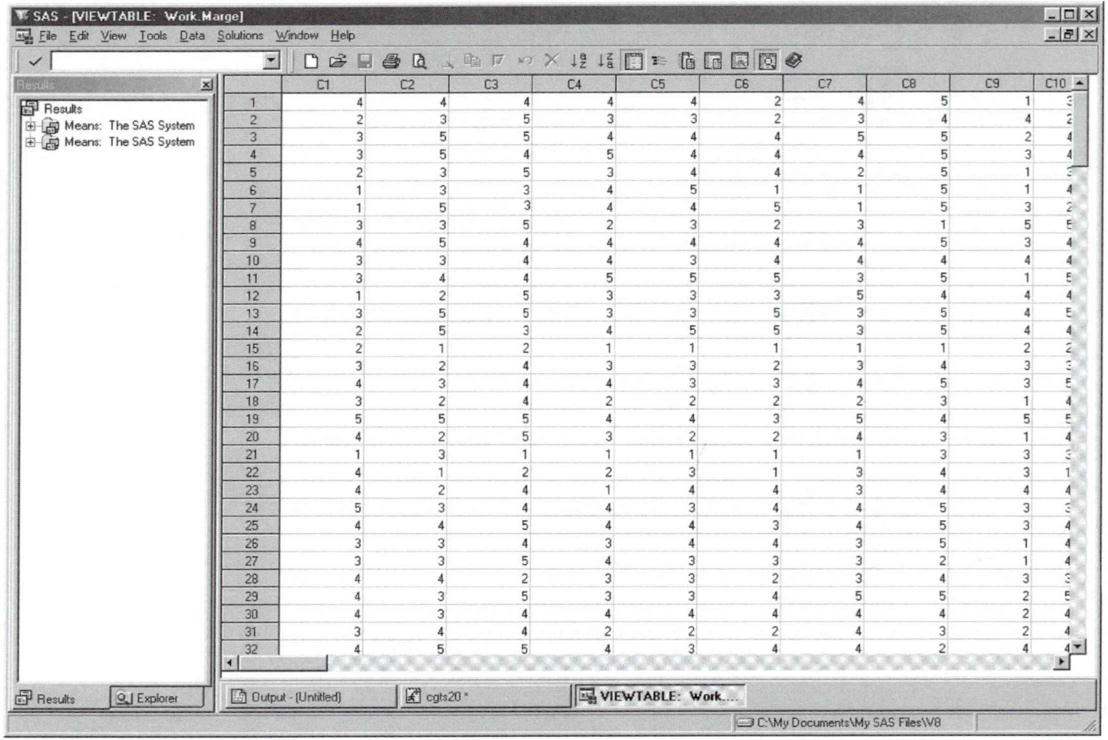

	C1	C2	C3	C4	C5	C6	C7	C8	C9	C10
1	4	4	4	4	4	2	4	5	1	3
2	2	3	5	3	3	2	3	4	4	2
3	3	5	5	4	4	4	5	5	2	4
4	3	5	4	5	4	4	4	5	3	4
5	2	3	5	3	4	4	2	5	1	3
6	1	3	3	4	5	1	1	5	1	4
7	1	5	3	4	4	5	1	5	3	2
8	3	3	5	2	3	2	3	1	5	5
9	4	5	4	4	4	4	4	5	3	4
10	3	3	4	4	3	4	4	4	4	4
11	3	4	4	5	5	5	3	5	1	5
12	1	2	5	3	3	3	5	4	4	4
13	3	5	5	3	3	5	3	5	4	5
14	2	5	3	4	5	5	3	5	4	4
15	2	1	2	1	1	1	1	1	2	2
16	3	2	4	3	3	2	3	4	3	3
17	4	3	4	4	3	3	4	5	3	5
18	3	2	4	2	2	2	2	3	1	4
19	5	5	5	4	4	3	5	4	5	5
20	4	2	5	3	2	2	4	3	1	4
21	1	3	1	1	1	1	1	3	3	3
22	4	1	2	2	3	1	3	4	3	1
23	4	2	4	1	4	4	3	4	4	4
24	5	3	4	4	3	4	4	5	3	3
25	4	4	5	4	4	3	4	5	3	4
26	3	3	4	3	4	4	3	5	1	4
27	3	3	5	4	3	3	3	2	1	4
28	4	4	2	3	3	2	3	4	3	3
29	4	3	5	3	3	4	5	5	2	5
30	4	3	4	4	4	4	4	4	2	4
31	3	4	4	2	2	2	4	3	2	4
32	4	5	5	4	3	4	4	2	4	4

Figure B.3.2   Commands for Inputting the 8×8 CGTS Correlation Matrix
Into SAS for Windows

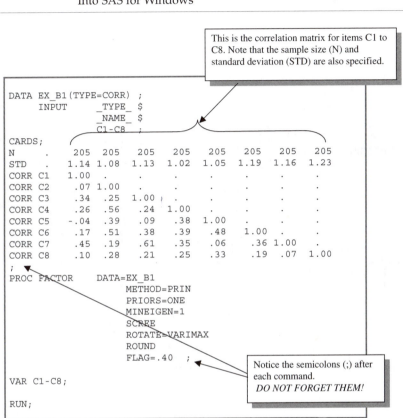

This is the correlation matrix for items C1 to C8. Note that the sample size (N) and standard deviation (STD) are also specified.

```
DATA EX_B1(TYPE=CORR)  ;
       INPUT        _TYPE_  $
                    _NAME_  $
                    C1-C8   ;
CARDS;
N         .     205  205   205   205   205   205   205   205
STD       .    1.14 1.08  1.13  1.02  1.05  1.19  1.16  1.23
CORR C1       1.00   .     .     .     .     .     .     .
CORR C2        .07 1.00    .     .     .     .     .     .
CORR C3        .34  .25  1.00    .     .     .     .     .
CORR C4        .26  .56   .24  1.00    .     .     .     .
CORR C5       -.04  .39   .09   .38  1.00    .     .     .
CORR C6        .17  .51   .38   .39   .48  1.00    .     .
CORR C7        .45  .19   .61   .35   .06   .36  1.00    .
CORR C8        .10  .28   .21   .25   .33   .19   .07  1.00
;
PROC FACTOR      DATA=EX_B1
                 METHOD=PRIN
                 PRIORS=ONE
                 MINEIGEN=1
                 SCREE
                 ROTATE=VARIMAX
                 ROUND
                 FLAG=.40   ;
VAR C1-C8;

RUN;
```

Notice the semicolons (;) after each command.
DO NOT FORGET THEM!

Table B3.1A   The Covariance Matrix and Descriptive Statistics Generated in SAS PROC
CORR for the 8-Item CGTS Scale

```
          EXAMPLE OF A CORRELATION AND COVARIANCE MATRIX GENERATED IN SAS

                              The CORR Procedure

        8  Variables:     C1    C2    C3    C4    C5    C6    C7    C8
```

Variance for Item C1 = 1.305

```
                                    Covariance Matrix, DF = 204
                              C1          C2          C3          C4

        C1    C1         1.30597     0.08046     0.43637     0.30449
        C2    C2         0.08046     1.17431     0.30595     0.61513
        C3    C3         0.43637     0.30595     1.28637     0.27704
        C4    C4         0.30449     0.61513     0.27704     1.04461
        C5    C5        -0.04325     0.44476     0.10674     0.40516
        C6    C6         0.23075     0.65100     0.51506     0.47274
        C7    C7         0.58871     0.23565     0.79949     0.41463
        C8    C8         0.14849     0.36872     0.29555     0.31743
```

Covariance for Item C1 and C3 = 0.436

```
                                    Covariance Matrix, DF = 204

                              C5          C6          C7          C8

        C1    C1        -0.04325     0.23075     0.58871     0.14849
        C2    C2         0.44476     0.65100     0.23565     0.36872
        C3    C3         0.10674     0.51506     0.79949     0.29555
        C4    C4         0.40516     0.47274     0.41463     0.31743
        C5    C5         1.10774     0.59146     0.07783     0.42467
        C6    C6         0.59146     1.41678     0.48708     0.28479
        C7    C7         0.07783     0.48708     1.33572     0.09540
        C8    C8         0.42467     0.28479     0.09540     1.52152

                              Simple Statistics

Variable    N      Mean     Std Dev      Sum      Minimum    Maximum   Label

   C1      205    3.11220   1.14279    638.00000   1.00000   5.00000     C1
   C2      205    3.63415   1.08366    745.00000   1.00000   5.00000     C2
   C3      205    3.91220   1.13418    802.00000   1.00000   5.00000     C3
   C4      205    3.47317   1.02207    712.00000   1.00000   5.00000     C4
   C5      205    3.20976   1.05250    658.00000   1.00000   5.00000     C5
   C6      205    3.17073   1.19029    650.00000   1.00000   5.00000     C6
   C7      205    3.56098   1.15574    730.00000   1.00000   5.00000     C7
   C8      205    3.68293   1.23350    755.00000   1.00000   5.00000     C8
```

Table B3.1B   Correlation Matrix Generated in SAS PROC CORR for the Eight-Item CGTS scale

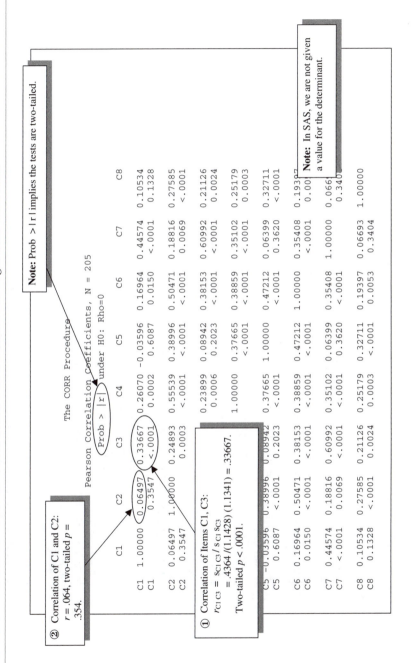

The CORR Procedure

Pearson Correlation Coefficients, N = 205
Prob > |r| under H0: Rho=0

	C1	C2	C3	C4	C5	C6	C7	C8
C1	1.00000	0.06497	0.33667	0.26070	-0.03596	0.16964	0.44574	0.10534
C1		0.3547	<.0001	0.0002	0.6087	0.0150	<.0001	0.1328
C2	0.06497	1.00000	0.24893	0.55539	0.38996	0.50471	0.18816	0.27585
C2	0.3547		0.0003	<.0001	<.0001	<.0001	0.0069	<.0001
C5	-0.03596	0.38996	0.08942	0.37665	1.00000	0.47212	0.06399	0.32711
C5	0.6087	<.0001	0.2023	<.0001		<.0001	0.3620	<.0001
C6	0.16964	0.50471	0.38153	0.38859	0.47212	1.00000	0.35408	0.19397
C6	0.0150	<.0001	<.0001	<.0001	<.0001		<.0001	0.0053
C7	0.44574	0.18816	0.60992	0.35102	0.06399	0.35408	1.00000	0.06693
C7	<.0001	0.0069	<.0001	<.0001	0.3620	<.0001		0.3404
C8	0.10534	0.27585	0.21126	0.25179	0.32711	0.19397	0.06693	1.00000
C8	0.1328	<.0001	0.0024	0.0003	<.0001	0.0053	0.3404	

Note: Prob > |r| implies the tests are two-tailed.

② Correlation of C1 and C2: $r = .064$, two-tailed $p = .354$.

① Correlation of Items C1, C3:
$r_{C1 C3} = s_{C1 C3} / s_{C1} s_{C3}$
= .4364 / ((1.1428)(1.1341)) = .33667.
Two-tailed $p < .0001$.

Note: In SAS, we are not given a value for the determinant.

247

Figure B3.3 SAS Program Commands Used to Generate Descriptive Statistics and the Covariance and Correlation Matrices for the Eight-Item CGTS Scale

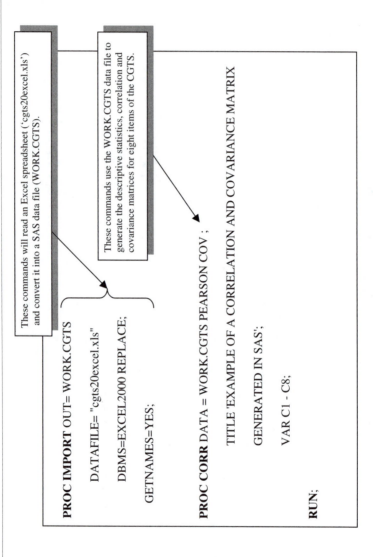

These commands will read an Excel spreadsheet ('cgts20excel.xls') and convert it into a SAS data file (WORK.CGTS).

These commands use the WORK.CGTS data file to generate the descriptive statistics, correlation and covariance matrices for eight items of the CGTS.

```
PROC IMPORT OUT= WORK.CGTS

    DATAFILE= "cgts20excel.xls"

    DBMS=EXCEL2000 REPLACE;

GETNAMES=YES;

PROC CORR DATA = WORK.CGTS PEARSON COV ;

    TITLE 'EXAMPLE OF A CORRELATION AND COVARIANCE MATRIX

    GENERATED IN SAS';

    VAR C1 - C8;

RUN;
```

Figure B3.4   SAS PROC FACTOR Program Commands Used to Generate the Measures of Sampling Adequacy

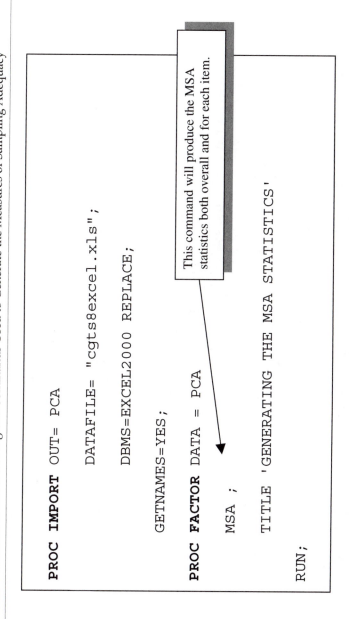

```
PROC IMPORT OUT= PCA

            DATAFILE= "cgts8excel.xls";

            DBMS=EXCEL2000 REPLACE;

    GETNAMES=YES;

PROC FACTOR DATA = PCA

    MSA ;

      TITLE 'GENERATING THE MSA STATISTICS'

RUN;
```

This command will produce the MSA statistics both overall and for each item.

Table B3.2   Measures of Sampling Adequacy (MSA) Generated in SAS PROC FACTOR

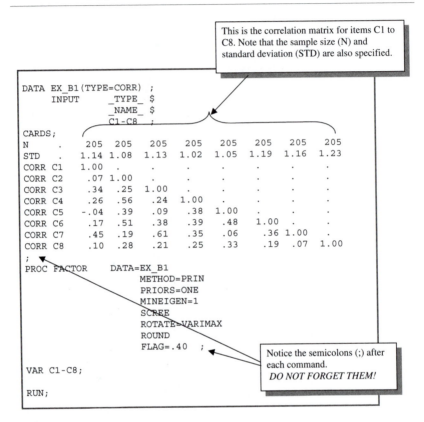

This is the correlation matrix for items C1 to C8. Note that the sample size (N) and standard deviation (STD) are also specified.

```
DATA EX_B1(TYPE=CORR) ;
     INPUT      _TYPE_  $
                _NAME_  $
                C1-C8   ;
CARDS;
N       .    205  205   205   205   205   205   205   205
STD     .   1.14 1.08  1.13  1.02  1.05  1.19  1.16  1.23
CORR C1     1.00   .     .     .     .     .     .     .
CORR C2      .07 1.00    .     .     .     .     .     .
CORR C3      .34  .25  1.00    .     .     .     .     .
CORR C4      .26  .56   .24  1.00    .     .     .     .
CORR C5     -.04  .39   .09   .38  1.00    .     .     .
CORR C6      .17  .51   .38   .39   .48  1.00    .     .
CORR C7      .45  .19   .61   .35   .06   .36  1.00    .
CORR C8      .10  .28   .21   .25   .33   .19   .07  1.00
;
PROC FACTOR      DATA=EX_B1
                 METHOD=PRIN
                 PRIORS=ONE
                 MINEIGEN=1
                 SCREE
                 ROTATE=VARIMAX
                 ROUND
                 FLAG=.40   ;

VAR C1-C8;

RUN;
```

Notice the semicolons (;) after each command.
DO NOT FORGET THEM!

Figure B4.2 SAS Commands Used to Generate the Initial Factors for the 8 × 8 CGTS Matrix

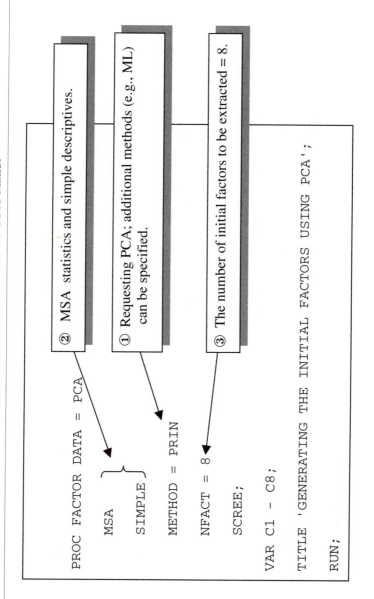

② MSA statistics and simple descriptives.

① Requesting PCA; additional methods (e.g., ML) can be specified.

③ The number of initial factors to be extracted = 8.

```
PROC FACTOR DATA = PCA

    MSA

    SIMPLE

    METHOD = PRIN

    NFACT = 8

    SCREE;

VAR C1 - C8;

TITLE 'GENERATING THE INITIAL FACTORS USING PCA';

RUN;
```

251

Table B4.1   SAS Computer-Generated Output for the Principal Components Analysis: Descriptive Statistics

```
                The FACTOR Procedure

Means and Standard Deviations from 205 Observations

Variable        Mean            Std Dev

  C1          3.1121951       1.1427939

  C2          3.6341463       1.0836598

  C3          3.9121951       1.1341826

  C4          3.4731707       1.0220664

  C5          3.2097561       1.0524958

  C6          3.1707317       1.1902883

  C7          3.5609756       1.1557355

  C8          3.6829268       1.2334994
```

Table B4.3   SAS Computer-Generated Output: The Factor Loading (Pattern) Matrix

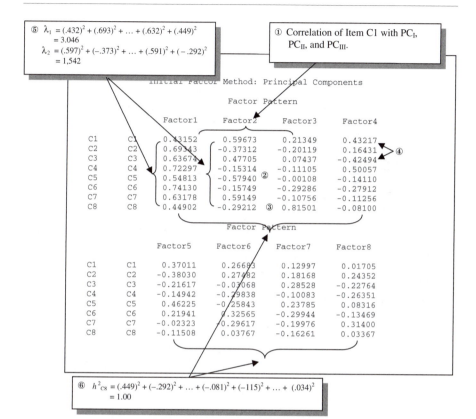

⑤ $\lambda_1 = (.432)^2 + (.693)^2 + \ldots + (.632)^2 + (.449)^2$
$= 3.046$
$\lambda_2 = (.597)^2 + (-.373)^2 + \ldots + (.591)^2 + (-.292)^2$
$= 1,542$

① Correlation of Item C1 with PC_I, PC_{II}, and PC_{III}.

Initial Factor Method: Principal Components

Factor Pattern

		Factor1	Factor2	Factor3	Factor4
C1	C1	0.43152	0.59673	0.21349	0.43217
C2	C2	0.69543	-0.37312	-0.20119	0.16431
C3	C3	0.63674	0.47705	0.07437	-0.42494
C4	C4	0.72297	-0.15314	-0.11105	0.50057
C5	C5	0.54813	-0.57940	-0.00108	-0.14110
C6	C6	0.74130	-0.15749	-0.29286	-0.27912
C7	C7	0.63178	0.59149	-0.10756	-0.11256
C8	C8	0.44902	-0.29212	0.81501	-0.08100

② ③ ④

Factor Pattern

		Factor5	Factor6	Factor7	Factor8
C1	C1	0.37011	0.26683	0.12997	0.01705
C2	C2	-0.38030	0.27482	0.18168	0.24352
C3	C3	-0.21617	-0.03068	0.28528	-0.22764
C4	C4	-0.14942	-0.29838	-0.10083	-0.26351
C5	C5	0.46225	-0.25843	0.23785	0.08316
C6	C6	0.21941	0.32565	-0.29944	-0.13469
C7	C7	-0.02323	0.29617	-0.19976	0.31400
C8	C8	-0.11508	0.03767	-0.16261	0.03367

⑥ $h^2_{C8} = (.449)^2 + (-.292)^2 + \ldots + (-.081)^2 + (-115)^2 + \ldots + (.034)^2$
$= 1.00$

Table B4.4 SAS Computer-Generated Output for the Total Variance Explained in PCA

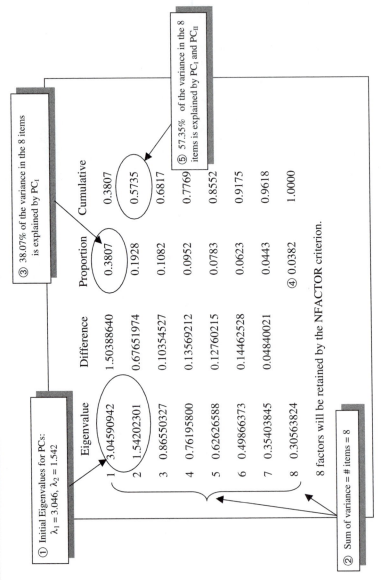

① Initial Eigenvalues for PCs:
$\lambda_1 = 3.046$, $\lambda_2 = 1.542$

③ 38.07% of the variance in the 8 items is explained by PC$_I$

⑤ 57.35% of the variance in the 8 items is explained by PC$_I$ and PC$_{II}$

② Sum of variance = # items = 8

	Eigenvalue	Difference	Proportion	Cumulative
1	3.04590942	1.50388640	0.3807	0.3807
2	1.54202301	0.67651974	0.1928	0.5735
3	0.86550327	0.10354527	0.1082	0.6817
4	0.76195800	0.13569212	0.0952	0.7769
5	0.62626588	0.12760215	0.0783	0.8552
6	0.49866373	0.14462528	0.0623	0.9175
7	0.35403845	0.04840021	0.0443	0.9618
8	0.30563824		④ 0.0382	1.0000

8 factors will be retained by the NFACTOR criterion.

Figure B.4.3 SAS Commands for Producing the Principal Axis Factoring Solution

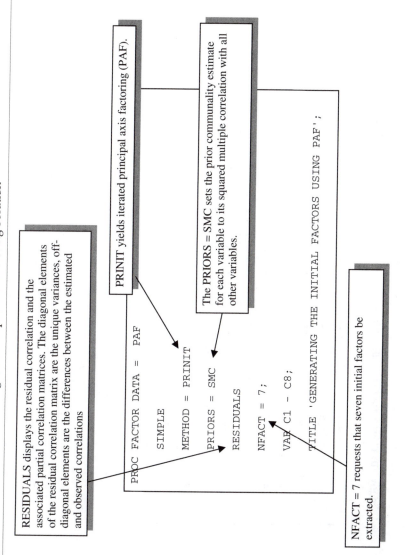

RESIDUALS displays the residual correlation and the associated partial correlation matrices. The diagonal elements of the residual correlation matrix are the unique variances, off-diagonal elements are the differences between the estimated and observed correlations

PRINT yields iterated principal axis factoring (PAF).

The PRIORS = SMC sets the prior communality estimate for each variable to its squared multiple correlation with all other variables.

NFACT = 7 requests that seven initial factors be extracted.

```
PROC FACTOR DATA = PAF
    SIMPLE
    METHOD = PRINIT
    PRIORS = SMC
    RESIDUALS
    NFACT = 7;
    VAR C1 - C8;
    TITLE 'GENERATING THE INITIAL FACTORS USING PAF';
```

Table B4.5 Initial Eigenvalues Generated from the Principal Axis Factoring (PAF) Solution Using SAS

	Eigenvalue	Difference	Proportion	Cumulative
1	2.45498042	1.53027209	0.8150	0.8150
2	0.92470833	0.76752503	0.3070	1.1219
3	0.15718330	0.05201721	0.0522	1.1741
4	0.10516609	0.11022867	0.0349	1.2090
5	-.00506259	0.10558553	-0.0017	1.2074
6	-.11064812	0.13244564	0.0367	1.1706
7	-.24309375	0.02780052	-0.0807	1.0899
8	-.27089427		-0.0899	1.0000

4 factors will be retained by the MINEIGEN criterion.

Four eigenvalues were negative. This is unacceptable in factor analysis (the minimum MINEIGEN criterion = 0). Therefore, according to SAS, only four factors will be retained.

Table B4.6   Comparison of Four-Factor Extraction in SPSS for Windows and SAS

Factor Matrix

	Factor			
	1	2	3	4
C1 Increase of personal control	.355	.382	-9.73E-02	.113
C2 Worry about uncertain diagnosis	.613	-.294	-2.72E-02	-7.81E-02
C3 What to do to manage risk	.574	.426	.187	8.402E-02
C4 Help reduce uncertainty about future	.761	-.208	-.560	1.565E-02
C5 Fear ambiguity of results	.476	.431	.148	-3.42E-02
C6 Worry about diagnosis I can't do anything about	.722	-.134	.314	-.340
C7 Hope to make better health, lifestyle choices	.612	.595	-1.45E-02	-2.57E-02
C8 Worried about loss of health, and life insurance coverage	.404	-.257	.203	.559

Extraction Method: Principal Axis Factoring.

Except for round-off, the loadings in SPSS for Windows and SAS are similar.

```
Factor Pattern
          Factor1        Factor2          Factor3          Factor4
C1        0.35352        0.38201         -0.08526          0.12283
C2        0.61147       -0.28805         -0.02299         -0.08252
C3        0.57091        0.42765          0.18944          0.06972
C4        0.77358       -0.21442         -0.57478          0.05672
C5        0.47525       -0.42536          0.14905         -0.05552
C6        0.72159       -0.12662          0.29412         -0.36967
C7        0.60959        0.59882         -0.01413         -0.01779
C8        0.40847       -0.26614          0.26004          0.55654
```

Table B4.7   Communality Estimates and Residual Correlation Matrix Generated in SAS Using Principal Axis Factoring With Four Factors

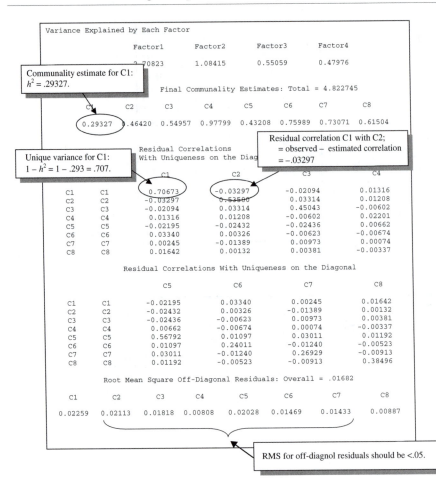

Variance Explained by Each Factor

	Factor1	Factor2	Factor3	Factor4
	2.70823	1.08415	0.55059	0.47976

Communality estimate for C1: $h^2 = .29327$.

Final Communality Estimates: Total = 4.822745

C1	C2	C3	C4	C5	C6	C7	C8
0.29327	0.46420	0.54957	0.97799	0.43208	0.75989	0.73071	0.61504

Residual correlation C1 with C2; = observed – estimated correlation = −.03297

Unique variance for C1: $1 - h^2 = 1 - .293 = .707$.

Residual Correlations With Uniqueness on the Diagonal

		C1	C2	C3	C4
C1	C1	0.70673	-0.03297	-0.02094	0.01316
C2	C2	-0.03297	0.53580	0.03314	0.01208
C3	C3	-0.02094	0.03314	0.45043	-0.00602
C4	C4	0.01316	0.01208	-0.00602	0.02201
C5	C5	-0.02195	-0.02432	-0.02436	0.00662
C6	C6	0.03340	0.00326	-0.00623	-0.00674
C7	C7	0.00245	-0.01389	0.00973	0.00074
C8	C8	0.01642	0.00132	0.00381	-0.00337

Residual Correlations With Uniqueness on the Diagonal

		C5	C6	C7	C8
C1	C1	-0.02195	0.03340	0.00245	0.01642
C2	C2	-0.02432	0.00326	-0.01389	0.00132
C3	C3	-0.02436	-0.00623	0.00973	0.00381
C4	C4	0.00662	-0.00674	0.00074	-0.00337
C5	C5	0.56792	0.01097	0.03011	0.01192
C6	C6	0.01097	0.24011	-0.01240	-0.00523
C7	C7	0.03011	-0.01240	0.26929	-0.00913
C8	C8	0.01192	-0.00523	-0.00913	0.38496

Root Mean Square Off-Diagonal Residuals: Overall = .01682

C1	C2	C3	C4	C5	C6	C7	C8
0.02259	0.02113	0.01818	0.00808	0.02028	0.01469	0.01433	0.00887

RMS for off-diagnol residuals should be <.05.

Table B4.8 Total Variance Explained by the Principal Axis Factoring Solution Using 4 Factors in SPSS for Window and SAS

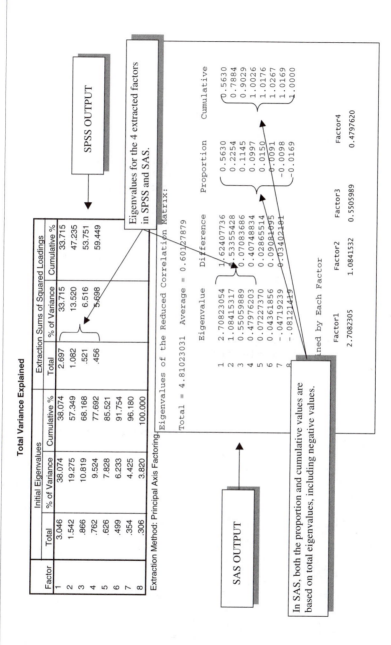

Total Variance Explained

Factor	Initial Eigenvalues			Extraction Sums of Squared Loadings		
	Total	% of Variance	Cumulative %	Total	% of Variance	Cumulative %
1	3.046	38.074	38.074	2.697	33.715	33.715
2	1.542	19.275	57.349	1.082	13.520	47.235
3	.866	10.819	68.168	.521	6.516	53.751
4	.762	9.524	77.692	.456	5.698	59.449
5	.626	7.828	85.521			
6	.499	6.233	91.754			
7	.354	4.425	96.180			
8	.306	3.820	100.000			

Extraction Method: Principal Axis Factoring

SPSS OUTPUT

Eigenvalues for the 4 extracted factors in SPSS and SAS.

SAS OUTPUT

In SAS, both the proportion and cumulative values are based on total eigenvalues, including negative values.

Eigenvalues of the Reduced Correlation Matrix:

Total = 4.81023031   Average = 0.60127879

	Eigenvalue	Difference	Proportion	Cumulative
1	2.70823054	1.62407736	0.5630	0.5630
2	1.08415317	0.53355428	0.2254	0.7884
3	0.55059889	0.07083686	0.1145	0.9029
4	0.47976203	0.40748834	0.0997	1.0026
5	0.07227370	0.02865514	0.0150	1.0176
6	0.04361856	0.09081095	0.0091	1.0267
7	-.04719239	0.03402181	-0.0098	1.0169
8	-.08121419		-0.0169	1.0000

...ned by Each Factor

Factor1	Factor2	Factor3	Factor4
2.7082305	1.0841532	0.5505989	0.4797620

259

Figure B4.4   SAS Commands Used to Generate the Initial Factors for the
8 × 8 CGTS Matrix Using PAF and the *Eigenvalues >1* Criteria

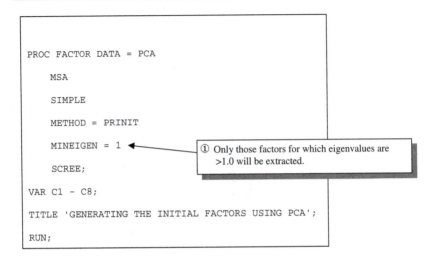

```
PROC FACTOR DATA = PCA

    MSA

    SIMPLE

    METHOD = PRINIT

    MINEIGEN = 1  ◄──────  ① Only those factors for which eigenvalues are
                                >1.0 will be extracted.
    SCREE;

VAR C1 - C8;

TITLE 'GENERATING THE INITIAL FACTORS USING PCA';

RUN;
```

Figure B4.5   Scree Plot Generated in SAS of the Eigenvalues Plotted
Against Their Principal Components

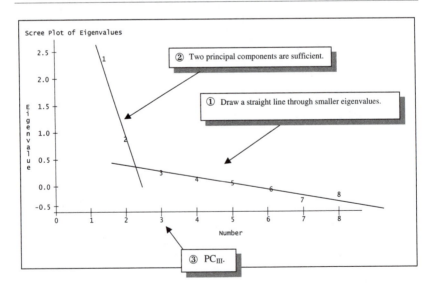

Table B4.9   Comparison of χ^2 Goodness-of-Fit Tests in SAS

A. Two Factors Extracted

```
Two factors:

     Test                            DF    Chi-Square    ChiSq

H0: No common factors               28      452.5124     <.0001

HA: At least one common factor

H0: 2 Factors are sufficient        13       46.4760     <.0001

HA: More factors are needed
```

① $p < .05$, χ^2 significant.

B. Three and Four Factors Extracted Using the Heywood Option.

```
Significance Tests Based on 205 observations

                        Test                    DF    Chi-Square    Pr >
                                                                    ChiSq

        H0: No common factors                   28    452.5124     <.0001
        HA: At least one common factor
        H0: 3 Factors are sufficient             7     20.9384      0.0039
        HA: More factors are needed


Significance Tests Based on 205 observations

                        Test                    DF    Chi-Square    Pr >
                                                                    ChiSq

        H0: No common factors                   28    452.5124     <.0001
        HA: At least one common factor
        H0: 4 Factors are sufficient             2      5.7016      0.0578

        HA: More factors are needed
```

② $p > .05$, χ^2 insignificant.

Figure B5.4   SAS Commands for Generating a Varimax Rotation of a
Two-Factor Principal Components Solution for Items C1 to C8
of the CGTS Scale

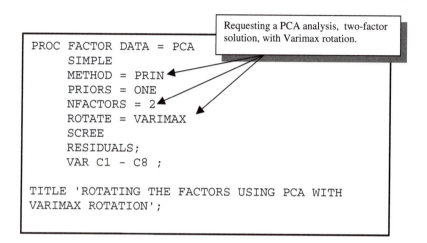

```
                                    ┌─────────────────────────────────┐
                                    │ Requesting a PCA analysis, two-factor │
PROC FACTOR DATA = PCA              │ solution, with Varimax rotation.      │
      SIMPLE                        └─────────────────────────────────┘
      METHOD = PRIN
      PRIORS = ONE
      NFACTORS = 2
      ROTATE = VARIMAX
      SCREE
      RESIDUALS;
      VAR C1 - C8 ;

TITLE 'ROTATING THE FACTORS USING PCA WITH
VARIMAX ROTATION';
```

Figure B5.5   SAS-Generated Plot of Rotated Varimax Solution for
Two-Factor Principal Component Solution, Items C1 to C8

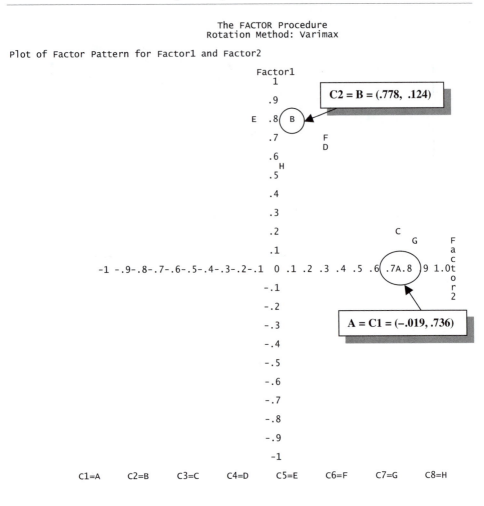

The FACTOR Procedure
Rotation Method: Varimax

Plot of Factor Pattern for Factor1 and Factor2

Table B5.3   Generated Output From SAS: Varimax Rotation of the Two Principal
Components for the Eight Items of the CGTS Scale

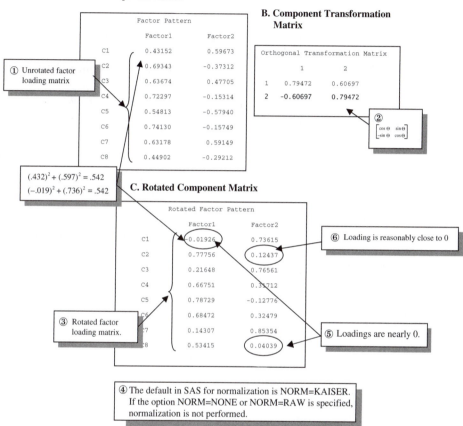

A. Component Matrix

Factor Pattern

	Factor1	Factor2
C1	0.43152	0.59673
C2	0.69343	-0.37312
C3	0.63674	0.47705
C4	0.72297	-0.15314
C5	0.54813	-0.57940
C6	0.74130	-0.15749
C7	0.63178	0.59149
C8	0.44902	-0.29212

① Unrotated factor loading matrix

B. Component Transformation Matrix

Orthogonal Transformation Matrix

	1	2
1	0.79472	0.60697
2	-0.60697	0.79472

② $\begin{bmatrix} \cos\Theta & \sin\Theta \\ -\sin\Theta & \cos\Theta \end{bmatrix}$

$(.432)^2 + (.597)^2 = .542$
$(-.019)^2 + (.736)^2 = .542$

C. Rotated Component Matrix

Rotated Factor Pattern

	Factor1	Factor2
C1	-0.01926	0.73615
C2	0.77756	0.12437
C3	0.21648	0.76561
C4	0.66751	0.33712
C5	0.78729	-0.12776
C6	0.68472	0.32479
C7	0.14307	0.85354
C8	0.53415	0.04039

⑥ Loading is reasonably close to 0

③ Rotated factor loading matrix.

⑤ Loadings are nearly 0.

④ The default in SAS for normalization is NORM=KAISER.
If the option NORM=NONE or NORM=RAW is specified,
normalization is not performed.

Table B5.4   Generated Output from SAS: PCA Analysis with Oblimin Rotation (delta = 0) of the Two Principal Components for the Eight Items of the CGTS Scale

A. Pattern Matrix From the Oblimin Rotation

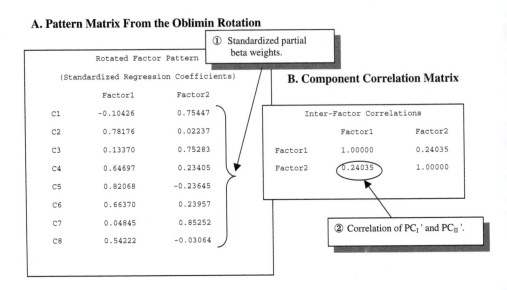

Rotated Factor Pattern

① Standardized partial beta weights.

(Standardized Regression Coefficients)

	Factor1	Factor2
C1	-0.10426	0.75447
C2	0.78176	0.02237
C3	0.13370	0.75283
C4	0.64697	0.23405
C5	0.82068	-0.23645
C6	0.66370	0.23957
C7	0.04845	0.85252
C8	0.54222	-0.03064

B. Component Correlation Matrix

Inter-Factor Correlations

	Factor1	Factor2
Factor1	1.00000	0.24035
Factor2	0.24035	1.00000

② Correlation of PC_I' and PC_{II}'.

C. Structure Matrix From the Oblimin

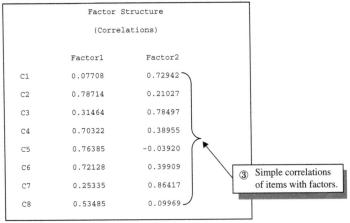

Factor Structure

(Correlations)

	Factor1	Factor2
C1	0.07708	0.72942
C2	0.78714	0.21027
C3	0.31464	0.78497
C4	0.70322	0.38955
C5	0.76385	-0.03920
C6	0.72128	0.39909
C7	0.25335	0.86417
C8	0.53485	0.09969

③ Simple correlations of items with factors.

Figure B5.10   Plot of the PCA Rotated Oblimin Solution Generated in SAS

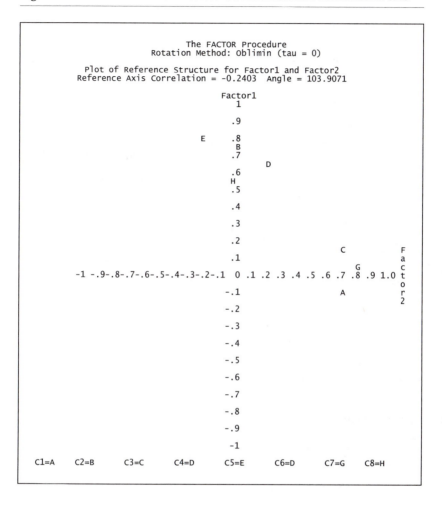

Table B5.5   Generated Output From SAS: PCA Analysis With Promax Rotation (kappa = 4) of the Two Principal Components for the Eight Items of the CGTS Scale

A. Factor Pattern Matrix

Rotation Method: Promax

(power = 4)

Rotated Factor Pattern

(Standardized Regression Coefficients)

	Factor1	Factor2
C1	-0.14590	0.77035
C2	0.78930	-0.00583
C3	0.09481	0.75999
C4	0.64164	0.21416
C5	0.84254	-0.27022
C6	0.65827	0.21915
C7	0.00325	0.86439
C8	0.54992	-0.05093

B. Component Correlation Matrix

Reference Axis Correlations

	Factor1	Factor2
Factor1	1.00000	-0.32227
Factor2	-0.32227	1.00000

C. Structure Matrix

Rotation Method: Promax

(Factor Structure (Correlations))

	Factor1	Factor2
C1	0.10236	0.72334
C2	0.78742	0.24854
C3	0.33973	0.79055
C4	0.71066	0.42094
C5	0.75545	0.00131
C6	0.72890	0.43130
C7	0.28182	0.86544
C8	0.53351	0.12629

Table B6.1   SAS Output for Evaluating the Factor Structure Matrix for High and Low Item-to-Factor Correlations

A.   All Loadings

```
                    Rotation Method: Oblimin (tau = 0)

                     Factor Structure (Correlations)
```

	Factor1	Factor2	Factor3	Factor4
C1	0.51372	0.09874	0.25079	-0.00498
C2	0.26854	0.75283	0.20109	0.27380
C3	0.78422	0.26775	0.27571	0.20920
C4	0.36889	0.65792		
C5	0.05285	0.66159		
C6	0.44813	0.61141	0.26377	0.38261
C7	0.73488	0.20765	0.16999	0.11643
C8	0.12971	0.36292	0.58420	-0.06413
C9	0.10615	0.23309	0.09845	0.72234
C10	0.72901	0.25157	0.31993	0.17028
C11	0.06871	0.19463	0.08194	0.61737
C12	0.63329	0.12225	0.26935	0.21978
C13	0.75170	0.33625	0.36945	0.32076
C14	0.41594	0.25046	0.28391	0.67666
C15	0.37783	0.74144	0.23432	0.37731
C16	0.65033	0.32835	0.22484	0.13708
C17	0.48556	0.15299	0.58187	0.32004
C18	0.36725	0.18590	0.80738	0.18639
C19	0.36907	0.25426	0.85896	0.23086
C20	0.71522	0.25398	0.56902	0.09136

① C1 correlates weakly with Factors 2 and 4.

② C20 is strongly correlated with Factors 1 and 3.

(Continued)

B.   Loadings <.40 Are Suppressed

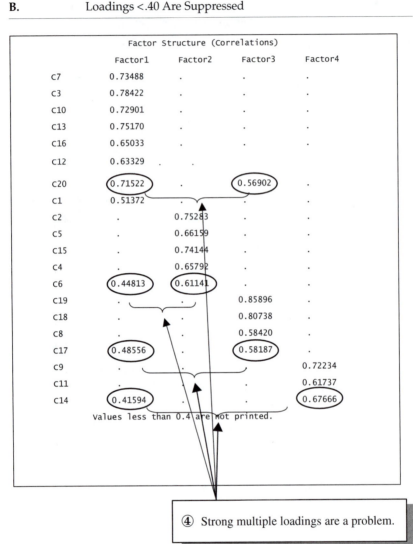

④ Strong multiple loadings are a problem.

Figure B6.1   SAS Commands Used to Generate Cronbach's Alpha
Coefficients

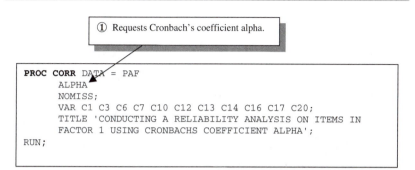

```
PROC CORR DATA = PAF
      ALPHA
      NOMISS;
      VAR C1 C3 C6 C7 C10 C12 C13 C14 C16 C17 C20;
      TITLE 'CONDUCTING A RELIABILITY ANALYSIS ON ITEMS IN
      FACTOR 1 USING CRONBACHS COEFFICIENT ALPHA';
RUN;
```

Table B6.3   Results of the SAS Reliability Analysis for Factor 1 of the
20-Item CGTS Scale

```
                        Cronbach Coefficient Alpha
                                                    ┌──────────────────────────────┐
                Variables                    Alpha  │ Coefficient alpha:           │
                                                    │ unstandardized and standardized.│
                                                    └──────────────────────────────┘

                        Raw                  0.879769  ⎫
                                                       ⎬
                        Standardized         0.882604  ⎭

              Cronbach Coefficient Alpha with Deleted Variable

                     Raw Variables              Standardized Variables
                     Correlation                      Correlation
  Deleted
  Variable       with Total        Alpha        with Total         Alpha
┌──────────────────────────────┐                ┌──────────────────────────────┐
│ Correlation with total scale.│                │ Scale alpha if item is deleted.│
└──────────────────────────────┘                └──────────────────────────────┘
    C1            0.432748       0.879274         0.432887         0.882590
    C3            0.736537       0.859665         0.738145         0.862984
    C6            0.498196       0.875422         0.495915         0.878668
    C7            0.649081       0.865363         0.650299         0.868785
    C10           0.672827       0.864460         0.670379         0.867471
    C12           0.584291       0.870600         0.585358         0.872991
    C13           0.724224       0.860561         0.729649         0.863551
    C14           0.458456       0.878817         0.456301         0.881141
    C16           0.606749       0.868278         0.613646         0.871168
    C17           0.507209       0.874379         0.507605         0.877934
    C20           0.679377       0.864087         0.682797         0.866654
```

Figure B7.1 SAS PROC FACTOR Commands Used to Sort the Factor Loading Matrix

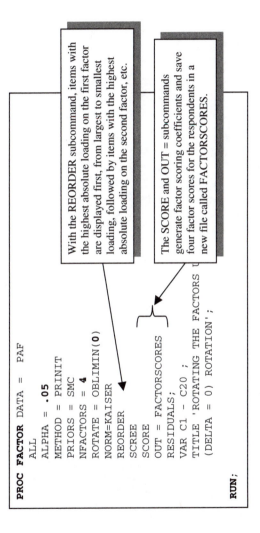

```
PROC FACTOR DATA = PAF
   ALL
   ALPHA = .05
   METHOD = PRINIT
   PRIORS = SMC
   NFACTORS = 4
   ROTATE = OBLIMIN(0)
   NORM=KAISER
   REORDER
   SCREE
   SCORE
   OUT = FACTORSCORES
   RESIDUALS;
   VAR C1 - C20 ;
   TITLE 'ROTATING THE FACTORS U
   (DELTA = 0) ROTATION';

RUN;
```

With the REORDER subcommand, items with the highest absolute loading on the first factor are displayed first, from largest to smallest loading, followed by items with the highest absolute loading on the second factor, etc.

The SCORE and OUT = subcommands generate factor scoring coefficients and save four factor scores for the respondents in a new file called FACTORSCORES.

273

Table B7.1   Factor Structure Matrix Generated in SAS Using the Reordered Loadings

These item loadings have been reordered from highest to lowest.

These are the next set of ordered loadings.

Factor Structure (Correlations)

	Factor1	Factor2	Factor3	Factor4
C7	0.73488	0.20765	0.16999	0.11643
C3	0.78422	0.26775	0.27571	0.20920
C10	0.72901	0.25157	0.31993	0.17028
C13	0.75170	0.33625	0.36945	0.32076
C16	0.65033	0.32835	0.22484	0.13708
C12	0.63329	0.12225	0.26935	0.21978
C20	0.71522	0.25398	0.56902	0.09136
C1	0.51372	0.09874	0.25079	-0.00498
C2	0.26854	0.75283	0.20109	0.27380
C5	0.05285	0.66159	0.21800	0.21876
C15	0.27783	0.74144	0.23432	0.37731
C4	0.36889	0.65792	0.27592	0.01017
C6	0.44813	0.61141	0.26377	0.38261
C19	0.36907	0.25426	0.85896	0.23086
C18	0.36725	0.18590	0.80738	0.18639
C8	0.12971	0.36292	0.58420	-0.06413
C17	0.48556	0.15299	0.58187	0.32004
C9	0.10615	0.23309	0.09845	0.72234
C11	0.06871	0.19463	0.08194	0.61737
C14	0.41594	0.25046	0.28391	

Table B7.3   Standardized Scoring Coefficients for the Factors Generated in SAS

```
                    Rotation Method: Oblimin (tau = 0)
                Scoring Coefficients Estimated by Regression

        Squared Multiple Correlations of the Variables with Each Factor
        Factor1          Factor2          Factor3          Factor4
       0.89574113       0.82820726       0.86431198       0.76043010

                        Standardized Scoring Coefficients
                  Factor1          Factor2          Factor3          Factor4
    C7            0.19501          0.01223         -0.03422         -0.05275
    C3            0.21721         -0.01440          0.00873         -0.00083
    C10           0.17617         -0.01683         -0.03112         -0.01344
    C13           0.15495          0.01376          0.02107          0.09118
    C16           0.08472          0.03173         -0.00941         -0.01516
    C12           0.11120         -0.05921         -0.01850          0.03447
    C20           0.16711          0.00352          0.10293         -0.09584
    C1            0.06215         -0.01839         -0.00359         -0.03552
    C2           -0.02664          0.29306          0.02670          0.01513
    C5           -0.07031          0.22496          0.05050          0.00336
    C15           0.04205          0.28461         -0.04152          0.09659
    C4            0.03574          0.20154          0.00897         -0.11062
    C6            0.04769          0.15497         -0.03244          0.08334
    C19           0.00177         -0.00023          0.51043          0.02829
    C18          -0.00668         -0.03269          0.31514          0.02245
    C8           -0.04669          0.10104          0.12921         -0.10076
    C17           0.04910         -0.03972          0.08723          0.07254
    C9           -0.02357         -0.00286         -0.07309          0.37971
    C11          -0.02081         -0.00124          0.00041          0.22261
    C14           0.02067         -0.01797          0.02399          0.32318
```

Figure B7.2   SAS Commands Used to Create a Factor-Based Scale Using the Items in Factor 1

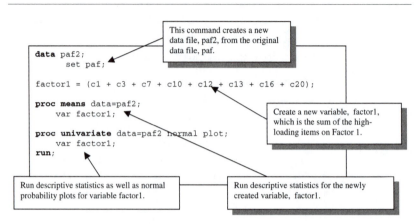

APPENDIX C

Output for
20-Item CGTS Scale

Table C3.1 20 × 20 Correlation Matrix for the 20-Item Concerns About Genetic Testing Scale

	C1	C2	C3	C4	C5	C6	C7	C8	C9	C10	C11	C12	C13	C14	C15	C16	C17	C18	C19	C20
C1	1.00	.07	.34	.26	-.04	.17	.45	.10	.00	.34	.04	.41	.44	.07	.17	.21	.17	.22	.29	.43
C2	.07	1.00	.25	.56	.39	.51	.19	.28	.32	.33	.20	.20	.28	.20	.63	.23	.11	.21	.19	.18
C3	.34	.25	1.00	.24	.09	.38	.61	.21	.08	.49	.07	.45	.65	.44	.34	.60	.40	.27	.21	.58
C4	.26	.56	.24	1.00	.38	.39	.35	.25	-.01	.29	.08	.21	.34	.14	.52	.26	.15	.27	.23	.32
C5	-.04	.39	.09	.38	1.00	.48	.06	.33	.26	.03	.14	-.10	.21	.18	.48	.19	.09	.13	.19	.14
C6	.17	.51	.38	.39	.48	1.00	.36	.19	.31	.32	.18	.32	.37	.43	.49	.41	.29	.15	.34	.38
C7	.45	.19	.61	.35	.06	.36	1.00	.07	.17	.50	-.05	.42	.54	.32	.15	.47	.24	.21	.15	.51
C8	.10	.28	.21	.25	.33	.19	.07	1.00	-.07	.10	-.03	.00	.15	.12	.19	.09	.26	.45	.47	.30
C9	.00	.32	.08	-.01	.26	.31	.17	-.07	1.00	.04	.46	.08	.20	.48	.19	.08	.21	.11	.22	.09
C10	.34	.33	.49	.29	.03	.32	.50	.10	.04	1.00	.08	.58	.62	.31	.33	.52	.38	.33	.35	.47
C11	.04	.20	.07	.08	.14	.18	-.05	-.03	.46	.08	1.00	.12	.25	.42	.32	-.01	.15	.14	.11	.00
C12	.41	.20	.45	.21	-.10	.32	.42	.00	.08	.58	.12	1.00	.40	.33	.30	.31	.35	.28	.33	.42
C13	.44	.28	.65	.34	.21	.37	.54	.15	.20	.62	.25	.40	1.00	.38	.42	.47	.47	.37	.34	.56
C14	.07	.20	.44	.14	.18	.43	.32	.12	.48	.31	.42	.33	.38	1.00	.37	.25	.35	.35	.27	.30
C15	.17	.63	.34	.52	.48	.49	.15	.19	.19	.33	.32	.30	.42	.37	1.00	.40	.26	.17	.27	.25
C16	.21	.23	.60	.26	.19	.41	.47	.09	.08	.52	-.01	.31	.47	.25	.40	1.00	.42	.16	.23	.52
C17	.17	.11	.40	.15	.09	.29	.24	.26	.21	.38	.15	.35	.47	.35	.26	.42	1.00	.51	.58	.43
C18	.22	.21	.27	.27	.13	.15	.21	.45	.11	.33	.14	.28	.37	.35	.17	.16	.51	1.00	.68	.52
C19	.29	.19	.21	.23	.19	.34	.15	.47	.22	.35	.11	.33	.34	.27	.27	.23	.58	.68	1.00	.52
C20	.43	.18	.58	.32	.14	.38	.51	.30	.09	.47	.00	.42	.56	.30	.25	.52	.43	.52	.52	1.00

Determinant = 1.995E−05.

Table C3.2   KMO and Bartlett's test for the 20-item CGTS Scale

KMO and Bartlett's Test

Kaiser-Meyer-Olkin Measure of Sampling Adequacy.		.763
Bartlett's Test of Sphericity	Approx. Chi-Square	2126.545
	df	190
	Sig.	.000

Table C4.2   Comparison of the Principal Component Analyses(PCA) and Principal Axis Factoring (PAF) Solutions for the 20-Item CGTS Generated in SPSS for Windows

A. Principal Components Solution

Total Variance Explained

Component	Initial Eigenvalues			Extraction Sums of Squared Loadings		
	Total	% of Variance	Cumulative %	Total	% of Variance	Cumulative %
1	6.698	33.490	33.490	6.698	33.490	33.490
2	2.294	11.469	44.959	2.294	11.469	44.959
3	1.764	8.819	53.778	1.764	8.819	53.778
4	1.655	8.274	62.052	1.655	8.274	62.052
5	1.055	5.274	67.326	1.055	5.274	67.326
6	.880	4.402	71.728			
7	.744	3.719	75.447			
8	.705	3.523	78.970			
9	.615	3.073	82.042			
10	.539	2.696	84.738			
11	.486	2.431	87.170			
12	.450	2.252	89.422			
13	.410	2.050	91.471			
14	.375	1.875	93.346			
15	.341	1.704	95.050			
16	.268	1.338	96.388			
17	.240	1.202	97.590			
18	.203	1.015	98.606			
19	.172	.858	99.463			
20	.107	.537	100.000			

① 5 factors meet the 5% criteria. Cumulative % = 67.326

Extraction Method: Principal Component Analysis.

B. Principal Axis Factoring Solution

Total Variance Explained

Factor	Initial Eigenvalues			Extraction Sums of Squared Loadings		
	Total	% of Variance	Cumulative %	Total	% of Variance	Cumulative %
1	6.698	33.490	33.490	6.284	31.420	31.420
2	2.294	11.469	44.959	1.852	9.260	40.679
3	1.764	8.819	53.778	1.382	6.909	47.588
4	1.655	8.274	62.052	1.183	5.916	53.504
5	1.055	5.274	67.326	.591	2.954	56.458
6	.880	4.402	71.728			
7	.744	3.719	75.447			
8	.705	3.523	78.970			
9	.615	3.073	82.042			
10	.539	2.696	84.738			
11	.486	2.431	87.170			
12	.450	2.252	89.422			
13	.410	2.050	91.471			
14	.375	1.875	93.346			
15	.341	1.704	95.050			
16	.268	1.338	96.388			
17	.240	1.202	97.590			
18	.203	1.015	98.606			
19	.172	.858	99.463			
20	.107	.537	100.000			

② 4 factors meet the 5% criteria.
Cumulative % = 53.504

Extraction Method: Principal Axis Factoring.

APPENDIX D

Tables for the Chi-Square and Normal Distribution

Table D.1   Critical values of the χ^2 Distribution

df	\multicolumn{7}{c}{Alpha (α)}
	0.250	0.100	0.050	0.025	0.010	.005	.001
1	1.3233	2.7055	3.8415	5.0239	6.6349	7.87944	10.8280
2	2.7726	4.6052	5.9915	7.3778	9.2103	10.5966	13.8160
3	4.1084	6.2514	7.8147	9.3484	11.3449	12.8381	16.2660
4	5.3853	7.7794	9.4877	11.1433	13.2767	14.8602	18.4670
5	6.6257	9.2364	11.0705	12.8325	15.0863	16.7496	20.5150
6	7.8408	10.6446	12.5916	14.4494	16.8119	18.5476	22.4580
7	9.0372	12.0170	14.0671	16.0128	18.4753	20.2777	24.3220
8	10.2188	13.3616	15.5073	17.5346	20.0902	21.9550	26.1250
9	11.3887	14.6837	16.9190	19.0228	21.6660	23.5893	27.8770
10	12.5489	15.9871	18.3070	20.4831	23.2093	25.1882	29.5880
11	13.7007	17.2750	19.6751	21.9200	24.7250	26.7569	31.2640
12	14.8454	18.5494	21.0261	23.3367	26.2170	28.2995	32.9090
13	15.9839	19.8119	22.3621	24.7356	27.6883	29.8194	34.5280
14	17.1770	21.0642	23.6848	26.1190	29.1413	31.3193	36.1230
15	18.2451	22.3072	24.9958	27.4884	30.5779	32.8013	37.6970
16	19.3688	23.5418	26.2962	28.8454	31.9999	34.2672	39.2520
17	20.4887	24.7690	27.5871	30.1910	33.4087	35.7185	40.7900
18	21.6049	25.9894	28.8693	31.5264	34.8053	37.1564	42.3120
19	22.7178	27.2036	30.1435	32.8523	36.1908	38.5822	43.8200
20	23.8277	28.4120	31.4104	34.1696	37.5662	39.9968	45.3150
21	24.9348	29.6151	32.6705	35.4789	38.9321	41.4010	46.7970
22	26.0393	30.8133	33.9244	36.7807	40.2894	42.7956	48.2680
23	27.1413	32.0069	35.1725	38.0757	41.6384	44.1813	49.7280
24	28.2412	33.1963	36.4151	39.3641	42.9798	45.5585	51.1790
25	29.3389	34.3816	37.6525	40.6465	44.3141	46.9278	52.6200
26	30.4345	35.5631	38.8852	41.9232	45.6417	48.2899	54.0520
27	31.5284	36.7412	40.1133	43.1944	46.9630	49.6449	55.4760
28	32.6205	37.9159	41.3372	44.4607	48.2782	50.9933	56.8920
29	33.7109	39.0875	42.5569	45.7222	49.5879	52.3356	58.3020
30	34.7998	40.2560	43.7729	46.9792	50.8922	53.6720	59.7030
40	45.6160	51.8050	65.7585	59.3417	63.6907	66.7659	73.4020
50	56.3336	63.1671	67.5048	71.4202	76.1539	79.4900	86.6610
60	66.9814	74.3970	79.0819	83.2976	88.3794	91.9517	99.6070
70	77.5766	85.5271	90.5312	95.0231	100.4250	104.2150	112.3170
80	88.1303	96.5782	101.8790	106.6290	112.3290	116.3210	124.8390
90	98.6499	107.565	113.1450	118.1360	124.1160	128.2990	137.2080
100	109.1410	118.4980	124.3420	129.5610	135.8070	140.1690	149.4490

SOURCE: This table was adapted from Table 8 of the *Biometrika Tables for Statisticians* (1970, Vol. 1, 3rd ed), E. S. Pearson and H. O. Hartley (eds.). Reproduced here by the kind permission of the trustees of *Biometrika*.

Table D.2   Cumulative Probabilities of the Normal Distribution

z	F(z)	1-F(z)	z	F(z)	1-F(z)	z	F(z)	1-F(z)	z	F(z)	1-F(z)
.00	.5000	.5000	.37	.6443	.3557	.74	.7704	.2296	1.11	.8665	.1335
.01	.5040	.4960	.38	.6480	.3520	.75	.7734	.2266	1.12	.8686	.1314
.02	.5080	.4920	.39	.6517	.3483	.76	.7764	.2236	1.13	.8708	.1292
.03	.5120	.4880	.40	.6554	.3446	.77	.7794	.2206	1.14	.8729	.1271
.04	.5160	.4840	.41	.6591	.3409	.78	.7823	.2177	1.15	.8749	.1251
.05	.5199	.4761	.42	.6628	.3372	.79	.7852	.2148	1.16	.8770	.1230
.06	.5239	.4721	.43	.6664	.3336	.80	.7881	.2119	1.17	.8790	.1210
.07	.5279	.4681	.44	.6700	.3300	.81	.7910	.2090	1.18	.8810	.1190
.08	.5319	.4641	.45	.6736	.3264	.82	.7939	.2061	1.19	.8830	.1170
.09	.5359	.4602	.46	.6772	.3228	.83	.7967	.2033	1.20	.8849	.1151
.10	.5398	.4562	.47	.6808	.3192	.84	.7995	.2005	1.21	.8869	.1131
.11	.5438	.4522	.48	.6844	.3156	.85	.8023	.1977	1.22	.8888	.1112
.12	.5478	.4483	.49	.6879	.3121	.86	.8051	.1949	1.23	.8907	.1093
.13	.5517	.4443	.50	.6915	.3085	.87	.8078	.1922	1.24	.8925	.1075
.14	.5557	.4404	.51	.6950	.3050	.88	.8106	.1894	1.25	.8944	.1056
.15	.5596	.4364	.52	.6985	.3015	.89	.8133	.1867	1.26	.8962	.1038
.16	.5636	.4364	.53	.7019	.2981	.90	.8159	.1841	1.27	.8980	.1020
.17	.5675	.4325	.54	.7054	.2946	.91	.8186	.1814	1.28	.8997	.1003
.18	.5714	.4286	.55	.7088	.2912	.92	.8212	.1788	1.29	.9015	.0985
.19	.5753	.4247	.56	.7123	.2877	.93	.8238	.1762	1.30	.9032	.0968
.20	.5793	.4207	.57	.7157	.2843	.94	.8264	.1736	1.31	.9049	.0951
.21	.5832	.4168	.58	.7190	.2810	.95	.8289	.1711	1.32	.9066	.0934
.22	.5871	.4129	.59	.7224	.2776	.96	.8315	.1685	1.33	.9082	.0918
.23	.5910	.4090	.60	.7257	.2743	.97	.8340	.1660	1.34	.9099	.0901
.24	.5949	.4051	.61	.7291	.2709	.98	.8365	.1635	1.35	.9115	.0885
.25	.5987	.4013	.62	.7324	.2676	.99	.8389	.1611	1.36	.9131	.0869
.26	.6026	.3974	.63	.7357	.2643	1.00	.8413	.1587	1.37	.9147	.0853
.27	.6064	.3936	.64	.7389	.2611	1.01	.8436	.1564	1.38	.9162	.0838
.28	.6103	.3987	.65	.7422	.2578	1.02	.8461	.1539	1.39	.9177	.0823
.29	.6141	.3859	.66	.7454	.2546	1.03	.8485	.1515	1.40	.9192	.0808
.30	.6179	.3821	.67	.7486	.2514	1.04	.8508	.1492	1.41	.9207	.0793
.31	.6217	.3783	.68	.7517	.2483	1.05	.8531	.1469	1.42	.9222	.0778
.32	.6255	.3745	.69	.7549	.2451	1.06	.8554	.1446	1.43	.9236	.0764
.33	.6293	.3707	.70	.7580	.2420	1.07	.8577	.1423	1.44	.9251	.0749
.34	.6331	.3669	.71	.7611	.2389	1.08	.8599	.1401	1.45	.9265	.0735
.35	.6368	.3632	.72	.7642	.2358	1.09	.8621	.1379	1.46	.9279	.0721
.36	.6406	.3594	.73	.7673	.2327	1.10	.8643	.1357	1.47	.9292	.0708

(Continued)

Table D.2   (Continued)

z	F(z)	1-F(z)	z	F(z)	1-F(z)	z	F(z)	1-F(z)	z	F(z)	1-F(z)
1.48	.9306	.0694	1.79	.9633	.0367	2.10	.9821	.0179	2.41	.9920	.0080
1.49	.9319	.0681	1.80	.9641	.0359	2.11	.9826	.0174	2.42	.9922	.0078
1.50	.9332	.0668	1.81	.9649	.0351	2.12	.9830	.0170	2.43	.9925	.0075
1.51	.9345	.0655	1.82	.9656	.0344	2.13	.9834	.0166	2.44	.9927	.0073
1.52	.9357	.0643	1.83	.9664	.0336	2.14	.9838	.0162	2.45	.9929	.0071
1.53	.9370	.0630	1.84	.9671	.0329	2.15	.9842	.0158	2.46	.9931	.0069
1.54	.9382	.0618	1.85	.9678	.0322	2.16	.9846	.0154	2.47	.9932	.0068
1.55	.9394	.0606	1.86	.9686	.0314	2.17	.9850	.0150	2.48	.9934	.0066
1.56	.9406	.0594	1.87	.9693	.0307	2.18	.9854	.0146	2.49	.9936	.0064
1.57	.9418	.0582	1.88	.9699	.0301	2.19	.9857	.0143	2.50	.9938	.0062
1.58	.9429	.0571	1.89	.9706	.0294	2.20	.9861	.0139	2.51	.9940	.0060
1.59	.9441	.0559	1.90	.9713	.0287	2.21	.9864	.0136	2.52	.9941	.0059
1.60	.9452	.0548	1.91	.9719	.0281	2.22	.9868	.0132	2.53	.9943	.0057
1.61	.9463	.0537	1.92	.9726	.0274	2.23	.9871	.0129	2.54	.9945	.0055
1.62	.9474	.0526	1.93	.9732	.0268	2.24	.9875	.0125	2.55	.9946	.0054
1.63	.9484	.0516	1.94	.9738	.0262	2.25	.9878	.0122	2.56	.9948	.0052
1.64	.9495	.0505	1.95	.9744	.0256	2.26	.9881	.0119	2.57	.9949	.0051
1.65	.9505	.0495	1.96	.9750	.0250	2.27	.9884	.0116	2.58	.9951	.0049
1.66	.9515	.0485	1.97	.9756	.0244	2.28	.9887	.0113	2.59	.9952	.0048
1.67	.9525	.0475	1.98	.9761	.0239	2.29	.9890	.0110	2.60	.9953	.0047
1.68	.9535	.0465	1.99	.9767	.0233	2.30	.9893	.0107	2.70	.9965	.0035
1.69	.9545	.0455	2.00	.9772	.0228	2.31	.9896	.0104	2.80	.9974	.0026
1.70	.9554	.0446	2.01	.9778	.0222	2.32	.9898	.0102	2.90	.9981	.0019
1.71	.9565	.0435	2.02	.9783	.0217	2.33	.9901	.0099	3.00	.9987	.0013
1.72	.9573	.0427	2.03	.9788	.0212	2.34	.9904	.0096	3.20	.9993	.0007
1.73	.9582	.0418	2.04	.9793	.0207	2.35	.9906	.0094	3.40	.9997	.0003
1.74	.9591	.0409	2.05	.9798	.0202	2.36	.9909	.0091	3.60	.9998	.0002
1.75	.9599	.0401	2.06	.9803	.0197	2.37	.9911	.0089	3.80	.9999	.0001
1.76	.9608	.0392	2.07	.9808	.0192	2.38	.9913	.0087	4.00	.9999	.0001
1.77	.9616	.0384	2.08	.9812	.0188	2.39	.9916	.0084			
1.78	.9625	.0375	2.09	.9817	.0183	2.40	.9918	.0082			

APPENDIX E

UNRAVELING THE MYSTERY
OF PRINCIPAL COMPONENT EXTRACTION

The purpose of Appendix E is to provide you with a detailed discussion of principal component extraction. As an illustrated example, we will extract the first two principal components for the first eight items of the Concerns About Genetic Testing Scale (CGTS) that was presented to you in Appendix A. The organization of this appendix is as follows. First, we will present you with a brief overview of the process of principal component extraction. Next, we will examine each step of the extraction process in greater detail using matrix algebra and the spreadsheet program Excel to extract the first two principal components. Throughout this endeavor, we will compare our results with that presented in the computer-generated printout obtained from SPSS for Windows.

As we indicated in Chapter 4, there are additional resources that you might want to examine as well. These include Bernstein (1988), Kline (1994), and Nunnally and Bernstein (1994).

BRIEF OVERVIEW OF THE PROCESS

To undertake a principal component analysis (PCA), we need to start with a correlation matrix. The correlation matrix that we will analyze is the eight-item matrix given in Figure E.1. This correlation matrix is a standardized representation of the relationships among the eight CGTS items to be examined. The 1s placed on the diagonal represent not only the correlation of the items with themselves (e.g., C1 with C1) but also

Figure E.1   The Eight-Item Correlation Matrix to Be Analyzed Using
Principal Component Analysis

	C1	C2	C3	C4	C5	C6	C7	C8
C1	1.00	.065	.337	.261	-.036	.170	.447	.104
C2	.065	1.000	.249	.555	.390	.505	.188	.276
C3	.337	.249	1.000	.239	.089	.382	.610	.211
C4	.261	.555	.239	1.000	.377	.389	.351	.252
C5	-.036	.390	.089	.377	1.000	.472	.064	.327
C6	.170	.505	.382	.389	.472	1.000	.354	.194
C7	.447	.188	.610	.351	.064	.354	1.000	.067
C8	.104	.276	.211	.252	.327	.194	.067	1.000

reflect the total variance for the given item because, for standardized items, $\bar{x} = 0$ and $s^2 = 1$.

The aim of PCA is to duplicate the correlation matrix using a set of factors (also called *components*) that are fewer in number and are linear combinations of the original set of items. PCA assumes that there is as much variance to be analyzed as observed variables and that all of the variance in an item can be explained by the extracted factors. The amount of variance to be estimated in our example, therefore, is 8 (i.e., $8 \times s^2 = 8 \times 1 = 8$). There will be no change in the correlation matrix because 1s are placed initially on the diagonal of the correlation matrix when it is being analyzed using PCA.

Extracting principal components from a correlation matrix consists of first identifying an initial principal component, PC_I, that is a linear combination of the original items (in our case, the eight items on the CGTS) such that it explains a maximum amount of the variance among the items. The influence of PC_I on the items being examined is then partialed out of the original correlation matrix. This results in a residual matrix, which represents the partial correlations of the items with each other, having first removed the influence of PC_I. The diagonal elements of this residual matrix represent the variance in the items that is not explained by PC_I. The elements on the off-diagonal represent the partial correlations of the items with each other after extracting the influence of PC_I.

Following the process used to obtain PC_I, the second principal component, PC_{II}, is extracted from this residual matrix. Because PC_{II} is obtained from the residual matrix and not the original correlation matrix, it is uncorrelated with (i.e., it is orthogonal to) PC_I. It also accounts for the second greatest proportion of variance that is remaining among the items having factored out the influence of PC$_I$. A second residual matrix is then created that consists of partial correlations of the items among themselves having removed the influence of PC$_I$ and PC$_{II}$. It is from this second residual matrix that PC$_{III}$ is extracted.

This process of extracting components is repeated on succeeding residual matrices until the elements in the residual variance-covariance matrix are reduced to random error. Each extracted principal component is orthogonal to the others and accounts for the greatest proportion of leftover variance after removing the influence of the previous components. In this way, the first extracted component accounts for the most variance and the last component accounts for the least variance. Although there are conceivably as many principal components as there are items, the process of extraction usually terminates sooner because the majority of the variance is typically accounted for by a relatively small number of components. Ideally, we would like to limit the extraction to include only those components that account for at least 5% of the total variance in the items.

Nunnally and Bernstein (1994) describe the process of finding principal components in PCA as *eigenanalysis*. That is, it is the process of finding a solution to the characteristic equation of the correlation matrix. To understand what a *characteristic equation* is, we need to define a few terms. These include *scalars, vectors, eigenvalues,* and *eigenvectors*.

Scalars and Vectors

A *scalar* in linear algebra is another way of referring to a single number (Fraleigh & Beauregard, 1987). An example of a scalar would be the number 2. A *vector*, on the other hand, is a matrix that has only one row or one column:

$$\mathbf{w} = \begin{bmatrix} 6 & 4 & 9 & 1 \end{bmatrix} \text{ or } \mathbf{v} = \begin{bmatrix} 2 \\ 3 \\ 6 \\ 7 \end{bmatrix}$$

The vector **w** presented above is referred to as a *row vector*, and the vector **v** is a *column vector*.

Eigenvalues and Eigenvectors

Let us assume that **R** is the 8×8 correlation matrix presented in Figure E.1. By definition, if $\mathbf{Rv} = \lambda\,\mathbf{v}$, where **v** is a nonzero 8×1 column vector and λ is a scalar, then λ is an *eigenvalue* of **R** and **v** is an *eigenvector* of **R** corresponding to the eigenvalue λ (Fraleigh & Beauregard, 1987, p. 226). These eigenvectors and eigenvalues have also been referred to in the literature as *characteristic vectors and characteristic values,* respectively.

In Chapter 3, we pointed out that there is a unique number called a *determinant* that is associated with every square matrix, including the correlation matrix, **R**. This determinant is denoted either by Det(**R**) or $|\mathbf{R}|$. The determinant can be used to find the eigenvalues and eigenvectors of a square matrix. For our 8×8 correlation matrix, an eigenvalue for this matrix is a value λ for which the following polynomial equation, $p(\lambda)$, holds:

$$p(\lambda) = \text{Det}(\mathbf{R} - \lambda\mathbf{I}) = 0$$

where

Det = determinant of the matrix $(\mathbf{R} - \lambda\mathbf{I})$

R = correlation matrix

λ = eigenvalue of the correlation matrix **R**; it is a scalar, or single number

I = identity matrix of the same size as the correlation matrix with 1s on the diagonal and 0s on the off diagonal

The polynomial, $p(\lambda)$, is called the *characteristic polynomial* of the matrix **R**, and the eigenvalues of **R** are the nontrivial solutions to the *characteristic equation,* $p(\lambda) = 0$. By solving this characteristic equation, we arrive at the eigenvalues of **R**.

There are at most n real solutions for λ when there is an $n \times n$ correlation matrix (Fraleigh, Beauregard, & Katz, 1994). For our 8×8 correlation matrix, therefore, there are at most *eight* solutions for λ. The eigenvectors of **R** corresponding to these eight possible eigenvalues, λs, can be found by solving the homogeneous matrix system $(\mathbf{R} - \lambda\mathbf{I})\mathbf{x} = \mathbf{0}$.

Sound clear as mud? As we indicated in Chapter 3, for better or worse, matrices and their multiplication are at the very foundation of factor analysis. Our goal is to find the eigenvectors that are associated with the correlation matrix, **R**. Once the eigenvalues and their corresponding eigenvectors have been obtained, the corresponding factor loadings for a principal component (e.g., PC_I) can be found by multiplying each element of a given eigenvector by the square root of its corresponding eigenvalue (Kline, 1994). Let us walk through this solution slowly.

IDENTIFYING THE FIRST PRINCIPAL COMPONENT, PC_I

Because the process is so labor intensive, we are not going to use the formulas presented above to solve for all eight of the eigenvalues and eigenvectors of **R**. Both Kline (1994) and Nunnally and Bernstein (1994) offer excellent systematic explanations of the iterative process involved in identifying the principal components of a matrix. It is their approach that we will use to identify the first two principal components for the 8×8 correlation matrix in Figure E.1. We will also compare our calculations for PC_I and PC_{II} using an Excel spreadsheet with those values obtained in SPSS for Windows.

The eigenvector that will determine the first principal component of the correlation matrix is obtained by first multiplying an arbitrary $1 \times n$ row vector, containing 1 row and n elements, into an $n \times n$ correlation matrix **R** (Kline, 1994; Nunnally & Bernstein, 1994). In our 8×8 CGTS example, this arbitrary 1×8 row vector will contain eight elements, e_1 to e_8. This vector will be multiplied into our 8×8 CGTS correlation matrix to produce the first 1×8 estimate of our eigenvector,

$$[e_1 \ e_2 \ \ldots \ e_1 \ e_8] \begin{bmatrix} 1.00 & \ldots & \ldots & \ldots & r_{18} \\ \vdots & & & & \vdots \\ \vdots & & & & \vdots \\ \vdots & & & & \vdots \\ r_{81} & \ldots & \ldots & \ldots & 1.00 \end{bmatrix} = [t_1 \ \ldots \ \ldots \ \ldots \ t_8]$$

[1 × 8 row vector] × [8 × 8 correlation matrix] = [1 × 8 estimate of the eigenvector T_{1A}]

Step 1:
Create an arbitrary vector by first summing the correlation coefficients in each column to produce the first trial eigenvector T_{1A}.

At this beginning step, the challenge is to decide on an initial 1×8 row vector to divide into our correlation matrix. Kline (1994) suggests that a good (but arbitrary) place to start is by first summing the correlation coefficients in each column of our correlation matrix to produce the 1×8 row vector, T_{1A} (Figure E.2, ①). This vector has eight elements, or *weights*, that will be used to generate a vector that will be multiplied into the correlation matrix.

Element 1 for this first trial vector T_{1A} was obtained by summing the correlations for item C1 in Column 1 ①:

$$\text{Element } 1 = \sum_{i=1}^{8} r_{C1Ci} = 1.00 + .065 + \cdots + .447 + .104 = 2.348$$

Element 2 was obtained in a similar fashion by summing the correlations for item C2:

$$\text{Element } 2 = \sum_{i=1}^{8} r_{C2Ci} = .065 + 1.000 + \cdots + .188 + .276 = 3.228$$

By summing the correlations in the rest of the columns of the correlation matrix, we arrive at a row vector that we will use as our beginning "guess" of what the first eigenvector for our correlation matrix will be:

$$T_{1A} = [2.348 \quad 3.228 \quad 3.117 \quad 3.424 \quad 2.683 \quad 3.466 \quad 3.080 \quad 2.432]$$

Now we need to refine this estimate.

Step 2:
Square the elements in T_{1A}. Sum them to obtain the "length" of the vector T_{1A}. Divide each element in T_{1A} by the square root of this length to produce the first normalized trial vector V_{1A}.

Obtaining the First Principal Component for the 8 × 8 Correlation Matrix

	C1	C2	C3	C4	C5	C6	C7	C8	Sum
C1	1.00	.065	.337	.261	-.036	.170	.447	.104	
C2	.065	1.000	.249	.555	.390	.505	.188	.276	
C3	.337	.249	1.000	.239	.089	.382	.610	.211	
C4	.261	.555	.239	1.000	.377	.389	.351	.252	
C5	-.036	.390	.089	.377	1.000	.472	.064	.322	
C6	.170	.505	.382	.389	.472	1.000	.354	.194	
C7	.447	.188	.610	.351	.064	.354	1.000	.067	
C8	.104	.276	.211	.252	.327	.194	.067	1.000	
T_{1A}	2.348	3.228	3.117	3.424	2.683	3.466	3.00008	2.432	
$(T_{1A})^2$	5.513	1.41	9.715	11.72	7.198	12.01	9.486	5.914	71.985
V_{1A}	.277	.380	.367	.404	.316	.409	.363	.287	
T_{1B}	.781	1.190	1.118	1.253	.949	1.278	1.108	.807	
$(T_{1B})^2$	.609	1.418	1.250	1.569	.901	1.634	1.227	.650	9.259
V_{1B}	.257	.391	.367	.412	.312	.420	.364	.265	
T_{1C}	.764	1.203	1.116	1.259	.952	1.289	1.107	.789	
$(T_{1C})^2$	.583	.448	1.245	1.586	.905	1.662	1.226	.623	9.279
V_{1C}	.251	.395	.366	.413	.312	.423	.363	.259	
T_{1D}	.756	1.209	1.113	1.262	.955	1.294	1.104	.784	
$(T_{1D})^2$	.571	1.462	1.238	1.591	.912	1.673	1.219	.616	9.280
$V_{1D} = V_{PC1}$	.248	.397	.365	.414	.313	.425	.362	.257	
PC_1	.433	.693	.638	.723	.547	.741	.633	.449	

① Sum of the correlation coefficients for C1.

② Sum of squared elements (e.g., T_{1A} and T_{1B}) = length of vector.

③ $2.348 / \sqrt{71.985} = 0.277$

⑤ $0.781 / \sqrt{9.259} = 0.257$

⑦ $0.764 / \sqrt{9.279} = 0.251$

⑧ $0.756 / \sqrt{9.280} = 0.248$

⑨ $\lambda_1 = \sqrt{9.280} = 3.046$

⑩ $\sqrt{3.046}\,(.248) = .433$

To refine this newly created, but arbitrary, row vector $\mathbf{T}_{1A}$, we need to *normalize* it. To normalize a vector means that we need to transform $\mathbf{T}_{1A}$ to be of unit length (i.e., make its length equal to 1). By definition, the *length* of a vector is the sum of its squared elements; therefore, normalizing such a vector means that we are setting the sum of its squared elements to be equal to 1.0 (Bernstein, 1988).

To normalize our vector $\mathbf{T}_{1A}$, we will first square each of its elements, ei, and sum them across the vector to obtain the vector's length (Figure E.2, ②):

$$length\ of\ vector\ T_{1A} = \sum_{i=1}^{8}e_i^2 = (2.348)^2 + (3.228)^2$$

$$+ \ldots + (3.081)^2 + (2.432)^2 = 71.985$$

Next we need to take the square root of this *vector length* ($\sqrt{71.986}$) and divide each of the structural elements in $\mathbf{T}_{1A}$ by this value to produce the first normalized trial vector, $\mathbf{V}_{1A}$ ③.

$$V_{1A} = \left[\frac{2.348}{\sqrt{71.985}} \quad \frac{3.228}{\sqrt{71.985}} \quad \frac{3.117}{\sqrt{71.985}} \quad \frac{3.424}{\sqrt{71.985}} \quad \frac{2.683}{\sqrt{71.985}} \right.$$

$$\left. \frac{3.466}{\sqrt{71.985}} \quad \frac{3.080}{\sqrt{71.985}} \quad \frac{2.432}{\sqrt{71.985}} \right]$$

$$= [.277 \quad .380 \quad .367 \quad .404 \quad .316 \quad .409 \quad .363 \quad .287]$$

Notice that if we were to square each element in the normalized vector $\mathbf{V}_{1A}$ and then sum these to obtain that vector's length, the resulting value would be 1.000:

$$(.277)^2 + (.380)^2 + \cdots + (.363)^2 + (.287)^2$$
$$= (.077) + (.145) + \cdots + (.132) + (.082) = 1.000$$

That is the definition of a normalized vector: its length is equal to 1.0.

Step 3:
Create a second estimate of the trial vector $\mathbf{T}_{1B}$ by multiplying the normalized vector $\mathbf{V}_{1A}$ into the correlation matrix, R.

This first *estimate* of the eigenvector for PC_1, V_{1A}, is exactly that: it is just an estimate. To come up with an even better estimate, we will multiply this normalized vector V_{1A} into the correlation matrix, R.

Multiplying a 1×8 row vector into an 8×8 correlation matrix is relatively straightforward using matrix algebra and can easily be undertaken in Excel. Each element in the column of the correlation matrix is multiplied by the set of eight elements in the normalized 1×8 row vector V_{1A} and the resulting value is summed. This produces a second 1×8 row vector, T_{1B}, as in Figure E.2 ④:

$$[.277 \ .380 \ ... \ .363 \ .287] \begin{bmatrix} 1.000 & .065 & \cdots & .447 & .104 \\ .065 & 1.000 & \cdots & .188 & .276 \\ \cdot & \cdot & \cdots & \cdot & \cdot \\ \cdot & \cdot & \cdots & \cdot & \cdot \\ \cdot & \cdot & \cdots & \cdot & \cdot \\ \cdot & \cdot & \cdots & \cdot & \cdot \\ .447 & .188 & \cdots & 1.000 & .067 \\ .104 & .276 & \cdots & .067 & 1.000 \end{bmatrix}$$

$$= [.781 \ 1.190 \ ... \ 1.108 \ .807]$$

$[1 \times 8$ row vector $V_{1A}] * [8 \times 8$ correlation matrix $R] = [1 \times 8$ row vector $T_{1B}]$

where

$$(.277)(1.00) + (.380)(.065) + \cdots + (.363)(.447) + (.287)(.104) = .781$$

$$(.277)(.065) + (.380)(1.000) + \cdots + (.363)(.188) + (.287)(.276) = 1.190$$

This matrix multiplication produces the second estimate of the principal component, T_{1B} (Figure E.2, ④):

$$T_{1B} = [.781 \ 1.190 \ 1.118 \ 1.253 \ 0.949 \ 1.278 \ 1.108 \ .807]$$

Step 4:
Create a second trial estimate of the normalized vector, V_{1B}, by dividing each element in T_{1B} by the square root of its length.

Remember that by *normalizing* a vector we are making it of unit length. As in Step 2, we do that by dividing each element in the vector by the square root of the vector's length. The length of the vector T_{1B} is the sum of the squares of its values ②:

$$\text{length of vector } T_{1B} = (.781)^2 + (1.19)^2 + \cdots + (1.108)^2 + (0.807)^2$$

$$= .609 + 1.418 + \cdots + 1.227 + 0.651 = 9.259$$

To obtain the new normalized vector V_{1B}, therefore, we will divide each value of T_{1B} by the square root of its length ($\sqrt{9.259}$):

$$C_1 = \frac{.781}{\sqrt{9.259}} = .257$$

$$C_2 = \frac{1.19}{\sqrt{9.259}} = .391$$

This creates our second estimate of the normalized vector V_{1B} (Figure E.2, ⑤):

$$V_{1B} = [.257 \quad .391 \quad .367 \quad .412 \quad .312 \quad .420 \quad .364 \quad .265]$$

Because V_{1B} is a normalized vector, the sum of its square elements (i.e., its length) equals 1.00:

$$(.257)^2 + (.391)^2 + \ldots + (.364)^2 + (.265)^2 = 1.000$$

Step 5:
Repeat the process in Steps 3 and 4 to obtain a third trial estimate of the normalized vector V_{1C}.

We now want to refine our estimate of the eigenvector for PC_I. To do this, V_{1B} is multiplied once again into the correlation matrix to create the vector T_{1C} (Figure E.2, ⑥):

$$\mathbf{T}_{1C} = [.257 \ .391 \ \dots \ .364 \ .265] \begin{bmatrix} 1.000 & .065 & \dots & .447 & .104 \\ .065 & 1.000 & \dots & .188 & .276 \\ \cdot & \cdot & \cdot \cdot \cdot & \cdot & \cdot \\ \cdot & \cdot & \cdot \cdot \cdot & \cdot & \cdot \\ \cdot & \cdot & \cdot \cdot \cdot & \cdot & \cdot \\ \cdot & \cdot & \cdot \cdot \cdot & \cdot & \cdot \\ .447 & .188 & \dots & 1.000 & .067 \\ .104 & .276 & \dots & .067 & 1.000 \end{bmatrix}$$

$$= [.764 \ 1.203 \ \dots \ 1.107 \ .789]$$

[1 × 8 row vector $\mathbf{V}_{1B}$] * [8 × 8 correlation matrix R] = [1 × 8 row vector $\mathbf{T}_{1C}$]

Each of the elements in $\mathbf{T}_{1C}$ are then squared and summed to produce the vector's new length (9.279):

$$\begin{aligned} \text{length of vector } \mathbf{T}_{1C} &= (.764)^2 + (1.203)^2 + \cdots + (1.107)^2 + (.789)^2 \\ &= (.583) + (1.148) + \cdots + (1.226) + (.623) \\ &= 9.279 \end{aligned}$$

To produce the third trial estimate of the normalized vector $\mathbf{V}_{1C}$, the elements in $\mathbf{T}_{1C}$ are again divided by the square root of its length ($\sqrt{9.279}$) ⑦:

$$\mathbf{V}_{1C} = \left[.764 \big/ \sqrt{9.279} \ 1.203 \big/ \sqrt{9.279} \ \dots \ 1.107 \big/ \sqrt{9.279} \ .789 \big/ \sqrt{9.279} \right]$$

$$= [.251 \quad .395 \quad .366 \quad .413 \quad .312 \quad .423 \quad .363 \quad .259]$$

Step 6:
Continue the process until convergence is reached.

This input-output process continues until the weights in the normalized output vector no longer differ substantially from the previously obtained normalized input vector. At that point, it is said that the solution has *converged* and the newly obtained normalized vector becomes the first eigenvector, $\mathbf{V}_{PC1}$, for the correlation matrix.

How do we determine when convergence has been achieved? Kline (1994) indicates that, for statistical computer programs, the general criterion for convergence is that "the sum of the squared differences between the pairs of elements in the two vectors is less than .00001" (p. 32).

For our two normalized vectors, V_{1B} and V_{1C}, the differences between the elements would be as follows:

$$= [.257 \quad .391 \quad .367 \quad .412 \quad .312 \quad .420 \quad .364 \quad .265] -$$
$$[.251 \quad .395 \quad .366 \quad .413 \quad .312 \quad .423 \quad .363 \quad .259]$$
$$= [.006 \quad -.004 \quad .001 \quad -.001 \quad .000 \quad -.003 \quad .001 \quad .006]$$

By squaring and summing the differences that these elements represent, we arrive at the sum of the squared differences:

$$[(.006)^2 + (-.004)^2 + (.001)^2 + (-.001)^2 + (.000)^2$$
$$+ (-.003)^2 + (.001)^2 + (.006)^2] = .00009$$

Because this value, .00009, though small, is still not less than the general criterion for convergence, .00001, we would need to continue with the input-output process until that criterion was reached.

Had we continued with this iterative process, we would have reached the .00001 criteria for convergence in two more steps. This 1×8 row matrix, V_{1D}, had the following elements (Figure E.2, ⑧):

$$V_{1D} = \left[.756 / \sqrt{9.280} \; 1.209 / \sqrt{9.280} \; \dots \; 1.104 / \sqrt{9.280} \; .784 / \sqrt{9.280} \right]$$

$$= [.248 \quad .397 \quad .365 \quad .414 \quad .313 \quad .425 \quad .362 \quad .257]$$

Step 7:
After convergence has been obtained, identify the eigenvector, eigenvalue, and factor loadings associated with the first principal component, PC_1.

Because convergence has been obtained with the normalized vector V_{1D}, it becomes the first eigenvector, V_{PCI}, for the correlation matrix R. The square root of the sums of squares of T_{1D}, 3.046, is also known as the square root of the vector V_{PCI}'s length (Figure E.2, ⑨). This value becomes the first eigenvalue, λ_1, for the correlation matrix (i.e., $\lambda_1 = \sqrt{9.279} = 3.046$). Remember that we used that eigenvalue, 3.046, to divide into the elements of T_{1C} to generate the normalized vector V_{1D} ⑧.

The factor loadings for PC_I are generated by multiplying the elements of the eigenvector, $\mathbf{V}_{PCI}$, by the square root of its eigenvalue, λ_1 (i.e., $\sqrt{\lambda_1} = \sqrt{3.046}$) (Figure E.2, ⑩):

factor loadings for $PC_I = \sqrt{3.046}$ [.248   .397   .365
.414   .313   .425   .362   .257]

$= [.433\ .693\ .638\ .723\ .547\ .741\ .633\ .449]$

Table E.1 summarizes the factor loadings on the first principal component, PC_I, for each of the eight items in the correlation matrix. These factor loadings indicate the extent to which each of the items in the correlation matrix correlate with the given principal component. Factor loadings can range from -1.0 to $+1.0$, with higher absolute values indicating a stronger correlation of the item with the principal component. From Table E.1, we can see that items C6, C4, and C2 load most strongly on this first factor (.741, .723, and .693, respectively) and C1 loads least strongly (.433). The square of these loadings is similar to r^2 in that it represents the amount of variance in the individual item that is explained by that factor. For item C1, for example, $(.433)^2 = .188$; therefore, 18.8% of the variance in C1 can be explained by PC_I.

If we had not already generated the eigenvalue for PC_I but had been presented with the factor loadings instead, we could calculate this eigenvalue, λ_1, by summing the squared factor loadings on PC_I:

$$\lambda_1 = (.433)^2 + (.693)^2 + (.638)^2 + (.723)^2$$
$$+ (.547)^2 + (.741)^2 + (.633)^2 + (.449)^2 = 3.046$$

This eigenvalue, 3.046, represents the amount of variance in *all* of the items that is explained by the first principal component, PC_I. We indicated earlier in this appendix that the total amount of variance that is available for eight standardized items is 8.0. Therefore, 3.046/8.00, or 38.074%, of the variance in all of the items is explained by our first principal component, PC_I.

Table E.1   Loadings of the Eight CGTS Items on the First Principal Component, PC_I

		Item Loadings
Item	Content Area	PCI
C1	It will increase my sense of personal control.	.433
C2	I worry about an uncertain diagnosis.	.693
C3	I want to know what to do to manage my risk.	.638
C4	It will help reduce my uncertainty about the future.	.723
C5	I fear the ambiguity of the results.	.547
C6	I worry about a diagnosis I cannot do anything about.	.741
C7	I hope to make better health and lifestyle choices as a result.	.633
C8	I am worried about loss of health and life insurance coverage.	.449

Comparison With Computer Printout From SPSS for Windows

Figure E.3 compares the SPSS-generated computer printout for the first two principal components when we ran the principal components analysis in Chapter 4 with our Excel-calculated factor loadings for PC_I.

As Figure E.3 indicates, our calculated factor loadings were in near perfect agreement with the SPSS-generated values ①. Only four items (C1, C3, C5, and C7) differed from the SPSS values by .001. The slight discrepancy in these four factor loadings may be attributed to round-off error. Our eigenvalue and percent of variance in the items that were explained by the first principal component were exactly the same as those presented in SPSS for Windows (3.046 and 38.074%, respectively) ②. Let us see now how successful we can be in generating the second principal component.

EXTRACTING THE SECOND PRINCIPAL COMPONENT

The procedure for extracting the second principal component, PC_{II}, follows the same format as that of PC_I. That is, using the iterative steps outlined in Steps 1 through 7, we will continue to extract and normalize a trial vector until we achieve satisfactory convergence with the

Figure E.3   SPSS Computer-Generated Printout for the First Two Principal
Components

Component Matrix [a]

	Component	
	1	2
C1 Increase of personal control	.432	.597
C2 Worry about uncertain diagnosis	.693	-.373
C3 What to do to manage risk	.637	.477
C4 Help reduce uncertainty about future	.723	-.153
C5 Fear ambiguity of results	.548	.579
C6 Worry about diagnosis I can't do anything about	.741	-.157
C7 Hope to make better health, lifestyle choices	.632	.591
C8 Worried about loss of health, and life insurance coverage	.449	-.292

Our PC$_I$

.433 ①
.693
.638
.723
.547
.741
.633
.449

Extraction Method: Principal Component Analysis.
a. 2 components extracted.

②   **Our PC$_I$**

$\lambda_1 = 3.046$ % Variance = $(3.046/8.000) \times 100 = 38.074$

Total Variance Explained

Component	Initial Eigenvalues			Extraction Sums of Squared Loadings		
	Total	% of Variance	Cumulative %	Total	% of Variance	Cumulative %
1	3.046	38.074	38.074	3.046	38.074	38.074
2	1.542	19.275	57.349	1.542	19.275	57.349
3	.866	10.819	68.168			
4	.762	9.524	77.692			
5	.626	7.828	85.521			
6	.499	6.233	91.754			
7	.354	4.425	96.180			
8	.306	3.820	100.000			

Extraction Method: Principal Component Analysis.

previous vector. This time, however, we will not use the original
correlation matrix for factor extraction. Instead, we will extract the trial
vectors from a *residual matrix,* one from which the influence of PC$_I$ has
been removed.

Step 8:
**Multiply the factor loadings of all item-pairs on PC$_I$ to create a
cross-product matrix.**

To create this residual matrix, the factor loadings for all possible pairs of items on PC_I are first multiplied together to form a cross-product matrix with the squared factor loadings of the items on the diagonal and the cross-product loadings on the off-diagonal, as in Figure E.4.

The squared loadings on the diagonal of the generated cross-product matrix in Figure E.4 represent the influence of the first principal component, PC_I, on the eight items of the CGTS. For example, (.191) × 100, or 19.1%, of the variance in the first item, C1, can be explained by the first principal component (Figure E.4, ①). In contrast, (.475) × 100, or 47.5%, of the variance in item C2 can be explained by PC_I ②.

Step 9:
Subtract the cross-products from the original correlation matrix to produce the residual matrix.

In the next step, the cross-product matrix is subtracted from the original correlation matrix to create a *residual* matrix. This residual matrix, which is presented in Figure E.5, represents the partial correlations of the items with each other, having first partialed out the influence of PC_I.

Because the variance of a standardized item is equal to 1.00, the diagonal elements of the residual matrix denote the amount of remaining variance in the items that is not explained by PC_I. The elements on the off-diagonal represent the partial correlations of the items with each other after extracting the influence of PC_I. For item C1, for example, (.809) × 100, or 80.9%, of the variance in item C1 is remaining after PC_I has been extracted (Figure E.5, ①). For item C2, (.525) × 100, or 52.5%, of its variance remains after extracting PC_I. Clearly, PC_I accounts for more variance in item C2 than it does in item C1.

Step 10:
"Reflect" the residual matrix to maximize the sum of the column elements.

The residual matrix will be the focus of our extraction of the second principal component, PC_{II}. However, there is a slight problem with this matrix. With the exception of Columns 1 and 8, the sum of the

Figure E.4 Multiplying PC$_I$ by Itself to Produce the Cross-Product Matrix

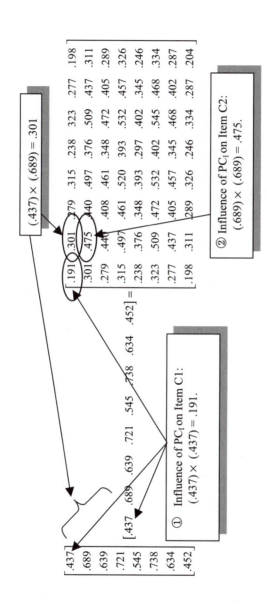

$[8 \times 1 \text{ factor loading matrix, PC}_I] * [1 \times 8 \text{ factor loading matrix, PC}_I] = [8 \times 8 \text{ cross-product matrix}]$

Figure E.5   Generating the Residual Matrix for the Eight CGTS Items

$$
\begin{bmatrix}
1.000 & .065 & \cdot & \cdot & \cdot & .447 & .104 \\
.065 & 1.000 & \cdot & \cdot & \cdot & .188 & .276 \\
\cdot & \cdot & & & & \cdot & \cdot \\
\cdot & \cdot & & \text{--} & & \cdot & \cdot \\
\cdot & \cdot & & & & \cdot & \cdot \\
.447 & .188 & \cdot & \cdot & \cdot & 1.000 & .067 \\
.104 & .276 & \cdot & \cdot & \cdot & .067 & 1.000
\end{bmatrix}
-
\begin{bmatrix}
.191 & .301 & \cdot & \cdot & \cdot & .277 & .198 \\
.301 & .475 & \cdot & \cdot & \cdot & .437 & .311 \\
\cdot & \cdot & & & & \cdot & \cdot \\
\cdot & \cdot & & & & \cdot & \cdot \\
\cdot & \cdot & & & & \cdot & \cdot \\
.277 & .437 & \cdot & \cdot & \cdot & .402 & .287 \\
.198 & .311 & \cdot & \cdot & \cdot & .287 & .204
\end{bmatrix}
=
$$

$$
\begin{bmatrix}
.809 & -.236 & .057 & -.054 & -.274 & -.153 & .170 & -.094 \\
-.236 & .525 & -.191 & .058 & .014 & -.003 & -.249 & .035 \\
.057 & -.191 & .592 & -.222 & -.259 & -.090 & .205 & -.078 \\
-.054 & .058 & -.222 & .480 & -.016 & -.143 & -.106 & -.074 \\
-.274 & .014 & -.239 & -.016 & .703 & .070 & -.281 & .081 \\
-.153 & -.003 & -.090 & -.143 & .070 & .455 & -.114 & -.140 \\
.170 & -.249 & .205 & -.106 & -.281 & -.114 & .598 & -.220 \\
-.094 & .035 & -.078 & -.074 & .081 & -.140 & -.220 & .796
\end{bmatrix}
$$

① Remaining variance in items C1 and C2.

② Σ column elements = −.117

[original correlation matrix] − [cross-product matrix of factor loadings] = [residual or partial correlation matrix, PC_1 removed] elements in each of the columns of this matrix is very close to zero. In Figure E.5, for example, the sum of the column elements in the partial correlation matrix for item C2 is –.119 ②. This low value will make it difficult to identify a suitable second principal component.

To circumvent this problem, some of the rows and columns will be *reflected* (Kline, 1994). This means that, for selected rows and columns, the signs for the elements other than those on the diagonal will be reversed (Figure E.6). That is, negative signs for the elements are made positive (e.g., –.236 in Row 2, Column 1 becomes +.236) and positive signs are made negative (e.g., .058 in Row 2, Column 4 becomes –.058). In addition, as we move from one column to another, some values (e.g., .058 in Row 2, Column 4) are twice reverse-coded because of their position in the matrix. The result of this reflection procedure is presented in Figure E.6.

For our residual matrix, the row and column elements for items C2, C4, C5, C6, and C8 have been reflected (Figure E.6, ①). These specific rows and columns were selected because, by changing the signs of their elements (except for those on the diagonal), we maximize the sum of the values in their respective columns. Notice that, as a result of our reflecting the matrix, the sum of the column elements for item C2 has gone from –.119 (Figure E.6, ②) to 1.235 ③.

What have we gained by reflecting the partial correlation matrix? Using this reflection procedure, we are able to maximize the sum of the elements in a particular row or column to the greatest extent possible. Kline (1994) indicates that this process is not statistical trickery because, once we obtain the factor loadings for PC_{II}, the loadings for the reflected items will be assigned negative values.

Step 11:
Generate a normalized trial vector, T_{2A}, for the second principal component, PC_{II}.

The process for extracting the second principal component, PC_{II}, is similar to the process we used to extract PC_I. Because the process is rather tedious to repeat a second time, we will summarize the process for you. The data that we will be using to generate the second principal component, PC_{II}, is presented in Figure E.7.

Figure E.6 Reflecting the 8 × 8 Residual Matrix

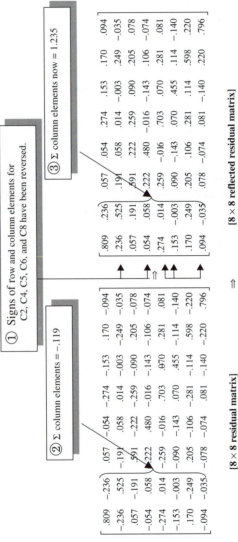

Figure E.7   Generating the Second Principal Component, PC_{II}

	C1	C2	C3	C4	C5	C6	C7	C8
C1	.809	.236	.057	.054	.274	.153	.170	.094
C2	.236	.525	.191	.058	.014	-.003	.249	-.035
C3	.057	.191	.591	.222	.259	.090	.205	.078
C4	.054	.058	.222	.480	-.016	-.143	.106	-.074
C5	.274	.014	.259	-.016	.703	.070	.281	.081
C6	.153	-.003	.090	-.143	.070	.455	.114	-.140
C7	.170	.249	.205	.106	.281	.114	.598	.220
C8	.094	-.035	.078	-.074	.081	-.140	.220	.796
① T_{2A}	1.847	1.235	1.693	.687	1.666	.596	1.942	1.019
$(T_{2A})^2$	3.411	1.525	2.866	.472	2.776	.355	3.771	1.038
④ V_{2A}	.459	.307	.420	.171	.414	.148	.482	.253
T_{2B}	.718	.476	.610	.222	.693	.198	.735	.372
$(T_{2B})^2$	.516	.227	.372	.049	.481	.039	.541	.139
V_{2B}	.467	.310	.397	.145	.451	.129	.478	.242
$(V_{2B} - V_{2A})^2$	.0001	.000009	.0006	.0007	.0013	.0004	.00002	.0001
V_{2C}	.473	.307	.388	.135	.462	.127	.476	.240
V_{2D}	.476	.305	.384	.130	.466	.128	.474	.239
V_{2E}	.477	.304	.382	.128	.468	.129	.474	.239
T_{2F}	.738	.469	.588	.197	.722	.200	.730	.368
$(T_{2F})^2$	.544	.220	.346	.039	.522	.040	.533	.135
V_{2F}	.478	.304	.381	.127	.468	.130	.474	.239
$(V_{2F} - V_{2E})^2$	6.69E-07	2.2E-07	6.7E-07	1.01E-06	3.38E-07	3.1E-07	8.5E-08	3.71E-08
PC_{II}	.594	.378	.473	.158	.581	.161	.589	.297
PC_{II}	.594	-.378	.473	-.158	-.581	-.161	.589	-.297

Annotation boxes:

② $\Sigma(e_{T2A})^2 = 16.214$

⑤ $\Sigma(e_{T2B})^2 = 2.364$

⑦ $\Sigma(V_{2B} - V_{2A})^2 = .0034$

⑪ $\lambda_2 = \sqrt{2.379} = 1.542$

③ $1.847 / \sqrt{16.214} = 0.459$

⑥ $0.718 / \sqrt{2.364} = 0.467$

⑧ $0.738 / \sqrt{2.379} = 0.478$

⑩ 3.29E-06

⑫ Factor loadings: $PC_{II} = \sqrt{1.542} \times V_{2F} = \sqrt{1.542} \times .478 = .594$.

⑬ Reflecting C2 on PC_{II}: .378 = -.378.

307

The first trial vector, T_{2A}, is first obtained by summing the column elements in the reflected residual matrix (Figure E.7, ①):

$$T_{2A} = [1.847 \quad 1.235 \quad 1.693 \quad 0.687 \quad 1.666 \quad 0.596 \quad 1.942 \quad 1.019]$$

Next, we square the elements in T_{2A} and sum them to obtain the vector's length, 16.214 (Figure E.7, ②). Then, by dividing each element in T_{2A} by the square root of this length, we obtain the first normalized trial vector, V_{2A} ③:

$$V_{2A} = [.459 \quad .307 \quad .420 \quad .171 \quad .414 \quad .148 \quad .482 \quad .253]$$

As with the other normalized vectors we produced for PC_I, the length of this vector is equal to 1.00.

Step 12:
Refine the normalized vector until convergence is reached.

You will recall from our discussion earlier in this appendix that vector convergence is reached when the sum of the squared differences between the pairs of elements in two normalized trial vectors is less than .00001 (Kline, 1994). In Figure E.7, five normalized vectors, V_{2B} through V_{2F}, were generated in an effort to reach that criterion. Trial vector V_{2B} was obtained by multiplying V_{2A} into the residual matrix. This produced the second trial vector, T_{2B} ④:

$$T_{2B} = [.718 \quad .476 \quad .610 \quad .222 \quad .693 \quad .198 \quad .735 \quad .372]$$

Next, each element in T_{2B} was squared and summed to obtain its length (2.364, ⑤). Then each element in T_{2B} was divided by the square root of that length ($\sqrt{2.364} = 1.538$) to obtain the second normalized trial vector, V_{2B} ⑥:

$$V_{2B} = \left[\frac{.718}{1.538} \quad \frac{.476}{1.538} \quad \frac{.610}{1.538} \quad \frac{.222}{1.538} \quad \frac{.693}{1.538} \quad \frac{.198}{1.538} \quad \frac{.735}{1.538} \quad \frac{.372}{1.538} \right]$$

$$= [.467 \quad .310 \quad .397 \quad .145 \quad .451 \quad .129 \quad .478 \quad .242]$$

Because the differences between the squared elements of V_{2A} and V_{2B} were much greater than .00001 (the sum of the squared differences for these first two vectors was .0034) (Figure E.7, ⑦), the input-output process continued until the normalized vector V_{2F} was produced ⑧:

$$V_{2F} = \begin{bmatrix} \dfrac{.738}{\sqrt{2.379}} & \dfrac{.469}{\sqrt{2.379}} & \dfrac{.588}{\sqrt{2.379}} & \dfrac{.197}{\sqrt{2.379}} \end{bmatrix}$$

$$\begin{matrix} \dfrac{.722}{\sqrt{2.379}} & \dfrac{.200}{\sqrt{2.379}} & \dfrac{.730}{\sqrt{2.379}} & \dfrac{.368}{\sqrt{2.379}} \end{matrix} \Bigg]$$

$$= [.478 \quad .304 \quad .381 \quad .127 \quad .468 \quad .130 \quad .474 \quad .239]$$

To assess convergence, the elements in the normalized vector V_{2F} were subtracted from the previously normalized vector V_{2E} ⑨. These differences were then squared and summed to obtain the value of 3.29E–06, or .00000329 ⑩. This value is less than our criterion of .00001; therefore, we will conclude our convergence efforts.

Step 13:
After convergence has been reached, identify the eigenvector, eigenvalue, and factor loadings associated with the second principal component, PC_{II}.

The normalized vector V_{2F} (Figure E.7, ⑧) becomes the second eigenvector, V_{PCII}, for the correlation matrix, R. The square root of the sums of squares of T_{2F}, which is also known as the square root of the vector's length, becomes the second eigenvalue, λ_2, for the correlation matrix. Our eigenvalue, λ_2, therefore is $\sqrt{2.379}$ or 1.542. This is the same eigenvalue, 1.542, which we used to divide into the eight elements of T_{2F} to obtain the normalized vector V_{2F}.

The factor loadings for PC_{II} are generated by multiplying the elements of the eigenvector, V_{2F}, by the square root of the eigenvalue, λ_2 (i.e., $\sqrt{1.542}$):

$$\textit{factor loadings for } PC_{II} = \sqrt{1.542}\ [.478 \quad .304 \quad .381 \quad .127 \quad .468 \quad .130 \quad .474 \quad .239]$$

$$= [.594 \quad .378 \quad .473 \quad .158 \quad .581 \quad .161 \quad .589 \quad .297]$$

Because we had reflected the rows and columns of items C2, C4, C5, C6, and C8 (i.e., changed the signs of their partial correlations with other items), we must now assign negative values to the loadings for these items:

$$\textit{reflected loadings for}$$
$$PC_{II} = [.594 \quad -.378 \quad .473 \quad -.158 \quad -.581 \quad -.161 \quad .589 \quad -.297]$$

Generated Factor Loadings for PC_I and PC_{II}

Table E.2 summarizes the factor loadings on the two principal components, PC_I and PC_{II}, for each of the eight items in the correlation matrix. As we indicated earlier in this appendix, these factor loadings indicate the extent to which each of the items in the correlation matrix correlate with the given principal component. Factor loadings can range from -1.0 to $+1.0$, with higher absolute values indicating a stronger correlation of the item with the principal component. From Table E.2, we can see that items C1, C7, C5, and C3 load most strongly on the second factor, PC_{II} (.594, .589, $-.581$, and .473, respectively), and C6 loads least strongly ($-.158$).

The square of these loadings represents the amount of variance in the individual item that is explained by this second factor. For item C1, for example, $(.594)^2 = .353$; therefore, 35.3% of the variance in C1 can be explained by PC_{II}.

If we did not have the eigenvalue, λ_2, we could generate it from Table E.2 by summing the squared factor loadings on PC_{II}:

$$\lambda_1 = (.594)^2 + (-.378)^2 + (.473)^2 + (-.158)^2 + (-.581)^2$$
$$+ (-.161)^2 + (.589)^2 + (-.297)^2$$
$$= 1.542$$

Table E.2   Loadings of the Eight CGTS Items on the First Two Principal
Components, PC_I and PC_{II}

		Item Loadings	
Item	*Content Area*	PC_I	PC_{II}
C1	It will increase my sense of personal control.	.433	.594
C2	I worry about an uncertain diagnosis.	.693	−.378
C3	I want to know what to do to manage my risk.	.638	.473
C4	It will help reduce my uncertainty about the future.	.723	−.158
C5	I fear the ambiguity of the results.	.547	−.581
C6	I worry about a diagnosis I cannot do anything about.	.741	−.161
C7	I hope to make better health and lifestyle choices as a result.	.633	.589
C8	I am worried about loss of health and life insurance coverage.	.449	−.297

This eigenvalue, 1.542, represents the amount of variance in the eight items that is explained by the second principal component, PC_{II}. Because the amount of variance that is available for eight standardized items is 8.00, 1.542/8.00, or 19.28%, of the variance in all of the items is explained by our second principal component, PC_{II}.

Comparison With the Computer
Printout From SPSS for Windows

Figure E.8 presents the computer printout for the first two principal components generated in SPSS for Windows when we ran the principal components analysis in Chapter 4. As with PC_I, our Excel-generated factor loadings for PC_{II} were in close agreement with the SPSS output; the differences between the loadings ranged from .002 for items C5 and C7 to .008 for item C4 (Figure E.8, ①). Our eigenvalue and percent of variance in the items that was explained by the second principal component were also similar: 1.542 and 19.28%, respectively ②. The slight discrepancy in the factor loadings may be due to round-off error. Together, the first two principal components explain 57.439% of the variance in the eight items of the CGTS.

Figure E.8   SPSS Computer-Generated Printout for the First Two Principal Components

Component Matrix [a]

	Component	
	1	2
C1 Increase of personal control	.432	.597
C2 Worry about uncertain diagnosis	.693	−.373
C3 What to do to manage risk	.637	.477
C4 Help reduce uncertainty about future	.723	−.153
C5 Fear ambiguity of results	.548	−.579
C6 Worry about diagnosis I can't do anything about	.741	−.157
C7 Hope to make better health, lifestyle choices	.632	.591
C8 Worried about loss of health, and life insurance coverage	.449	−.292

Our PC$_{II}$

.594
−.378
.473
−.161
−.581
−.161
.589
−.297

Extraction Method: Principal Component Analysis.

a. 2 components extracted.

Our PC$_{II}$

$\lambda_2 = 1.542$ % Variance $= 1.542/8.000 \times 100$
$= 19.28$

Total Variance Explained

Component	Initial Eigenvalues			Extraction Sums of Squared Loadings		
	Total	% of Variance	Cumulative %	Total	% of Variance	Cumulative %
1	3.046	38.074	38.074	3.046	38.074	38.074
2	1.542	19.275	57.349	1.542	19.275	57.349
3	.866	10.819	68.168			
4	.762	9.524	77.692			
5	.626	7.828	85.521			
6	.499	6.233	91.754			
7	.354	4.425	96.180			
8	.306	3.820	100.000			

Extraction Method: Principal Component Analysis.

Completing the Extractions

In this appendix, we have tried to provide you with an in-depth understanding of the process of identifying the first two principal components of the 8×8 correlation matrix for the eight items of the Concerns About Genetic Testing Scale. Had we chosen to do so, we could have continued this extraction process and extracted as many as eight principal components. Each of the additional components would have been extracted from a residual partial correlation matrix that had the influence of the prior identified components removed. We would have continued with this process until the coefficients in the residual matrix were so small that the remaining item variance to be extracted was negligible.

If all eight potential components in our 8×8 correlation matrix had been extracted, then only 0s would appear in the remaining residual matrix. Given that a goal of factor analysis is to explain the most amount of variance in the items with the fewest number of factors, we would clearly have terminated the process sooner. For a discussion of the criteria for deciding on when to terminate this input process, let us return to Chapter 4.

REFERENCES

Allen, M. J., & Yen, W. M. (1979). *Introduction to measurement theory.* Monterey, CA: Brooks/Cole.

American Psychological Association. (1985). *Standards for educational and psychological testing.* Washington, DC: Author.

Anderson, T. W., & Rubin, H. (1956). Statistical inference in factor analysis. *Proceedings of the 3rd Berkeley Symposium on Mathematical Statistics and Probability, 5,* 111-150.

Barnum, B. J. S. (1998). *Nursing theory, analysis, application, evaluation* (5th ed.). Philadelphia: Lippincott, Williams & Wilkins.

Bartlett, M. S. (1950). Tests of significance in factor analysis. *British Journal of Psychology (Statistical Section), 3,* 77-85.

Beck, A. T. (1976). *Cognitive therapy and the emotional disorders.* New York: International Universities Press.

Beck, A. T., Steer, R. A., & Garbin, M. G. (1988). Psychometric properties of the Beck Depression Inventory: Twenty-five years of evaluation. *Clinical Psychology Review, 8,* 77-100.

Bentler, P. (1985). *Theory and implementation of EQS. A structural equations program.* Los Angeles: BMDP Statistical Software.

Bentler, P., & Bonett, D. G. (1980). Significance tests and goodness of fit in the analysis of covariance structures. *Psychological Bulletin, 88,* 588-606.

Bernstein, I. H. (1988). *Applied multivariate analysis.* New York: Springer-Verlag.

Bickel, P. J., & Doksum, K. A. (1977). *Mathematical statistics.* San Francisco: Holden-Day.

Boyle, J. S. (1994). Styles of ethnography. In J. M. Morse (Ed.), *Critical issues in qualitative research methods* (pp. 159-185). Thousand Oaks, CA: Sage.

Brink, P. J., & Wood, M. J. (1998). Descriptive designs. In P. J. Brink & M. J. Wood (Eds.), *Advanced design in nursing research* (2nd ed., pp. 287-307). Thousand Oaks, CA: Sage.

Broome, M. E. (2000). Integrative literature reviews for the development of concepts. In B. L. Rodgers & K. A. Knafl (Eds.), *Concept development in nursing: Foundations, techniques, and applications* (2nd ed.). Philadelphia: W. B. Saunders.

Byrne, B. (1989). *A primer of LISREL: Basic applications and programming for confirmatory factor analytic models.* New York: Springer-Verlag.

Burns, N., & Grove, S. K. (2001). *The practice of nursing research: Conduct, critique, & utilization.* Philadelphia: W. B. Saunders.

Burt, C. (1939). The factor analysis of emotional traits. *Character and Personality, 7,* 238-254, 285-299.

Burt, C. (1941). *The factors of the mind: An introduction to factor analysis in psychology.* New York: Macmillan.

Burt, C. (1966). The early history of multivariate techniques in psychological research. *Multivariate Behavior Research, 1,* 24-42.

Carpenter, D. R. (1999). Phenomenology as method. In H. J. Streubert & D. R. Carpenter (Eds.), *Qualitative research in nursing: Advancing the humanistic imperative* (2nd ed., pp. 43-63). Philadelphia: Lippincott.

Carroll, J. B. (1953). An analytic solution for approximating simple structure in factor analysis. *Psychometrika, 18,* 23-38.

Carry, M. A. (1994). The group effect in focus groups: Planning, implementing, and interpreting focus group research. In J. M. Morse (Ed.), *Critical issues in qualitative research methods* (pp. 225-241). Thousand Oaks, CA: Sage.

Cattell, R. B. (1965). Factor analysis: An introduction to essentials. I. The purpose and underlying models. *Biometrics, 21,* 190-215.

Cattell, R. B. (1966). The scree test for the number of factors. *Multivariate Behavioral Research, 1,* 245-276.

Cattell, R. B. (1978). *The scientific use of factor analysis in the behavioral and life sciences.* New York: Plenum.

Cattell, R. B., & Jaspars, J. (1967). A general plasmode (No. 30-10-5-2) for factor analytic exercises and research. *Multivariate Behavioral Research Monographs, 67*(3).

Chinn, P. K., & Kramer, M. K. (1999). *Theory and nursing: Integrated knowledge development* (5th ed.). St. Louis: Mosby.

Cody, R. P., & Smith, J. K. (1997). *Applied statistics and the SAS programming language* (4th ed.). Upper Saddle River, NJ: Prentice Hall.

Colaizzi, P. F. (1978). Psychological research as the phenomenologist views it. In R. Valle & M. King (Eds.), *Existential phenomenological alternatives for psychology* (pp. 48-71). New York: Oxford University Press.

Comrey, A. L., & Lee, H. B. (1992). *A first course in factor analysis.* Hillsdale, NJ: Lawrence Erlbaum.

Cooper, H. (1989). *Integrating research: A guide for literature reviews.* Newbury Park, CA: Sage.

Cooper, H., & Hedges, L. (1994). *The handbook of research synthesis.* New York: Russell Sage Foundation.

Crabtree, B. F., & Miller, W. L. (Eds.). (1992). *Doing qualitative research.* Newbury Park, CA: Sage.

Cramer, E. M. (1974). On Browne's solution for oblique Procrustes rotation. *Psychometrika, 39,* 159-163.

Creswell, J. W. (1994). *Research design: Qualitative and quantitative approaches.* Thousand Oaks, CA: Sage.

Crocker, L., & Algina, J. (1986). *Introduction to classical and modern test theory.* New York: Holt, Rinehart & Winston.

Cronbach, L. J. (1951). Coefficient alpha and the internal structure of tests. *Psychometrika, 16,* 297-334.

Cronbach, L. J. (1984). *Essentials of psychological testing* (4th ed.). New York: Harper.

Cronbach, L. J., Gleser, G. C., Nanda, H., & Rajaratnam, N. (1972). *The depend-ability of behavioral measurements: Theory of generalizability for scores and profiles.* New York: Wiley.

Crowne, D., & Marlowe, D. (1964). *The approval motive: Studies in evaluation dependence.* New York: John Wiley.

Croyle, R. T. (1995). *Psychological effects of screening for disease and detection prevention.* New York: Oxford University.

Croyle, R. T., & Lerman, C. (1995). Psychological impact of genetic testing. In R. T. Croyle (Ed.), *Psychological effects of screening for disease and detection prevention.* New York: Oxford University.

Cureton, E. E., & D'Agostino (1983). *Factor analysis: An applied approach.* Hillsdale, NJ: Lawrence Erlbaum.

Delwiche, L. D., & Slaughter, S. J. (1998). *The little SAS book: A primer* (2nd ed.). Cary, NC: SAS Publishing.

Denzin, N. K., & Lincoln, Y. S. (Eds.). (1998). *Strategies of qualitative inquiry.* Thousand Oaks, CA: Sage.

Der, G., & Everitt, B. S. (2002). *Handbook of statistical analyses using SAS* (2nd ed.). Boca Raton, FL: Chapman & Hall.

Derogatis, L., Lipman, R., & Covi, L. (1973). SCL-90: An outpatient psychiatric rating scale—Preliminary report. *Psychopharmacology Bulletin, 9,* 13-23.

DeVellis, R. F. (1991). *Scale development: Theory and applications.* Newbury Park, CA: Sage.

Dodd, S. C. (1929). On the sampling theory of intelligence. *British Journal of Psychology, 19,* 306-327.

Ebel, R. L. (1979). *Essentials of educational measurement.* Englewood Cliffs, NJ: Prentice Hall.

Edwards, A. (1970). *The measurement of personality traits by scales and inventories.* New York: Holt, Rinehart & Winston.

Erlandson, D., Harris, E., Skipper, B., & Allen, S. (1993). *Doing naturalistic inquiry: A guide to methods.* Newbury Park, CA: Sage.

Fava, G. A., Kellner, R., Munari, F., Pavan, L., & Pesarin, F. (1982). Losses, hos-tility, and depression. *Journal of Nervous and Mental Diseases, 150,* 474-478.

Fawcett, J. (1997). The structural hierarchy of nursing knowledge: Components and their definitions. In I. M. King & J. Fawcett (Eds.), *The language of nurs-ing theory and metatheory.* Indianapolis, IN: Sigma Theta Tau International.

Fraleigh, J. B., Beauregard, R. A., & Katz, V. J. (1994). *Linear algebra* (3rd ed.). Boston: Addison-Wesley-Longman.

Fry, E. (1977). Fry's readability graph: Clarifications, validity, and extension to level 17. *Journal of Reading, 21,* 249.

Gardner, R. C. (2001). *Psychological statistics using SPSS for Windows.* Upper Saddle River, NJ: Prentice Hall.

Garnett, J. C. M. (1919). On certain independent factors in mental measure-ment. *Proceedings of the Royal Society of London, 96,* 91-111.

George, D., & Mallery, P. (2000). *SPSS for Windows step by step: A simple guide and reference, 10.0 update.* Boston: Allyn & Bacon.

Gift, A. G. (1996). Introduction. *Scholarly Inquiry for Nursing Practice: An International Journal, 10,* 179-183.

Giorgi, A. (1985). *Phenomenology and psychological research.* Pittsburgh: Duquesne University.

Goddard, J., & Kirby, A. (1976). *An introduction to factor analysis.* Norwich, UK: Geo Abstracts.

Gorsuch, R. L. (1983). *Factor analysis* (2nd ed.). Hillsdale, NJ: Lawrence Erlbaum.

Green, S. B., Salkind, N. J., & Akey, T. M. (2000). *Using SPSS for Windows: Analyzing and understanding data* (2nd ed.). Upper Saddle River, NJ: Prentice Hall.

Guba, E. G. (1978). *Toward a methodology of naturalistic inquiry in educational evaluation* (CSE Monograph Series in Evaluation No. 8). Los Angeles: University of California, Los Angeles, Center for the Study of Evaluation.

Guilford, J. P. (1977). The invariance problem in factor analysis. *Educational and Psychological Measurement, 37,* 11-19.

Gulliksen, H. (1974). Looking back and ahead in psychometrics. *American Psychologist, 29,* 251-161.

Guttman, L. (1953). Image theory for the structure of quantitative variables. *Psychometrika, 18,* 277-296.

Guttman, L. (1954). Some necessary conditions for common-factor analysis. *Psychometrika, 19,* 149-161.

Guttman, L. (1956). Best possible estimates of communalities. *Psychometrika, 21,* 273-285.

Hair, J. F., Anderson, R. E., Tatham, R. L., & Black, W. C. (1995). *Multivariate data analysis with readings* (4th ed.). Englewood Cliffs, NJ: Prentice Hall.

Harman, H. H. (1976). *Modern factor analysis* (3rd ed.). Chicago: University of Chicago.

Harris, C. W., & Kaiser, H. F. (1964). Oblique factor analytic solutions by orthogonal transformations. *Psychometrika, 29,* 347-362.

Hatcher, L. (1994). *A step-by-step approach to using the SAS system for factor analysis and structural equation modeling.* Cary, NC: SAS Publishing.

Hathaway, S. R. (1942). *The Minnesota Multiphasic Personality Inventory.* Minneapolis: University of Minnesota.

Hays, W. L. (1994). *Statistics* (5th ed.). Fort Worth, TX: Harcourt Brace.

Hendrickson, A. E., & White, P. O. (1964). Promax: A quick method for rotation to oblique simple structure. *British Journal of Statistical Psychology, 17,* 65-70.

Hinkle, D. E., Wiersma, W., & Jurs, S. G. (1998). *Applied statistics for the behavioral sciences* (4th ed.). Boston: Houghton Mifflin.

Hoehn-Saric, R., & McLeod, D. (1993). *Biology of anxiety disorders.* Washington, DC: American Psychiatric Press.

Horn, J. L. (1967). On subjectivity in factor analysis. *Educational and Psychological Measurement, 27,* 811-820.

Hotelling, H. (1933). Analysis of a complex of statistical variables into principal components. *Journal of Educational Psychology, 24,* 417-441, 498-520.

Hupcey, J. E., Morse, J. M., Lenz, E. R., & Tason, M. C. (1996). Wilsonian methods of concept analysis: A critique. *Scholarly Inquiry for Nursing Practice: An International Journal, 10,* 185-209.

Hurley, J., & Cattell, R. B. (1962). The Procrustes program: Producing direct rotation to test a hypothetical factor structure. *Behavioral Science, 7,* 258-262.

Hutchinson, S. A. (2001). Grounded theory: The method. In P. L. Munhall (Ed.), *Nursing research: A qualitative perspective* (3rd ed., pp. 180-212). Sudbury, MA: Jones & Bartlett.

Isaac, S., & Michael, W. B. (1981). *Handbook in research and evaluation.* San Diego: EdITS.

Jacobsen, P. B., Valdimarsdottir, H. B., Brown, K. L., & Offit, K. (1997). Decision-making about genetic testing among women at familial risk for breast cancer. *Psychosomatic Medicine, 59,* 459-466.

Jacobson, L., Brown, R., & Ariza, M. (1983). A revised multidimensional social desirability inventory. *Bulletin of the Psychonomic Society, 21,* 391-392.

Jennrich, R. I., & Sampson, P. F. (1966). Rotation for simple loadings. *Psychometrika, 31,* 313-323.

Jöreskog, K. G. (1967). Some contributions to maximum likelihood factor analysis. *Psychometrika, 32,* 443-482.

Jöreskog, K. G. (1969). A general approach to confirmatory maximum likelihood factor analysis. *Psychometrika, 34,* 183-202.

Jöreskog, K. G. (1970). A general method for analysis of covariance structures. *Biometrika, 57,* 239-251.

Jöreskog, K. G. (1977). Factor analysis by least-squares and maximum likelihood methods. In K. Enslein, A. Ralston, & H. S. Wilf (Eds.), *Statistical methods for digital computers.* New York: John Wiley & Sons.

Jöreskog, K. G., & Goldberger, A. S. (1972). Factor analysis by generalized least squares. *Psychometrika, 37,* 243-250.

Jöreskog, K. G., & Sörbom, D. (1989). *LISREL 7: A guide to the program and applications* (2nd ed.). Chicago: SPSS, Inc.

Kachigan, S. K. (1986). *Statistical analysis: An interdisciplinary introduction to univariate and multivariate methods.* New York: Radius.

Kaiser, H. F. (1958). The Varimax criterion for analytic rotation in factor analysis. *Pyschometrika, 23,* 187-200.

Kaiser, H. F. (1959). Computer program for Varimax rotation in factor analysis. *Educational and Psychological Measurement, 19,* 413-420.

Kaiser, H. F. (1960). The application of electronic computers to factor analysis. *Educational and Psychology Measurement, 20,* 141-151.

Kaiser, H. F. (1963). Image analysis. In C. S. Harris (Ed.), *Problems in measuring change* (pp. 156-166). Madison: University of Wisconsin.

Kaiser, H. F. (1970). A second-generation Little Jiffy. *Psychometrika, 35,* 401-415.

Kaiser, H. F. (1974). An index of factorial simplicity. *Psychometrika, 39,* 32-36.

Kaiser, H. F., & Rice, J. (1974). Little Jiffy, Mark IV. *Educational and Psychology Measurement, 34,* 111-117.

Kaplan, A. (1963). *The conduct of inquiry: Methodology for behavioral science.* San Francisco: Chandler.

Keck, J. F. (1998). Terminology of theory development. In A. M. Tomey & M. A. Alligood (Eds.), *Nursing theorists and their work* (4th ed., pp. 16-24). St. Louis: Mosby.

Kelly, P. T. (1992). Informational needs of individuals and families with hereditary cancers. *Seminars in Oncology Nursing, 8*, 288-292.

Kim, J., & Mueller, C. W. (1978). *Factor analysis: Statistical methods and practical issues.* Beverly Hills, CA: Sage.

Kinney, A. Y., Choi, Y., DeVellis, B., Millikan, R., Kobetz, E., & Sandler, R. S. (2000). Attitudes toward genetic testing in patients with colorectal cancer. *Cancer Practice, 8*, 178-186.

Kirchhoff, K. T. (1999). Design of questionnaires and structured interviews. In M. A. Mateo & K. T. Kirchhoff (Eds.), *Using and conducting nursing research in the clinical setting* (2nd ed., pp. 229-239). Philadelphia: W. B. Saunders.

Kirkevold, M. (1997). Integrative nursing research—An important strategy to further development of nursing science and practice. *Journal of Advanced Nursing, 25*, 977-984.

Kissinger, J. A. (1998). Overconfidence: A concept analysis. *Nursing Forum, 33*, 18-26.

Kline, P. (1986). *A handbook of test construction.* New York: Methuen.

Kline, P. (1994). *An easy guide to factor analysis.* New York: Routledge.

Kline, P. (2000a). *The handbook of psychological testing* (2nd ed.). London: Routledge.

Kline, P. (2000b). *A psychometrics primer.* London: Free Association Books.

Knapp, T. R. (1998). *Quantitative nursing research.* Thousand Oaks, CA: Sage.

Kuder, G. F., & Richardson, M. W. (1937). The theory of the estimation of test reliability. *Psychometrika, 2*, 151-160.

Lackey, N. R., & Wingate, A. L. (1998). The pilot study: One key to research success. In P. J. Brink & M. J. Wood (Eds.), *Advanced design in nursing research* (2nd ed., pp. 375-386). Thousand Oaks, CA: Sage.

Lawley, D. N., & Maxwell, A. E. (1971). *Factor analysis as a statistical method* (2nd ed.). London: Butterworth.

Lazarus, R. S., & Folkman, S. (1991). The concept of coping. In A. Monat & R. S. Lazarus (Eds.), *Stress and coping: An anthology* (3rd ed., pp. 189-206). New York: Columbia University.

Ledermann, W. (1937). On the rank of the reduced correlation matrix in multiple-factor analysis. *Psychometrika, 2*, 85-93.

Ledermann, W. (1938). The orthogonal transformations of a factorial matrix into itself. *Psychometrika, 3*, 181-187.

Leininger, M. M. (1985). *Qualitative research methods in nursing.* St. Louis: Harcourt.

Lerman, C., & Croyle, R. (1994). Psychological issues in genetic testing for breast cancer susceptibility. *Archives of Internal Medicine, 154*, 609-616.

Lerman, C., Marshall, J., Audrain, J., & Gomez-Caminero, A. (1996). Genetic testing for colon cancer susceptibility: Anticipated reactions of patients and challenges to providers. *International Journal of Cancer, 69*, 58-61.

Lerman, C., & Rimer, B. K. (1995). In R. T. Croyle (Ed.), *Psychological effects of screening for disease and detection prevention.* New York: Oxford University Press.

Leske, J. S. (1991). Internal psychometric properties of the Critical Care Family Needs Inventory. *Heart & Lung, 20*, 236-244.

Likert, R. (1932). A technique for the measurement of attitudes. *Archives of Psychology, 140,* 44-53.

Lincoln, Y. S., & Guba, E. G. (1985). *Naturalistic inquiry.* Beverly Hills, CA: Sage.

Lynn, M. (1989). Meta-analysis: An appropriate tool for the integration of nursing research. *Nursing Research, 38,* 302-305.

Maykut, P., & Morehouse, R. (1994). *Beginning qualitative research: A philosophic and practical guide.* London: Falmer.

McCubbin, H. I., Thompson, A. I., & McCubbin, M. A. (1996). A-COPE: Adolescent-Coping Orientation for Problem Experiences. In H. I. McCubbin, A. I. Thompson, & M. A. McCubbin (Eds.), *Family assessment: Resiliency, coping, and adaptation: Inventories for research and practice* (pp. 537-583). Madison: University of Wisconsin.

McCutcheon, A. L. (1987). *Latent class analysis.* Newbury Park, CA: Sage.

McDonald, R. P., & Burr, E. J. (1967). A comparison of four methods of constructing factor scores. *Psychometrika, 32,* 381-401.

McDonald, R. P., & Mulaik, S. A. (1979). Determinacy of common factors: A nontechnical review. *Psychological Bulletin, 86,* 297-306.

McIver, J. P., & Carmines, E. G. (1981). *Unidimensional scaling.* Beverly Hills, CA: Sage.

Meili, R. (1930). A propos de la theorie des facteurs Response a M. C. Spearman [Concerning the factor theory. A reply to C. Spearman]. *Archives de Psychologie, 22,* 328-332.

Miles, M. B., & Huberman, A. M. (1994). *Qualitative data analysis: An expanded sourcebook.* Thousand Oaks, CA: Sage.

Miller, D. E. (1991). *Handbook of research design and social measurement* (5th ed.). Newbury Park, CA: Sage.

Miner, J. B. (1912). Correlation. *Psychological Bulletin, 9,* 222-231.

Miner, J. B. (1920). Correlation. *Psychological Bulletin, 17,* 338-396.

Mishel, M. H. (1998). Methodological studies: Instrument development. In P. J. Brink & M. J. Wood (Eds.), *Advanced design in nursing research* (2nd ed., pp. 235-282). Thousand Oaks, CA: Sage.

Moran, D. (2000). *Introduction to phenomenology.* London: Routledge.

Morse, J. M. (Ed.). (1994). *Critical issues in qualitative research methods.* Thousand Oaks, CA: Sage.

Morse, J. M., & Field, P. A. (1995). *Qualitative research methods for health professionals* (2nd ed.). Thousand Oaks, CA: Sage.

Moustakas, C. (1994). *Phenomenological research methods.* Thousand Oaks, CA: Sage.

Mulaik, S. A. (1986). Factor analysis and psychometrika: Major developments. *Psychometrika, 5,* 23-33.

Munhall, P. L. (1994). *Revisioning phenomenology: Nursing and health science research.* New York: National League for Nursing.

Neuhaus, J. O., & Wrigley, C. (1954). The quartimax method: An analytic approach to orthogonal simple structure. *British Journal of Statistical Psychology, 7,* 81-91.

Nieswiadomy, R. M. (2001). *Foundations of nursing research* (4th ed.). Paramus, NJ: Prentice Hall.

Norbeck, J. S. (1985). What constitutes a publishable report of instrument development? *Nursing Research, 34,* 380-382.

Norris, C. A. (1982). *Concept clarification in nursing.* Rockville, MD: Aspen Systems.

Norusis, M. J. (2000). *SPSS 10.0 guide to data analysis.* Upper Saddle River, NJ: Prentice Hall.

Nunnally, J. C. (1978). *Psychometric theory* (2nd ed.). New York: McGraw-Hill.

Nunnally, J. C., & Bernstein, I. H. (1994). *Psychometric theory* (3rd ed.). New York: McGraw-Hill.

Oberst, M. T. (1994). Preparing reports of new instruments: Getting the recipe right. *Research in Nursing and Health, 17,* 399.

Patton, M. Q. (1990). *Qualitative evaluation and research methods* (2nd ed.). Newbury Park, CA: Sage.

Pearson, K. (1901). On lines and planes of closest fit to systems of points in space. *Philosophical Magazine, 2*(series 6), 559-572.

Pearson, E. S., & Hartley, H. O. (1970). *Biometrika tables for statisticians* (Vol. 1, 3rd ed.). New York: Cambridge University Press.

Pedhazur, E. J., & Schmelkin, L. P. (1991). *Measurement, design, and analysis: An integrated approach.* Hillsdale, NJ: Lawrence Erlbaum.

Pett, M. A. (1997). *Nonparametric statistics for health care research.* Thousand Oaks, CA: Sage.

Pett, M. A., & Johnson, M. J. (2002). Measurement characteristics of the Revised College Students' Hassles Scale (RUSHS). Manuscript in preparation.

Pett, M. A., Wampold, B. E., Turner, C. W., & Vaughan-Cole, B. (1999). *Journal of Family Psychology, 13,* 145-164.

Polit, D. F., & Hungler, B. P. (1999). *Nursing research: Principles and methods* (6th ed.). Philadelphia: Lippincott.

Rempusheski, V. F. (1990). The proliferation of unreliable and invalid questionnaires. *Applied Nursing Research, 3,* 174-176.

Rice, J. A. (1994). *Mathematical statistics and data analysis.* Belmont, CA: Wadsworth.

Rodgers, B. L., & Knafl, K. A. (2000). *Concept development in nursing: Foundations, techniques, and applications* (2nd ed.). Philadelphia: W. B. Saunders.

Rosenthal, R., & Rosnow, R. L. (1991). *Essentials of behavioral research: Methods and data analysis* (2nd ed.). Boston: McGraw-Hill.

SAS Institute, Inc. (2000). *SAS online doc, version 8 with PDF files,* Cary, NC: SAS Institute, Inc.

SAS Institute, Inc. (1985). *SAS user's guide: Statistics* (version 5 ed.). Cary, NC: SAS Institute, Inc.

Saunders, D. R. (1960). A computer program to find the best-fitting orthogonal factors for a given hypothesis. *Psychometrika, 25,* 199-205.

Saunders, D. R. (1962). Trans-Varimax. *Psychometrika, 26,* 395.

Schönemann, P. H., & Wang, M. M. (1972). Some new results in factor indeterminacy. *Psychometrika, 37,* 61-91.

Schwarz, N., Knauper, B., Hippler, H.-J., Noelle-Neumann, E., & Clark, L. (1991). Rating scales: Numeric values may change the meaning of scale labels. *Public Opinion Quarterly, 55,* 570-582.

Shavelson, R. J., & Webb, N. M. (1991). *Generalizability theory: A primer.* Newbury Park, CA: Sage.

Silverman, D. (Ed.). (1997). *Qualitative research: Theory, method and practice.* London: Sage.

Smith, K. R., & Croyle, R. T. (1995). Attitudes toward genetic testing for colon cancer risk. *American Journal of Public Health, 85,* 1435-1438.

Smith, M. C., & Stullenbarger, E. (1991). A prototype for integrative review and meta-analysis of nursing research. *Journal of Advanced Nursing, 16,* 1272-1283.

Smith, M. C., & Stullenbarger, E. (1995). An integrative review and meta-analysis of oncology nursing research: 1981-1990. *Cancer Nursing, 18*(3), 167-179.

Sokolowski, R. (2000). *Introduction to phenomenology.* Cambridge, UK: Cambridge University Press.

Sörbom, D. (1974). A general method for studying differences in factor means and factor structure between groups. *British Journal of Mathematical and Statistical Psychology, 27,* 229-239.

Spearman, C. (1904). General intelligence, objectively determined and measured. *American Journal of Psychology, 15,* 201-293.

Spearman, C. (1922). Recent contributions to the theory of "two factors." *British Journal of Psychology, 13,* 26-30.

Spearman, C. (1923). Further note on the "theory of two factors." *British Journal of Psychology, 13,* 266-270.

Spearman, C. (1927). *The abilities of man.* New York: Macmillan.

Spearman, C. (1928). Pearson's contribution to the theory of two factors. *British Journal of Psychology, 19,* 95-101.

Spearman, C. (1929). The uniqueness of "G." *Journal of Educational Psychology, 20,* 212-216.

Spearman, C. (1930a). A truce to "barking in." *Journal of Educational Psychology, 21,* 110-111.

Spearman, C. (1930b). La theorie des facteurs. *Archives de Psychologie, 22,* 313-327.

Spearman, C., & Holzinger, K. J. (1924). The sampling error in the theory of two factors. *British Journal of Psychology, 15,* 17-19.

Spector, P. E. (1992). *Summated rating scale construction, an introduction.* Newbury Park, CA: Sage.

SPSS, Inc. (1993). *SPSS base system syntax reference guide* (release 6.0). Chicago: SPSS, Inc.

SPSS, Inc. (1999). *SPSS base system syntax reference guide* (release 10.0). Chicago: SPSS, Inc.

SPSS, Inc. (2002). *SPSS base 11. Users guide.* Chicago: SPSS, Inc.

Stake, R. E. (1998). Case studies. In N. K. Denzin & Y. S. Lincoln (Eds.), *Strategies of qualitative inquiry* (pp. 86-109). Thousand Oaks, CA: Sage.

Steiger, J. H. (1996). Coming full circle in the history of factor indeterminacy. *Multivariate Behavioral Research, 31,* 617-630.

Stevens, J. P. (2001). *Applied multivariate statistics for the social sciences* (4th ed.). Mahwah, NJ: Lawrence Erlbaum.

Stevens, S. S. (1951). Mathematics, measurement and psychophysics. In S. S. Stevens (Ed.), *Handbook of experimental psychology* (pp. 1-49). New York: John Wiley.

Stevens, S. S. (1959). Measurement, psychophysics, and utility. In C. W. Churchman & P. Ratoosh (Eds.), *Measurement: Definitions and theories* (pp. 18-63). New York: John Wiley.

Stevens, S. S. (1968). Measurement, statistics, and the schemapiric view. *Science, 161*, 849-856.

Strauss, A. L. (1987). *Qualitative analysis for social scientists.* Cambridge, UK: Cambridge University.

Streiner, D. L., & Norman, G. R. (1995). *Health measurement scales: A practical guide to their development and use* (2nd ed.). Oxford, UK: Oxford University Press.

Streubert, H. J. (1991). Phenomenological research as a theoretic initiative in community health nursing. *Public Health Nursing, 8*(2), 119-123.

Streubert, H. J., & Carpenter, D. R. (1999). *Qualitative research in nursing: Advancing the humanistic imperative* (2nd ed.). Philadelphia: Lippincott, Williams & Wilkins.

Sudman, S., & Bradburn, N. M. (1982). *Asking questions: A practical guide to questionnaire design.* San Francisco: Jossey-Bass.

Tabachnick, B. G., & Fidell, L. S. (2001). *Using multivariate statistics* (4th ed.). Boston: Allyn & Bacon.

Thomson, G. H. (1934). Hotelling's method modified to give Spearman's g. *Journal of Educational Psychology, 25*, 366-374.

Thomson, G. H. (1936). Boundary conditions in the common-factor-space, in the factorial analysis of ability. *Psychometrika, 1*, 155-163.

Thomson, G. H. (1938). Methods of estimating mental factors. *Nature, 141*, 46.

Thurstone, L. L. (1931). Multiple factor analysis. *Psychological Review, 38*, 406-427.

Thurstone, L. L. (1935). *The vectors of mind.* Chicago: University of Chicago.

Thurstone, L. L. (1937a). Current misuse of the factorial methods. *Psychometrika, 2*, 3-6.

Thurstone, L. L. (1937b). Psychology as a quantitative rational science. *Science, 85*, 227-232.

Thurstone, L. L. (1940). Current issues in factor analysis. *Psychological Bulletin, 37*, 189-236.

Thurstone, L. L. (1947). *Multiple factor analysis.* Chicago: University of Chicago.

Thurstone, L. L. (1948). Psychological implications of factor analysis. *American Psychologist, 3*, 402-408.

Thurstone, L. L. (1954). An analytic method for simple structure. *Psychometrika, 19*, 173-182.

Tucker, L. R. (1971). Relations of factor score estimates to their use. *Psychometrika, 36*, 427-436.

Tucker, L. R., Koopman, R. F., & Linn, R. I. (1969). Evaluation of factor analytic research procedures by means of simulated correlation matrices. *Psychometrika, 34*, 421-459.

van Kaam, A. (1959). A phenomenological analysis exemplified by the feeling of being really understood. *Individual Psychology, 15*, 66-72.

van Manen, M. (1984). Practicing phenomenological writing. *Phenomenology and Pedagogy, 2,* 36-69.

Vogt, W. P. (1993). *Dictionary of statistics and methodology: A nontechnical guide for the social sciences.* Newbury Park, CA: Sage.

Walker, L. O., & Avant, K. C. (1995). *Strategies for theory construction in nursing* (3rd ed.). Norwalk, CT: Appleton & Lange.

Waltz, C. F., Strickland, O. L., & Lenz, E. R. (1991). *Measurement in nursing research.* Philadelphia: F. A. Davis.

Ware, J. E., Snow, K. K., & Kosinski, M. (2000). *SF-36 Health Survey: Manual and Interpretation Guide.* Lincoln, RI: QualityMetric Inc.

Ware, J. E., Snyder, M. K., McClure, R. E., & Jarett, I. M. (1972). *The measurement of health concepts* (Technical Report No. HCP-72-5). Springfield, VA: U.S. Department of Commerce, National Technical Information Service.

Weisberg, H. F., Krosnick, J. A., & Bowen, B. D. (1996). *An introduction to survey research, polling, and data analysis* (3rd ed.). Thousand Oaks, CA: Sage.

Wilson, E. B. (1928). On hierarchical correlational systems. *Proceedings of the National Academy of Sciences, 14,* 283-291.

Wilson, H. S. (1985). *Research in nursing.* Menlo Park, CA: Addison-Wesley.

Woods, N. (1988). Designing prescription-testing studies. In N. Woods & M. Catanzaro (Eds.), *Nursing research: Theory and practice* (pp. 202-218). St. Louis: Mosby.

Zimmerman, B. B., & Zimmerman, S. S. (1998). *New perspectives on Microsoft® Word 97.* Cambridge, MA: Course Technology.

INDEX

Page references followed by n indicate notes. References followed by t or f indicate tables or figures, respectively.

ABOUT THE AUTHORS

Marjorie A. Pett, MStat, DSW, is a Research Professor in both the University of Utah Colleges of Nursing and Health, Salt Lake City. She has been on the faculty of the College of Nursing since 1980. By her own admission, she is a "collector" of academic degrees: BA (Brown University), MS in Sociology (University of Stockholm, Sweden), MSW (Smith College), MStat (University of Utah), and DSW (University of Utah).

Dr. Pett is the author of numerous articles and presentations related to both to her federally funded research on family interaction in married and divorced families and to her interests in statistics. Her textbook, *Nonparametric Statistics for Health Care Research* (Sage, 1997), has received much praise from the health care community. Dr. Pett has a strong commitment to facilitating the practical application of statistics in the social, behavioral, and biological sciences, especially among practitioners in health care settings. She has taught statistics to doctoral students from a variety of disciplines, both at the beginning and advanced levels. In addition to her year-long doctoral level statistics class, her elective course offerings include seminars on nonparametric statistics, multivariate statistics, structural equation modeling (SEM), hierarchical linear modeling (HLM), and factor analysis.

In 2002 she received a Faculty Teaching Award from the College of Nursing and will receive a University Distinguished Teaching Award from the University of Utah at its commencement exercises in 2003.

Nancy R. Lackey, RN, PhD, holds the Loewenberg Chair of Excellence in the Loewenberg School of Nursing at The University of Memphis. She has a BSN from Indiana University, MSN from Marquette University, and a PhD from Texas Woman's University. She was awarded a two-year postdoctoral fellowship to the University of Utah in the School of Nursing, where she studied family theories, family research methodologies and issues, and psychometrics. During her academic career she has designed and taught undergraduate and graduate courses in nursing theory, theory development, qualitative and quantitative research methodologies, psychometrics, as well as various adult medical-surgical clinical courses. The focus of her research interest is the psychosocial needs of cancer patients, their caregivers and families. She has also developed the Cancer Patient's Need Survey and has assisted with the development and refinement of other psychosocial instruments.

John J. Sullivan, PhD, was a Research Professor in the University of Utah College of Nursing and Department of Surgery. Trained originally as an experimental psychologist (learning), Dr. Sullivan's primary interest in his later academic career was in the multivariate analysis of health and medical problems. Dr. Sullivan had more than 25 years of practical experience in test construction and applications of measurement theory to health care issues.